KODOCHA

ANA'S STAGE

2

KODOCHA
SANA'S STAGE

Vol. 2

Written and Illustrated by Miho Obana
English Adaptation by Sarah Dyer

TOKYOPOP®
Los Angeles - Tokyo

Story and Art - Miho Obana

Translator - Yukio Ichimura
English Adaption - Sarah Dyer
Reprint Editor - Mark Paniccia
Retouch and Lettering - Kyle Plummer
Cover Layout - Raseel El Djoundi
Graphic Designer - Anna Kernbaum

Senior Editor - Julie Taylor
Production Manager - Jennifer Miller
Art Director - Matthew Alford
VP of Production & Manufacturing - Ron Klamert
President & C.O.O. - John Parker
Publisher - Stuart Levy

Email: editor@TOKYOPOP.com
Come visit us online at www.TOKYOPOP.com

A ⬤ TOKYOPOP® Manga

TOKYOPOP® is an imprint of Mixx Entertainment Inc.
5900 Wilshire Blvd. Suite 2000, Los Angeles, CA 90036

ISBN: 1-931514-51-8

First TOKYOPOP® printing: July 2002

10 9 8 7 6 5 4 3
Printed in Canada

KODOCHA
SANA'S STAGE

Vol. 2

CONTENTS

MAIN CHARACTERS

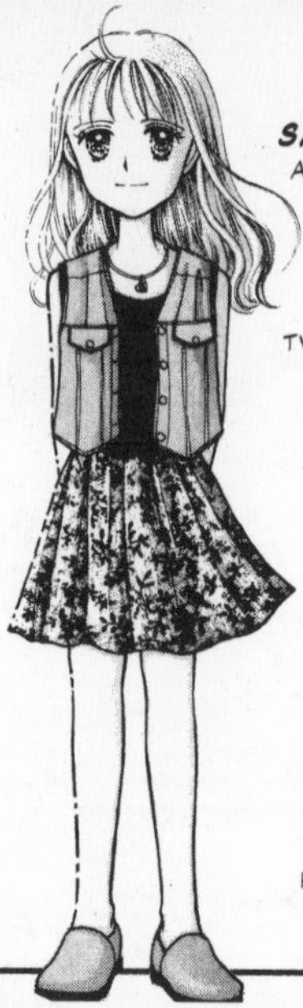

SANA KURATA:
A CHEERFUL 6TH GRADER WHO APPEARS ON A POPULAR TV SHOW, CHILD'S TOY.

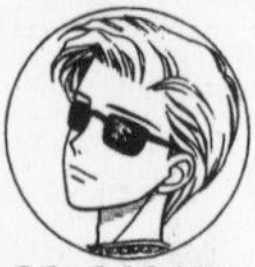

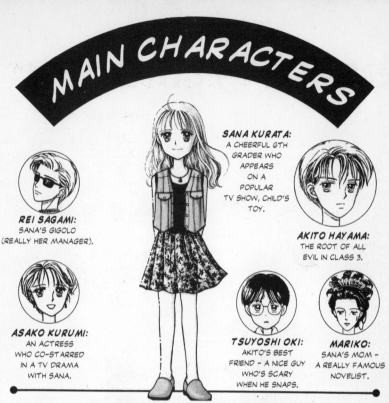

REI SAGAMI:
SANA'S GIGOLO (REALLY HER MANAGER).

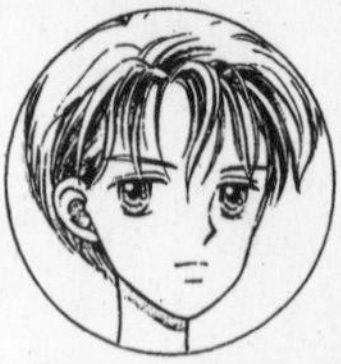

AKITO HAYAMA:
THE ROOT OF ALL EVIL IN CLASS 3.

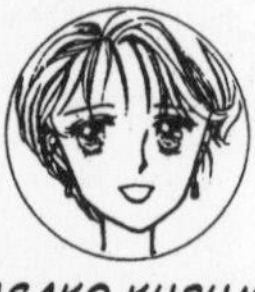

ASAKO KURUMI:
AN ACTRESS WHO CO-STARRED IN A TV DRAMA WITH SANA.

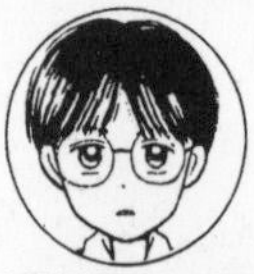

TSUYOSHI OKI:
AKITO'S BEST FRIEND - A NICE GUY WHO'S SCARY WHEN HE SNAPS.

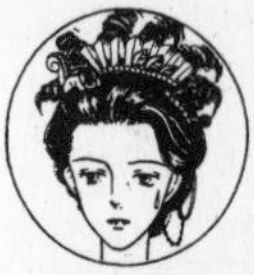

MARIKO:
SANA'S MOM - A REALLY FAMOUS NOVELIST.

SYNOPSIS FROM BOOK 1

SANA KURATA IS A POPULAR CHILD ACTRESS, MAINLY FAMOUS FOR APPEARING ON "CHILD'S TOY", A TV SHOW. SHE HAS A GOOD HOME LIFE WITH HER FUNNY (MOSTLY WEIRD-FUNNY) NOVELIST MOTHER, MISAKO, AND HER MANAGER, REI. BUT SCHOOL IS A DIFFERENT STORY, A BOY GANG TOOK OVER SANA'S 6TH GRADE CLASSROOM (CLASS 3) AND TERRORIZED THE ENTIRE CLASS! APPEALS TO THE GANG'S RINGLEADER, AKITO HAYAMA, DIDN'T ACCOMPLISH ANYTHING. SANA TRIED TO STAY OUT OF IT, BUT FINALLY SHE LOST PATIENCE AND GOT INVOLVED. SHE WASN'T DOING WELL AGAINST HAYAMA AT FIRST, BUT FINALLY SHE GOT AN EMBARRASSING PHOTO OF HIM (BLACKMAIL!), AND THE PROBLEM WAS SOLVED. SHE REALLY HATED HAYAMA UNTIL SHE FOUND OUT THAT HE ACTED SO ROTTEN BECAUSE HE WAS SO UNHAPPY AT HOME. HIS MOTHER DIED GIVING BIRTH TO HIM, AND HE GREW UP WITH A DISTANT FATHER AND A SISTER WHO CALLED HIM A "DEMON CHILD". SANA GETS A JOB AS A CHARACTER IN A TV MOVIE WHO IS IN THE SAME CIRCUMSTANCES - EXCEPT WITH A HAPPY ENDING. SO SHE WORKS VERY HARD ON THE MOVIE, HOPING THE HAYAMA FAMILY WILL WATCH IT AND SEE THEMSELVES IN IT. THE DRAMA IS A SUCCESS AND WHEN THE HAYAMAS SEE IT, IT REALLY SEEMS TO CHANGE THEIR LIVES...

CHILD'S TOY EXTRA:

CHiLD'S TOY WEATHER REPORT

Sana's version

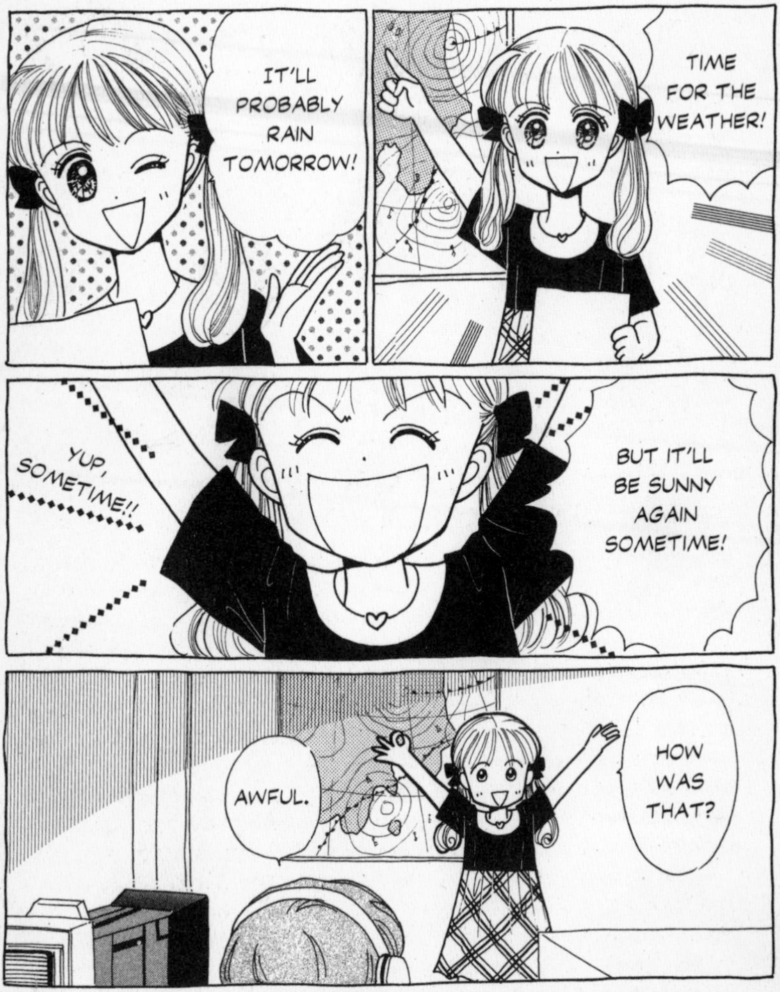
TIME FOR THE WEATHER!
IT'LL PROBABLY RAIN TOMORROW!
BUT IT'LL BE SUNNY AGAIN SOMETIME!
YUP, SOMETIME!!
HOW WAS THAT?
AWFUL.

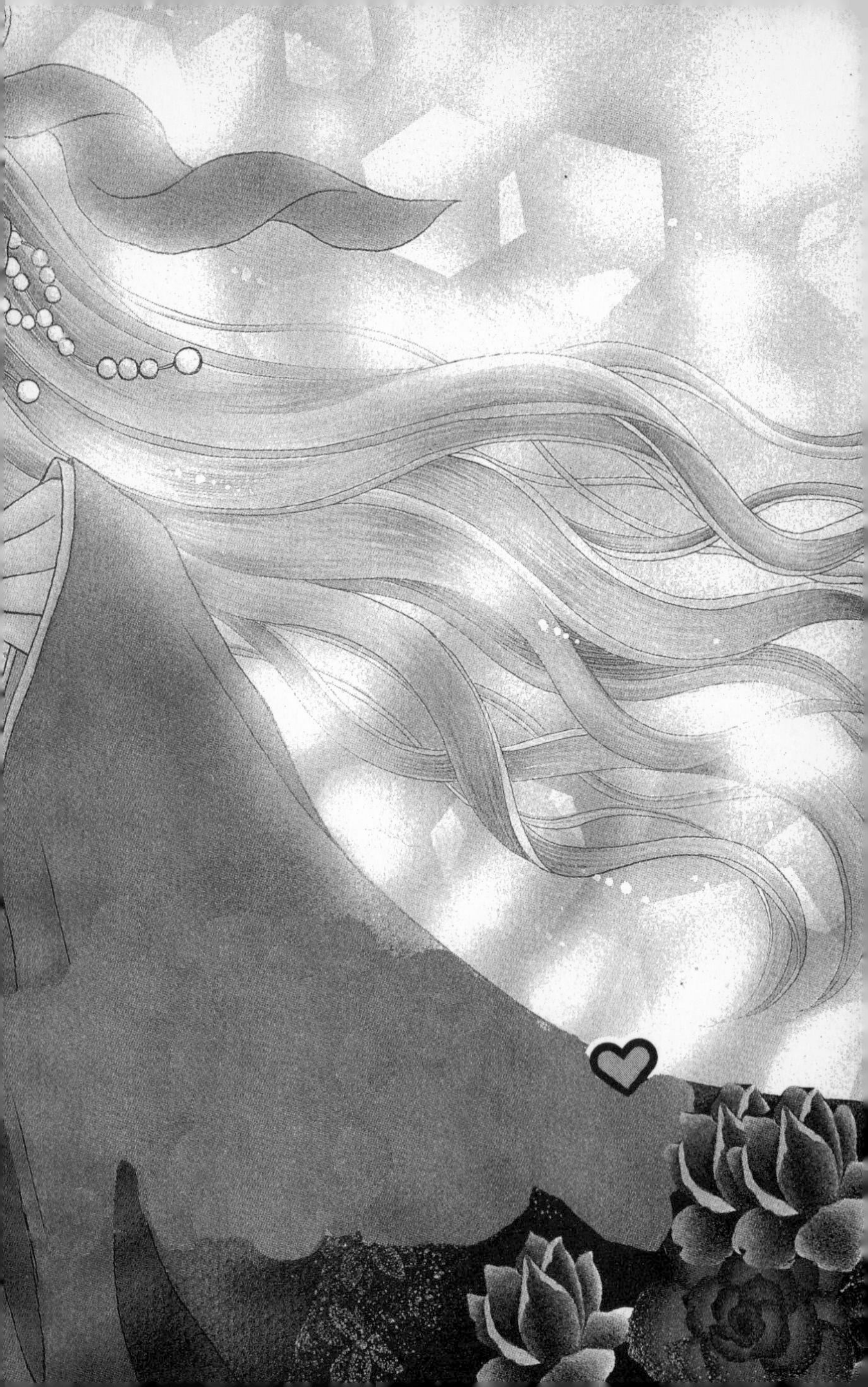

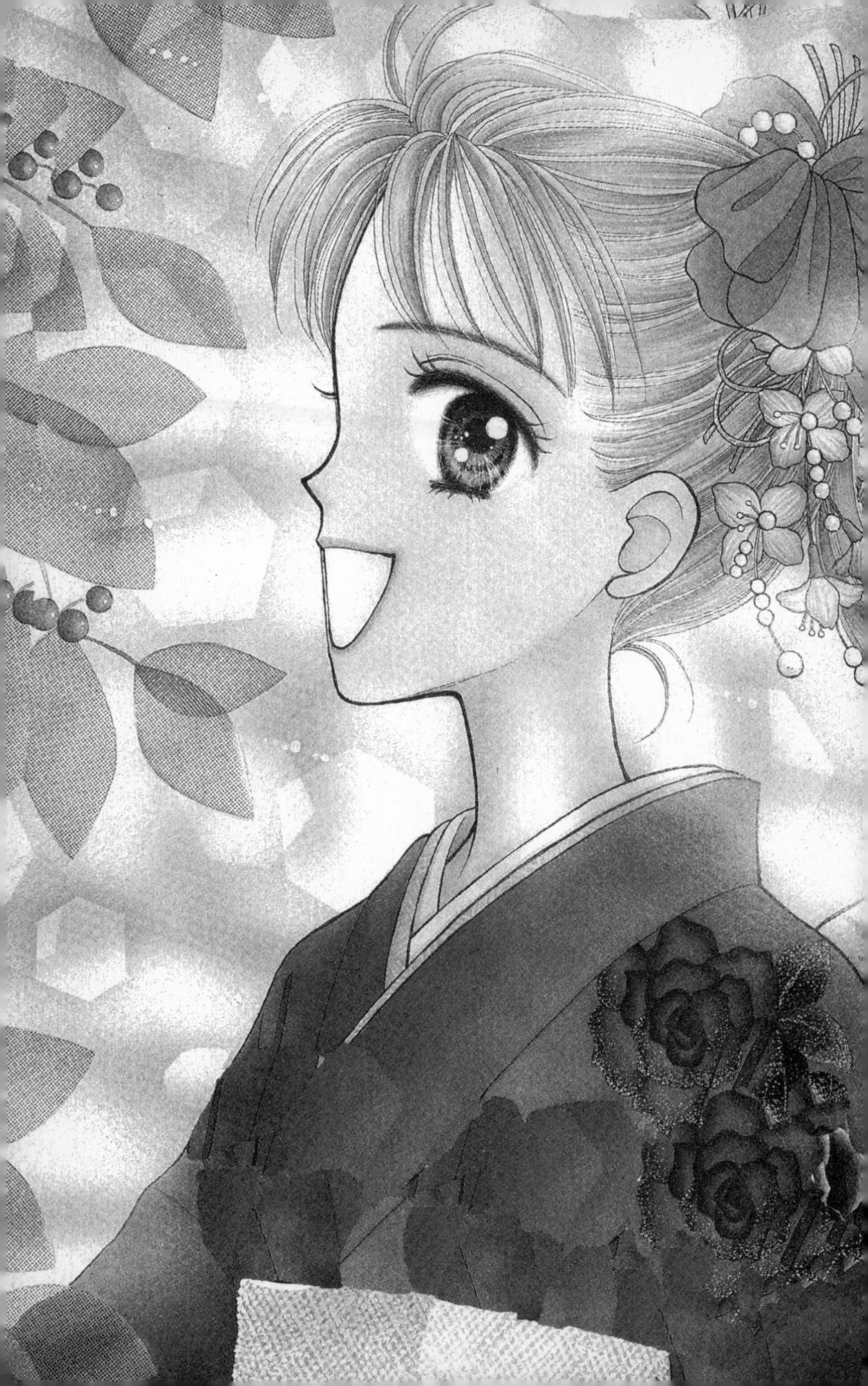

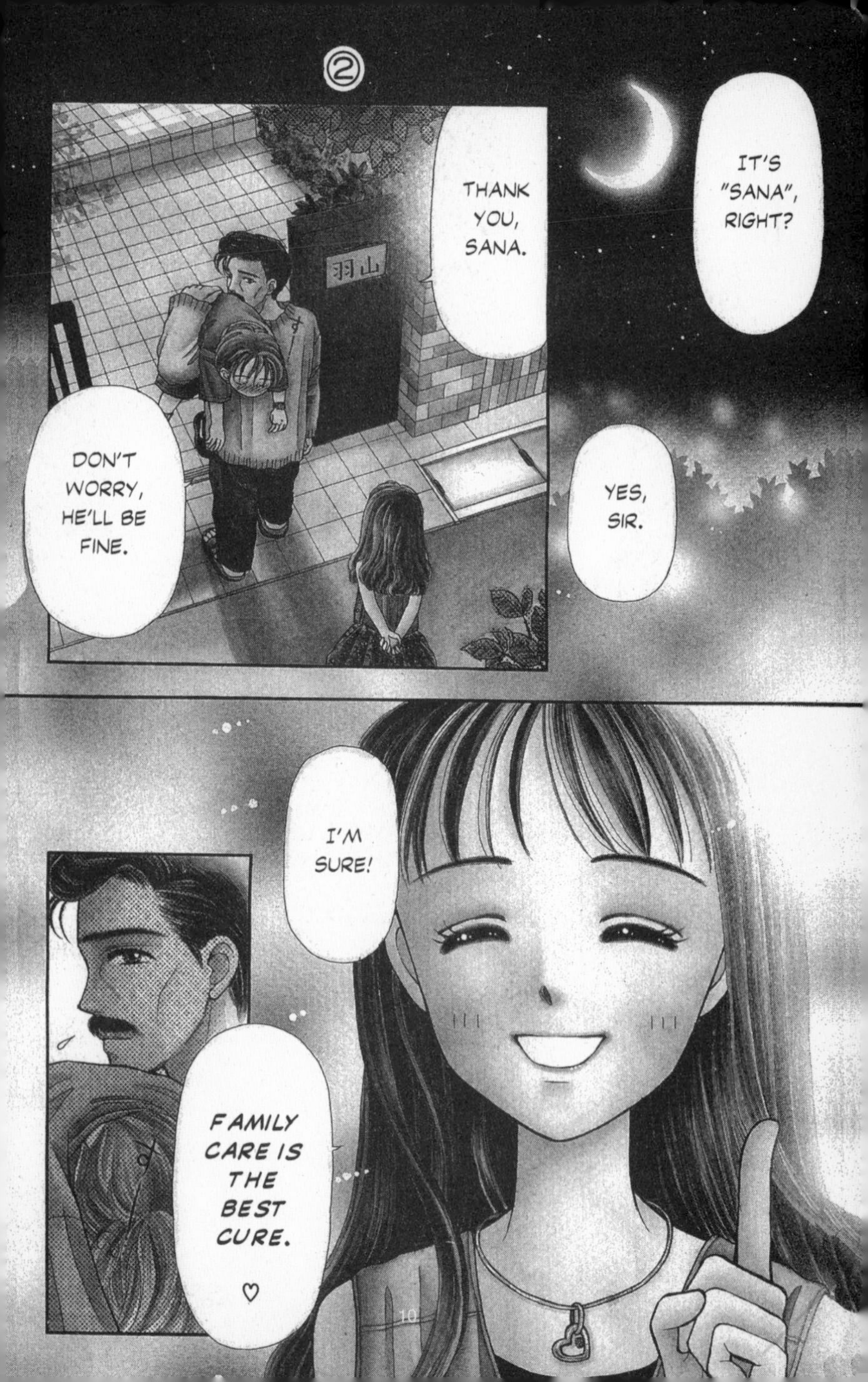
②
IT'S "SANA", RIGHT?
YES, SIR.
THANK YOU, SANA.
DON'T WORRY, HE'LL BE FINE.
I'M SURE!
FAMILY CARE IS THE BEST CURE. ♡

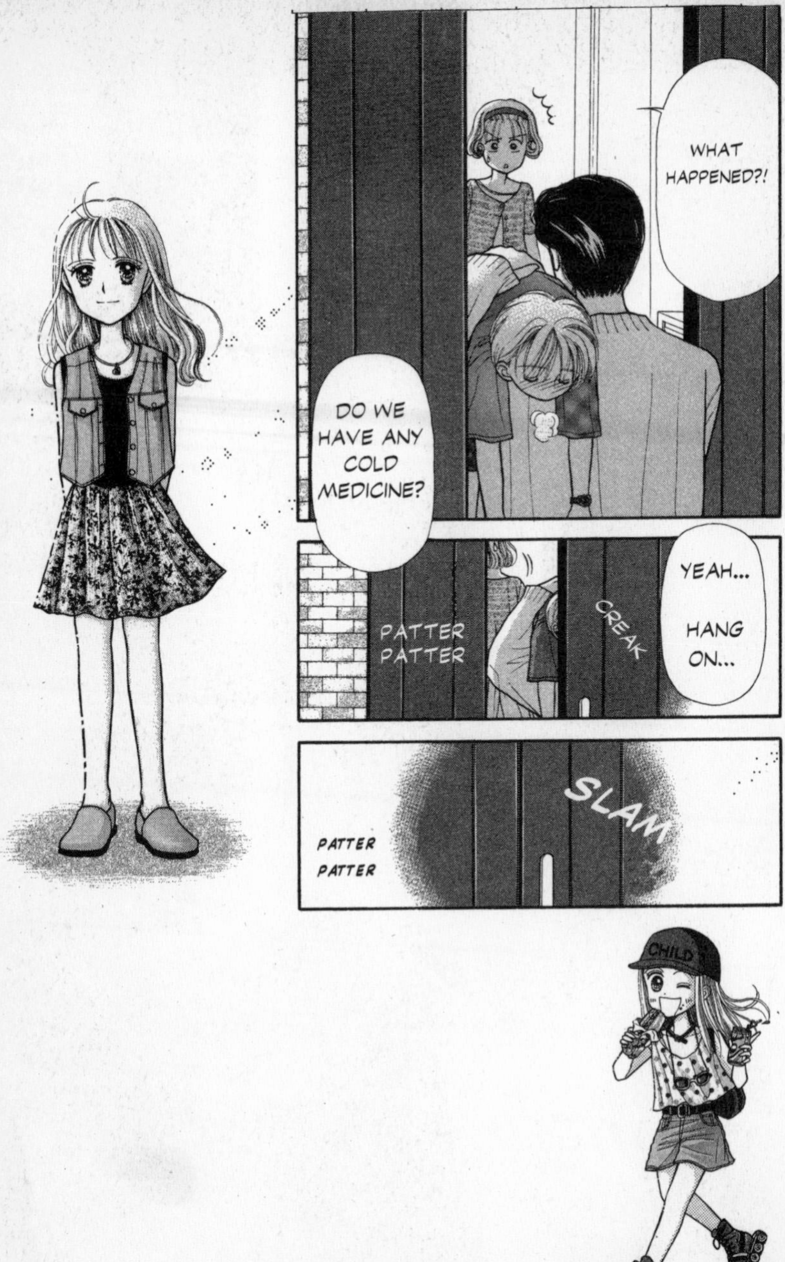

WHAT HAPPENED?!
DO WE HAVE ANY COLD MEDICINE?
YEAH... HANG ON...
CREAK
PATTER PATTER
SLAM
PATTER PATTER
CHILD

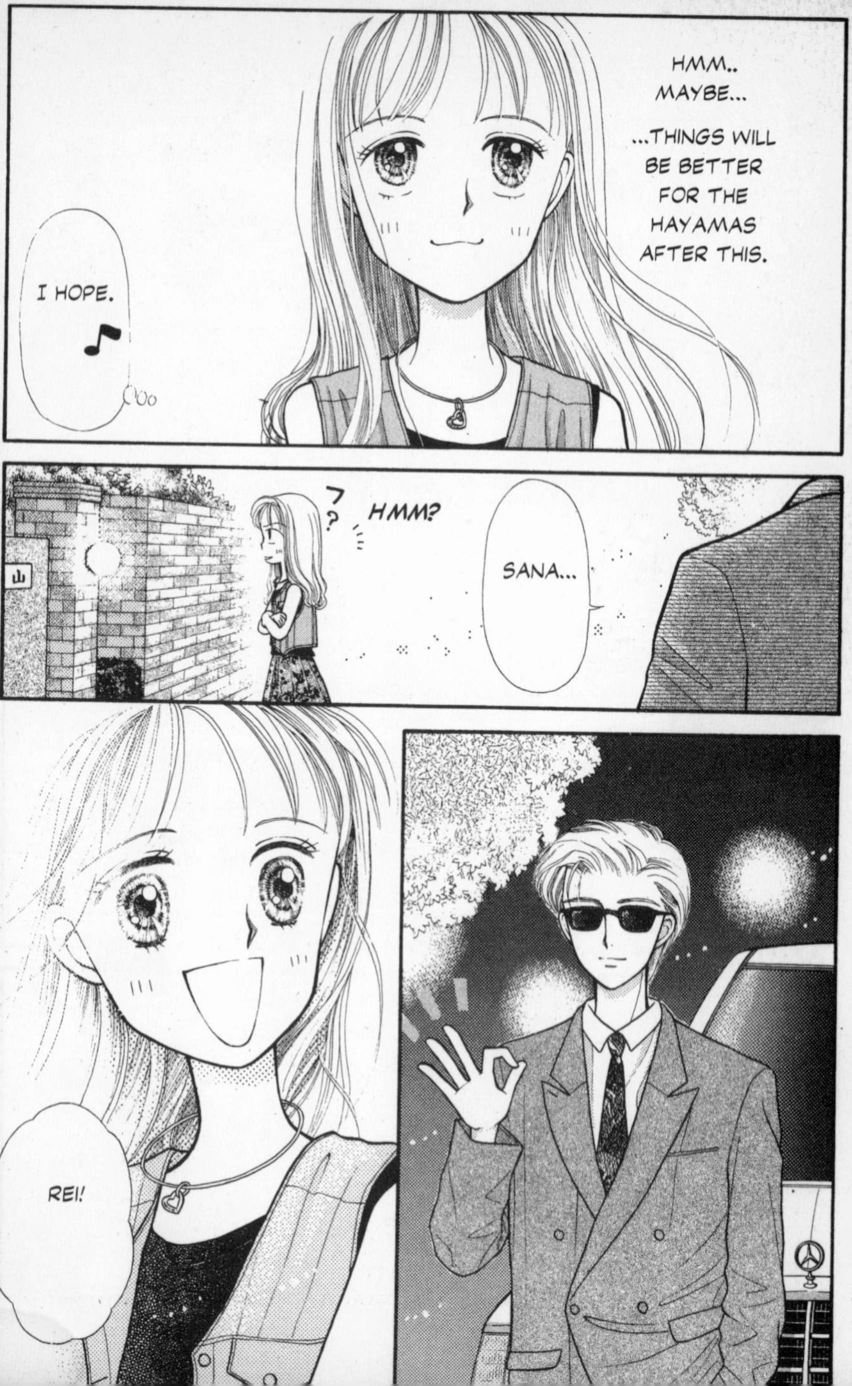
HMM.. MAYBE...
...THINGS WILL BE BETTER FOR THE HAYAMAS AFTER THIS.
I HOPE.
SANA...
HMM?
山
REI!

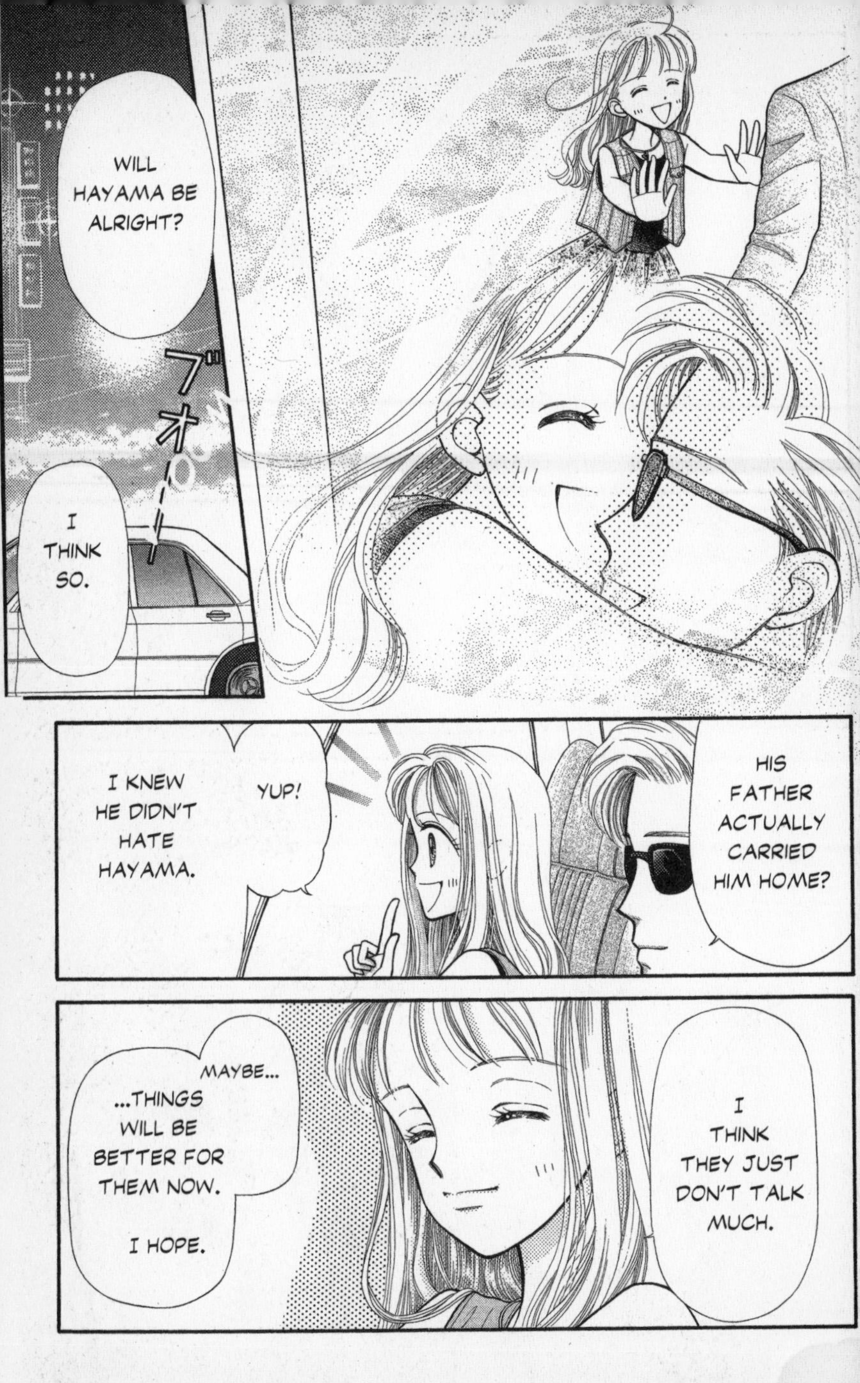
WILL HAYAMA BE ALRIGHT?
I THINK SO.
HIS FATHER ACTUALLY CARRIED HIM HOME?
YUP!
I KNEW HE DIDN'T HATE HAYAMA.
I THINK THEY JUST DON'T TALK MUCH.
MAYBE... ...THINGS WILL BE BETTER FOR THEM NOW.
I HOPE.

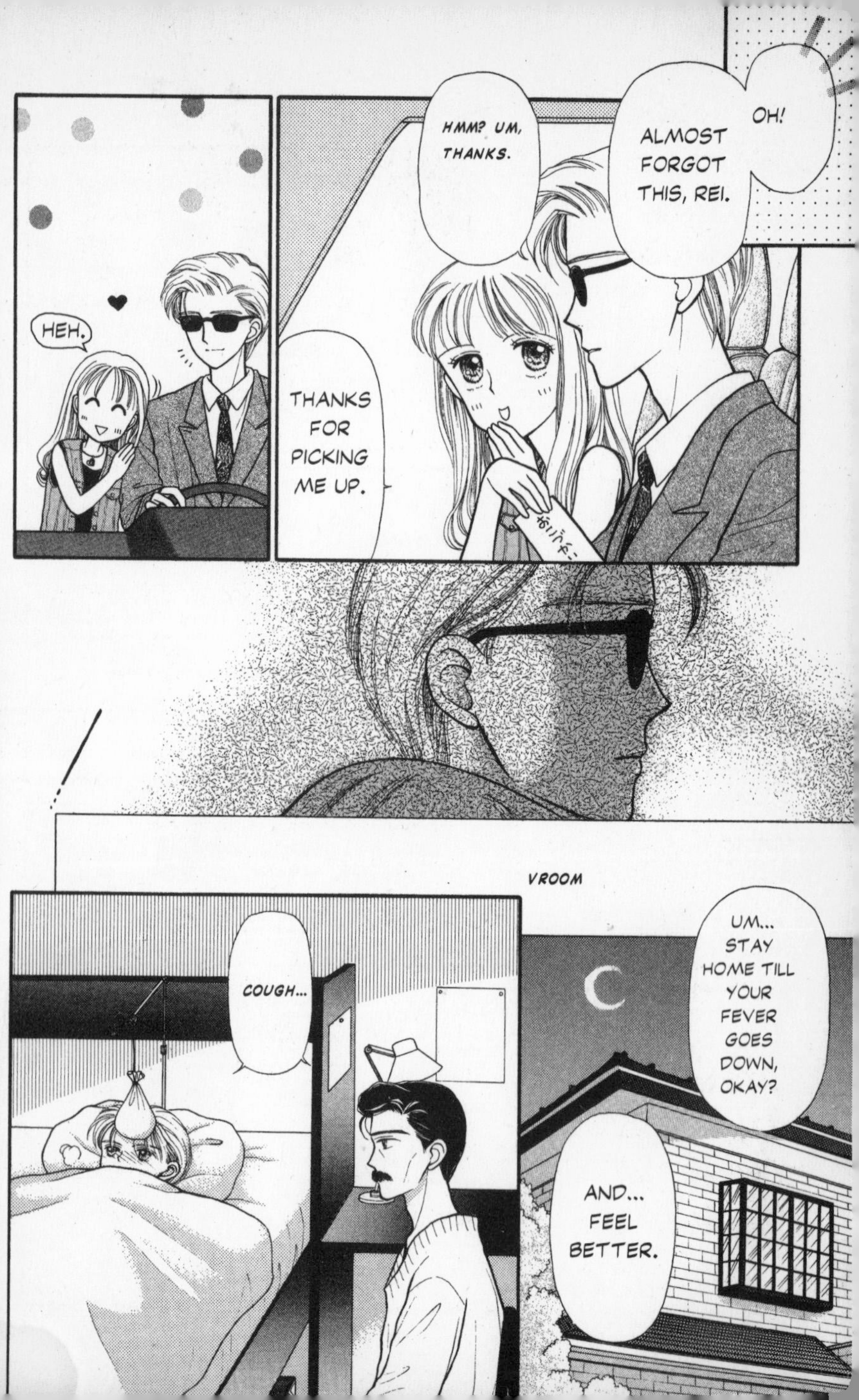
OH!
ALMOST FORGOT THIS, REI.
HMM? UM, THANKS.
THANKS FOR PICKING ME UP.
HEH.
VROOM
UM... STAY HOME TILL YOUR FEVER GOES DOWN, OKAY?
AND... FEEL BETTER.
COUGH...

Obana's Incoherent Babbling

Hello! It's me, Obana! And here's Book 2 of Kodocha. I'm super-busy these days, thanks to you guys! I didn't know a comic book artist could be so busy! Normally, I'm really lazy — I always had trouble finishing things I started. But because of you, I can keep doing this hard job! Thanks, fans! And I want you to know, I really do read all your mail. I get a lot of letters, so I can't reply to them all. (I'm sorry!) But they're very important to me as the feedback for my work. Thanks for your support! I'll keep doing my best, ok?

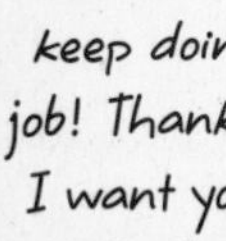

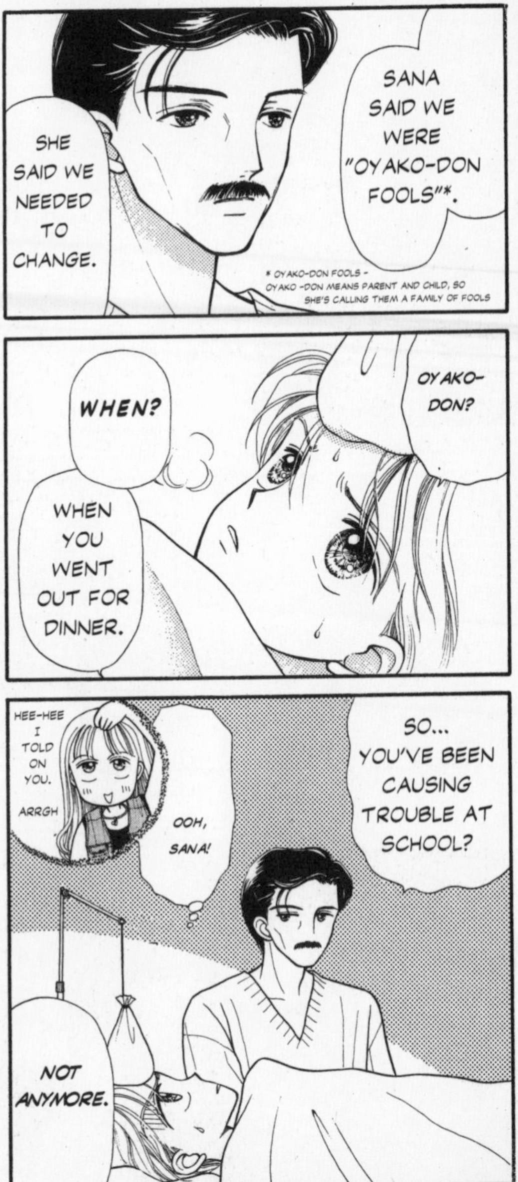
SANA SAID WE WERE "OYAKO-DON FOOLS"*.
SHE SAID WE NEEDED TO CHANGE.
* OYAKO-DON FOOLS - OYAKO-DON MEANS PARENT AND CHILD, SO SHE'S CALLING THEM A FAMILY OF FOOLS
OYAKO-DON?
WHEN?
WHEN YOU WENT OUT FOR DINNER.
SO... YOU'VE BEEN CAUSING TROUBLE AT SCHOOL?
OOH, SANA!
HEE-HEE I TOLD ON YOU.
ARRGH
NOT ANYMORE.

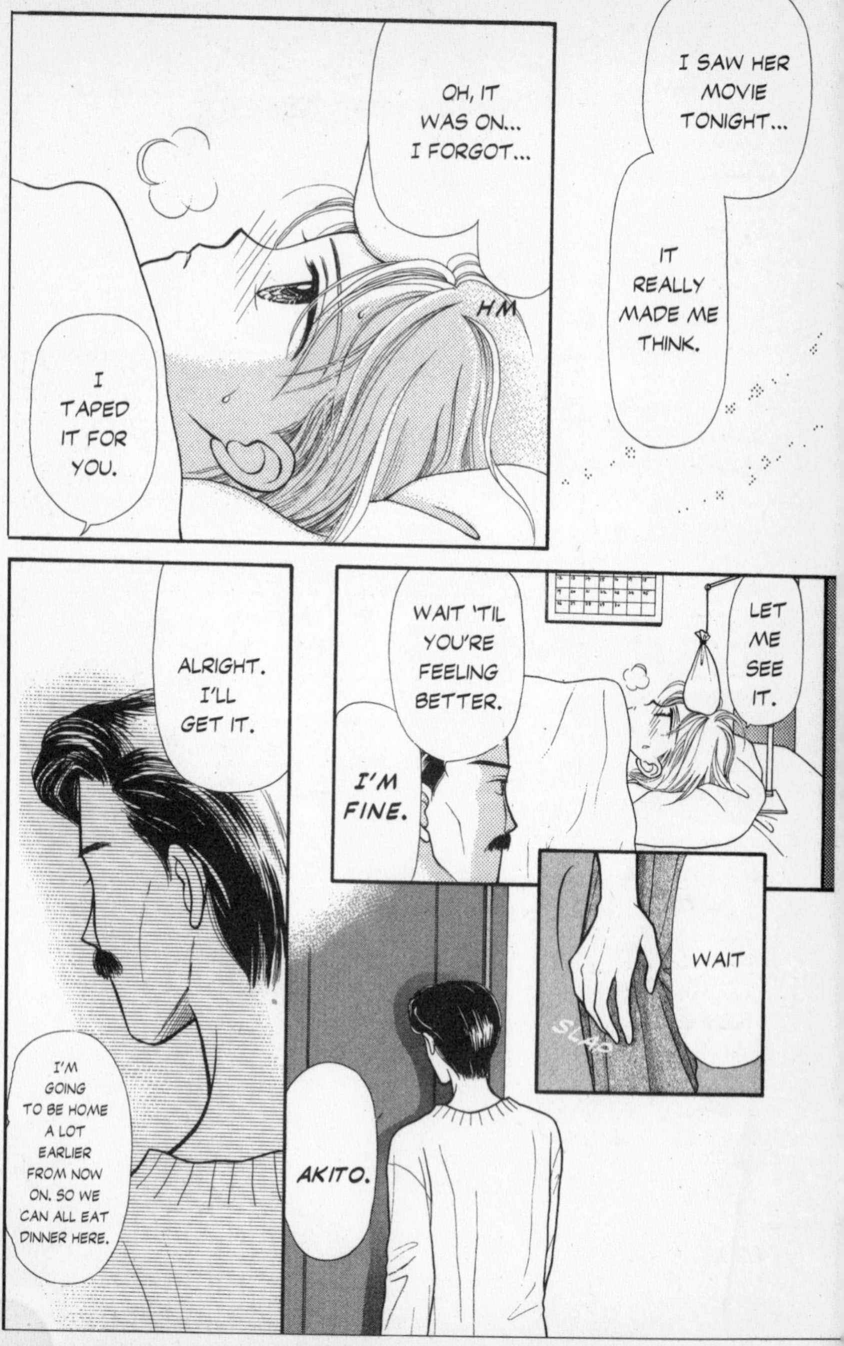
I SAW HER MOVIE TONIGHT...
IT REALLY MADE ME THINK.
OH, IT WAS ON... I FORGOT...
HM
I TAPED IT FOR YOU.
LET ME SEE IT.
WAIT 'TIL YOU'RE FEELING BETTER.
I'M FINE.
WAIT
SLAP
ALRIGHT. I'LL GET IT.
AKITO.
I'M GOING TO BE HOME A LOT EARLIER FROM NOW ON. SO WE CAN ALL EAT DINNER HERE.

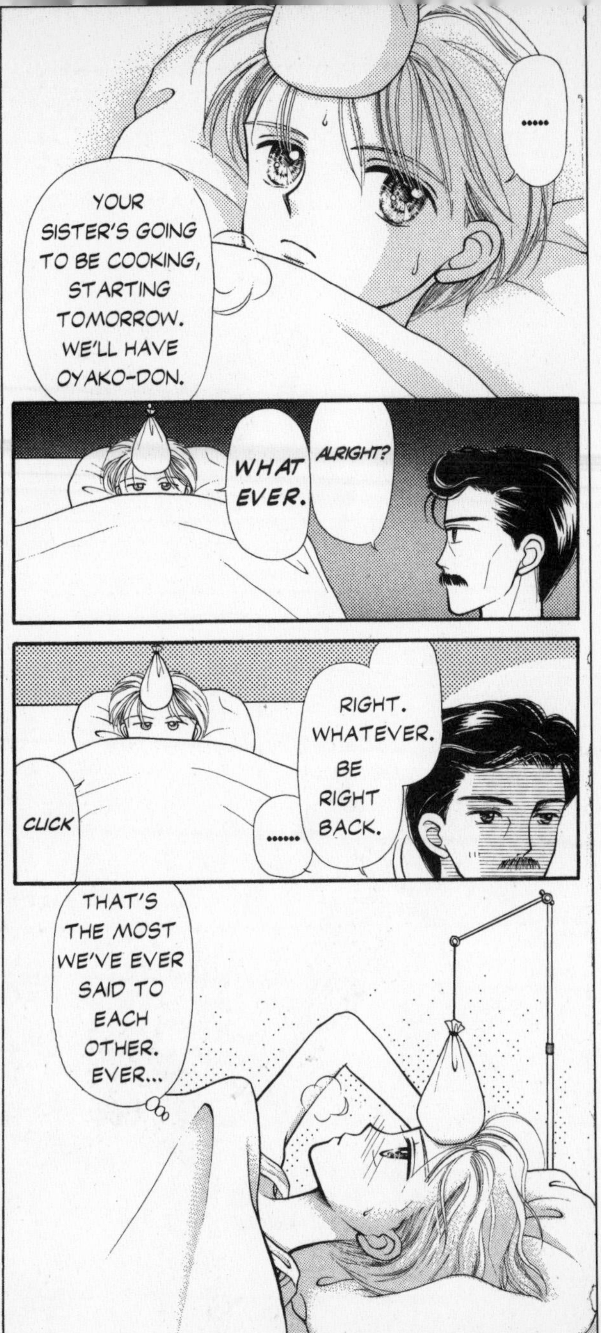
.....
YOUR SISTER'S GOING TO BE COOKING, STARTING TOMORROW. WE'LL HAVE OYAKO-DON.
ALRIGHT?
WHAT EVER.
RIGHT. WHATEVER. BE RIGHT BACK.
......
CLICK
THAT'S THE MOST WE'VE EVER SAID TO EACH OTHER. EVER...

About the Anime

A Kodocha animated video will soon be released in Japan. (In fact, it'll be out when this book is published.) To be honest, I wasn't interested in animation at first. But once we started doing real work on it — designing the characters, picking voice actors — I got really into it. Animation is actually a lot of fun! Sometimes people ask me not to animate my comics because it'll be different from the image they have in their head — but, it's supposed to be different! The pictures you're used to seeing on paper move and the characters talk — there's music and sound and it's a whole different medium. I'm interested in seeing how it turns out. But I appreciate that you all love the original too — thanks!

(To be continued.)

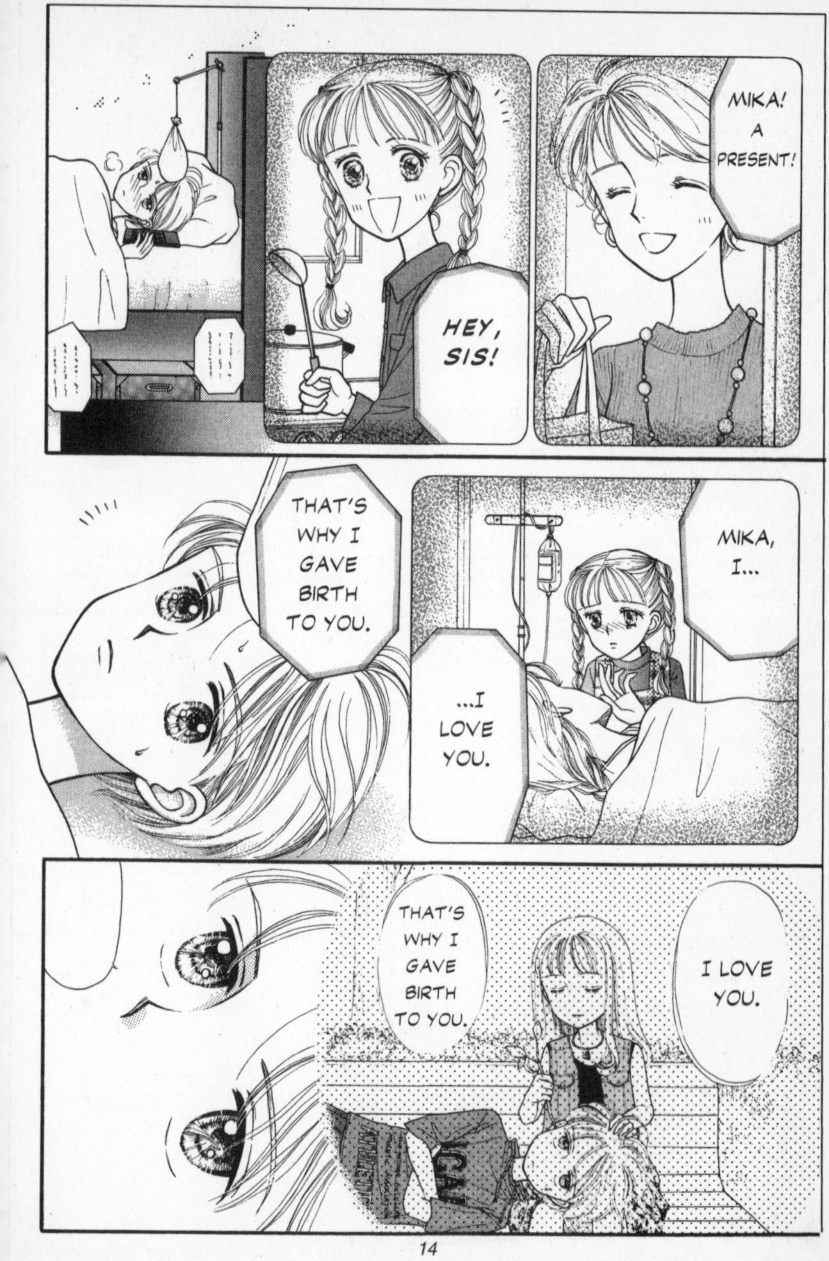
MIKA! A PRESENT!
HEY, SIS!
MIKA, I...
...I LOVE YOU.
THAT'S WHY I GAVE BIRTH TO YOU.
I LOVE YOU.
THAT'S WHY I GAVE BIRTH TO YOU.

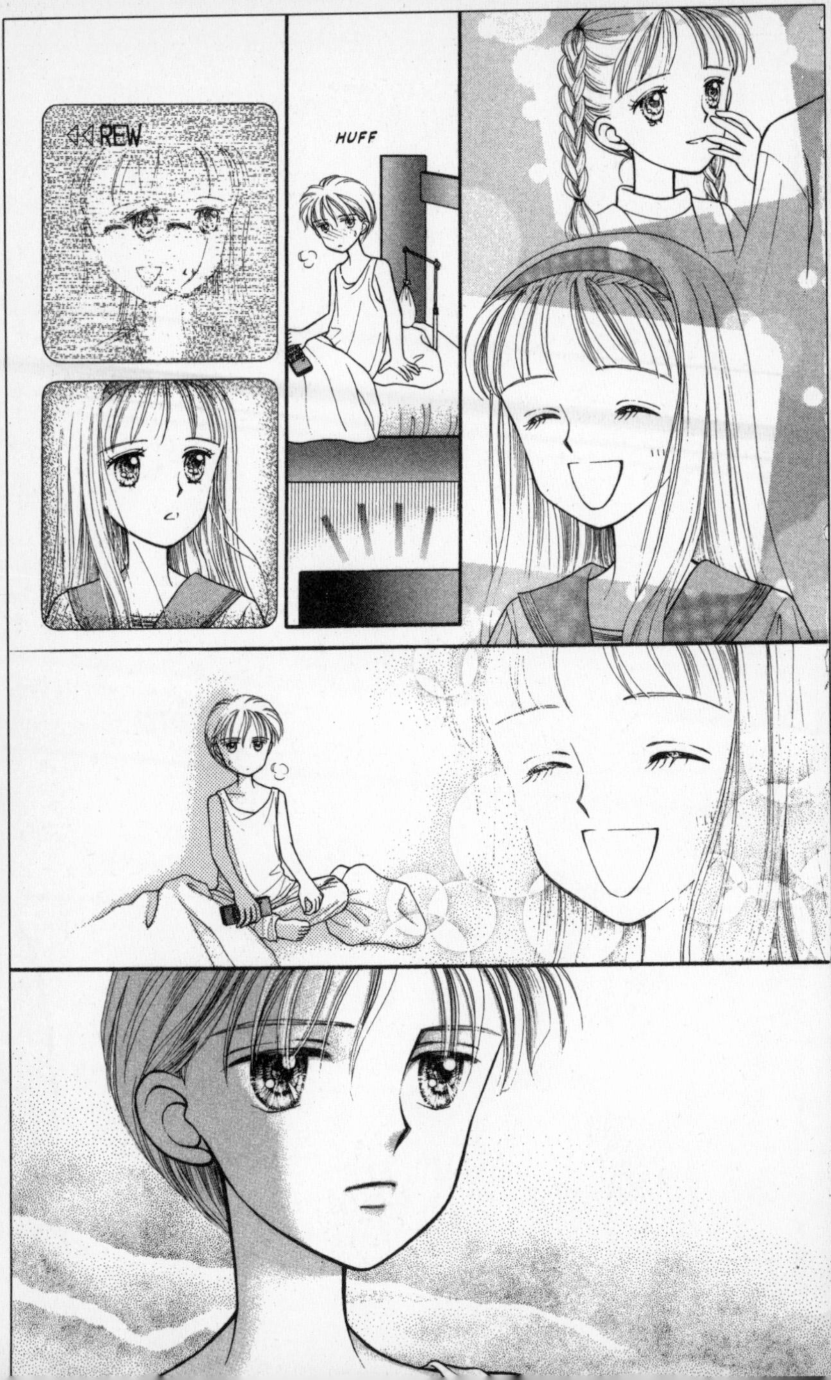
HUFF
REW

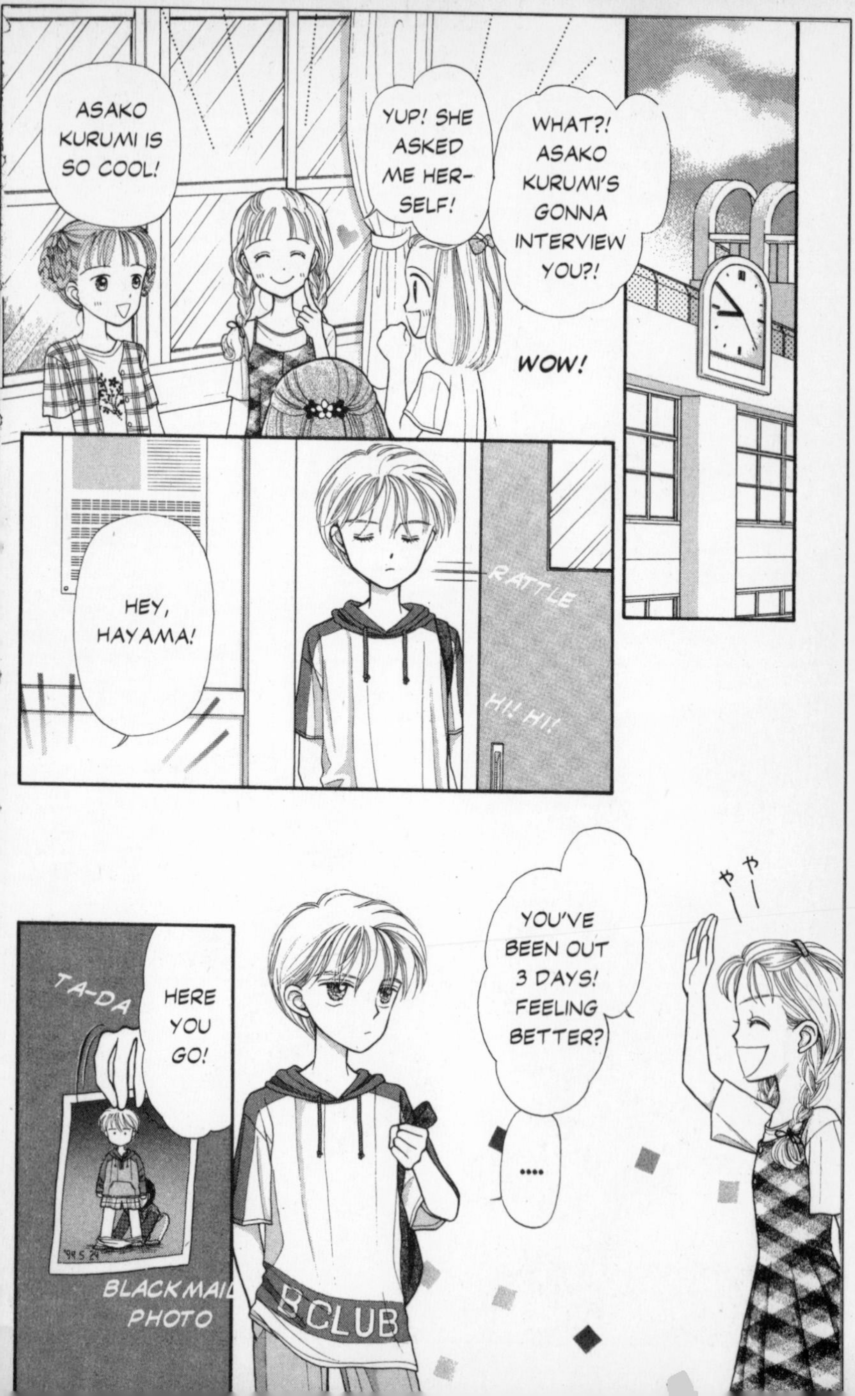
WHAT?! ASAKO KURUMI'S GONNA INTERVIEW YOU?!
WOW!
YUP! SHE ASKED ME HER-SELF!
ASAKO KURUMI IS SO COOL!
RATTLE
HI! HI!
HEY, HAYAMA!
ヤー ヤー
YOU'VE BEEN OUT 3 DAYS! FEELING BETTER?
....
TA-DA
HERE YOU GO!
BLACKMAIL PHOTO

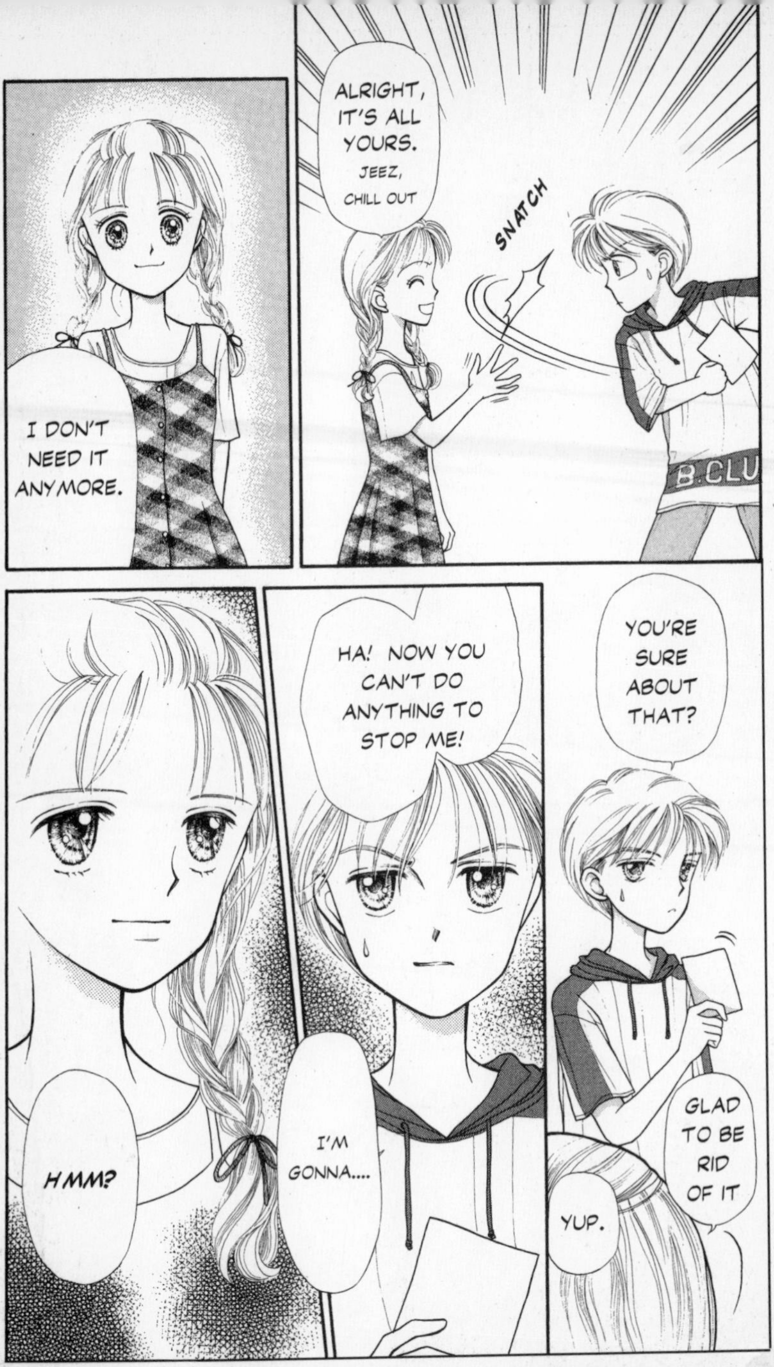
ALRIGHT, IT'S ALL YOURS.
JEEZ, CHILL OUT
SNATCH
I DON'T NEED IT ANYMORE.
YOU'RE SURE ABOUT THAT?
GLAD TO BE RID OF IT
YUP.
HA! NOW YOU CAN'T DO ANYTHING TO STOP ME!
I'M GONNA....
HMM?

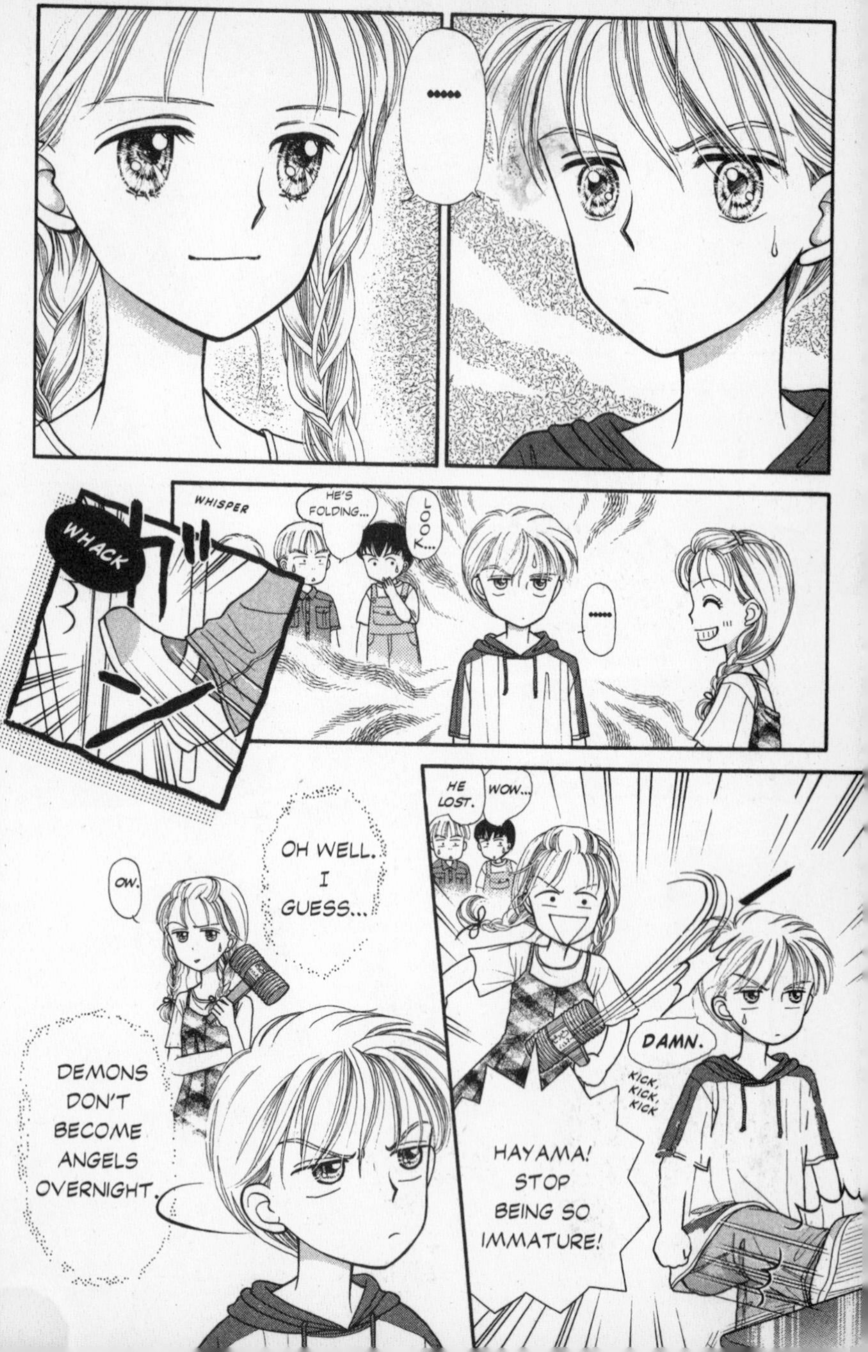
.....
.....
LOOK...
HE'S FOLDING...
WHISPER
WHACK
WOW...
HE LOST.
DAMN.
KICK, KICK, KICK
HAYAMA! STOP BEING SO IMMATURE!
OH WELL. I GUESS...
OW.
DEMONS DON'T BECOME ANGELS OVERNIGHT.

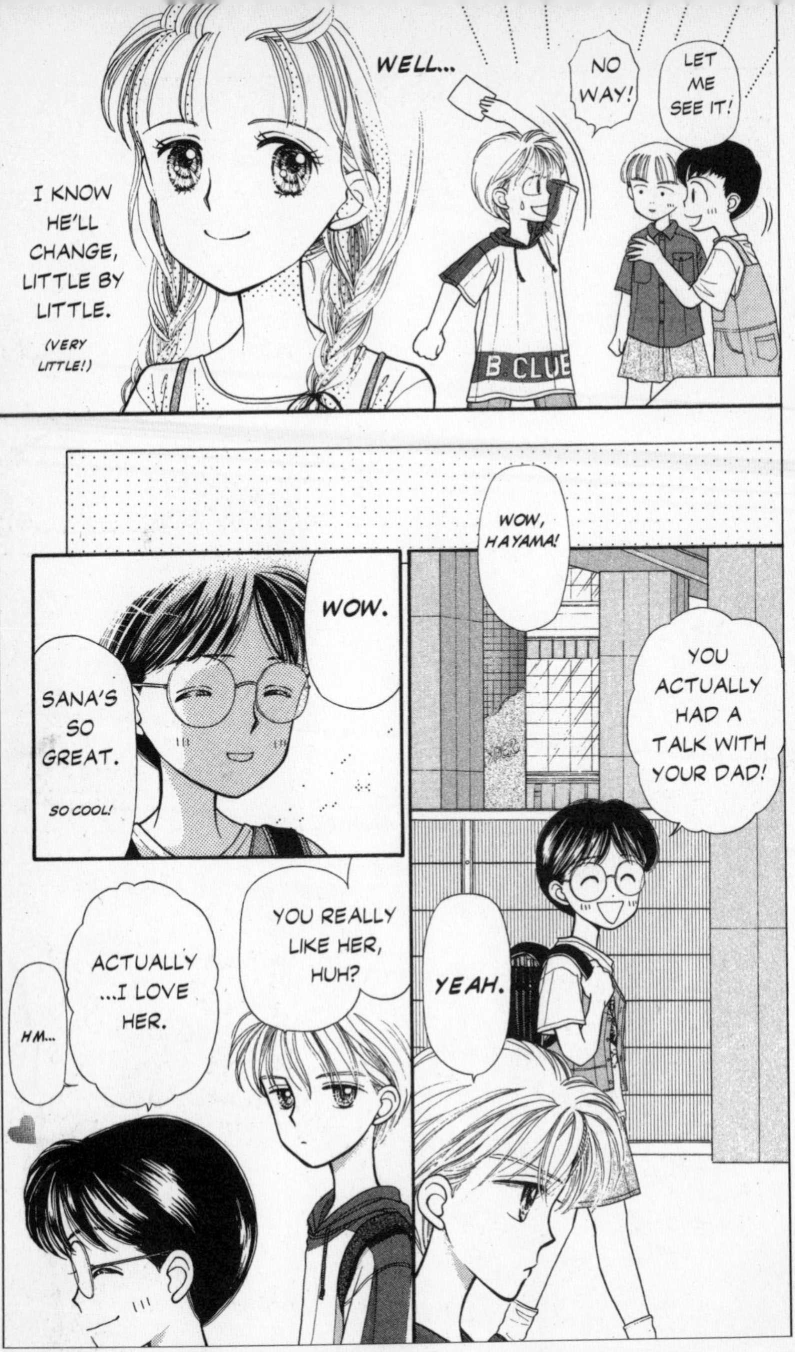
LET ME SEE IT!
NO WAY!
WELL...
I KNOW HE'LL CHANGE, LITTLE BY LITTLE.
(VERY LITTLE!)
WOW, HAYAMA!
YOU ACTUALLY HAD A TALK WITH YOUR DAD!
WOW.
SANA'S SO GREAT.
SO COOL!
YEAH.
YOU REALLY LIKE HER, HUH?
ACTUALLY ...I LOVE HER.
HM...

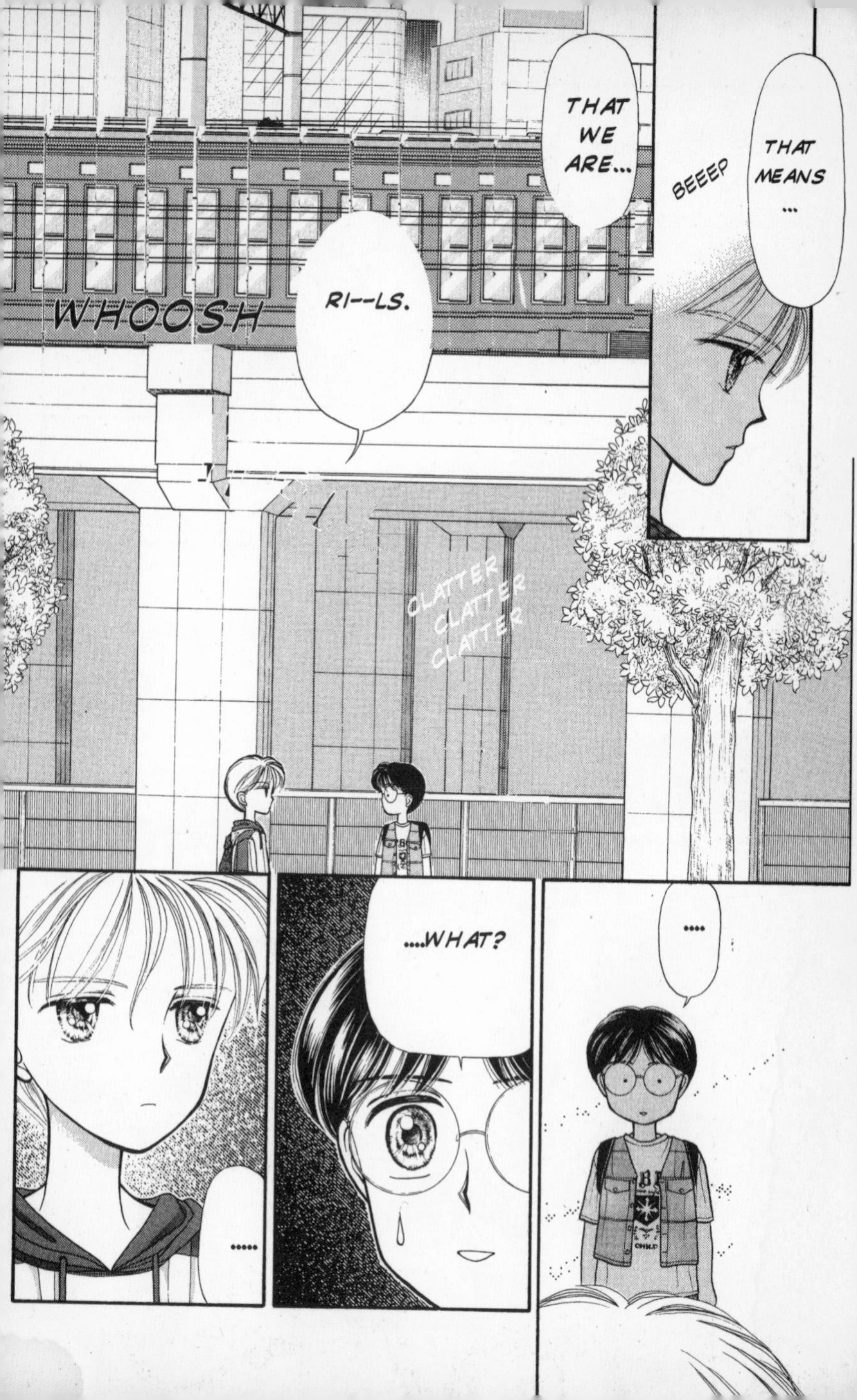
THAT MEANS ...
BEEEP
THAT WE ARE...
RI--LS.
WHOOSH
CLATTER CLATTER CLATTER
....
....WHAT?
.....

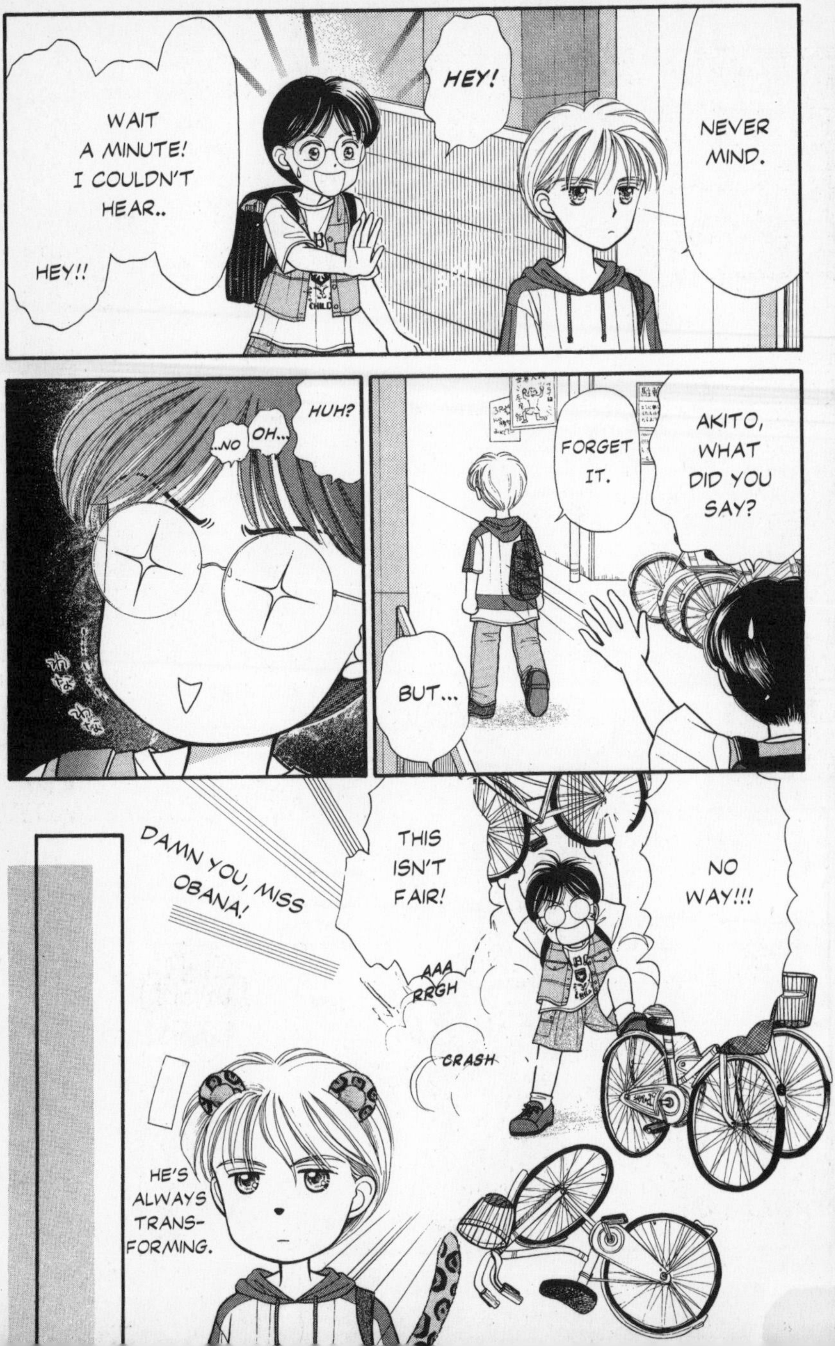
NEVER MIND.
HEY!
WAIT A MINUTE! I COULDN'T HEAR..
HEY!!
AKITO, WHAT DID YOU SAY?
FORGET IT.
BUT...
HUH?
OH...
...NO
NO WAY!!!
THIS ISN'T FAIR!
DAMN YOU, MISS OBANA!
AAARRGH
CRASH
HE'S ALWAYS TRANS-FORMING.

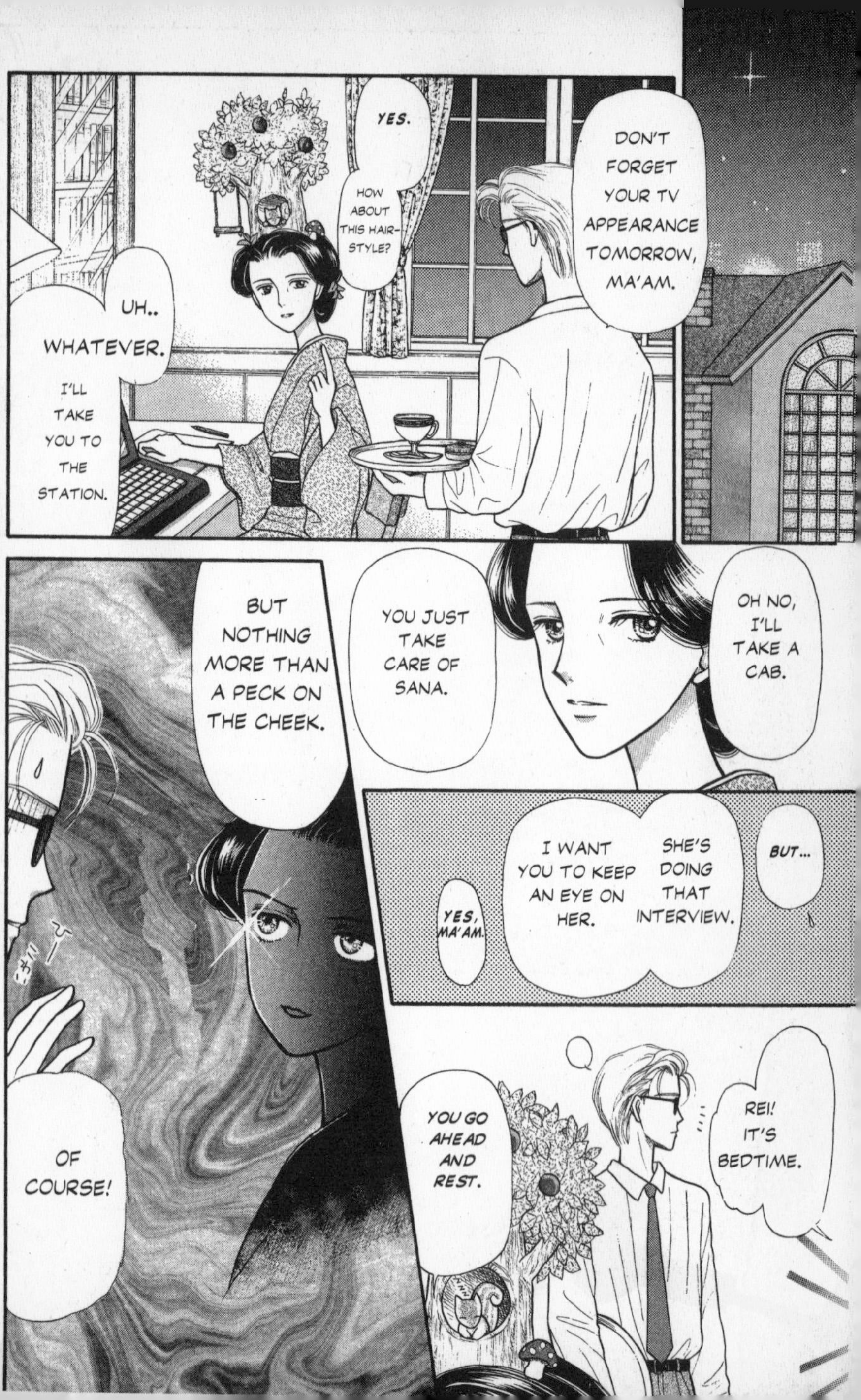
DON'T FORGET YOUR TV APPEARANCE TOMORROW, MA'AM.
YES.
HOW ABOUT THIS HAIR-STYLE?
UH.. WHATEVER.
I'LL TAKE YOU TO THE STATION.
OH NO, I'LL TAKE A CAB.
YOU JUST TAKE CARE OF SANA.
BUT...
SHE'S DOING THAT INTERVIEW.
I WANT YOU TO KEEP AN EYE ON HER.
YES, MA'AM.
BUT NOTHING MORE THAN A PECK ON THE CHEEK.
OF COURSE!
REI! IT'S BEDTIME.
YOU GO AHEAD AND REST.

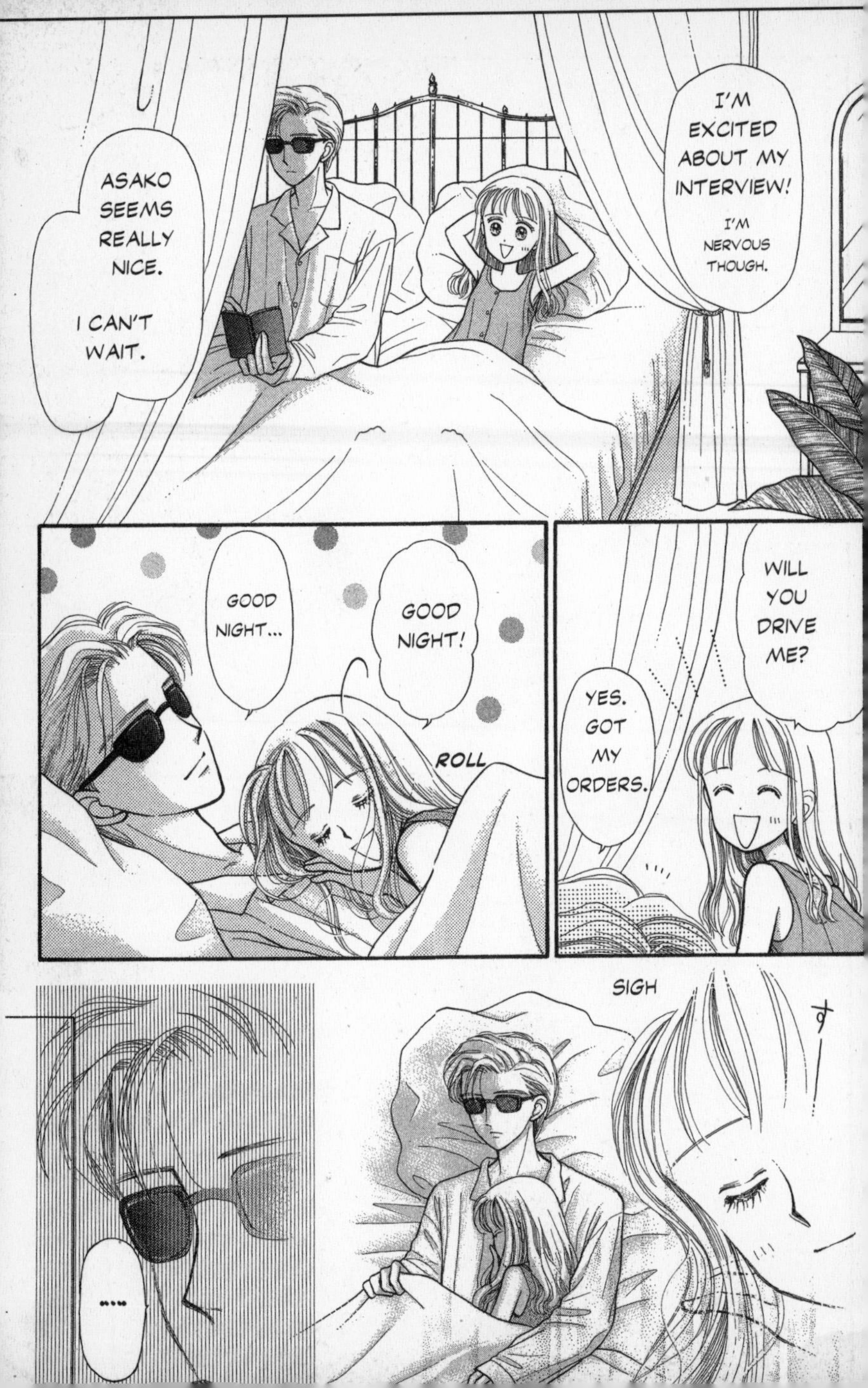
I'M EXCITED ABOUT MY INTERVIEW!
I'M NERVOUS THOUGH.
ASAKO SEEMS REALLY NICE.
I CAN'T WAIT.
WILL YOU DRIVE ME?
YES. GOT MY ORDERS.
GOOD NIGHT!
GOOD NIGHT...
ROLL
SIGH
す
....

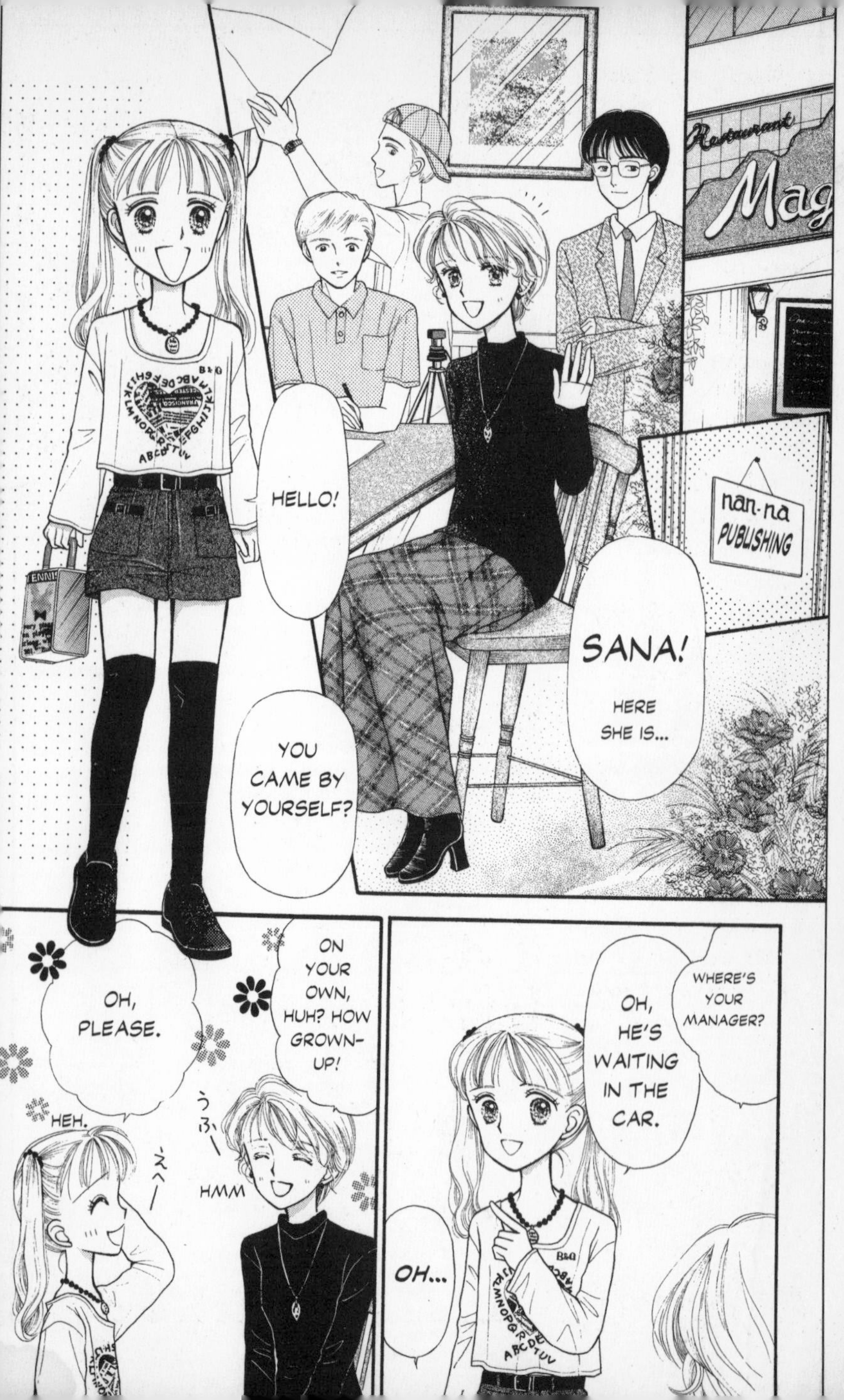
Restaurant
Mag
nan-na PUBUSHING
SANA! HERE SHE IS...
HELLO!
YOU CAME BY YOURSELF?
WHERE'S YOUR MANAGER?
OH, HE'S WAITING IN THE CAR.
OH...
ON YOUR OWN, HUH? HOW GROWN-UP!
OH, PLEASE.
うふー
HMM
HEH.
えへー

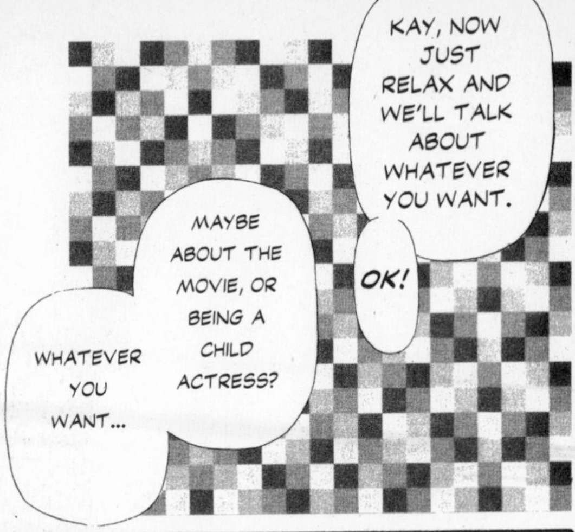
KAY, NOW JUST RELAX AND WE'LL TALK ABOUT WHATEVER YOU WANT.
OK!
MAYBE ABOUT THE MOVIE, OR BEING A CHILD ACTRESS?
WHATEVER YOU WANT...

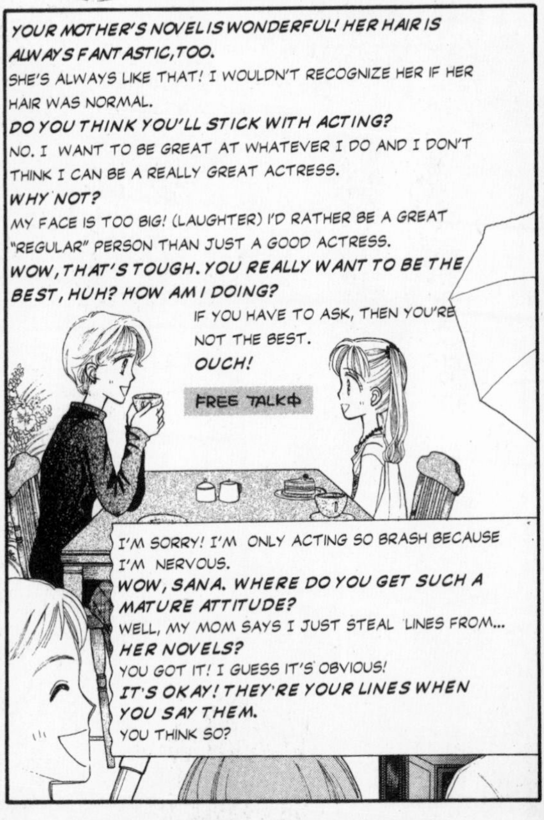
YOUR MOTHER'S NOVEL IS WONDERFUL! HER HAIR IS ALWAYS FANTASTIC, TOO.
SHE'S ALWAYS LIKE THAT! I WOULDN'T RECOGNIZE HER IF HER HAIR WAS NORMAL.
DO YOU THINK YOU'LL STICK WITH ACTING?
NO. I WANT TO BE GREAT AT WHATEVER I DO AND I DON'T THINK I CAN BE A REALLY GREAT ACTRESS.
WHY NOT?
MY FACE IS TOO BIG! (LAUGHTER) I'D RATHER BE A GREAT "REGULAR" PERSON THAN JUST A GOOD ACTRESS.
WOW, THAT'S TOUGH. YOU REALLY WANT TO BE THE BEST, HUH? HOW AM I DOING?
IF YOU HAVE TO ASK, THEN YOU'RE NOT THE BEST.
OUCH!
FREE TALK♂
I'M SORRY! I'M ONLY ACTING SO BRASH BECAUSE I'M NERVOUS.
WOW, SANA. WHERE DO YOU GET SUCH A MATURE ATTITUDE?
WELL, MY MOM SAYS I JUST STEAL LINES FROM...
HER NOVELS?
YOU GOT IT! I GUESS IT'S OBVIOUS!
IT'S OKAY! THEY'RE YOUR LINES WHEN YOU SAY THEM.
YOU THINK SO?

Making the Video

So, the Kodocha video has a lot of funny lines — even more than the original. I cracked up when I saw the finished script! I'm sure you'll love it, too. Check it out if you get the chance! The main voice talents are:
Sana: Chisa Yokoyama,
Akito: Emi Ogata,
Tsuyoshi: Minami Takayama,
Rei: Masami Kikuchi.
I didn't actually know who they were, but they're all well-known voice actors. (Thank you, guys!) They had the recording 3 days ago, but I couldn't go because I was so close to my deadline! Man. But as I worked, I thought about how my characters were being given life at that moment and it made me happy.
(To be continued.)

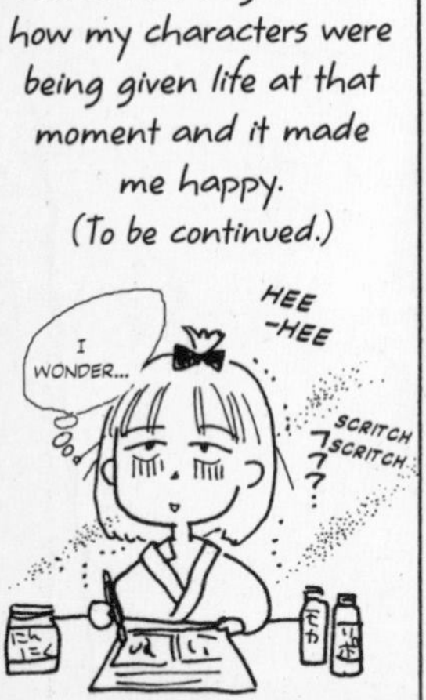
I WONDER...
HEE -HEE
SCRITCH SCRITCH

FREE TALK

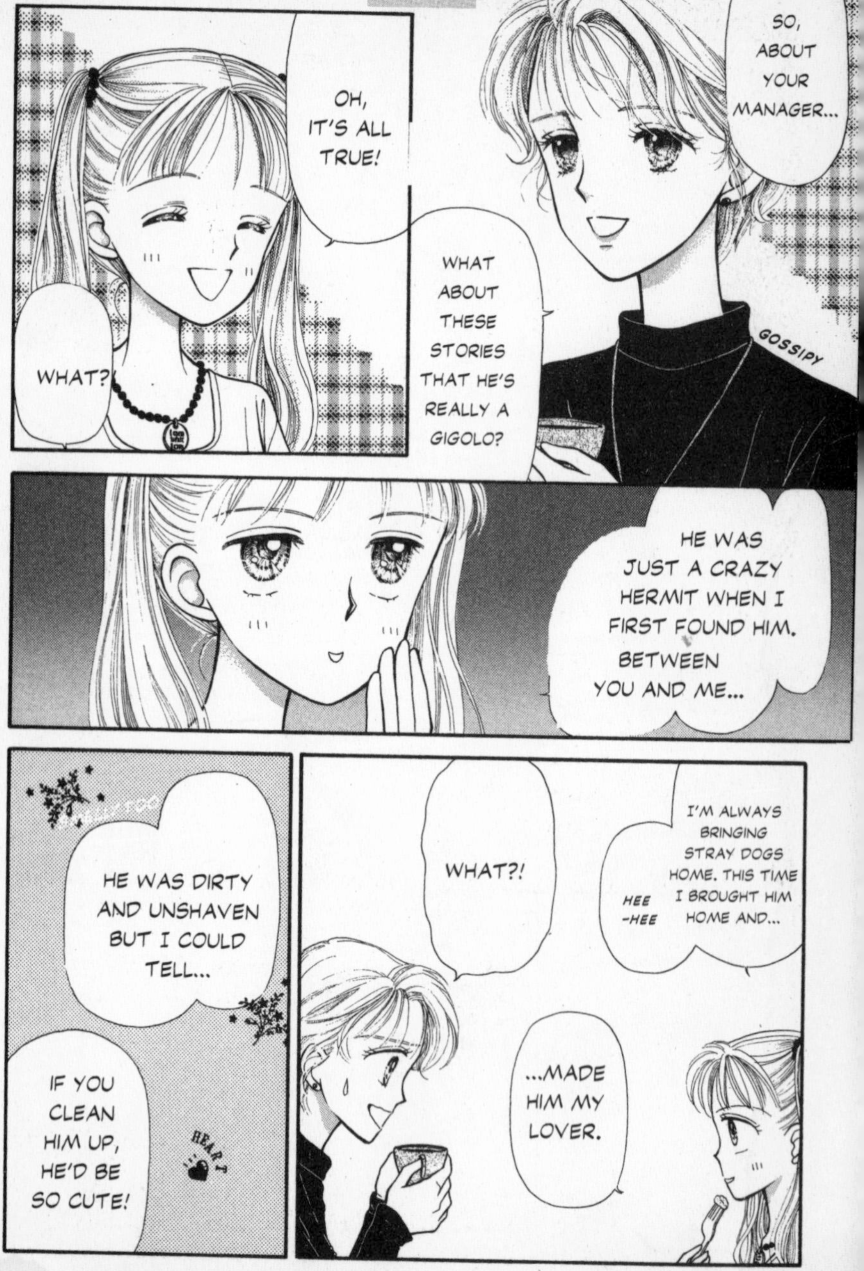
SO, ABOUT YOUR MANAGER...
GOSSIPY
WHAT ABOUT THESE STORIES THAT HE'S REALLY A GIGOLO?
OH, IT'S ALL TRUE!
WHAT?
HE WAS JUST A CRAZY HERMIT WHEN I FIRST FOUND HIM. BETWEEN YOU AND ME...
I'M ALWAYS BRINGING STRAY DOGS HOME. THIS TIME I BROUGHT HIM HOME AND...
HEE -HEE
WHAT?!
...MADE HIM MY LOVER.
HE WAS DIRTY AND UNSHAVEN BUT I COULD TELL...
IF YOU CLEAN HIM UP, HE'D BE SO CUTE!
HEART

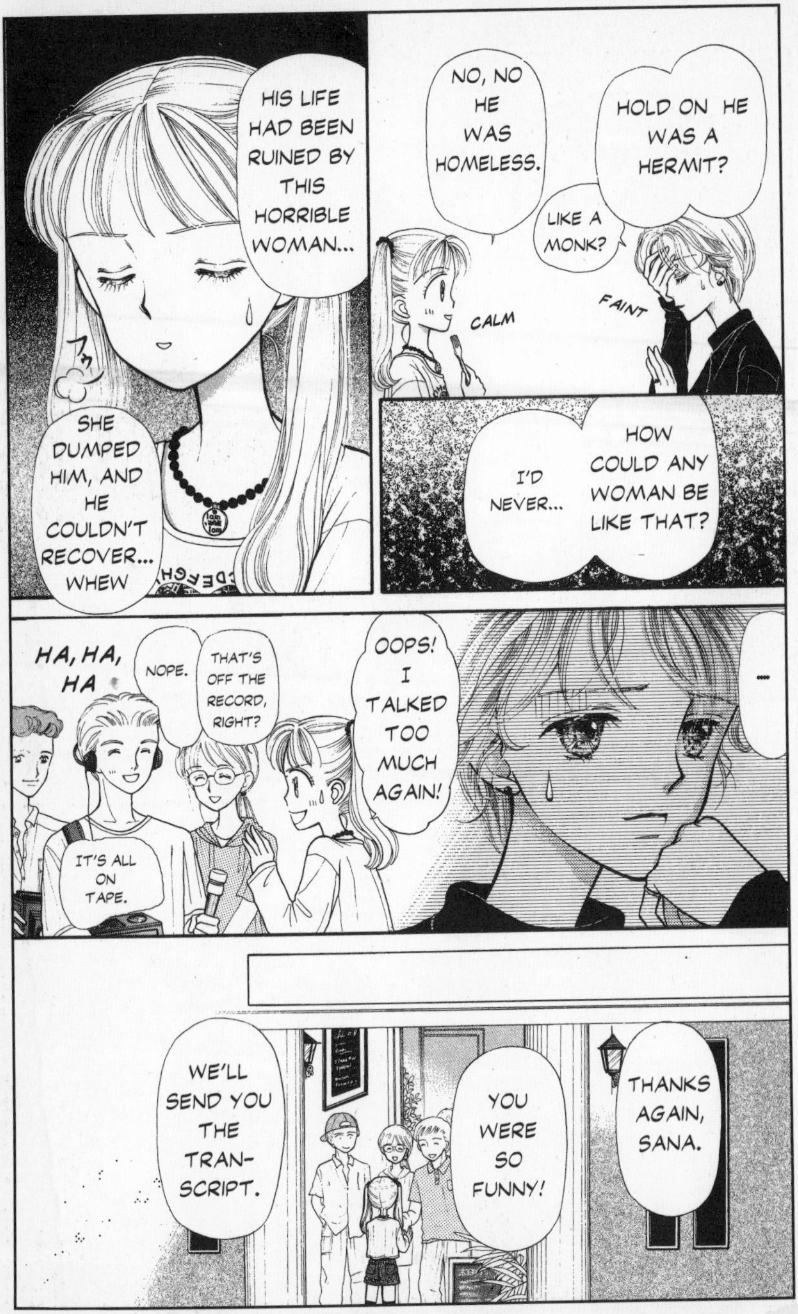
HOLD ON HE WAS A HERMIT?
NO, NO HE WAS HOMELESS.
LIKE A MONK?
FAINT
CALM
HOW COULD ANY WOMAN BE LIKE THAT?
I'D NEVER...
HIS LIFE HAD BEEN RUINED BY THIS HORRIBLE WOMAN...
フゥ
SHE DUMPED HIM, AND HE COULDN'T RECOVER... WHEW
...
OOPS! I TALKED TOO MUCH AGAIN!
THAT'S OFF THE RECORD, RIGHT?
NOPE.
HA, HA, HA
IT'S ALL ON TAPE.
THANKS AGAIN, SANA.
YOU WERE SO FUNNY!
WE'LL SEND YOU THE TRAN-SCRIPT.

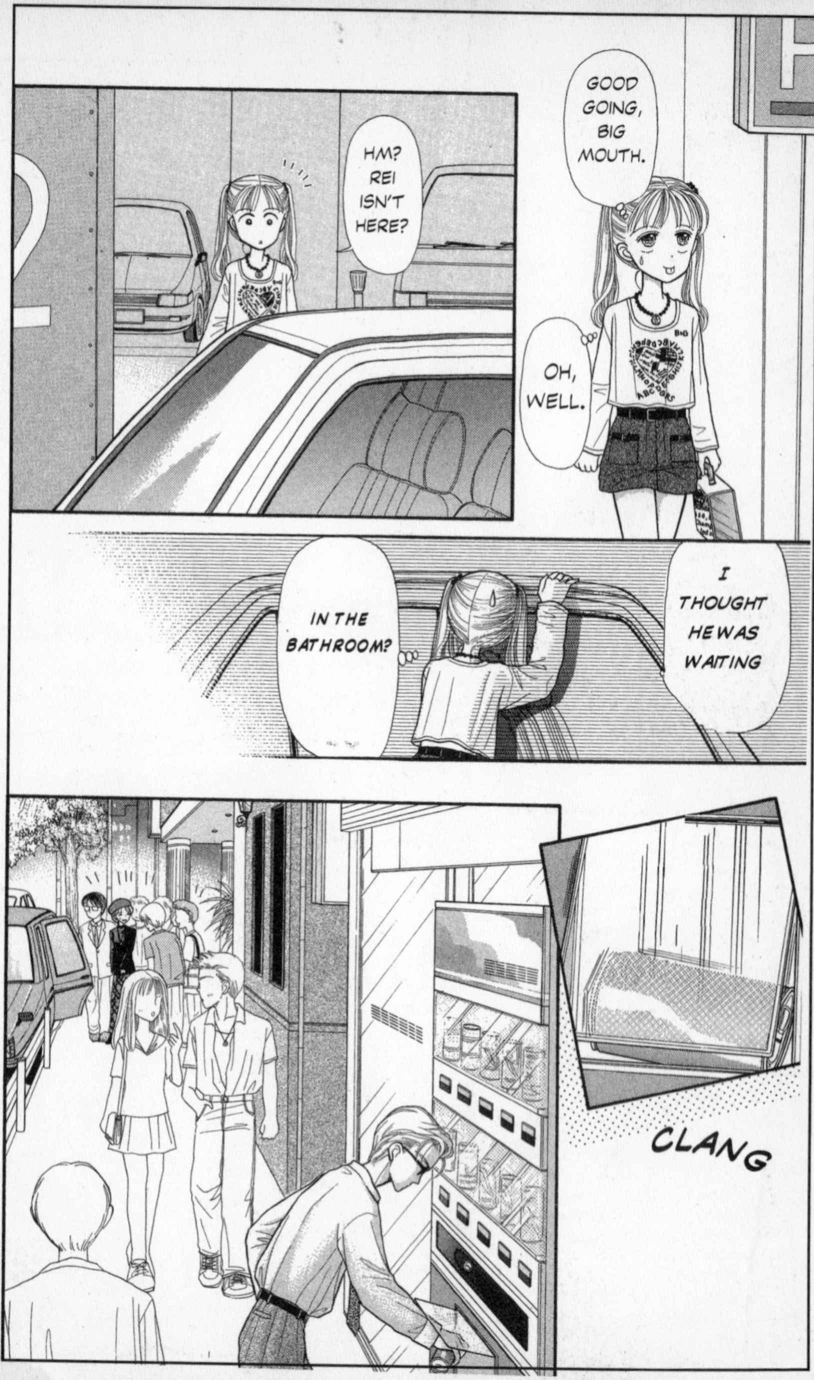
GOOD GOING, BIG MOUTH.
OH, WELL.
HM? REI ISN'T HERE?
I THOUGHT HE WAS WAITING
IN THE BATHROOM?
CLANG

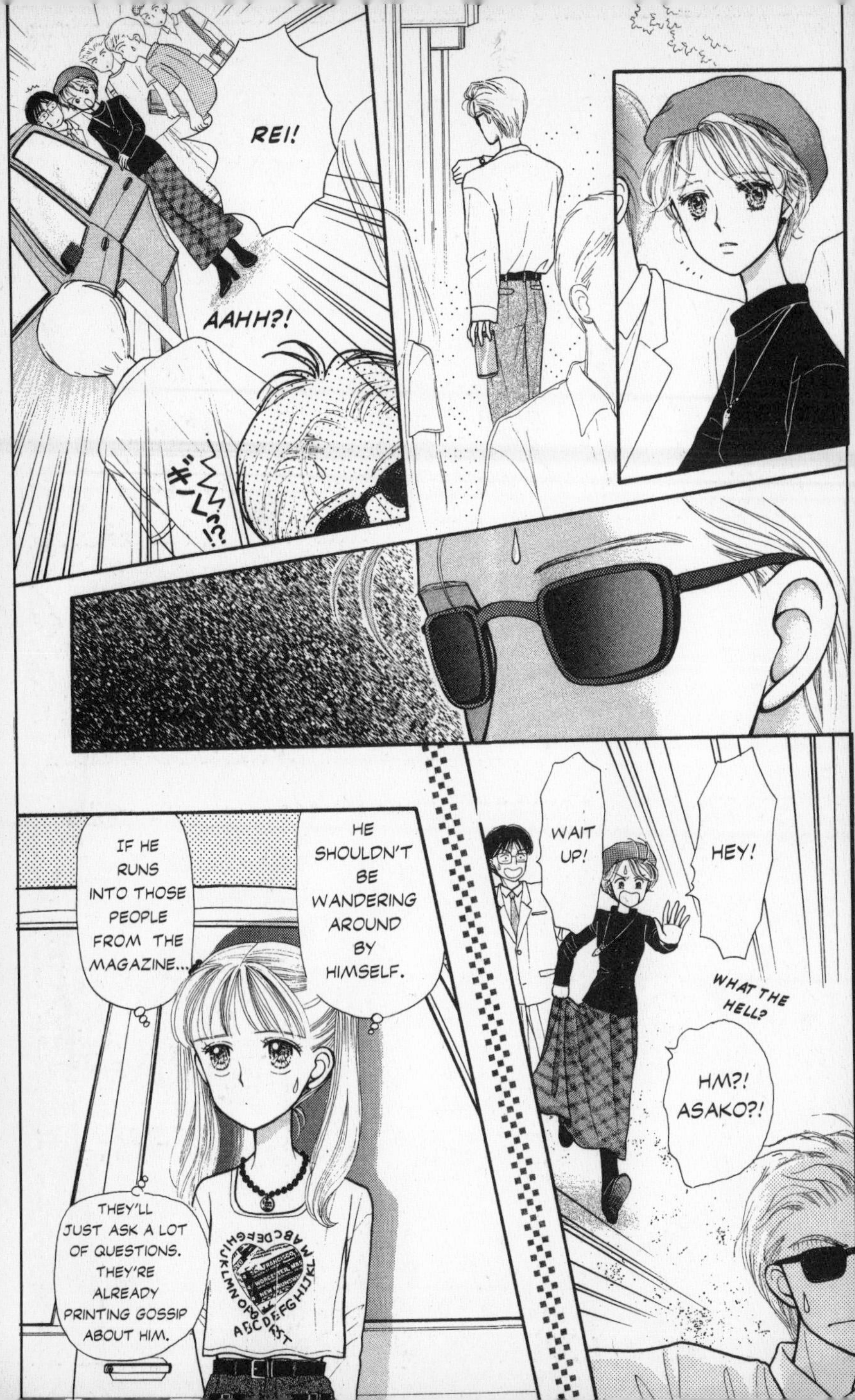
REI!
AAHH?!
HEY!
WAIT UP!
WHAT THE HELL?
HM?! ASAKO?!
HE SHOULDN'T BE WANDERING AROUND BY HIMSELF.
IF HE RUNS INTO THOSE PEOPLE FROM THE MAGAZINE...
THEY'LL JUST ASK A LOT OF QUESTIONS. THEY'RE ALREADY PRINTING GOSSIP ABOUT HIM.

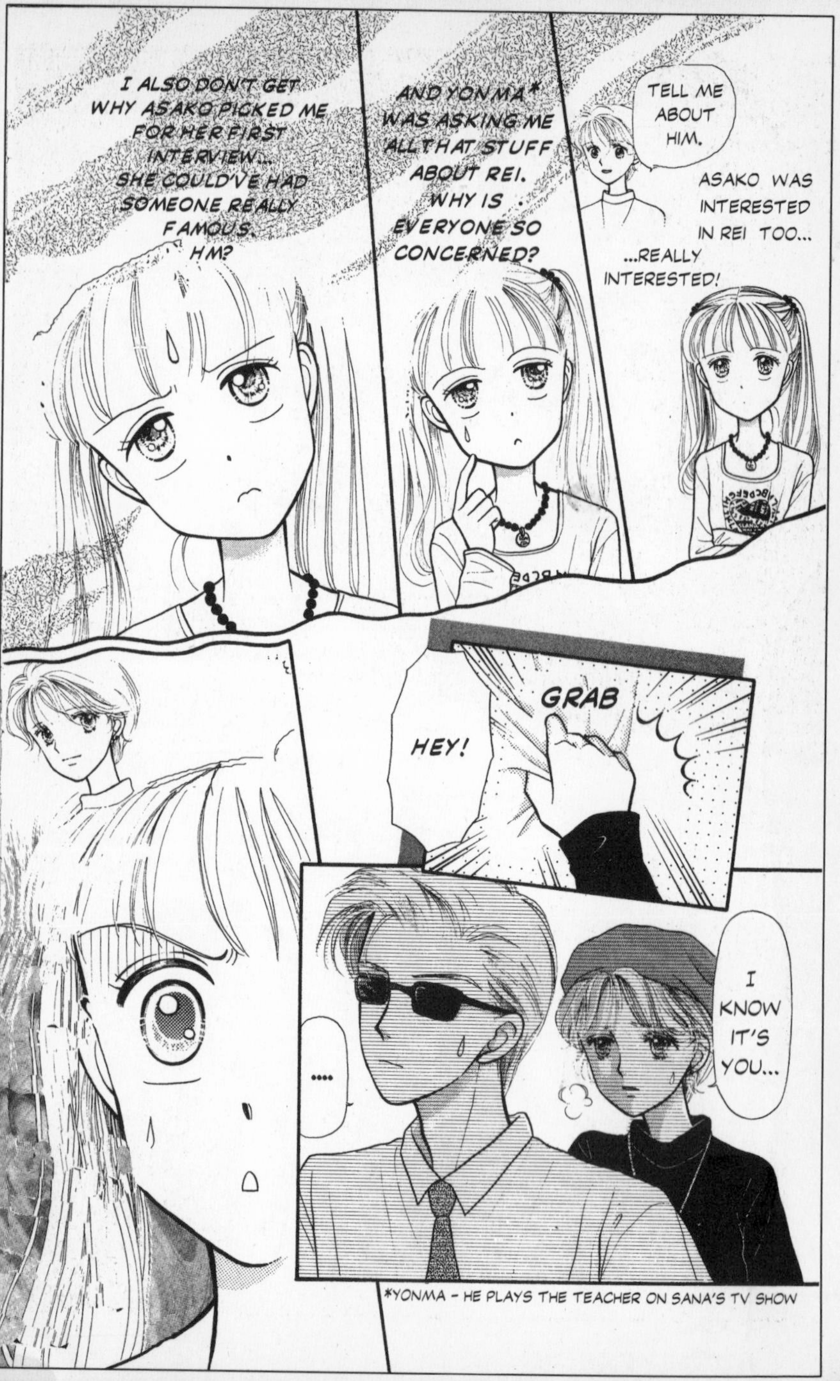
TELL ME ABOUT HIM.
ASAKO WAS INTERESTED IN REI TOO...
...REALLY INTERESTED!
AND YONMA* WAS ASKING ME ALL THAT STUFF ABOUT REI. WHY IS EVERYONE SO CONCERNED?
I ALSO DON'T GET WHY ASAKO PICKED ME FOR HER FIRST INTERVIEW... SHE COULD'VE HAD SOMEONE REALLY FAMOUS. HM?
GRAB
HEY!
I KNOW IT'S YOU...
....

*YONMA - HE PLAYS THE TEACHER ON SANA'S TV SHOW

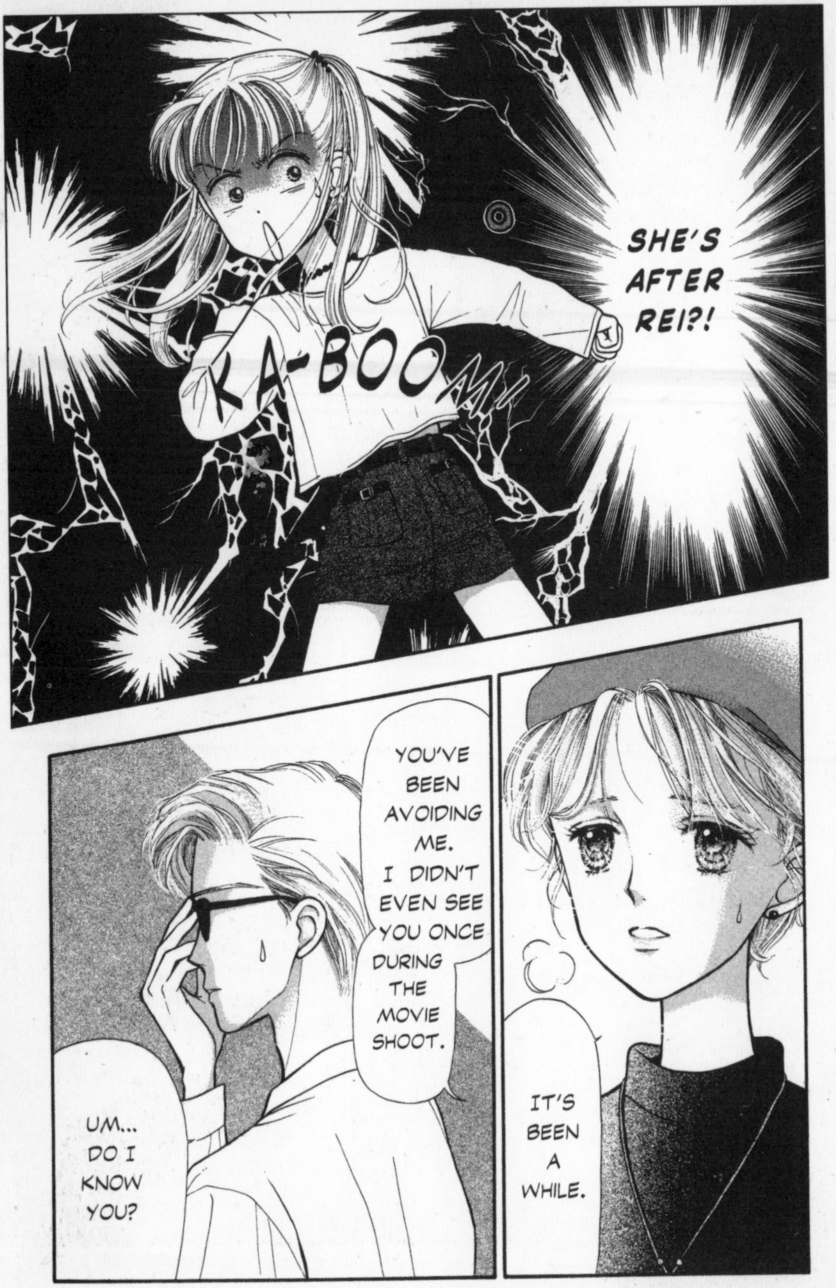
SHE'S AFTER REI?!
KA-BOOM!!
IT'S BEEN A WHILE.
YOU'VE BEEN AVOIDING ME. I DIDN'T EVEN SEE YOU ONCE DURING THE MOVIE SHOOT.
UM... DO I KNOW YOU?

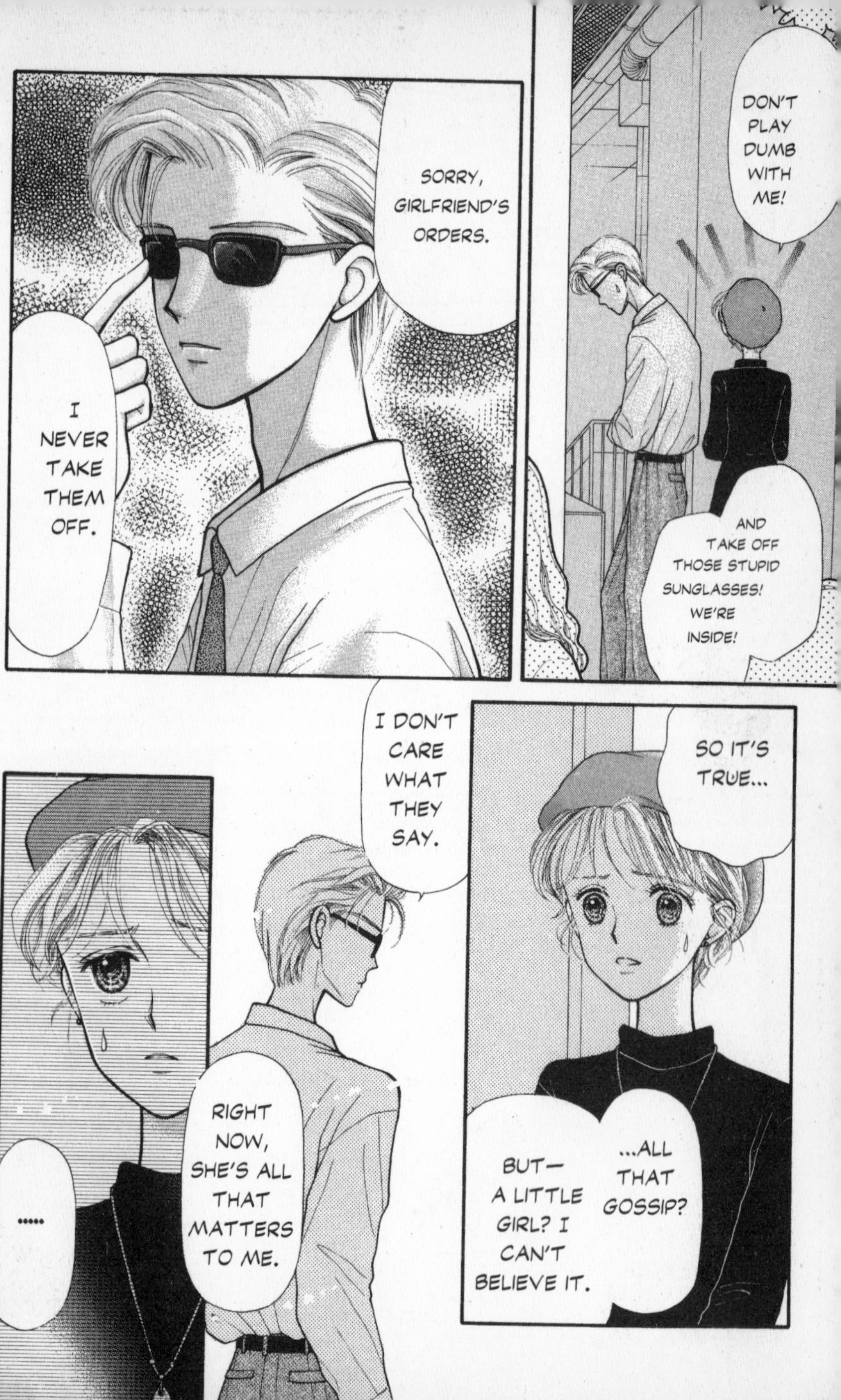
DON'T PLAY DUMB WITH ME!
AND TAKE OFF THOSE STUPID SUNGLASSES! WE'RE INSIDE!
SORRY, GIRLFRIEND'S ORDERS.
I NEVER TAKE THEM OFF.
SO IT'S TRUE...
...ALL THAT GOSSIP?
BUT— A LITTLE GIRL? I CAN'T BELIEVE IT.
I DON'T CARE WHAT THEY SAY.
RIGHT NOW, SHE'S ALL THAT MATTERS TO ME.
......

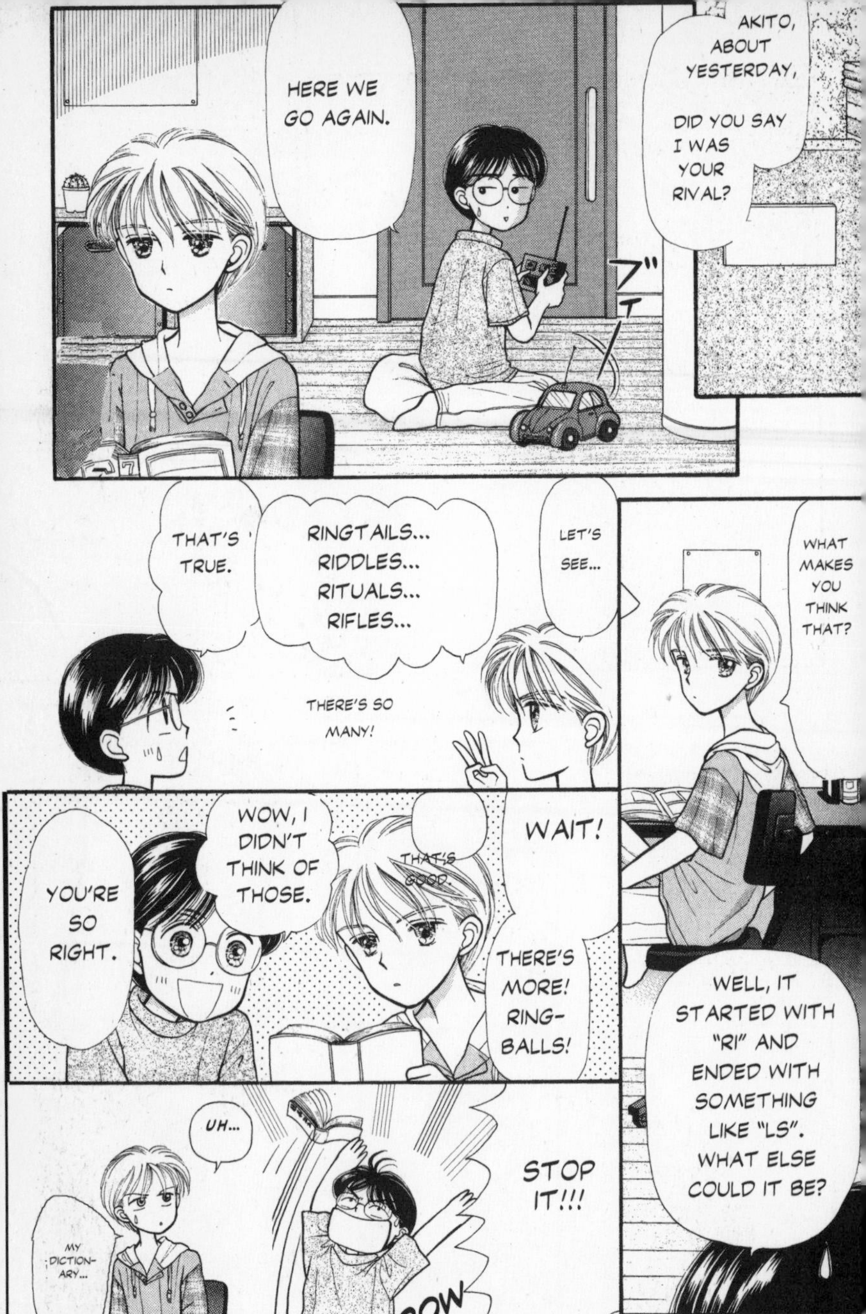
AKITO, ABOUT YESTERDAY, DID YOU SAY I WAS YOUR RIVAL?
HERE WE GO AGAIN.
WHAT MAKES YOU THINK THAT?
WELL, IT STARTED WITH "RI" AND ENDED WITH SOMETHING LIKE "LS". WHAT ELSE COULD IT BE?
LET'S SEE...
RINGTAILS... RIDDLES... RITUALS... RIFLES...
THAT'S TRUE.
THERE'S SO MANY!
WAIT!
THERE'S MORE! RING-BALLS!
THAT'S GOOD.
WOW, I DIDN'T THINK OF THOSE.
YOU'RE SO RIGHT.
STOP IT!!!
POW
UH...
MY DICTION-ARY...

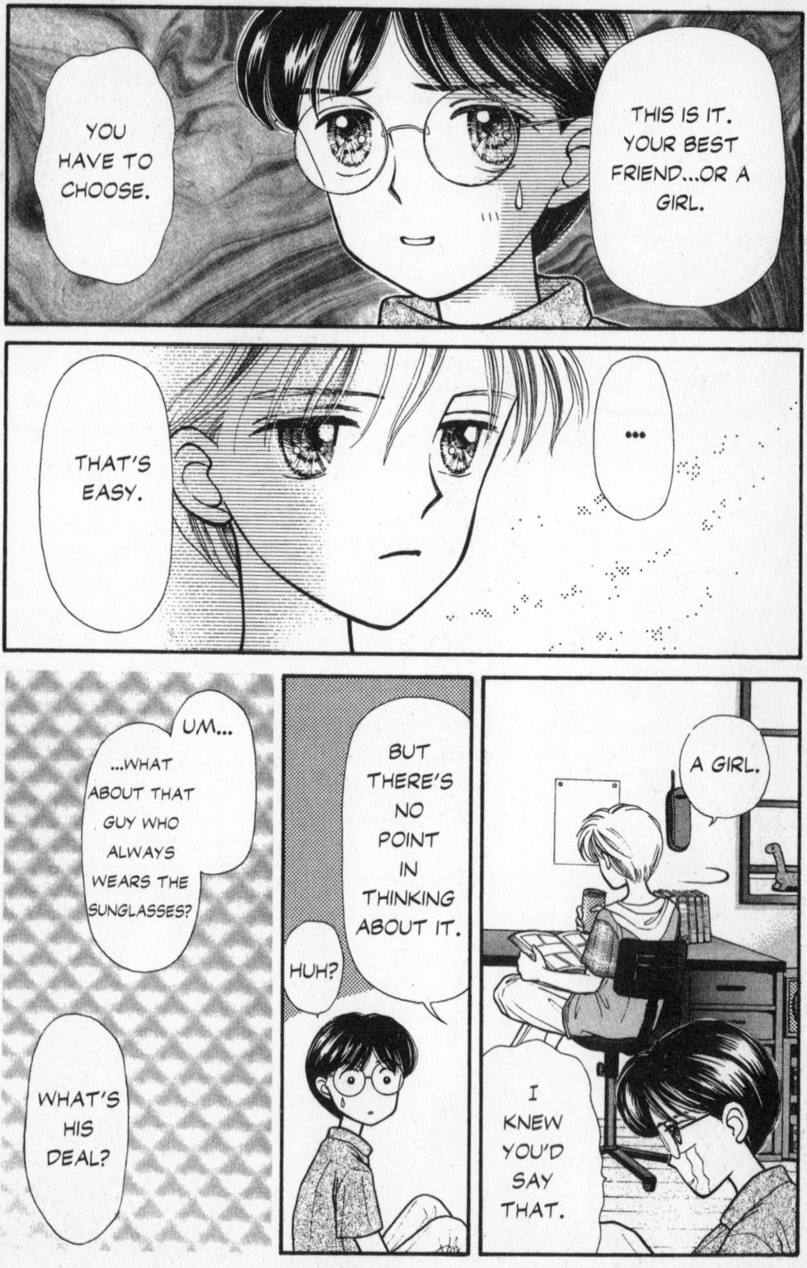
THIS IS IT. YOUR BEST FRIEND...OR A GIRL.
YOU HAVE TO CHOOSE.
...
THAT'S EASY.
A GIRL.
I KNEW YOU'D SAY THAT.
BUT THERE'S NO POINT IN THINKING ABOUT IT.
HUH?
UM...
...WHAT ABOUT THAT GUY WHO ALWAYS WEARS THE SUNGLASSES?
WHAT'S HIS DEAL?

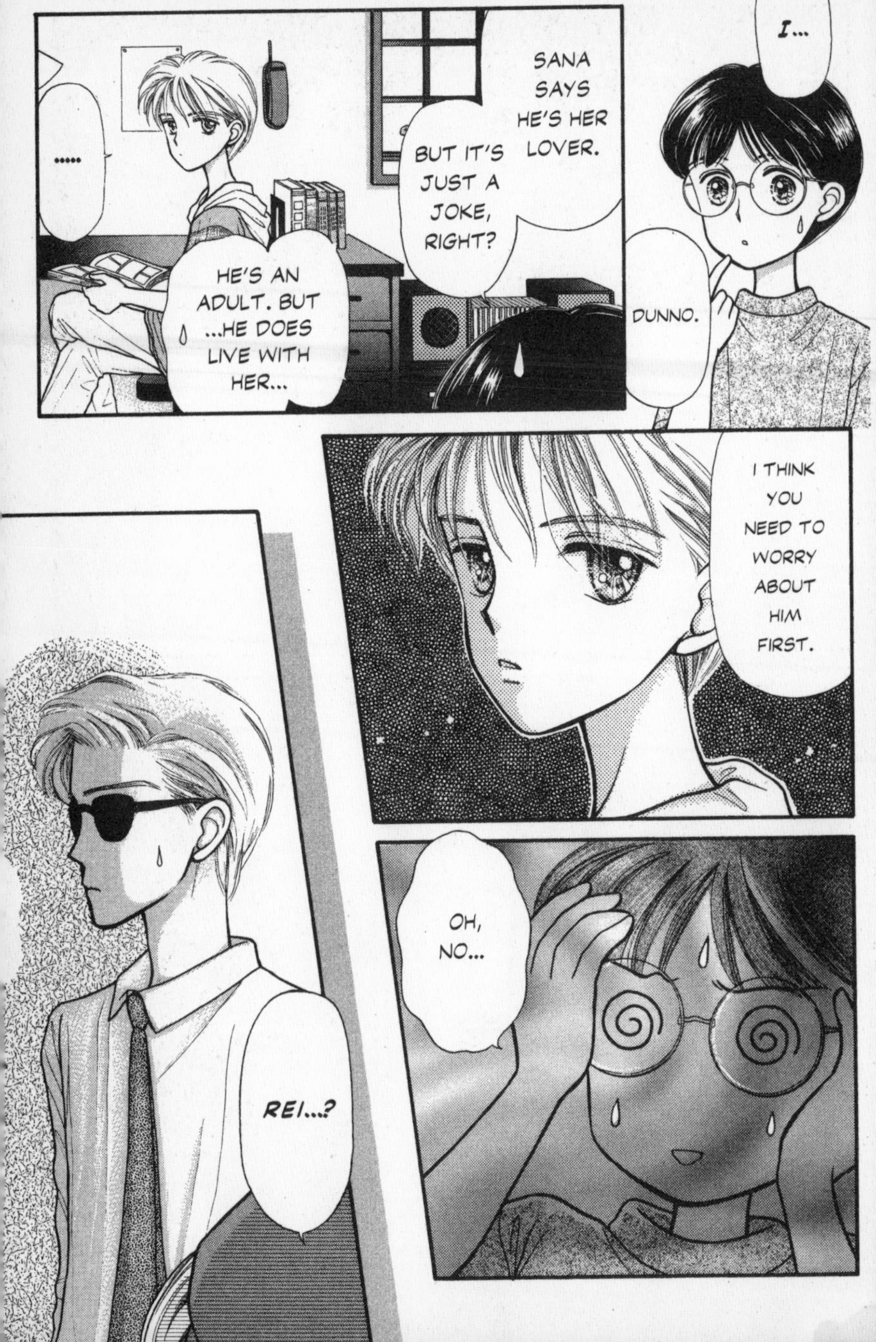
I...
SANA SAYS HE'S HER LOVER.
BUT IT'S JUST A JOKE, RIGHT?
DUNNO.
.....
HE'S AN ADULT. BUT ...HE DOES LIVE WITH HER...
I THINK YOU NEED TO WORRY ABOUT HIM FIRST.
OH, NO...
REI...?

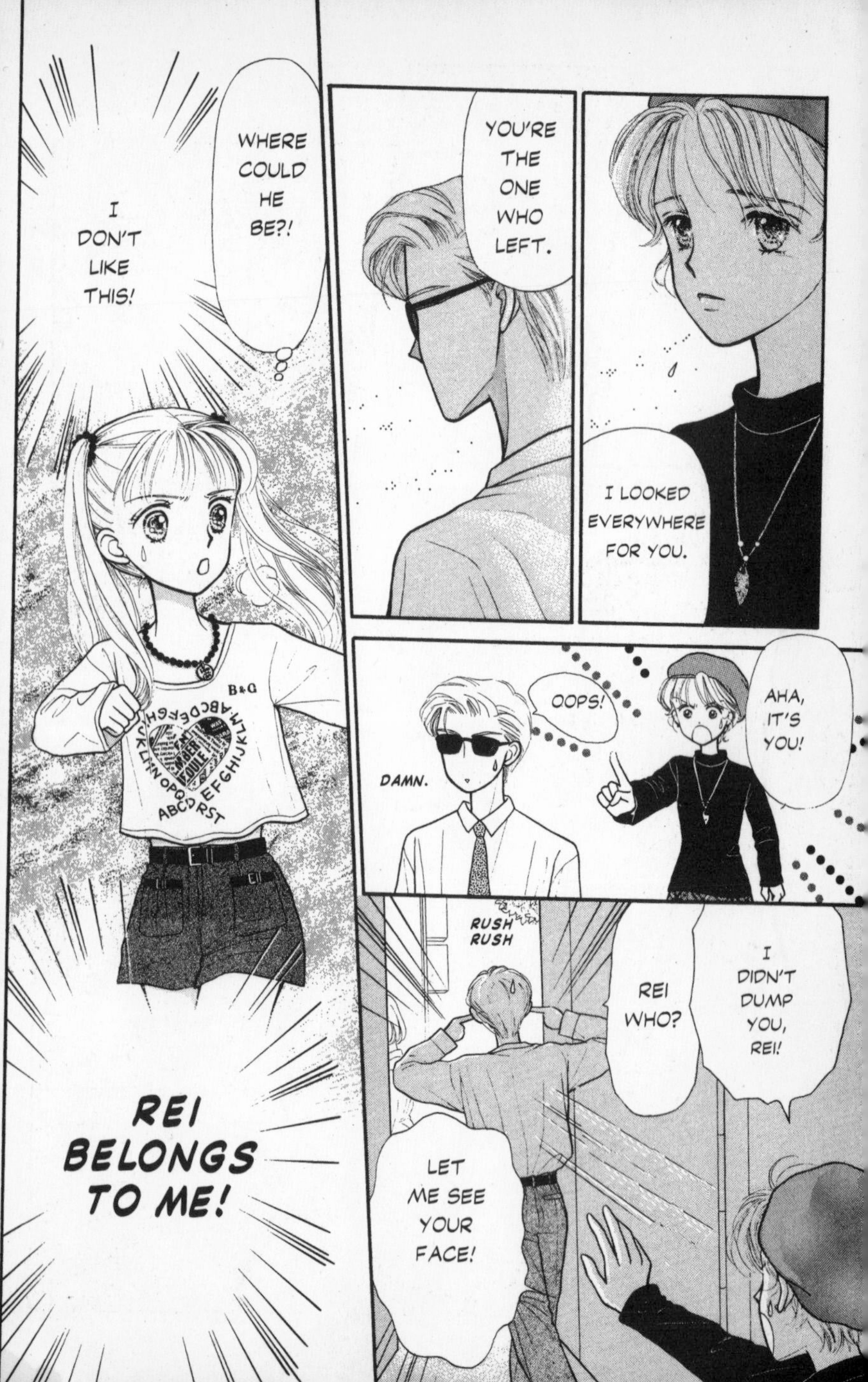
I LOOKED EVERYWHERE FOR YOU.
YOU'RE THE ONE WHO LEFT.
AHA, IT'S YOU!
OOPS!
DAMN.
I DIDN'T DUMP YOU, REI!
REI WHO?
RUSH RUSH
LET ME SEE YOUR FACE!
WHERE COULD HE BE?!
I DON'T LIKE THIS!
REI BELONGS TO ME!

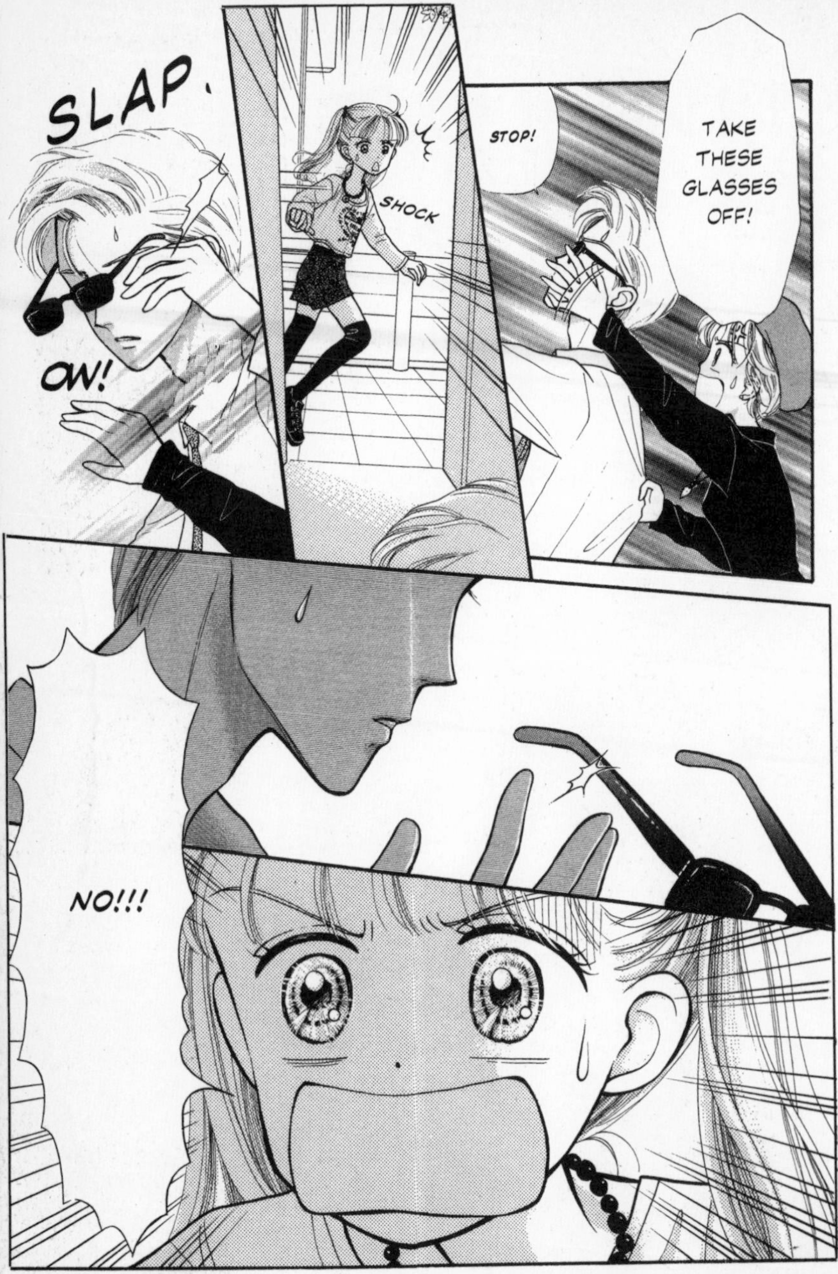
TAKE THESE GLASSES OFF!
STOP!
SHOCK
SLAP.
OW!
NO!!!

CHILD'S TOY EXTRA:

CHILD'S TOY WEATHER REPORT

Hayama's version

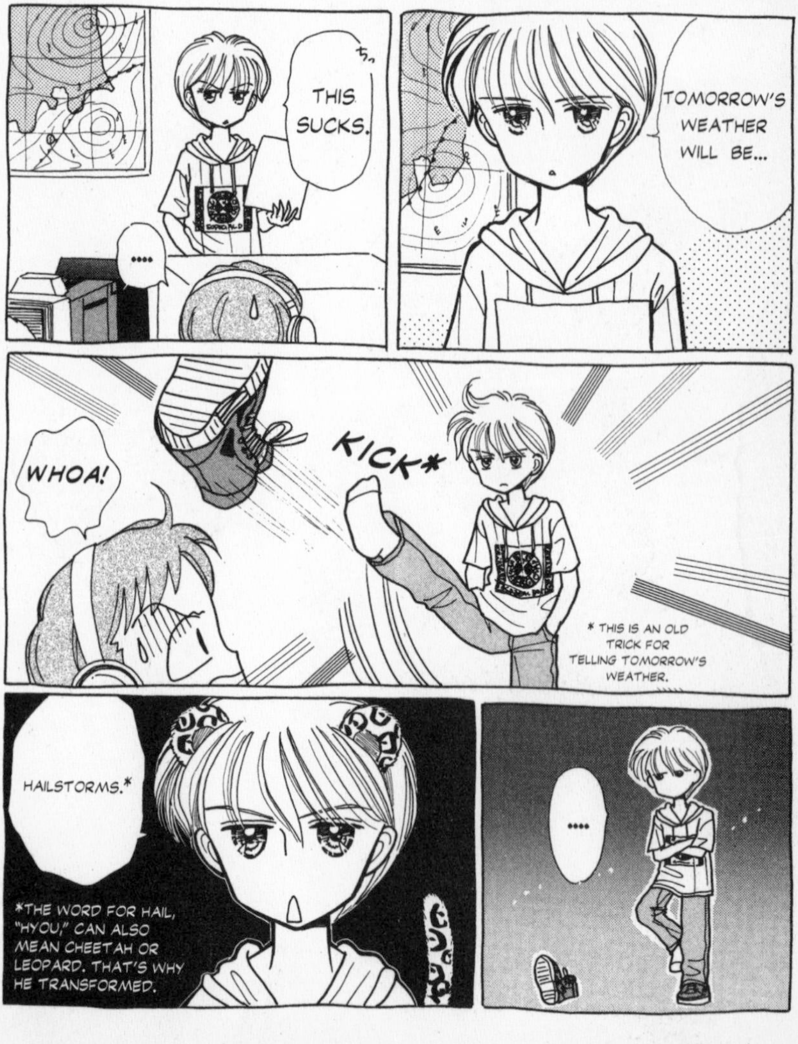
TOMORROW'S WEATHER WILL BE...
THIS SUCKS.
....
KICK*
WHOA!
* THIS IS AN OLD TRICK FOR TELLING TOMORROW'S WEATHER.
....
HAILSTORMS.*
*THE WORD FOR HAIL, "HYOU," CAN ALSO MEAN CHEETAH OR LEOPARD. THAT'S WHY HE TRANSFORMED.

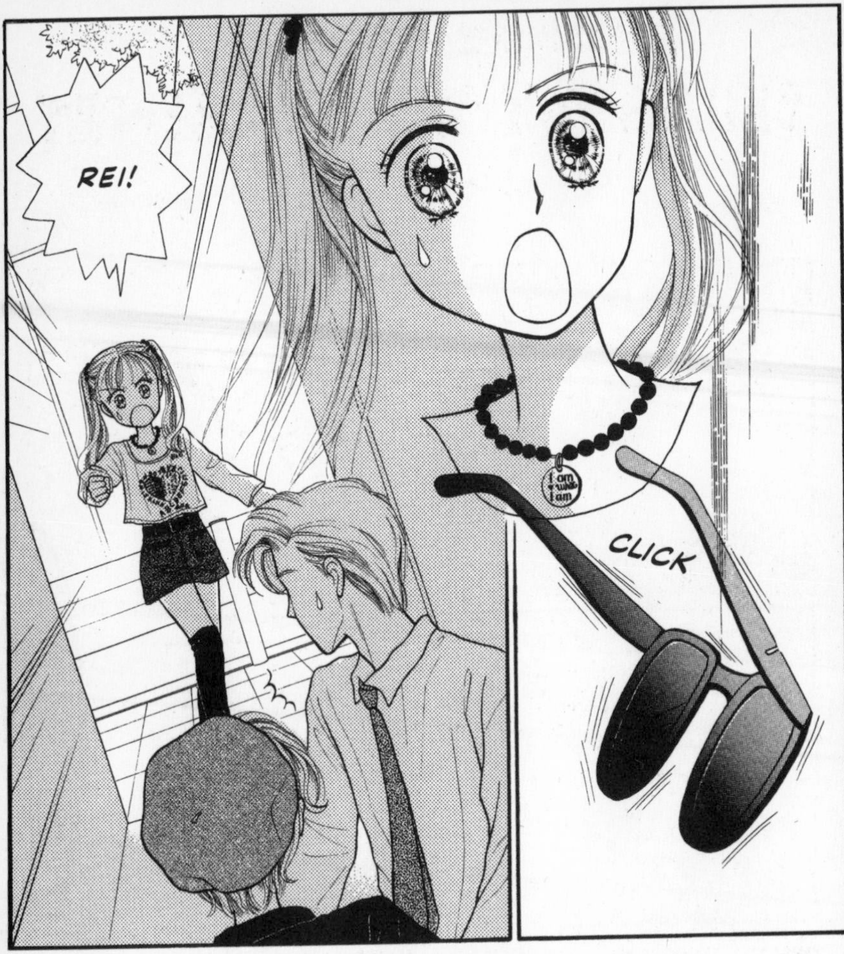
CLICK
REI!

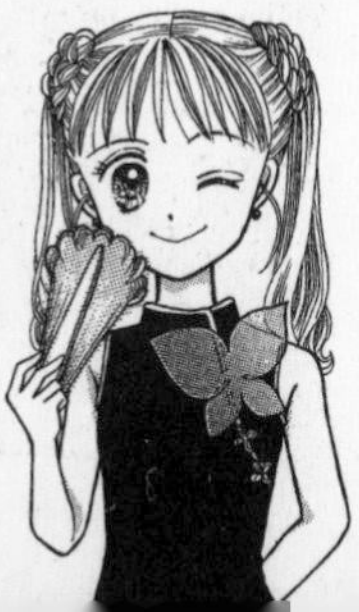

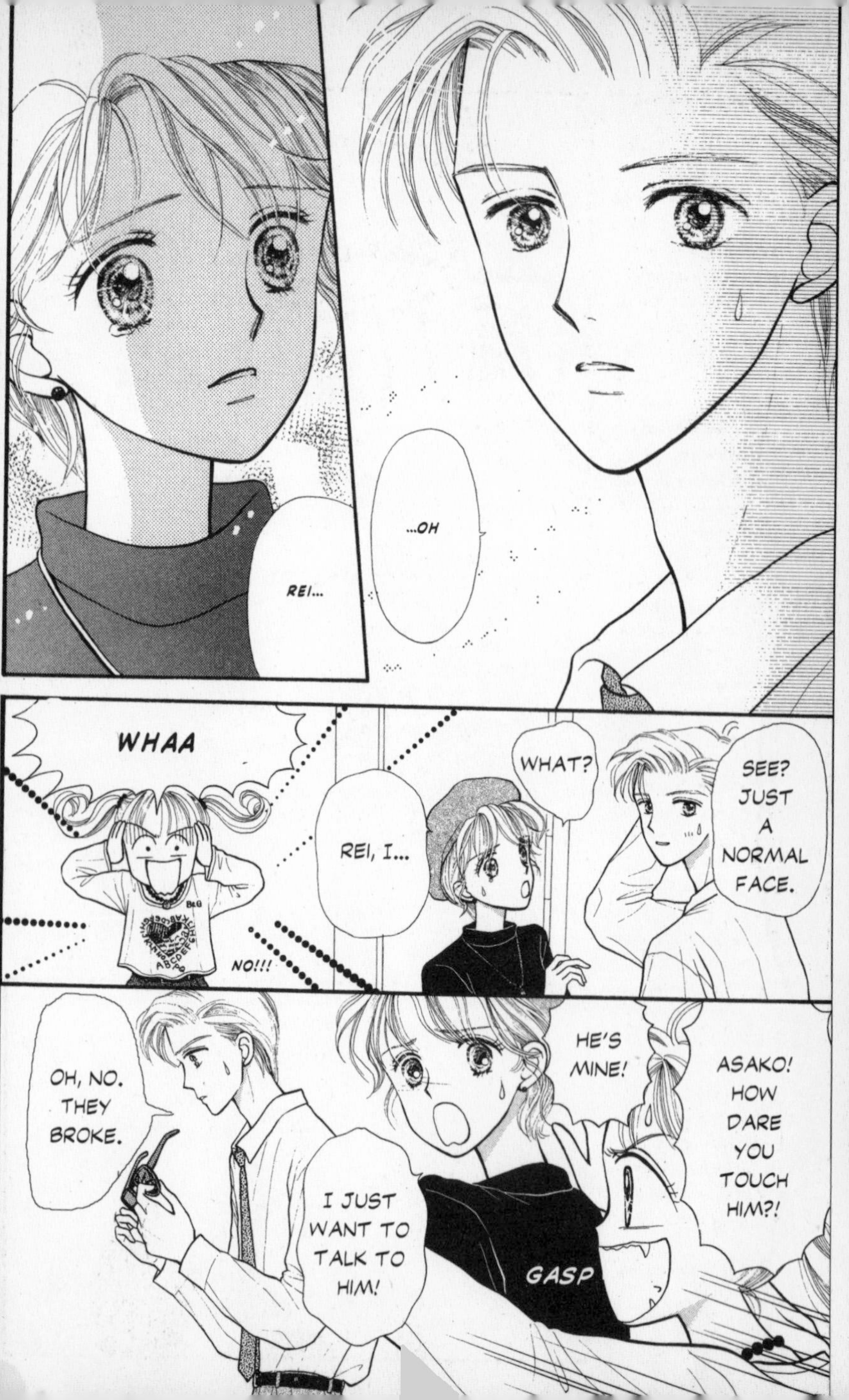
...OH
REI...
SEE? JUST A NORMAL FACE.
WHAT?
REI, I...
WHAA
NO!!!
ASAKO! HOW DARE YOU TOUCH HIM?!
HE'S MINE!
GASP
I JUST WANT TO TALK TO HIM!
OH, NO. THEY BROKE.

Playin' My Song

They let me write the theme song for the video! I thought maybe a pro should do it but I did it anyway. Ha, ha. It's very amateur-ish and embarrassing. (Oh, well. I'm an amateur.) This is the only time you'll hear a song I wrote, so check it out! I have to admit, I didn't really think about it actually being sung when I wrote it. So, it might not be so easy to sing. (The singer, Miss Chisa Yokoyama, is also the voice of Sana in the video.) I actually wrote three different songs at first 1: Serious; 2: Funny; and 3: Just plain goofy. (Hee-hee.) And they ended up picking the serious one to record. I dunno, maybe it's too serious for Kodocha. Please sing it in your music class in school! (Hee-hee.) I told them I couldn't write songs! But I wrote the music, and then I thought it would be embarrassing to ask a professional to add words to an amateur's melody. So I gave it a try! I hope you like it!

(To be continued.)

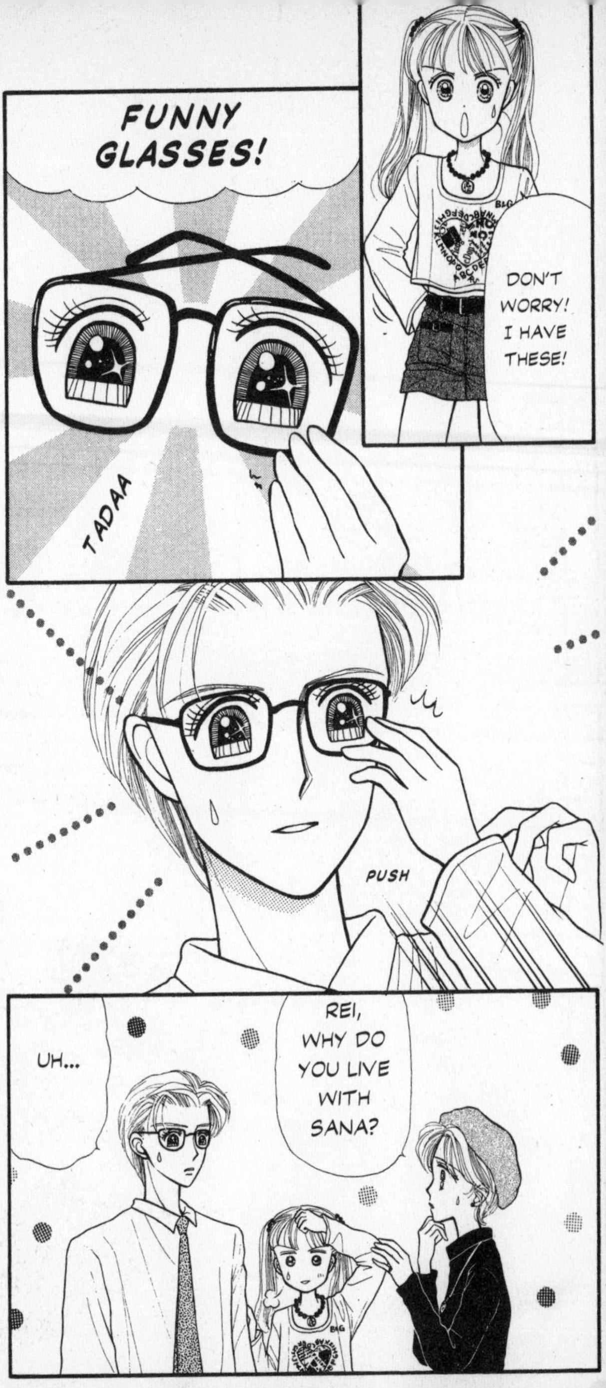
DON'T WORRY! I HAVE THESE!
FUNNY GLASSES!
TADAA
PUSH
REI, WHY DO YOU LIVE WITH SANA?
UH...

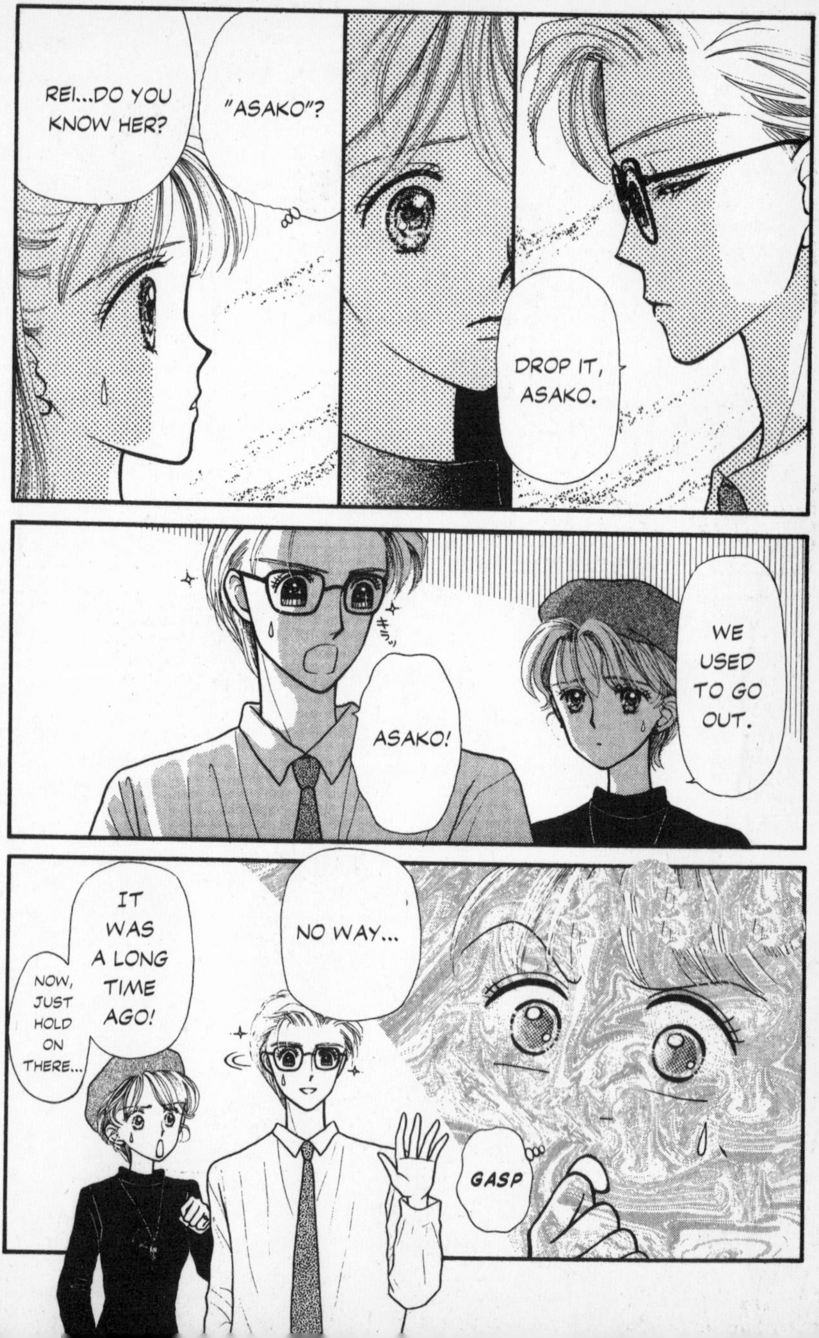
DROP IT, ASAKO.
"ASAKO"?
REI...DO YOU KNOW HER?
WE USED TO GO OUT.
ASAKO!
GASP
NO WAY...
IT WAS A LONG TIME AGO!
NOW, JUST HOLD ON THERE...

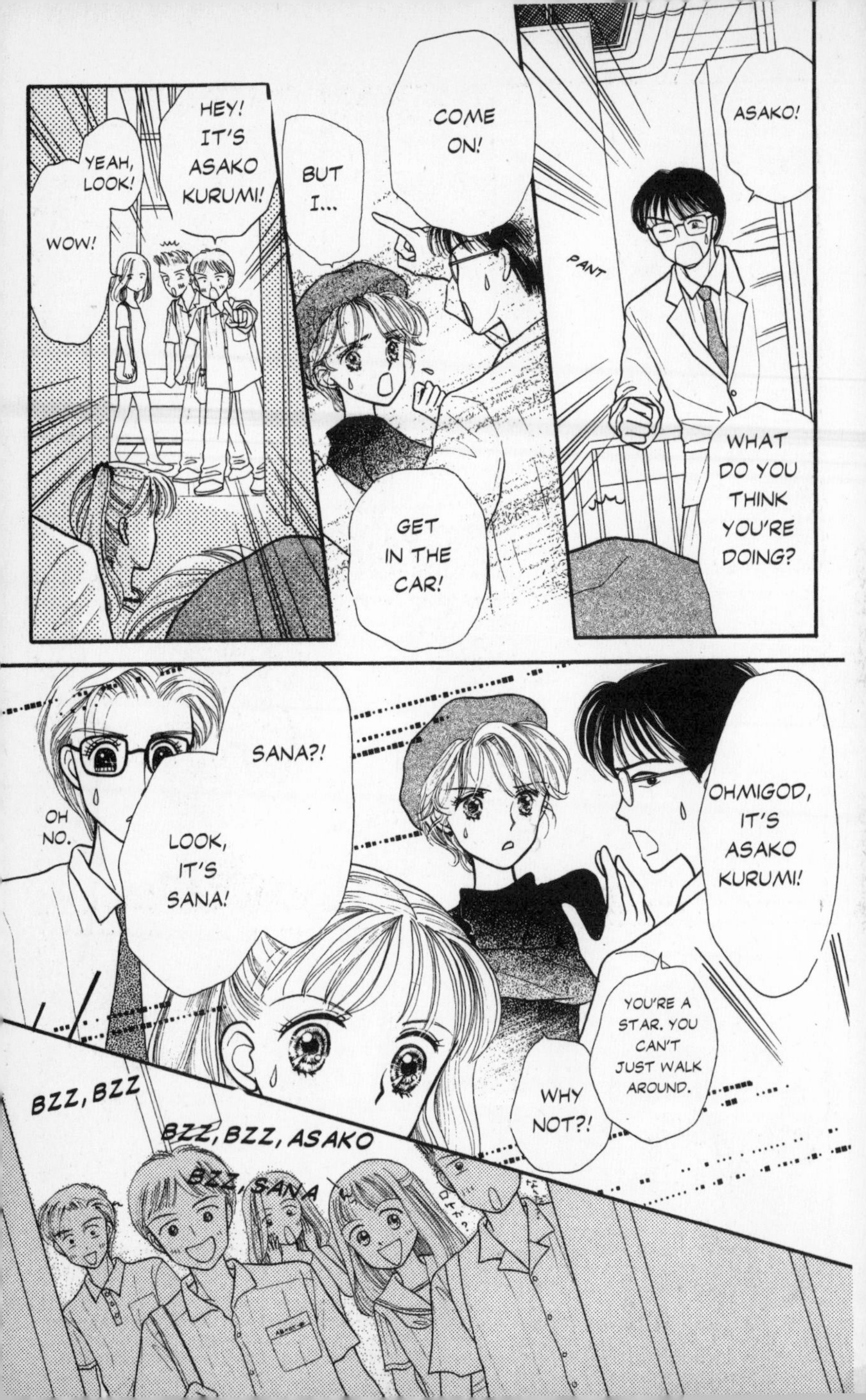
ASAKO!
PANT
WHAT DO YOU THINK YOU'RE DOING?
COME ON!
BUT I...
GET IN THE CAR!
HEY! IT'S ASAKO KURUMI!
YEAH, LOOK!
WOW!
OHMIGOD, IT'S ASAKO KURUMI!
SANA?!
LOOK, IT'S SANA!
OH NO.
YOU'RE A STAR. YOU CAN'T JUST WALK AROUND.
WHY NOT?!
BZZ, BZZ
BZZ, BZZ, ASAKO
BZZ, SANA

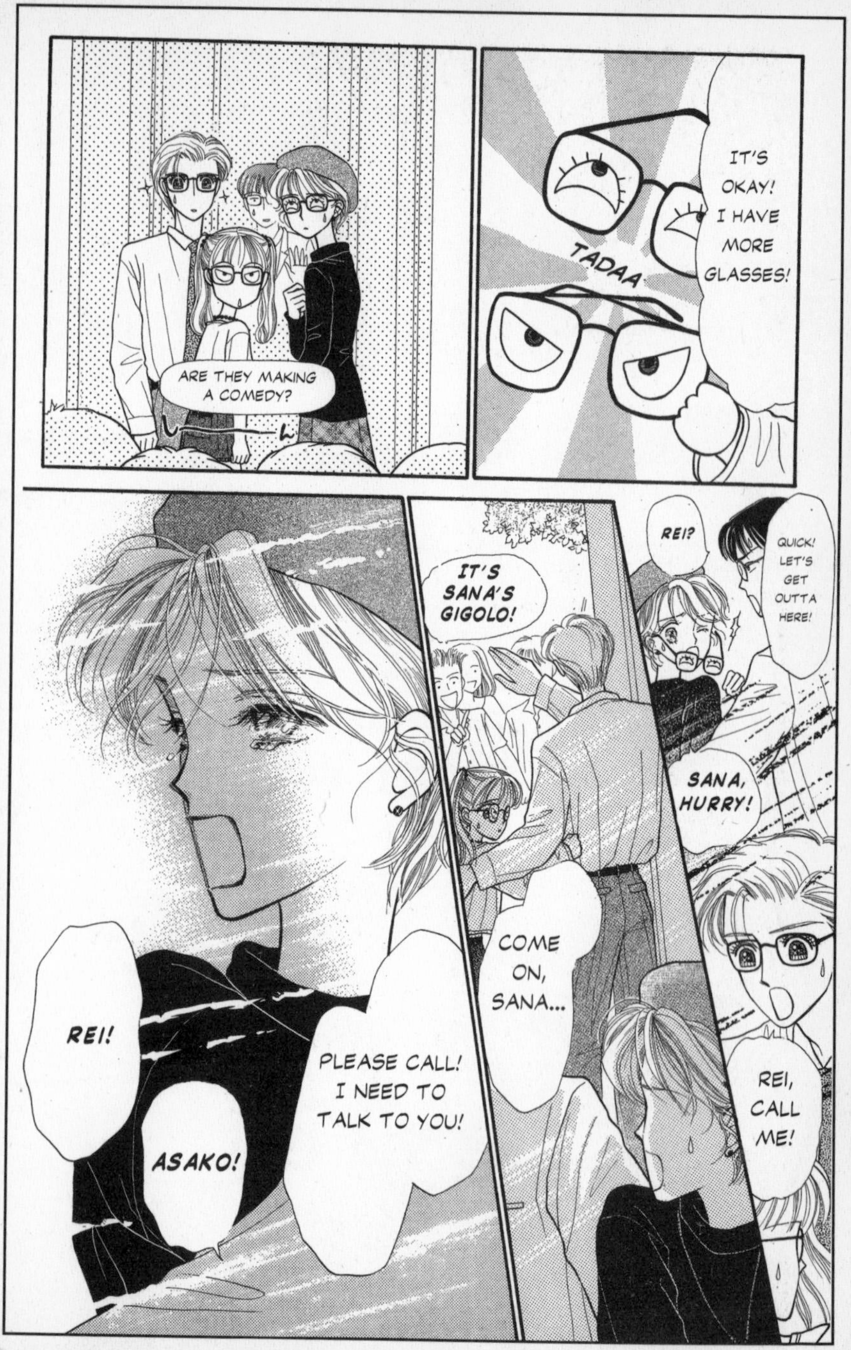
IT'S OKAY! I HAVE MORE GLASSES!
TADAA
ARE THEY MAKING A COMEDY?
QUICK! LET'S GET OUTTA HERE!
REI?
IT'S SANA'S GIGOLO!
SANA, HURRY!
REI, CALL ME!
COME ON, SANA...
PLEASE CALL! I NEED TO TALK TO YOU!
REI!
ASAKO!

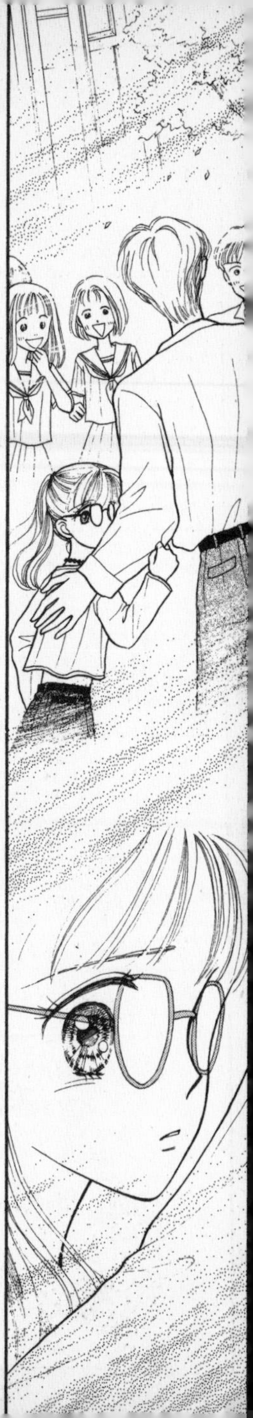
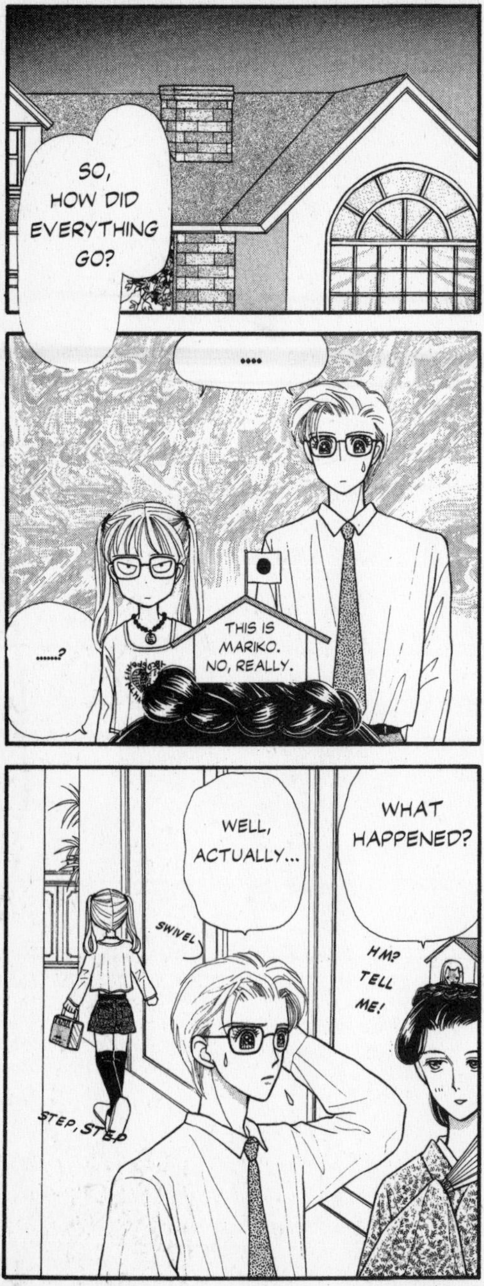
SO, HOW DID EVERYTHING GO?
....
THIS IS MARIKO. NO, REALLY.
......?
WHAT HAPPENED?
WELL, ACTUALLY...
HM? TELL ME!
SWIVEL
STEP, STEP

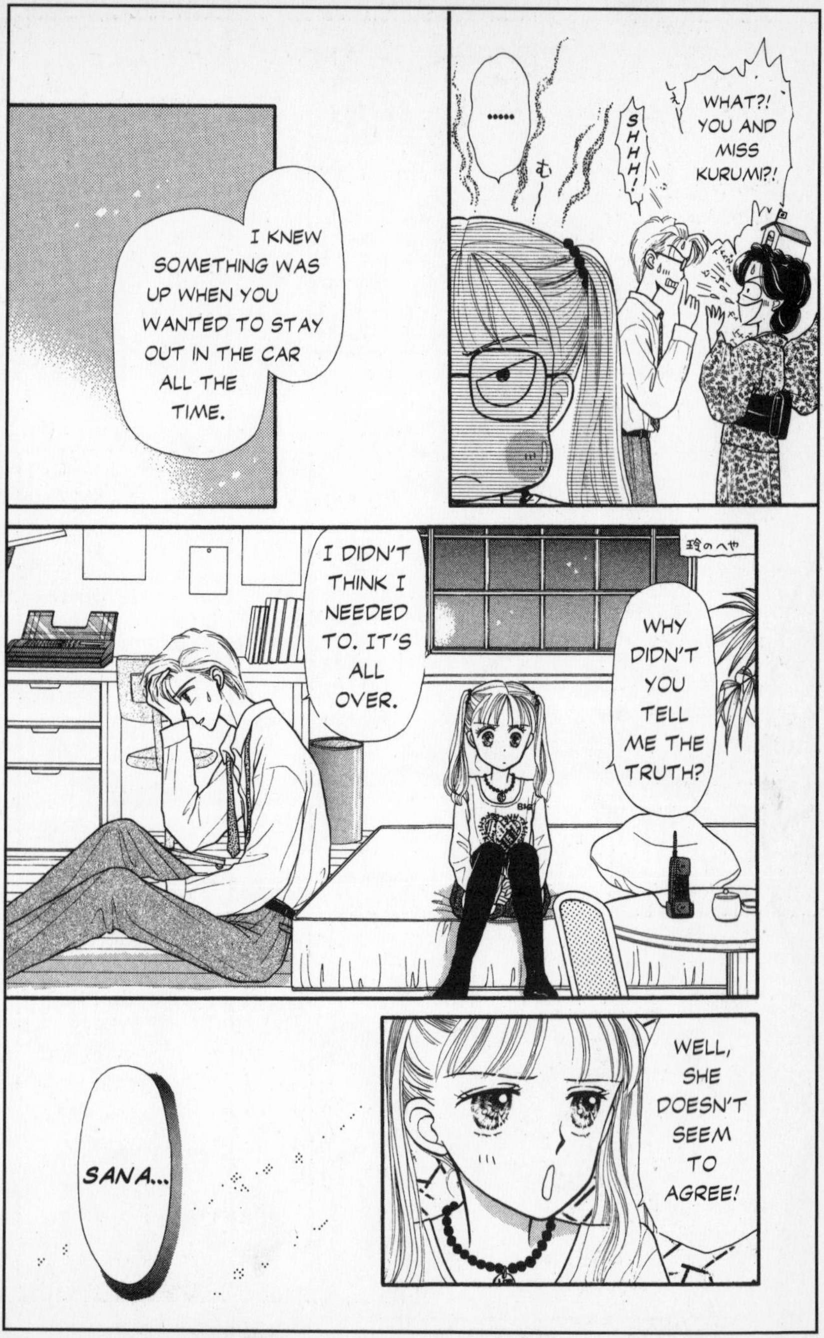
WHAT?! YOU AND MISS KURUMI?!
SHHH!
......
む
I KNEW SOMETHING WAS UP WHEN YOU WANTED TO STAY OUT IN THE CAR ALL THE TIME.
玲のへや
WHY DIDN'T YOU TELL ME THE TRUTH?
I DIDN'T THINK I NEEDED TO. IT'S ALL OVER.
WELL, SHE DOESN'T SEEM TO AGREE!
SANA...

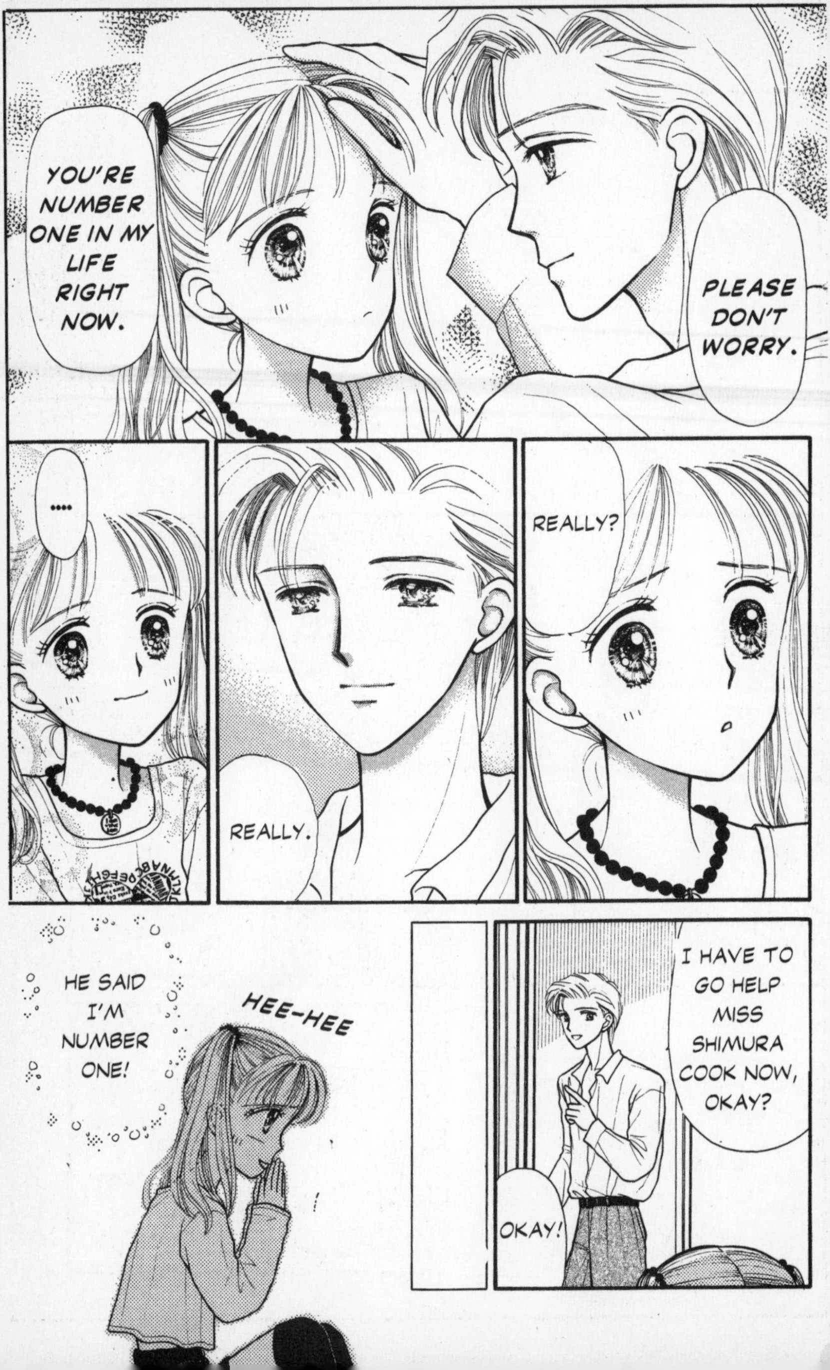
PLEASE DON'T WORRY.
YOU'RE NUMBER ONE IN MY LIFE RIGHT NOW.
REALLY?
REALLY.
....
I HAVE TO GO HELP MISS SHIMURA COOK NOW, OKAY?
OKAY!
HEE-HEE
HE SAID I'M NUMBER ONE!

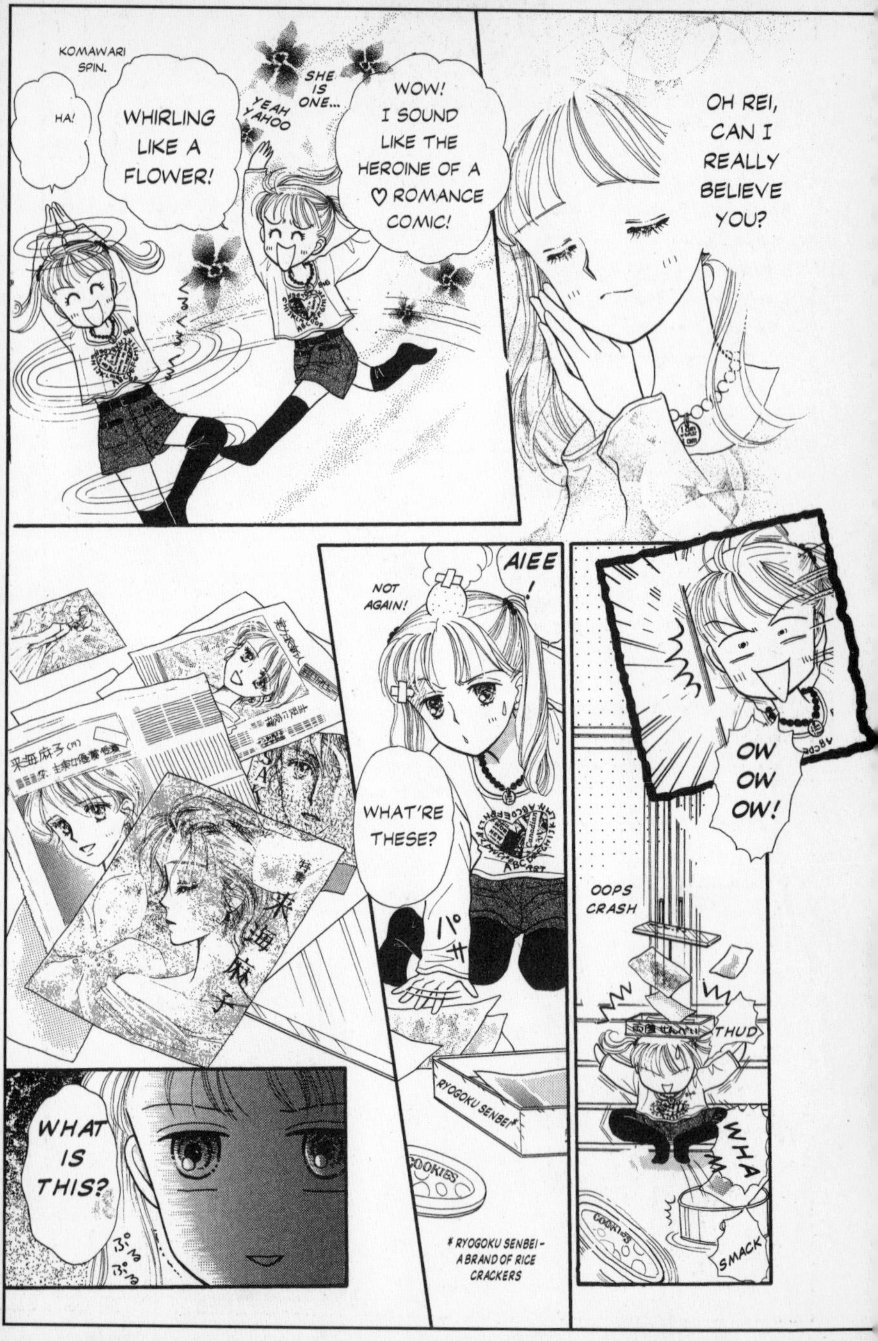
OH REI, CAN I REALLY BELIEVE YOU?
WOW! I SOUND LIKE THE HEROINE OF A ♡ ROMANCE COMIC!
SHE IS ONE...
YEAH YAHOO
KOMAWARI SPIN.
WHIRLING LIKE A FLOWER!
HA!
OW OW OW!
OOPS CRASH
THUD
WHA
SMACK
AIEE!
NOT AGAIN!
WHAT'RE THESE?
パキ
RYOGOKU SENBEI*
COOKIES
* RYOGOKU SENBEI - A BRAND OF RICE CRACKERS
WHAT IS THIS?

The Write Stuff

Mr. Hongo from Syuei-sya (the production company) helped me write the theme. (He also did the arrangement.) Thank you, Mr. Hongo! I'm used to showing editors my work for feedback and changing things after their input (from doing my comics), so our session went smoothly. The lyrics are written from Sana's point of view, and the song is called "Child's Feeling". Check it out! I really like playing musical instruments, so I enjoyed writing the music for the song, too. I can play almost everything at least a little bit, but I play the piano and saxophone a lot. (And drums and guitar, too.) I played the saxophone for three years in junior high band! I still perform in public sometimes. I go and play my saxophone in a neighborhood park. But I can't play it like I used to! I used to take such huge breaths, people thought I could just keep playing with out ever stopping to breathe. But I can't play that way any more since I started smoking!

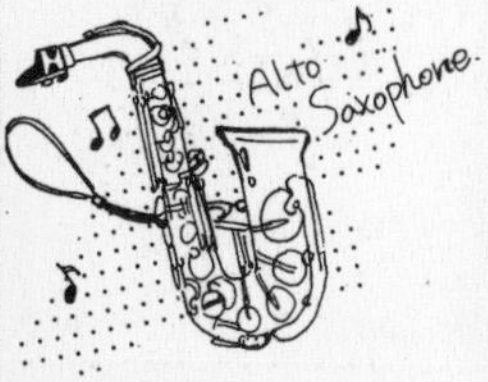
Alto Saxophone

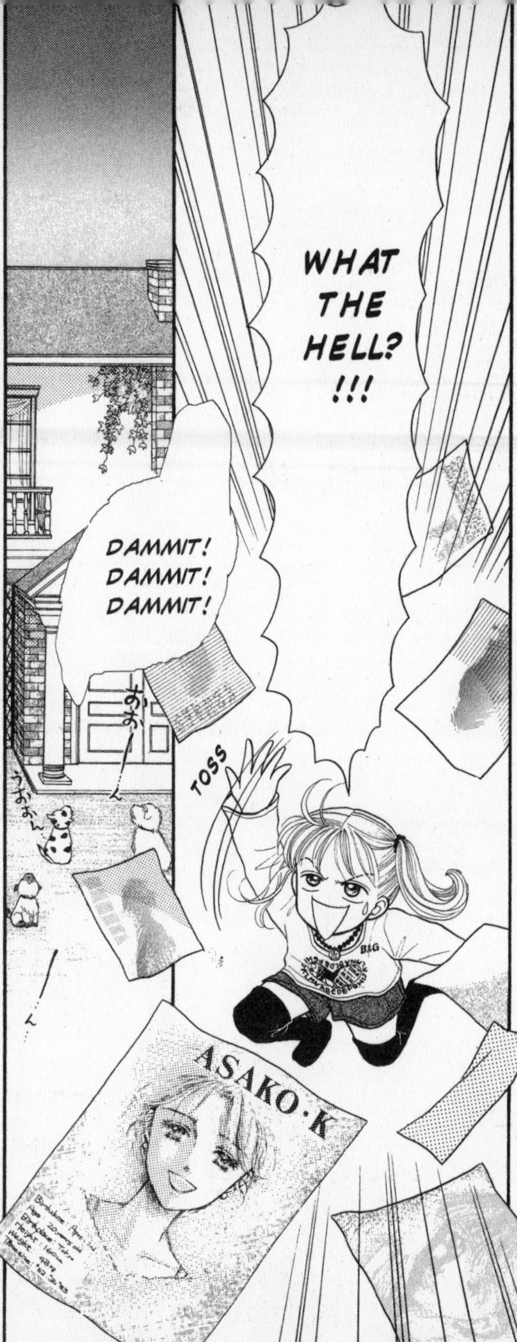
WHAT THE HELL? !!!
TOSS
DAMMIT! DAMMIT! DAMMIT!
ASAKO·K

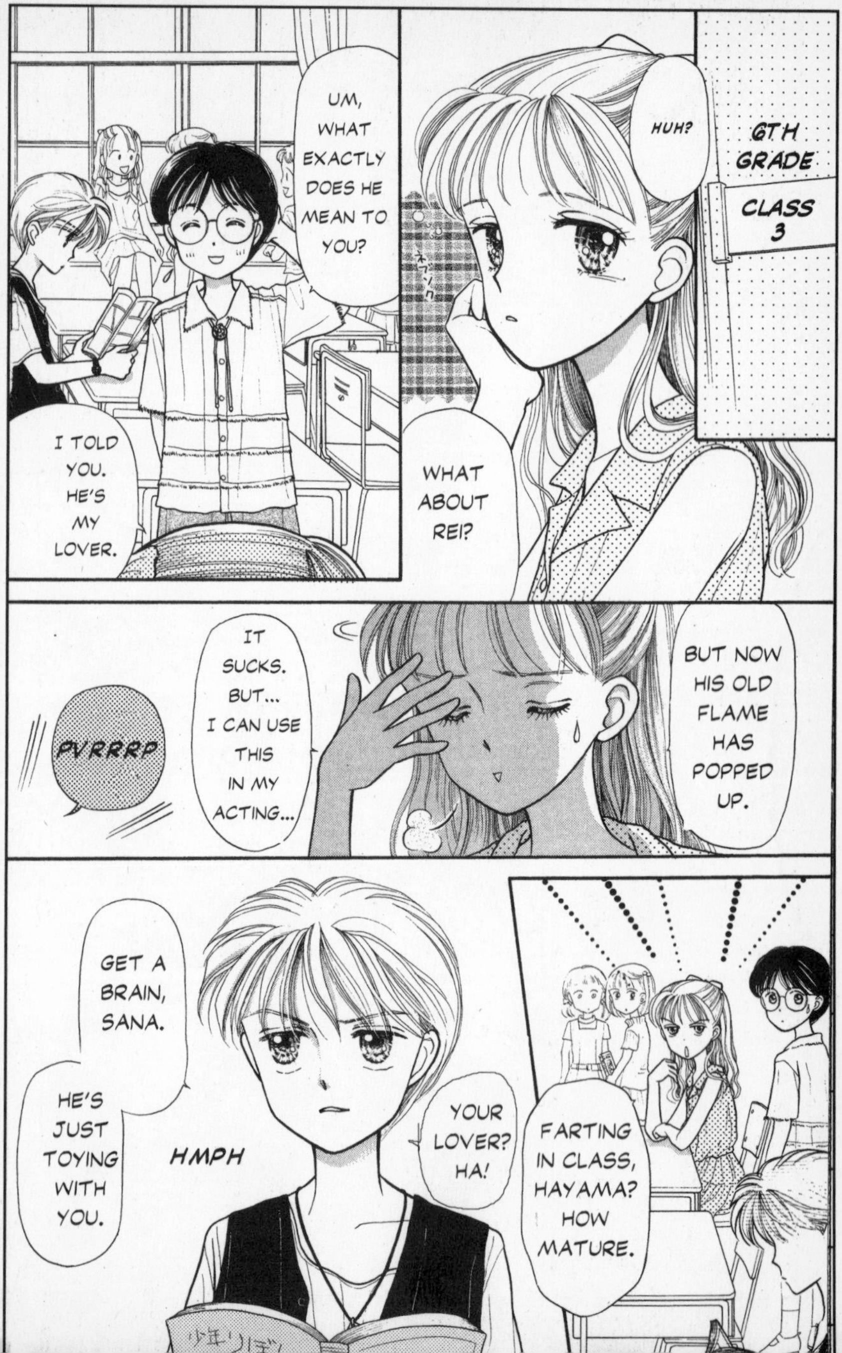
6TH GRADE CLASS 3
HUH?
WHAT ABOUT REI?
UM, WHAT EXACTLY DOES HE MEAN TO YOU?
I TOLD YOU. HE'S MY LOVER.
BUT NOW HIS OLD FLAME HAS POPPED UP.
IT SUCKS. BUT... I CAN USE THIS IN MY ACTING...
PVRRRP
FARTING IN CLASS, HAYAMA? HOW MATURE.
YOUR LOVER? HA!
HMPH
GET A BRAIN, SANA.
HE'S JUST TOYING WITH YOU.

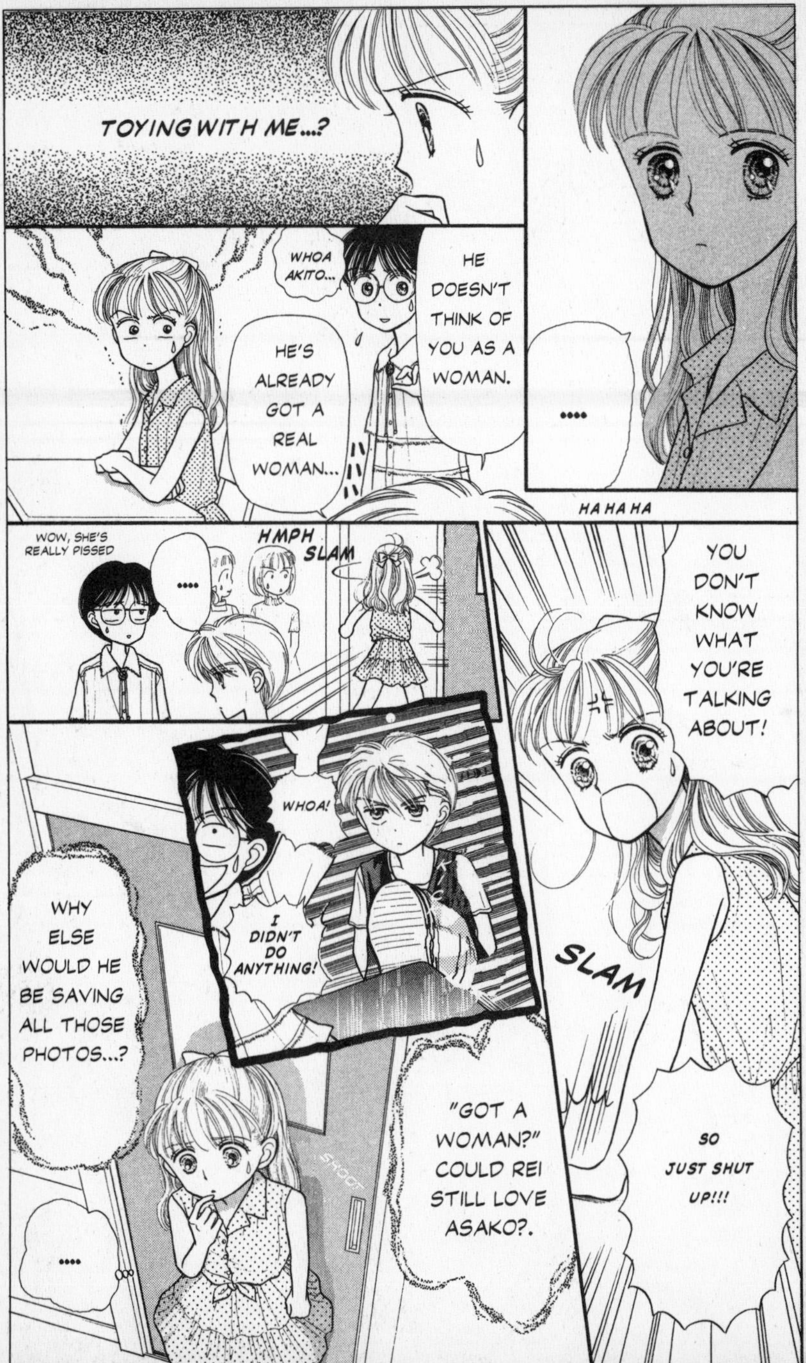
....
HA HA HA
TOYING WITH ME...?
HE DOESN'T THINK OF YOU AS A WOMAN.
WHOA AKITO...
HE'S ALREADY GOT A REAL WOMAN...
YOU DON'T KNOW WHAT YOU'RE TALKING ABOUT!
SLAM
SO JUST SHUT UP!!!
HMPH
SLAM
....
WOW, SHE'S REALLY PISSED
WHOA!
I DIDN'T DO ANYTHING!
"GOT A WOMAN?" COULD REI STILL LOVE ASAKO?.
WHY ELSE WOULD HE BE SAVING ALL THOSE PHOTOS...?
....

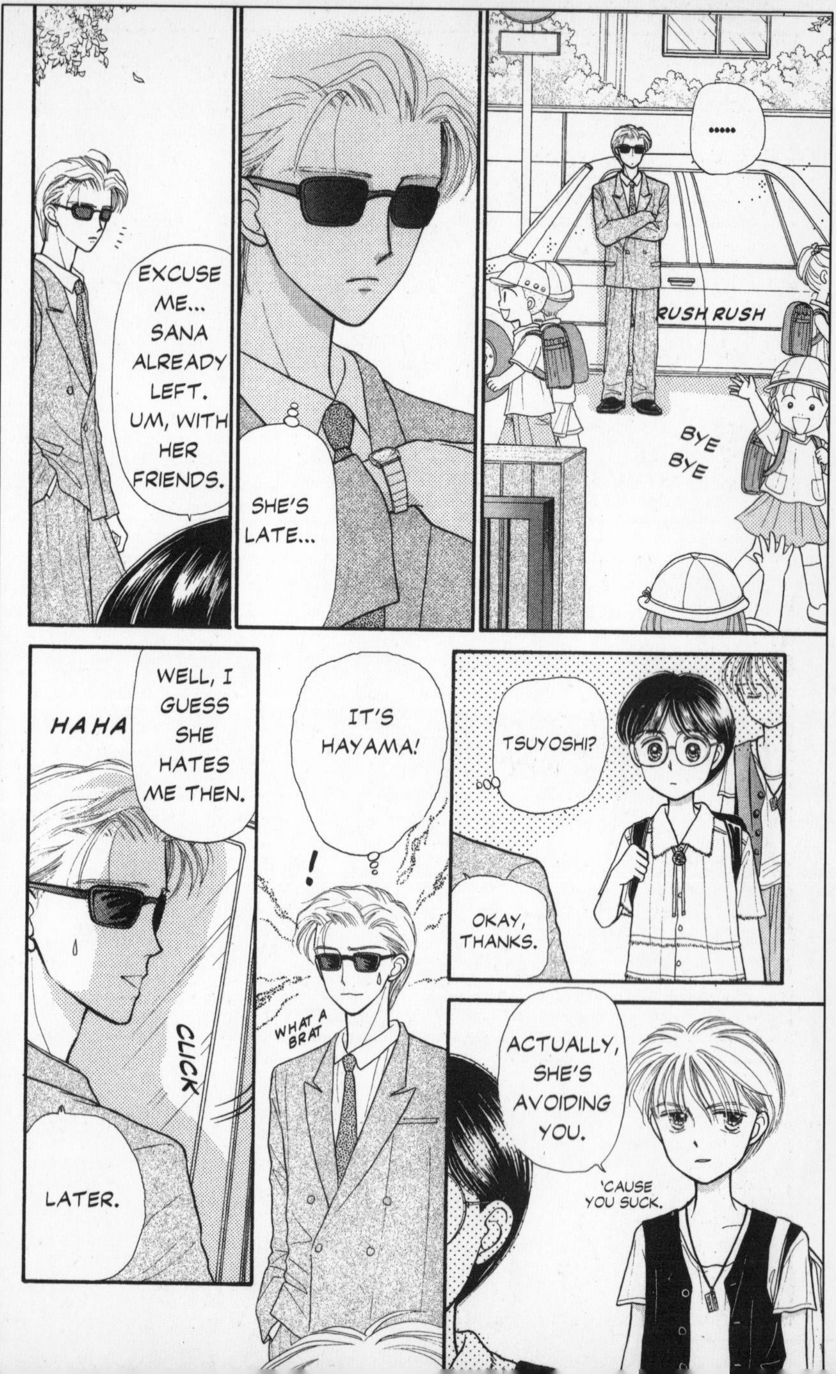
......
RUSH RUSH
BYE BYE
SHE'S LATE...
EXCUSE ME... SANA ALREADY LEFT. UM, WITH HER FRIENDS.
TSUYOSHI?
OKAY, THANKS.
ACTUALLY, SHE'S AVOIDING YOU.
'CAUSE YOU SUCK.
!
IT'S HAYAMA!
WHAT A BRAT
HAHA
WELL, I GUESS SHE HATES ME THEN.
CLICK
LATER.

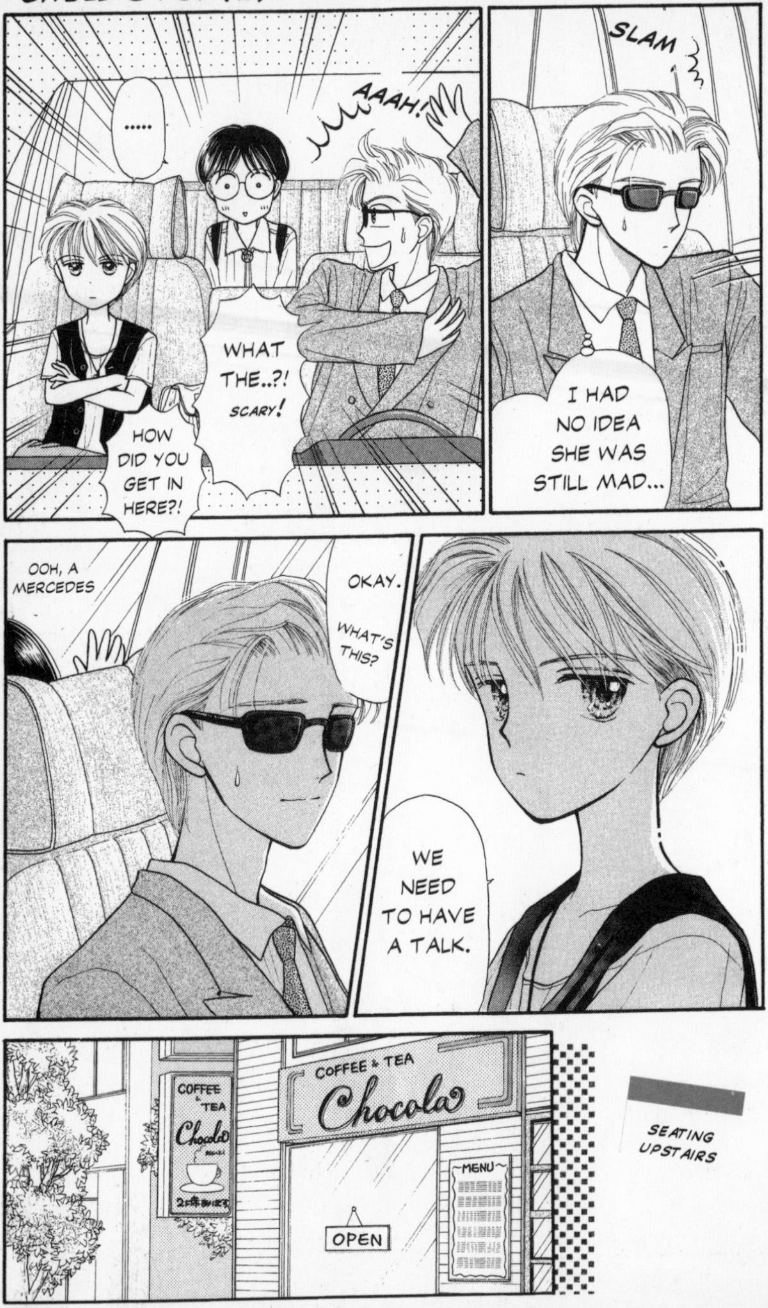
SLAM
I HAD NO IDEA SHE WAS STILL MAD...
AAAH!
......
WHAT THE..?! SCARY!
HOW DID YOU GET IN HERE?!
WE NEED TO HAVE A TALK.
OKAY.
WHAT'S THIS?
OOH, A MERCEDES
SEATING UPSTAIRS
COFFEE & TEA Chocola
COFFEE & TEA Chocola
MENU
OPEN

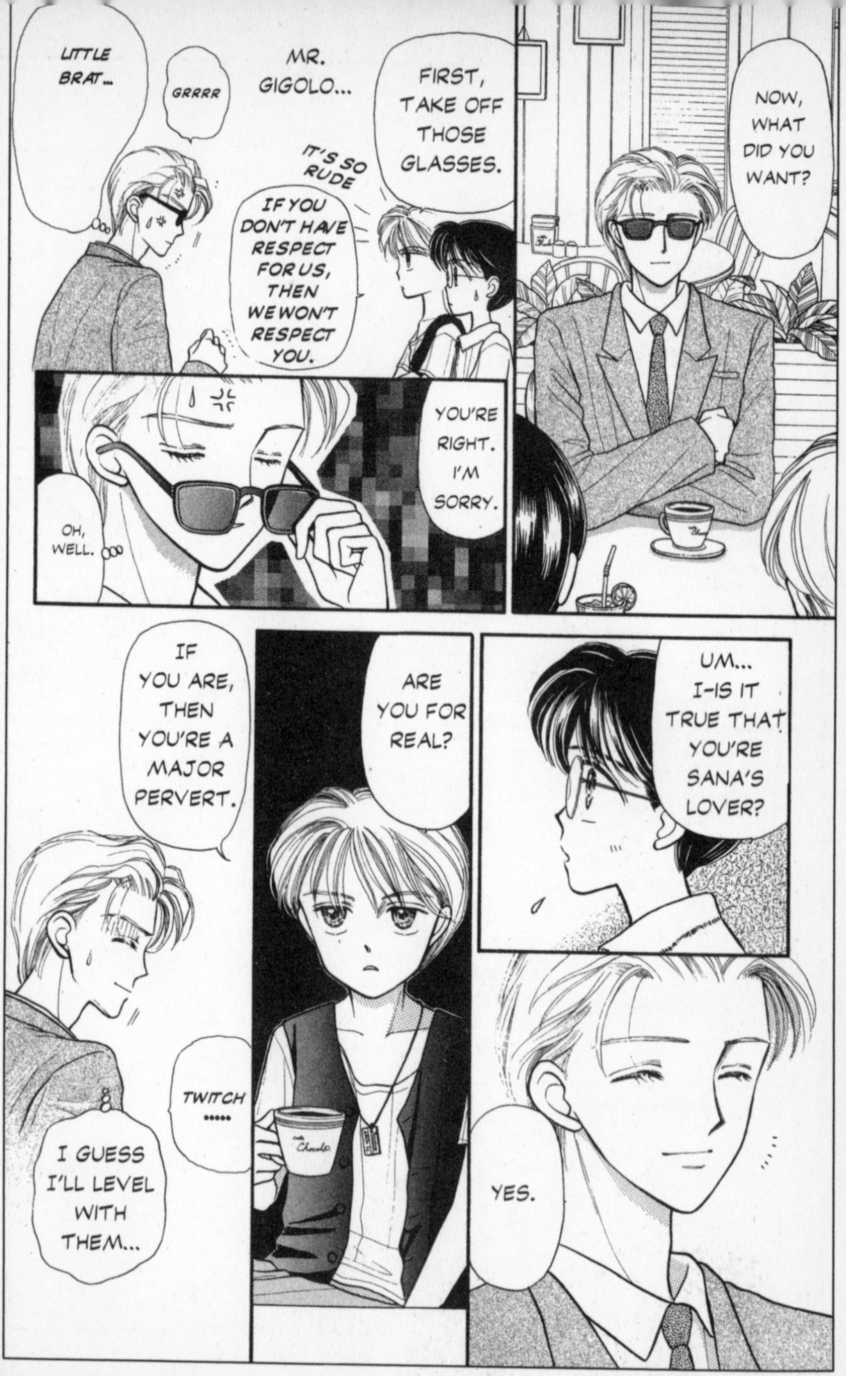
NOW, WHAT DID YOU WANT?
FIRST, TAKE OFF THOSE GLASSES.
MR. GIGOLO...
IT'S SO RUDE
IF YOU DON'T HAVE RESPECT FOR US, THEN WE WON'T RESPECT YOU.
GRRRR
LITTLE BRAT...
YOU'RE RIGHT. I'M SORRY.
OH, WELL.
UM... I-IS IT TRUE THAT YOU'RE SANA'S LOVER?
YES.
ARE YOU FOR REAL?
IF YOU ARE, THEN YOU'RE A MAJOR PERVERT.
TWITCH .....
I GUESS I'LL LEVEL WITH THEM...

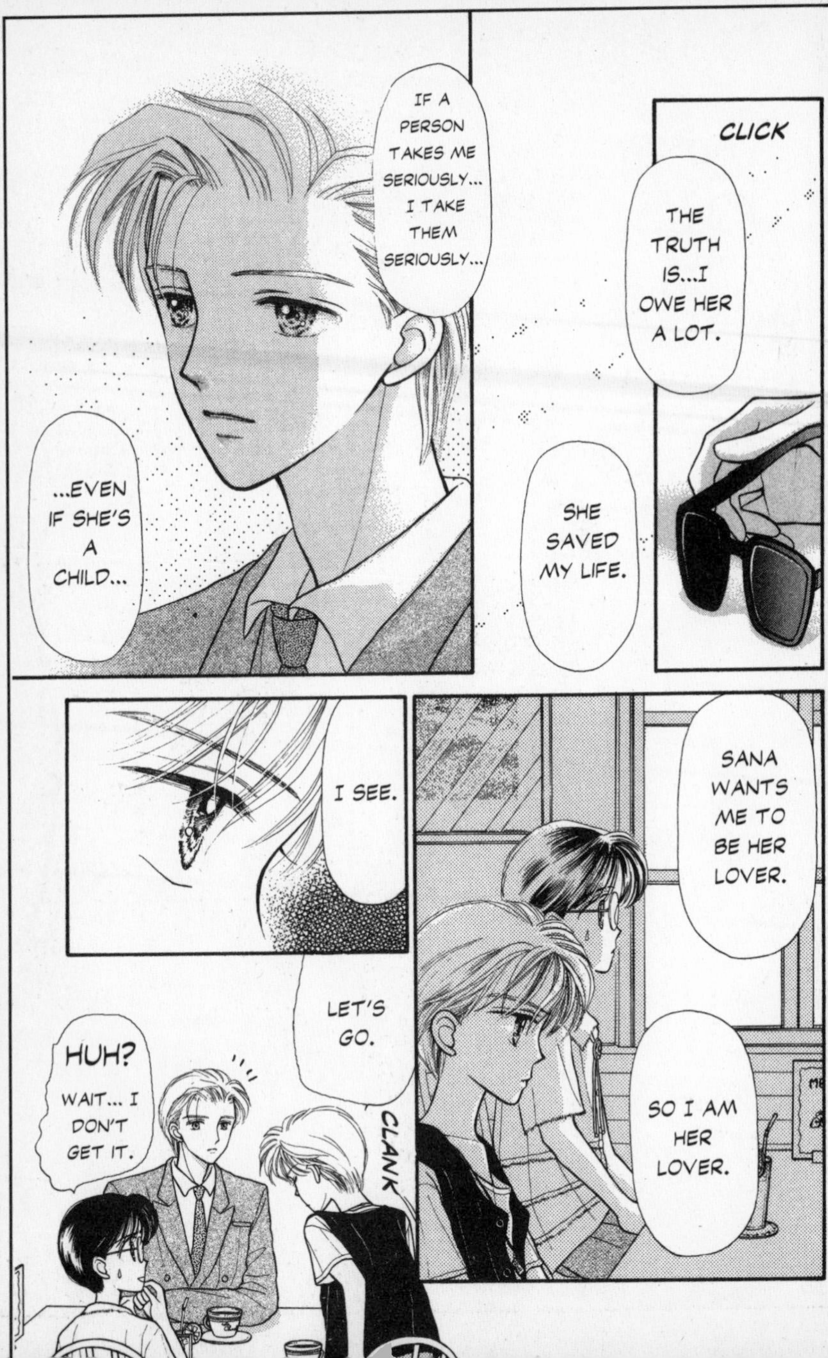
CLICK
THE TRUTH IS...I OWE HER A LOT.
SHE SAVED MY LIFE.
IF A PERSON TAKES ME SERIOUSLY... I TAKE THEM SERIOUSLY...
...EVEN IF SHE'S A CHILD...
SANA WANTS ME TO BE HER LOVER.
SO I AM HER LOVER.
I SEE.
LET'S GO.
CLANK
HUH?
WAIT... I DON'T GET IT.

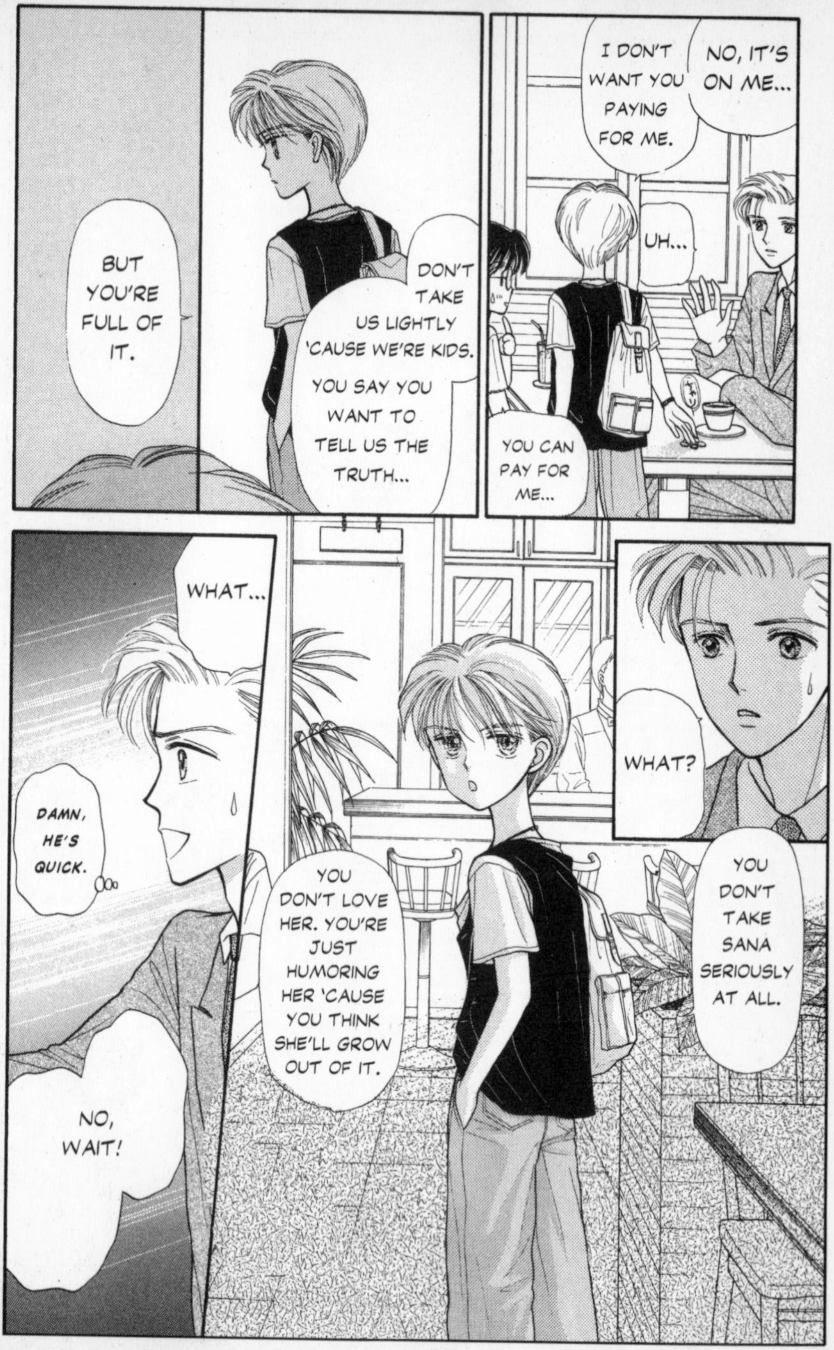

NO, IT'S ON ME...
I DON'T WANT YOU PAYING FOR ME.
UH...
YOU CAN PAY FOR ME...
DON'T TAKE US LIGHTLY 'CAUSE WE'RE KIDS.
YOU SAY YOU WANT TO TELL US THE TRUTH...
BUT YOU'RE FULL OF IT.
WHAT?
YOU DON'T TAKE SANA SERIOUSLY AT ALL.
YOU DON'T LOVE HER. YOU'RE JUST HUMORING HER 'CAUSE YOU THINK SHE'LL GROW OUT OF IT.
WHAT...
DAMN, HE'S QUICK.
NO, WAIT!

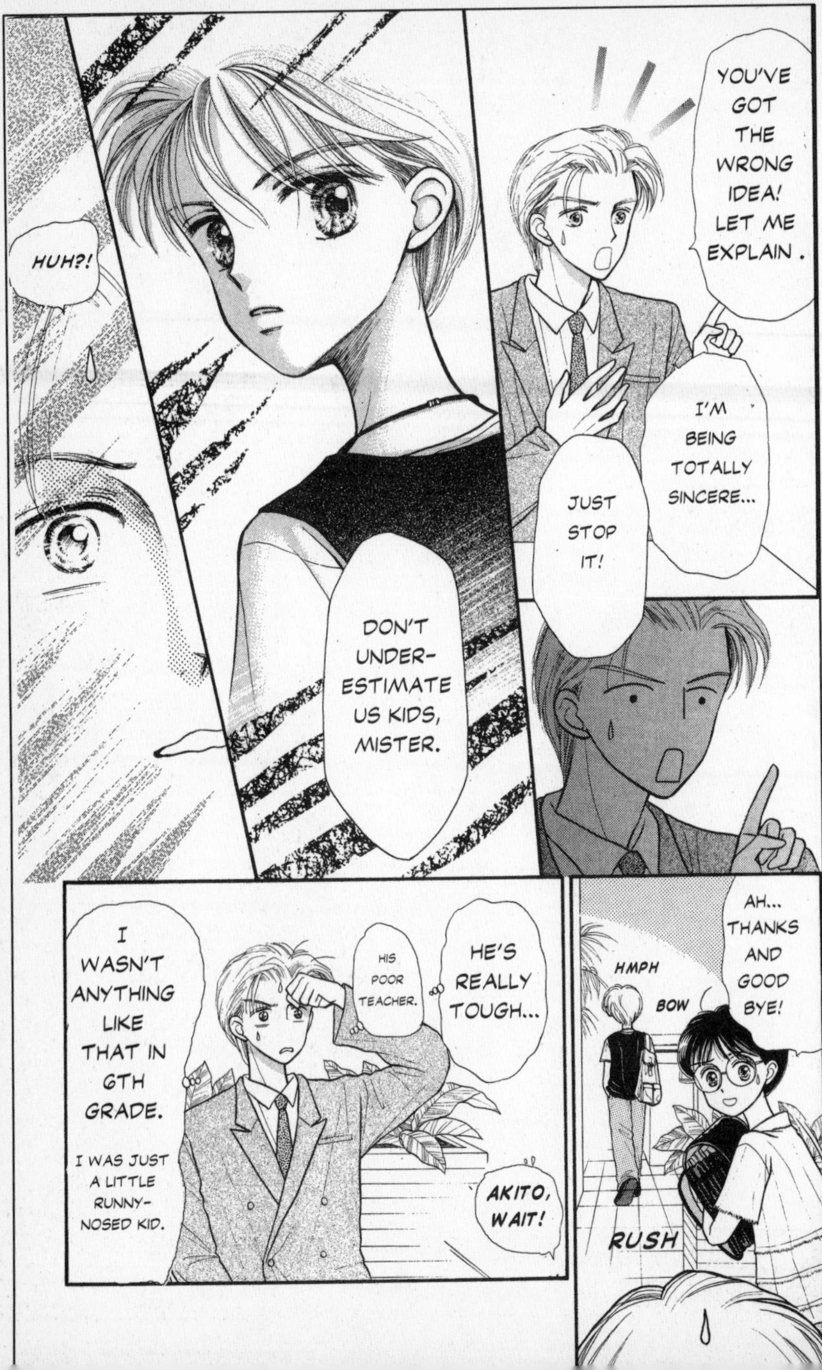
YOU'VE GOT THE WRONG IDEA! LET ME EXPLAIN.
I'M BEING TOTALLY SINCERE...
JUST STOP IT!
DON'T UNDER-ESTIMATE US KIDS, MISTER.
HUH?!
AH... THANKS AND GOOD BYE!
BOW
HMPH
RUSH
HE'S REALLY TOUGH...
HIS POOR TEACHER.
AKITO, WAIT!
I WASN'T ANYTHING LIKE THAT IN 6TH GRADE.
I WAS JUST A LITTLE RUNNY-NOSED KID.

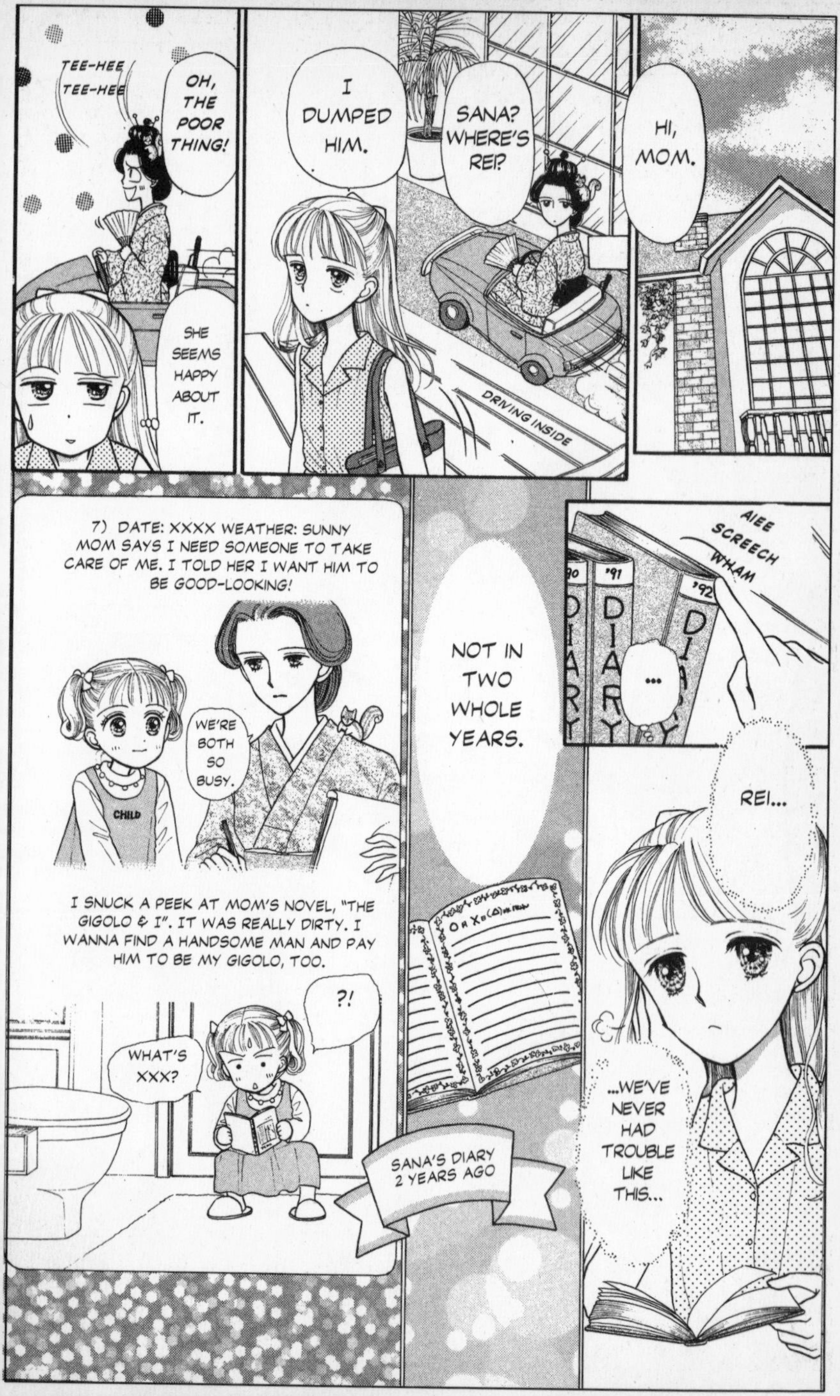
HI, MOM.
SANA? WHERE'S REI?
DRIVING INSIDE
I DUMPED HIM.
OH, THE POOR THING!
TEE-HEE TEE-HEE
SHE SEEMS HAPPY ABOUT IT.
AIEE SCREECH WHAM
'90 '91 '92
DIARY DIARY DIARY
...
REI...
...WE'VE NEVER HAD TROUBLE LIKE THIS...
NOT IN TWO WHOLE YEARS.
SANA'S DIARY 2 YEARS AGO
7) DATE: XXXX WEATHER: SUNNY
MOM SAYS I NEED SOMEONE TO TAKE CARE OF ME. I TOLD HER I WANT HIM TO BE GOOD-LOOKING!
WE'RE BOTH SO BUSY.
CHILD
I SNUCK A PEEK AT MOM'S NOVEL, "THE GIGOLO & I". IT WAS REALLY DIRTY. I WANNA FIND A HANDSOME MAN AND PAY HIM TO BE MY GIGOLO, TOO.
?!
WHAT'S XXX?

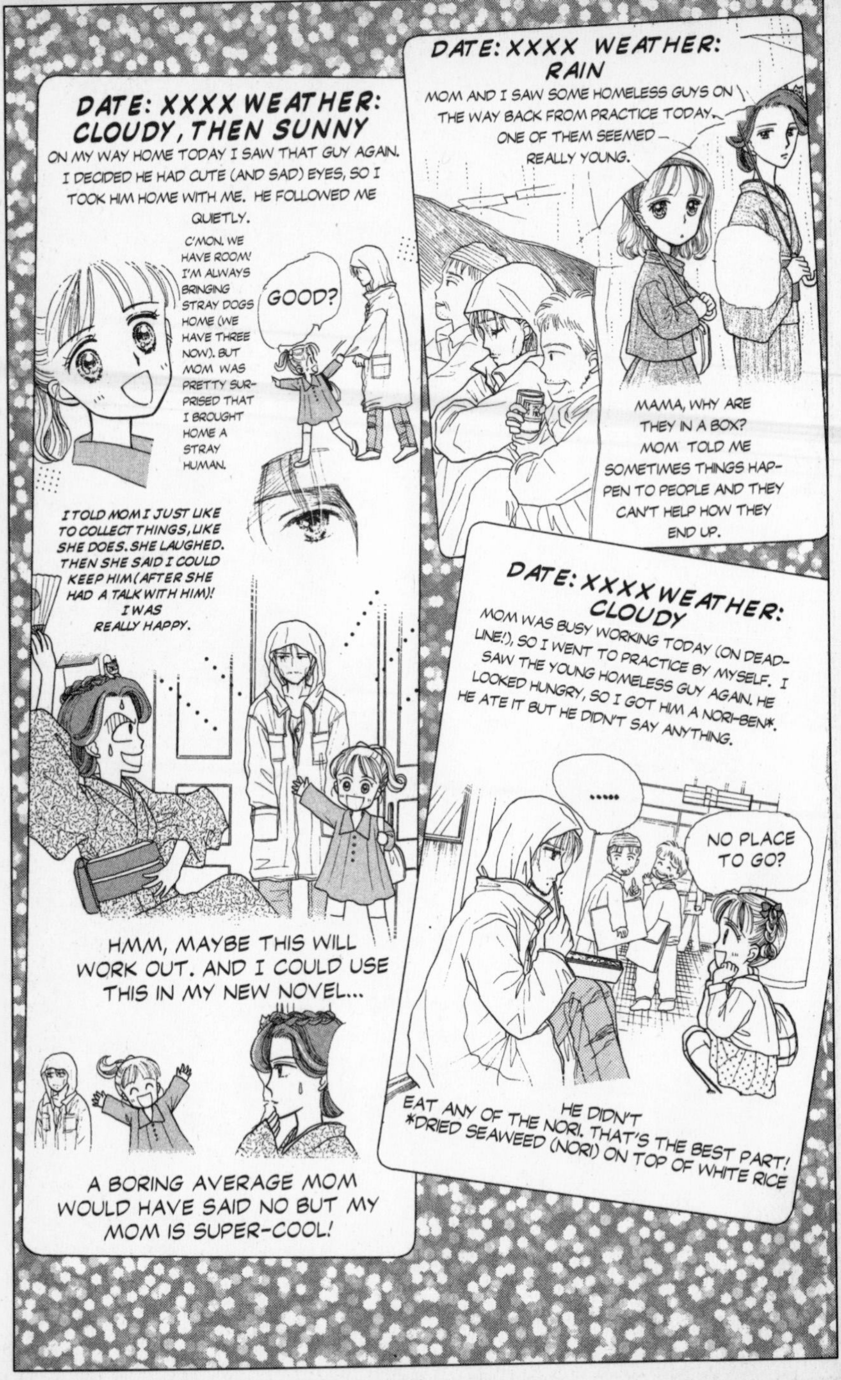
DATE: XXXX WEATHER: RAIN
MOM AND I SAW SOME HOMELESS GUYS ON THE WAY BACK FROM PRACTICE TODAY. ONE OF THEM SEEMED REALLY YOUNG.
MAMA, WHY ARE THEY IN A BOX? MOM TOLD ME SOMETIMES THINGS HAPPEN TO PEOPLE AND THEY CAN'T HELP HOW THEY END UP.
DATE: XXXX WEATHER: CLOUDY
MOM WAS BUSY WORKING TODAY (ON DEADLINE!), SO I WENT TO PRACTICE BY MYSELF. I SAW THE YOUNG HOMELESS GUY AGAIN. HE LOOKED HUNGRY, SO I GOT HIM A NORI-BEN*. HE ATE IT BUT HE DIDN'T SAY ANYTHING.
NO PLACE TO GO?
......
HE DIDN'T EAT ANY OF THE NORI. THAT'S THE BEST PART!
*DRIED SEAWEED (NORI) ON TOP OF WHITE RICE
DATE: XXXX WEATHER: CLOUDY, THEN SUNNY
ON MY WAY HOME TODAY I SAW THAT GUY AGAIN. I DECIDED HE HAD CUTE (AND SAD) EYES, SO I TOOK HIM HOME WITH ME. HE FOLLOWED ME QUIETLY.
GOOD?
C'MON. WE HAVE ROOM! I'M ALWAYS BRINGING STRAY DOGS HOME (WE HAVE THREE NOW). BUT MOM WAS PRETTY SURPRISED THAT I BROUGHT HOME A STRAY HUMAN.
I TOLD MOM I JUST LIKE TO COLLECT THINGS, LIKE SHE DOES. SHE LAUGHED. THEN SHE SAID I COULD KEEP HIM (AFTER SHE HAD A TALK WITH HIM)! I WAS REALLY HAPPY.
HMM, MAYBE THIS WILL WORK OUT. AND I COULD USE THIS IN MY NEW NOVEL...
A BORING AVERAGE MOM WOULD HAVE SAID NO BUT MY MOM IS SUPER-COOL!

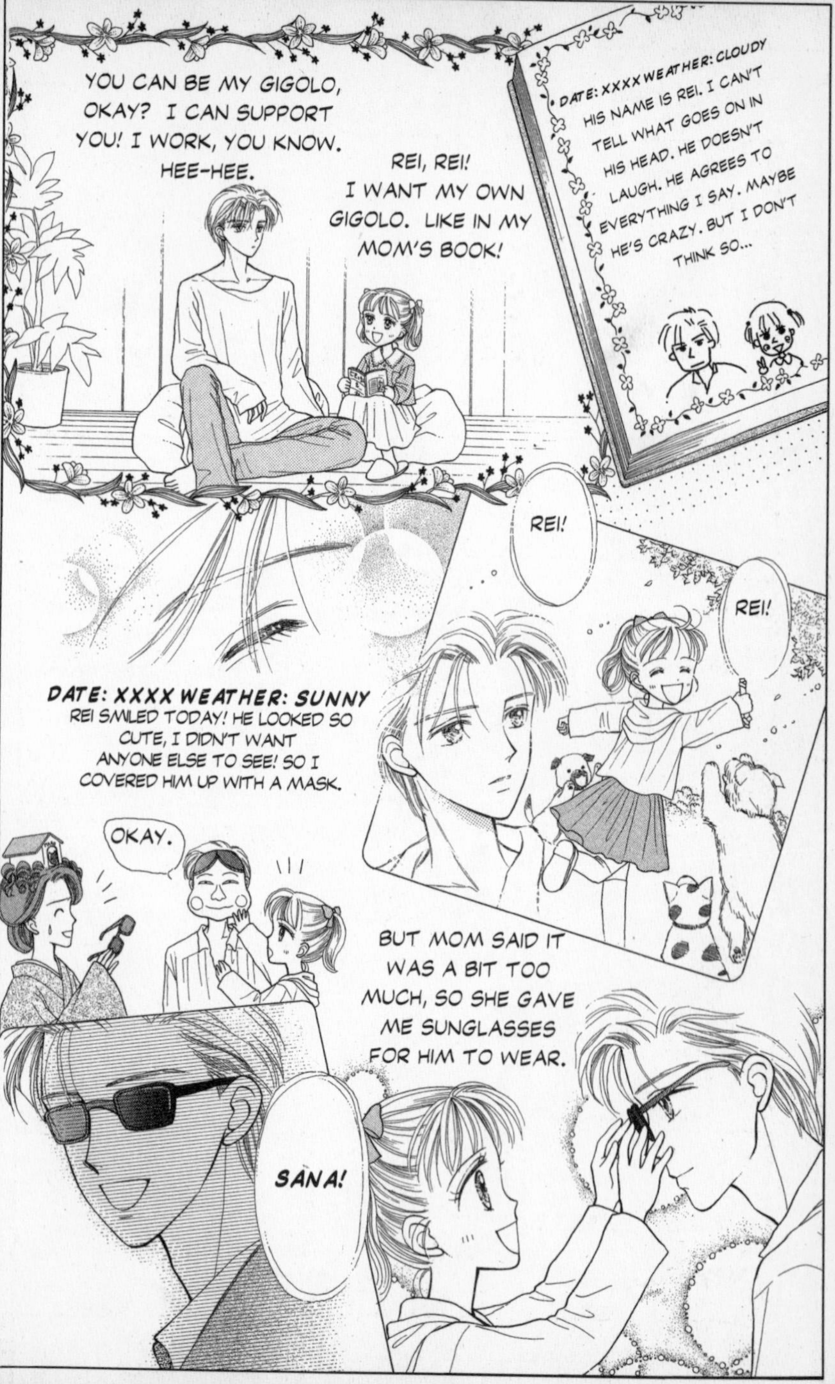

DATE: XXXX WEATHER: CLOUDY
HIS NAME IS REI. I CAN'T TELL WHAT GOES ON IN HIS HEAD. HE DOESN'T LAUGH. HE AGREES TO EVERYTHING I SAY. MAYBE HE'S CRAZY. BUT I DON'T THINK SO...
REI, REI! I WANT MY OWN GIGOLO. LIKE IN MY MOM'S BOOK!
YOU CAN BE MY GIGOLO, OKAY? I CAN SUPPORT YOU! I WORK, YOU KNOW. HEE-HEE.
REI!
REI!
DATE: XXXX WEATHER: SUNNY
REI SMILED TODAY! HE LOOKED SO CUTE, I DIDN'T WANT ANYONE ELSE TO SEE! SO I COVERED HIM UP WITH A MASK.
OKAY.
BUT MOM SAID IT WAS A BIT TOO MUCH, SO SHE GAVE ME SUNGLASSES FOR HIM TO WEAR.
SANA!

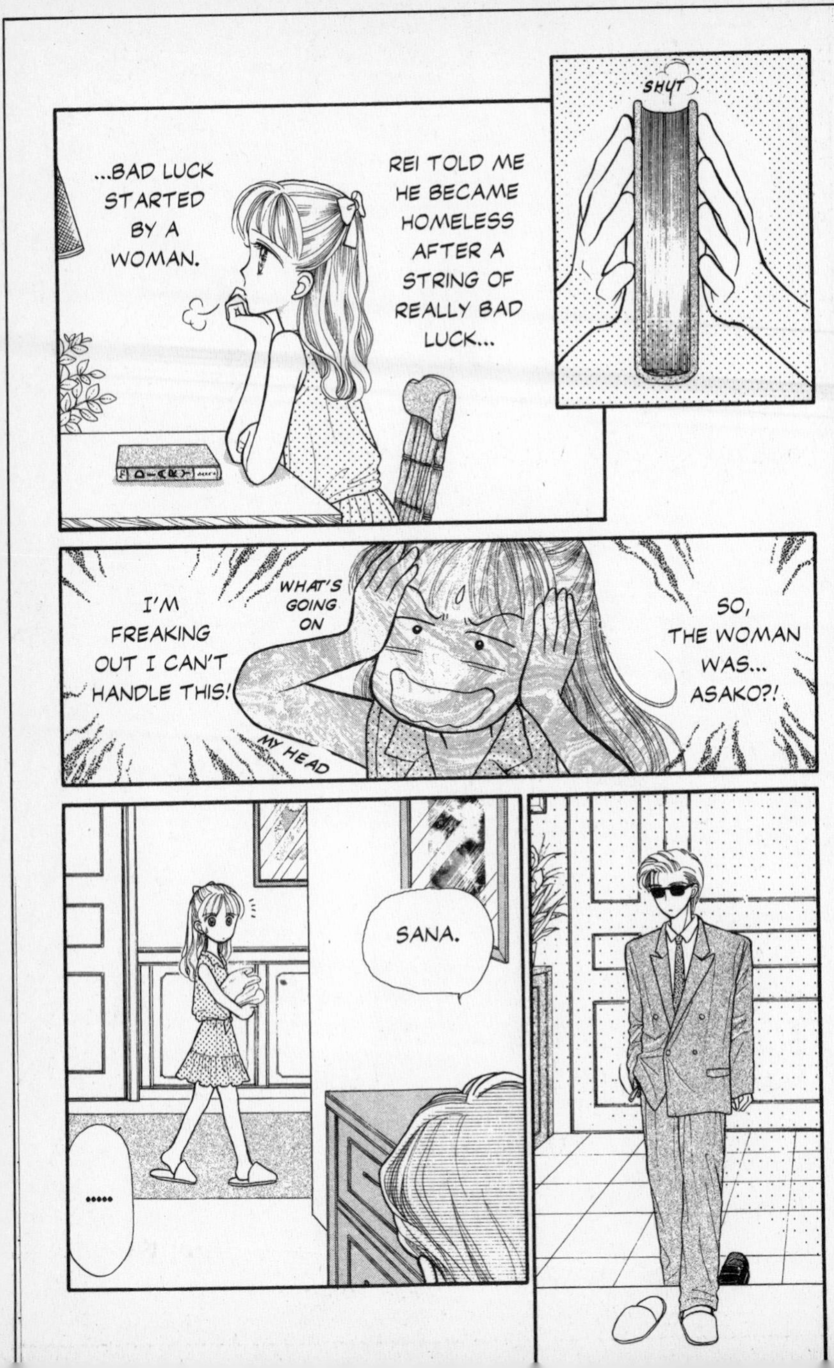
SHUT
REI TOLD ME HE BECAME HOMELESS AFTER A STRING OF REALLY BAD LUCK...
...BAD LUCK STARTED BY A WOMAN.
SO, THE WOMAN WAS... ASAKO?!
WHAT'S GOING ON
MY HEAD
I'M FREAKING OUT I CAN'T HANDLE THIS!
SANA.
.....

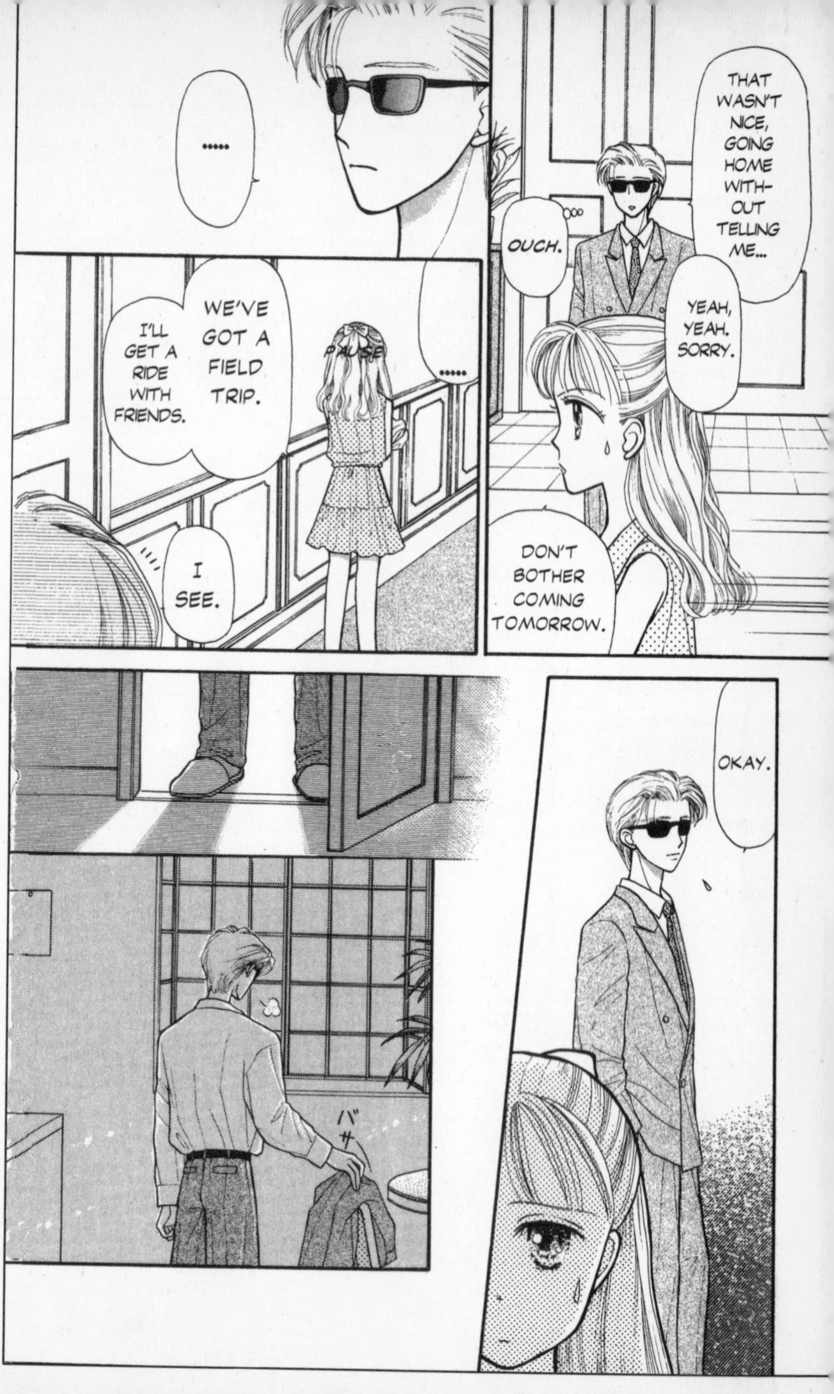
THAT WASN'T NICE, GOING HOME WITH-OUT TELLING ME...
OUCH.
YEAH, YEAH. SORRY.
DON'T BOTHER COMING TOMORROW.
.....
.....
WE'VE GOT A FIELD TRIP.
I'LL GET A RIDE WITH FRIENDS.
PAUSE
I SEE.
OKAY.
バサ

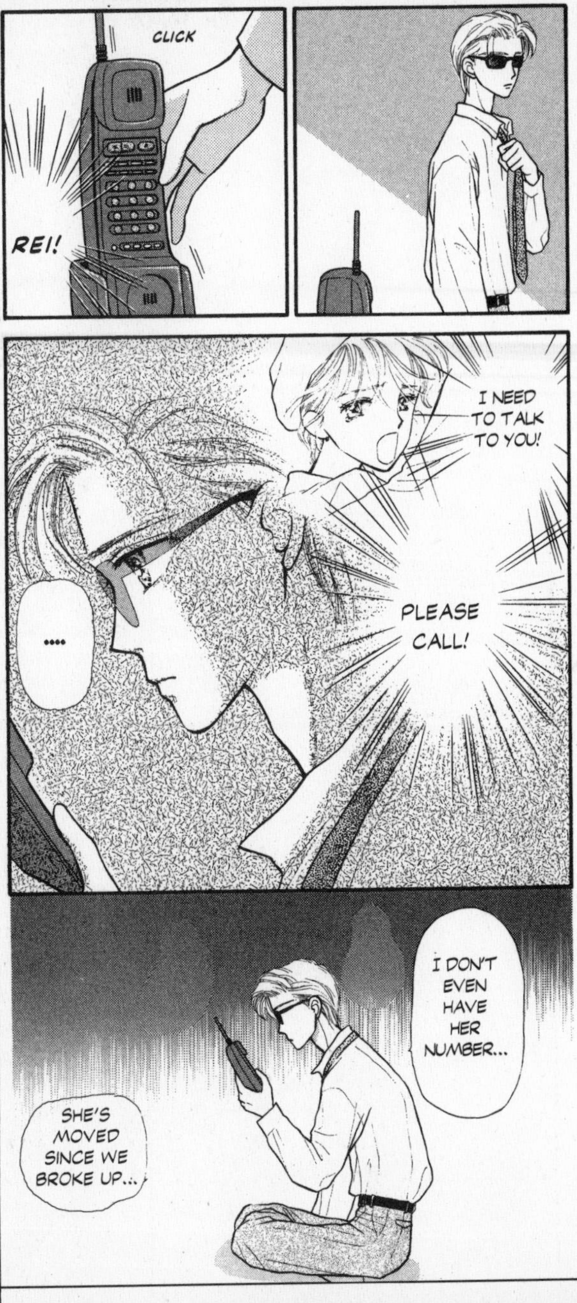
CLICK
REI!
I NEED TO TALK TO YOU!
PLEASE CALL!
....
I DON'T EVEN HAVE HER NUMBER...
SHE'S MOVED SINCE WE BROKE UP...

All about the Himawari Theater

In book 1, I told you about my friend "S", who Sana is partly based on. Let me tell you some more about her! "S" was in Himawari Theater (which I based Sana's Himawari Theater on), and was on TV a lot. She did lots of stuff. She was on regular shows and did commercials. I've even seen her face on a toy box! At one point (in elementary school), I wanted to be just like her. So can you guess what I did? I auditioned for the Himawari Theater! I really did!

Can you believe it?

(To be continued.)

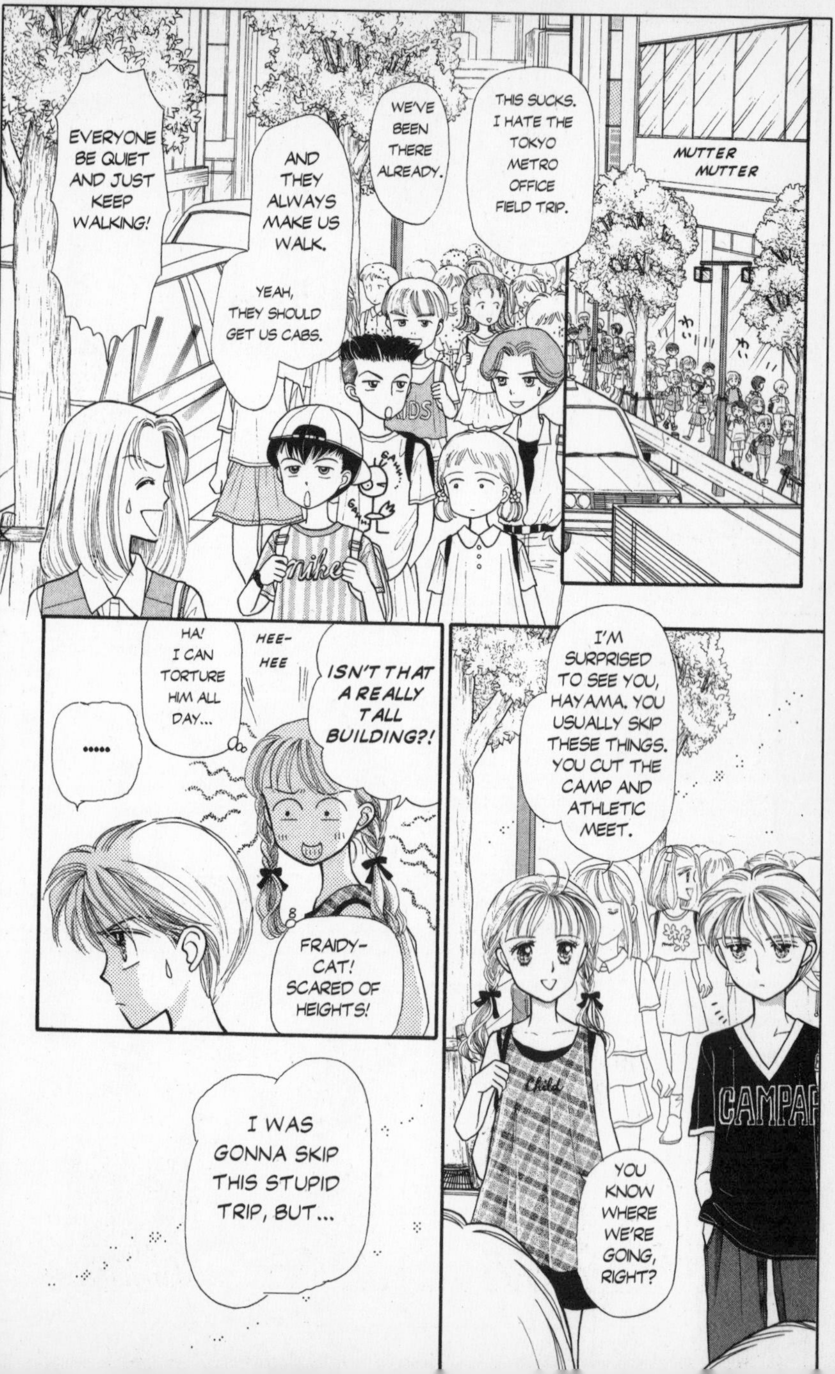
MUTTER MUTTER
THIS SUCKS. I HATE THE TOKYO METRO OFFICE FIELD TRIP.
WE'VE BEEN THERE ALREADY.
AND THEY ALWAYS MAKE US WALK.
YEAH, THEY SHOULD GET US CABS.
EVERYONE BE QUIET AND JUST KEEP WALKING!
I'M SURPRISED TO SEE YOU, HAYAMA. YOU USUALLY SKIP THESE THINGS. YOU CUT THE CAMP AND ATHLETIC MEET.
YOU KNOW WHERE WE'RE GOING, RIGHT?
ISN'T THAT A REALLY TALL BUILDING?!
HEE-HEE
HA! I CAN TORTURE HIM ALL DAY...
FRAIDY-CAT! SCARED OF HEIGHTS!
.....
I WAS GONNA SKIP THIS STUPID TRIP, BUT...

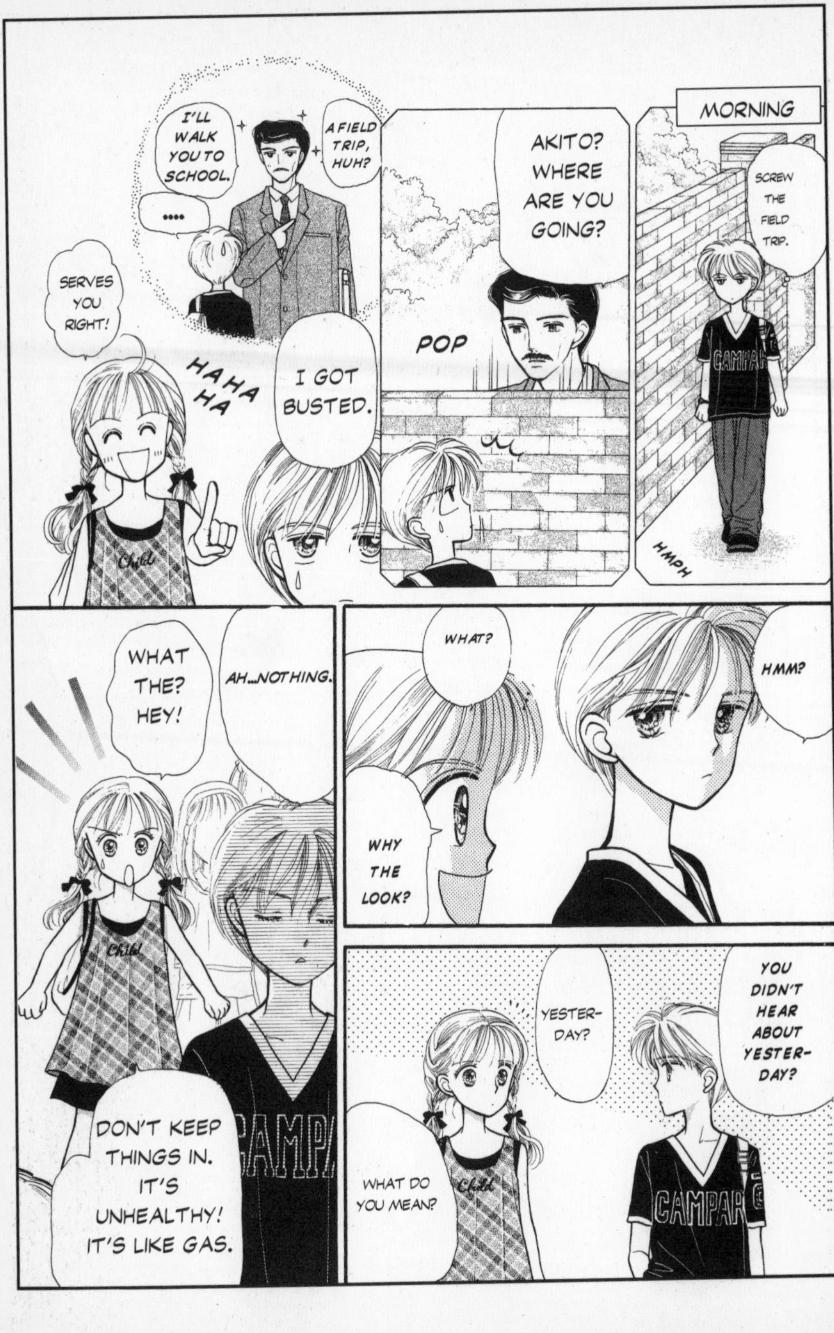
MORNING
SCREW THE FIELD TRIP.
HMPH
AKITO? WHERE ARE YOU GOING?
POP
A FIELD TRIP, HUH?
I'LL WALK YOU TO SCHOOL.
....
I GOT BUSTED.
SERVES YOU RIGHT!
HAHA HA
HMM?
WHAT?
WHY THE LOOK?
YOU DIDN'T HEAR ABOUT YESTER-DAY?
YESTER-DAY?
WHAT DO YOU MEAN?
AH...NOTHING.
WHAT THE? HEY!
DON'T KEEP THINGS IN. IT'S UNHEALTHY! IT'S LIKE GAS.

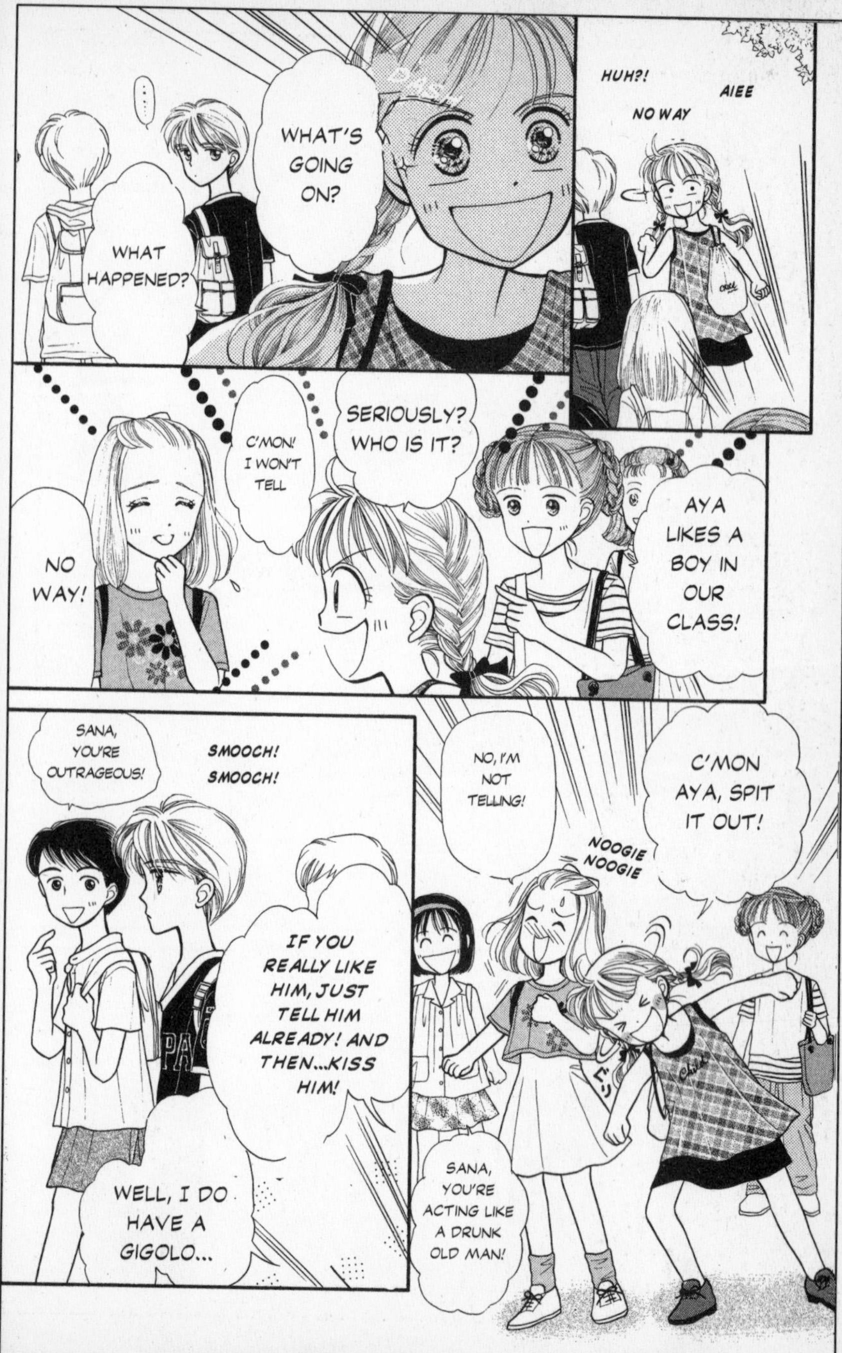
HUH?!
AIEE
NO WAY
WHAT'S GOING ON?
...
WHAT HAPPENED?
AYA LIKES A BOY IN OUR CLASS!
SERIOUSLY? WHO IS IT?
C'MON! I WON'T TELL
NO WAY!
C'MON AYA, SPIT IT OUT!
NOOGIE NOOGIE
NO, I'M NOT TELLING!
SANA, YOU'RE ACTING LIKE A DRUNK OLD MAN!
IF YOU REALLY LIKE HIM, JUST TELL HIM ALREADY! AND THEN...KISS HIM!
SMOOCH! SMOOCH!
SANA, YOU'RE OUTRAGEOUS!
WELL, I DO HAVE A GIGOLO...

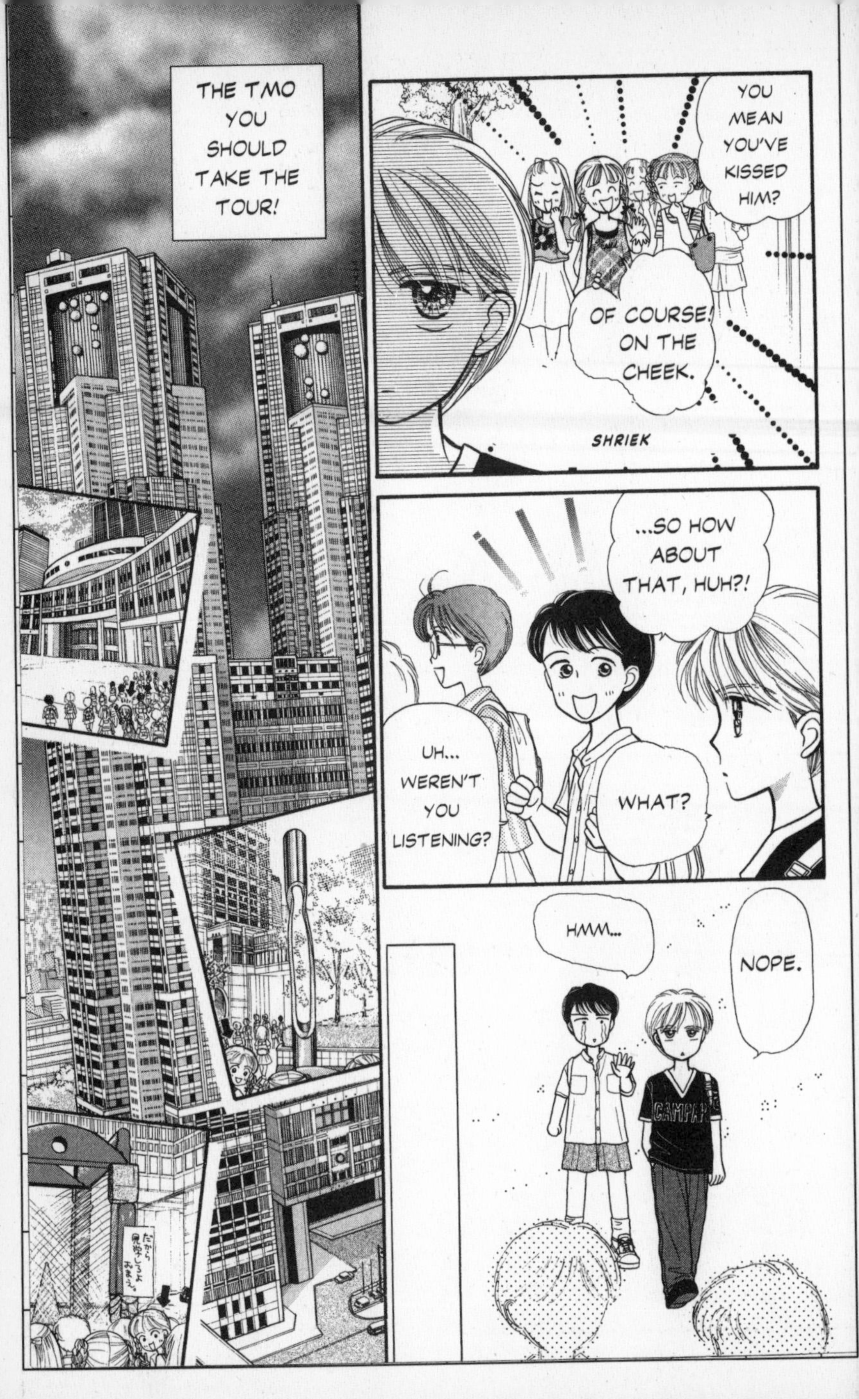
YOU MEAN YOU'VE KISSED HIM?
OF COURSE! ON THE CHEEK.
SHRIEK
...SO HOW ABOUT THAT, HUH?!
WHAT?
UH... WEREN'T YOU LISTENING?
NOPE.
HMM...
THE TMO YOU SHOULD TAKE THE TOUR!
だから見学しろよおまえ。

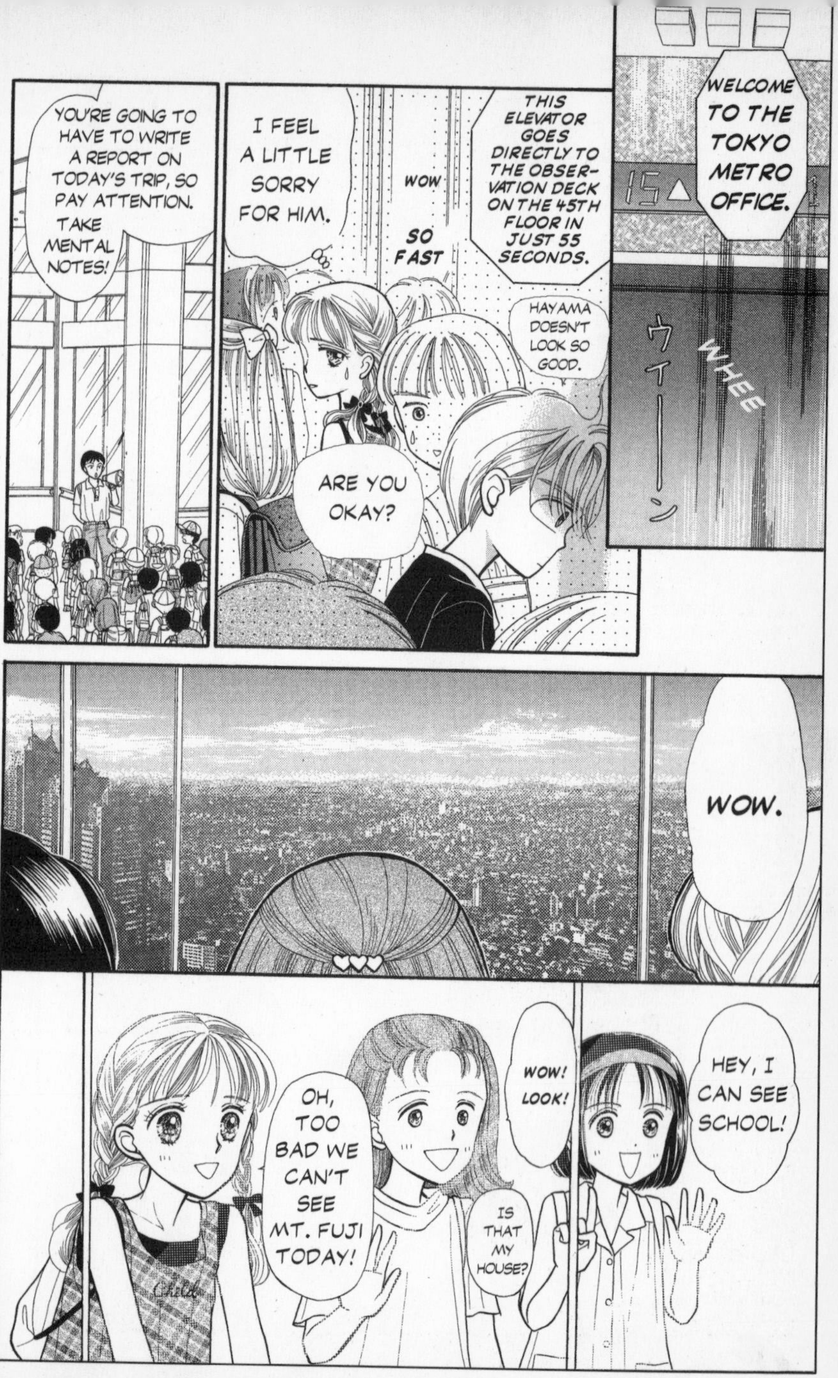
WELCOME TO THE TOKYO METRO OFFICE.
15
ウィーン
WHEE
THIS ELEVATOR GOES DIRECTLY TO THE OBSERVATION DECK ON THE 45TH FLOOR IN JUST 55 SECONDS.
WOW
SO FAST
I FEEL A LITTLE SORRY FOR HIM.
HAYAMA DOESN'T LOOK SO GOOD.
ARE YOU OKAY?
YOU'RE GOING TO HAVE TO WRITE A REPORT ON TODAY'S TRIP, SO PAY ATTENTION. TAKE MENTAL NOTES!
WOW.
HEY, I CAN SEE SCHOOL!
WOW! LOOK!
IS THAT MY HOUSE?
OH, TOO BAD WE CAN'T SEE MT. FUJI TODAY!

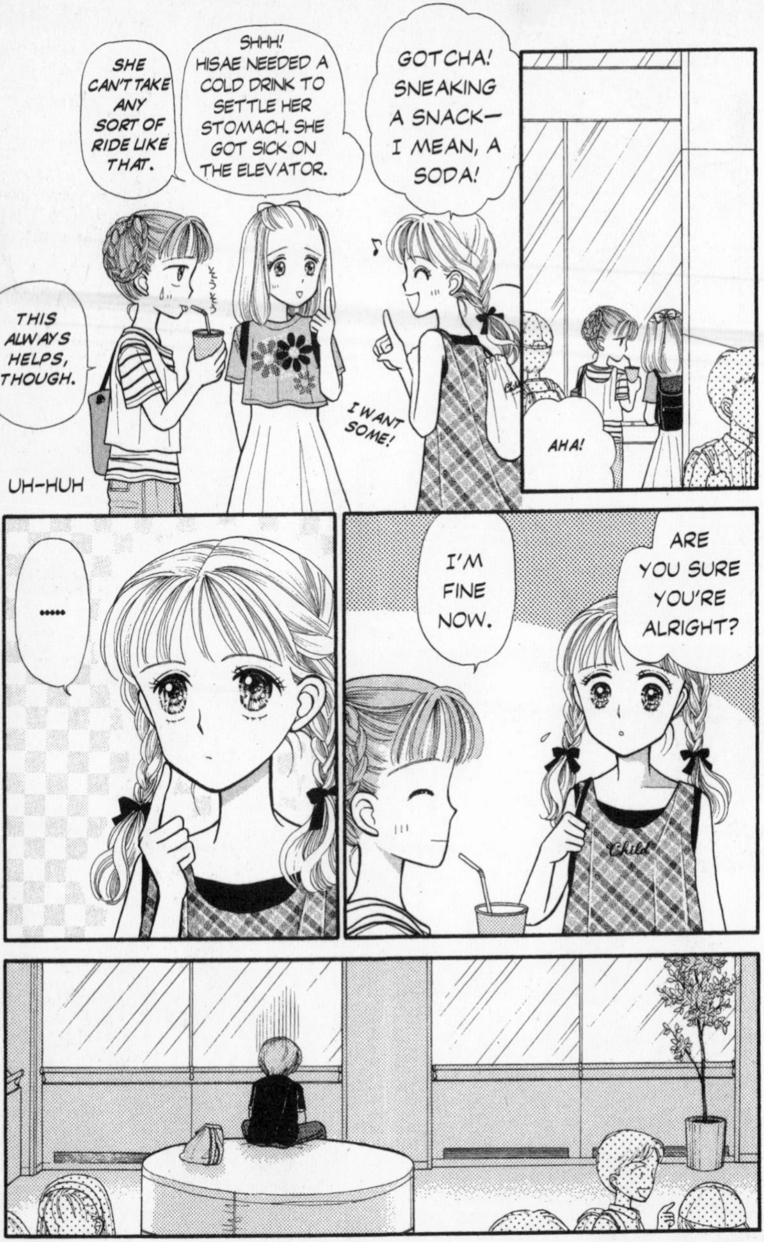
AHA!
GOTCHA! SNEAKING A SNACK—I MEAN, A SODA!
SHHH! HISAE NEEDED A COLD DRINK TO SETTLE HER STOMACH. SHE GOT SICK ON THE ELEVATOR.
SHE CAN'T TAKE ANY SORT OF RIDE LIKE THAT.
I WANT SOME!
THIS ALWAYS HELPS, THOUGH.
UH-HUH
ARE YOU SURE YOU'RE ALRIGHT?
I'M FINE NOW.
......

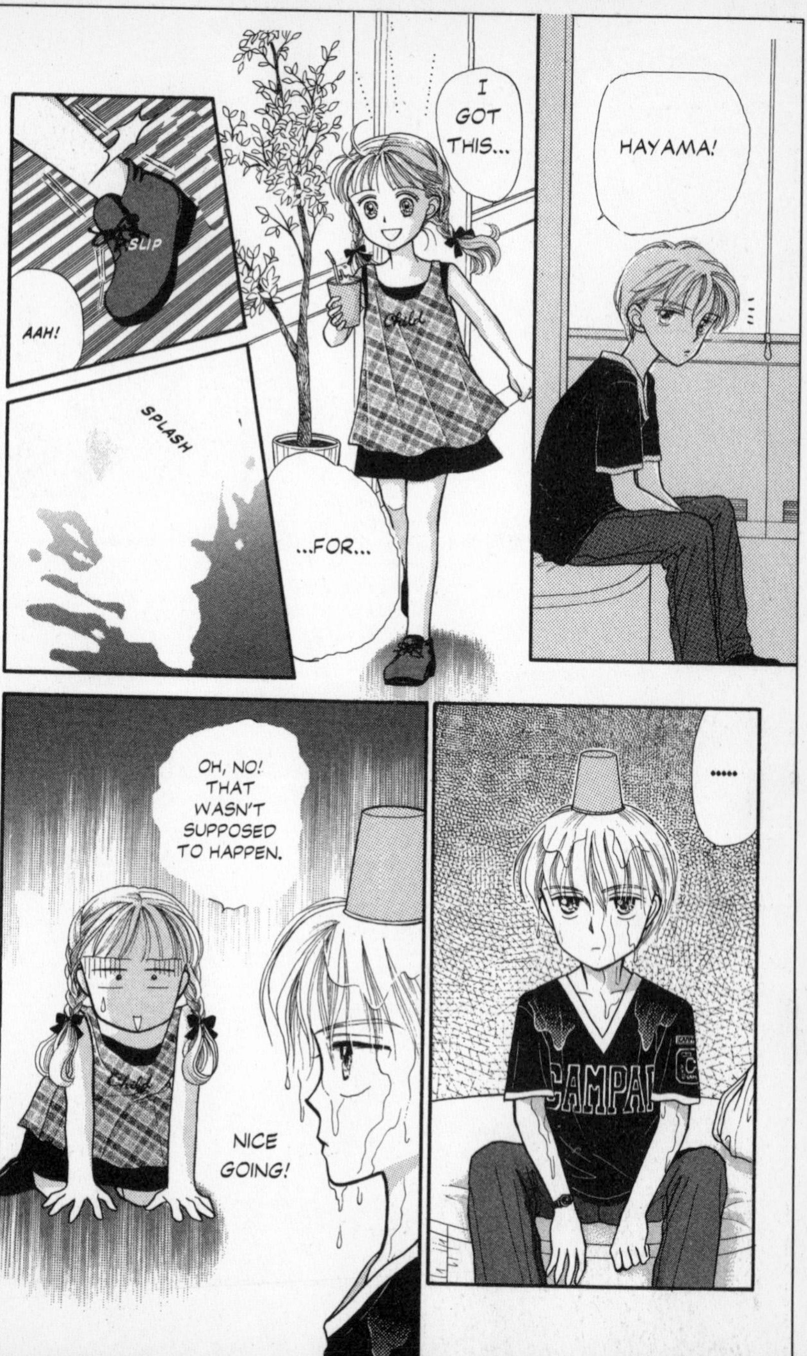
HAYAMA!
I GOT THIS...
...FOR...
SLIP
AAH!
SPLASH
......
OH, NO! THAT WASN'T SUPPOSED TO HAPPEN.
NICE GOING!

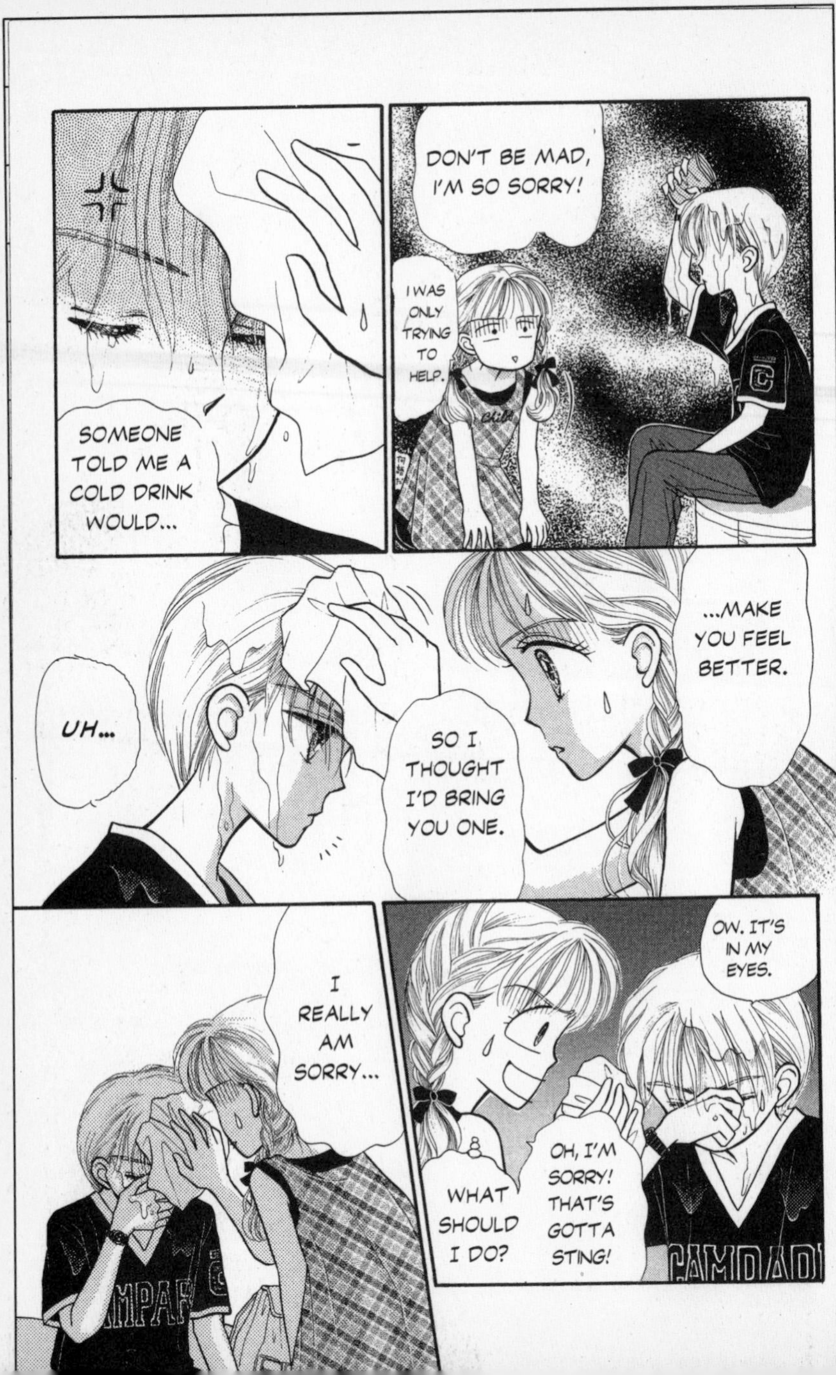
DON'T BE MAD, I'M SO SORRY!
I WAS ONLY TRYING TO HELP.
SOMEONE TOLD ME A COLD DRINK WOULD...
...MAKE YOU FEEL BETTER.
SO I THOUGHT I'D BRING YOU ONE.
UH...
OW. IT'S IN MY EYES.
OH, I'M SORRY! THAT'S GOTTA STING!
WHAT SHOULD I DO?
I REALLY AM SORRY...

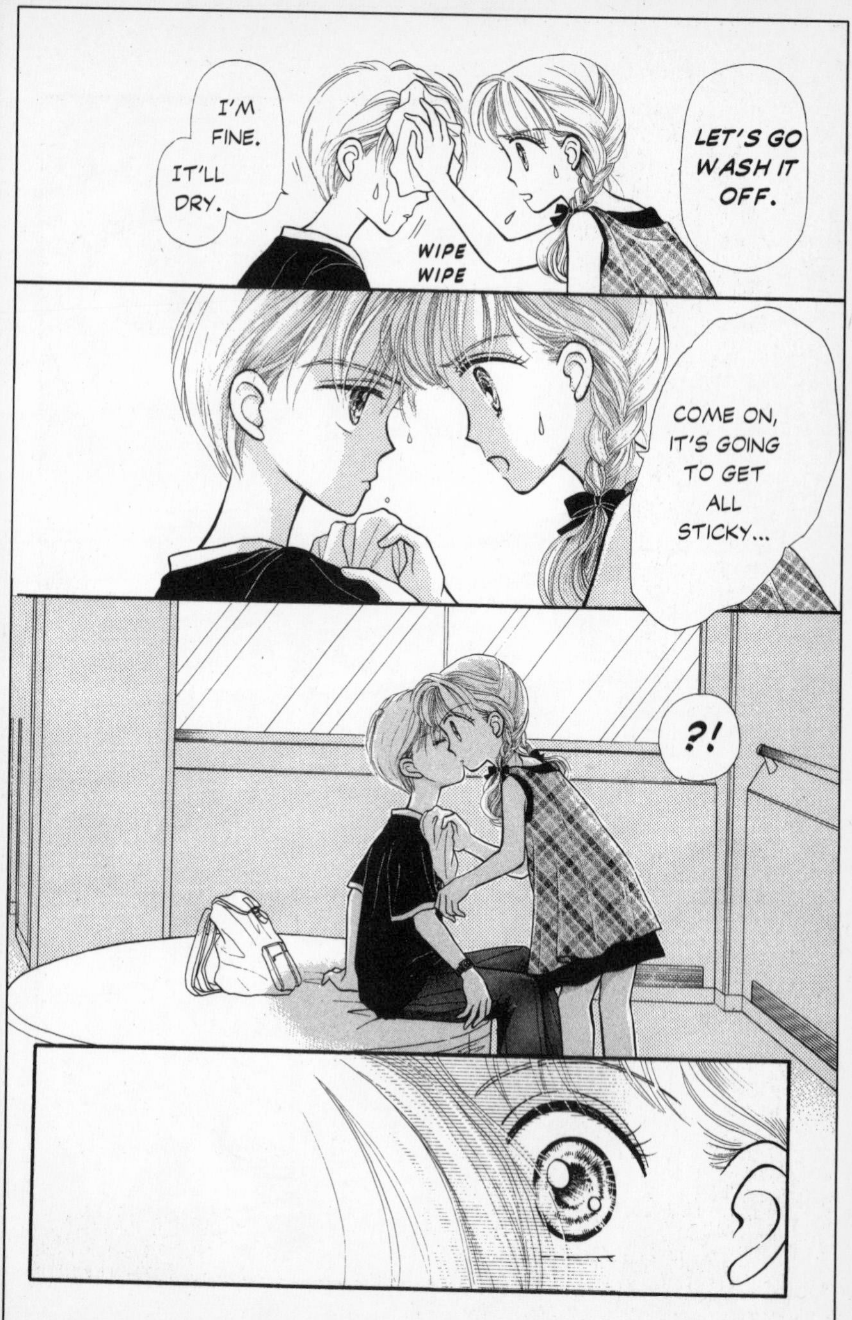
LET'S GO WASH IT OFF.
WIPE WIPE
I'M FINE. IT'LL DRY.
COME ON, IT'S GOING TO GET ALL STICKY...
?!

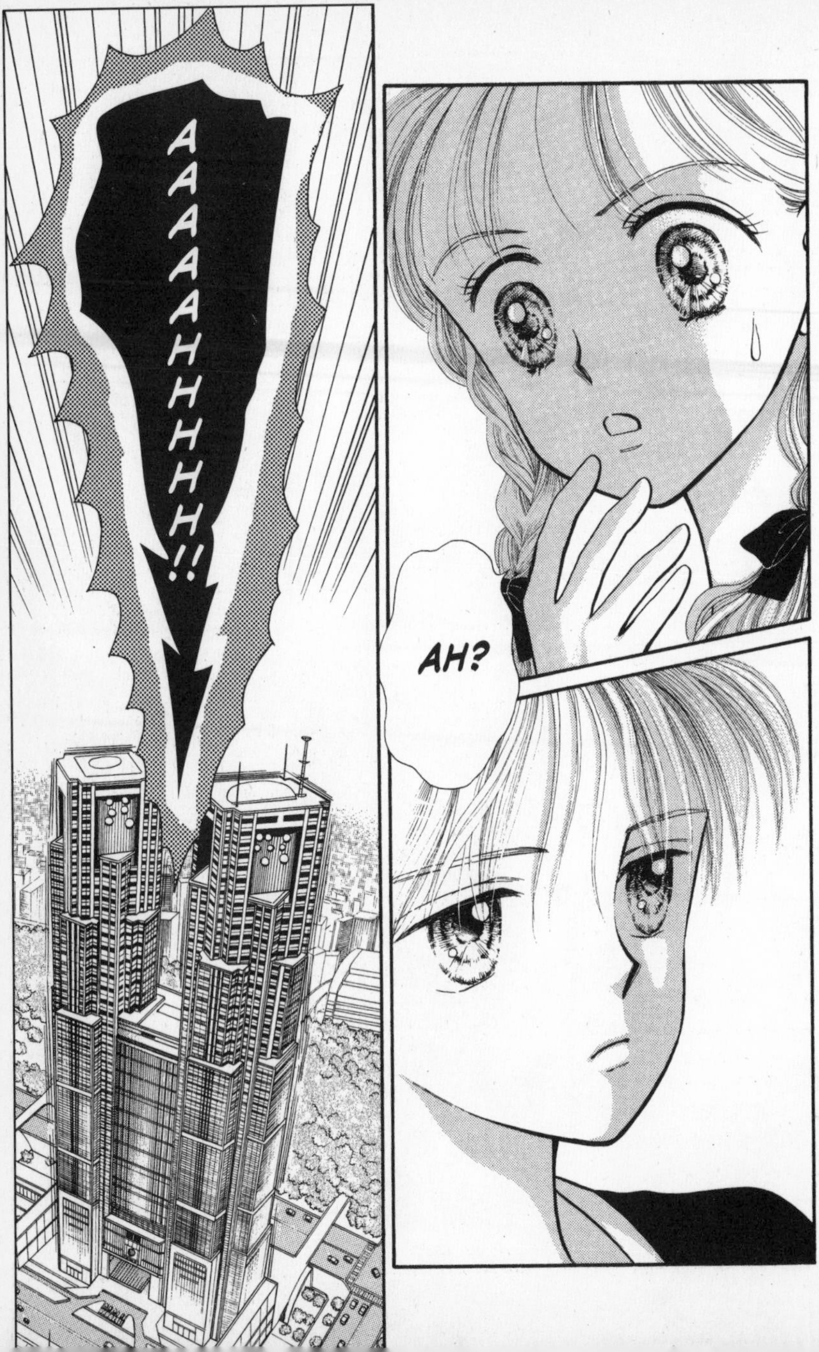
AH?
AAAAAHHHHH!!

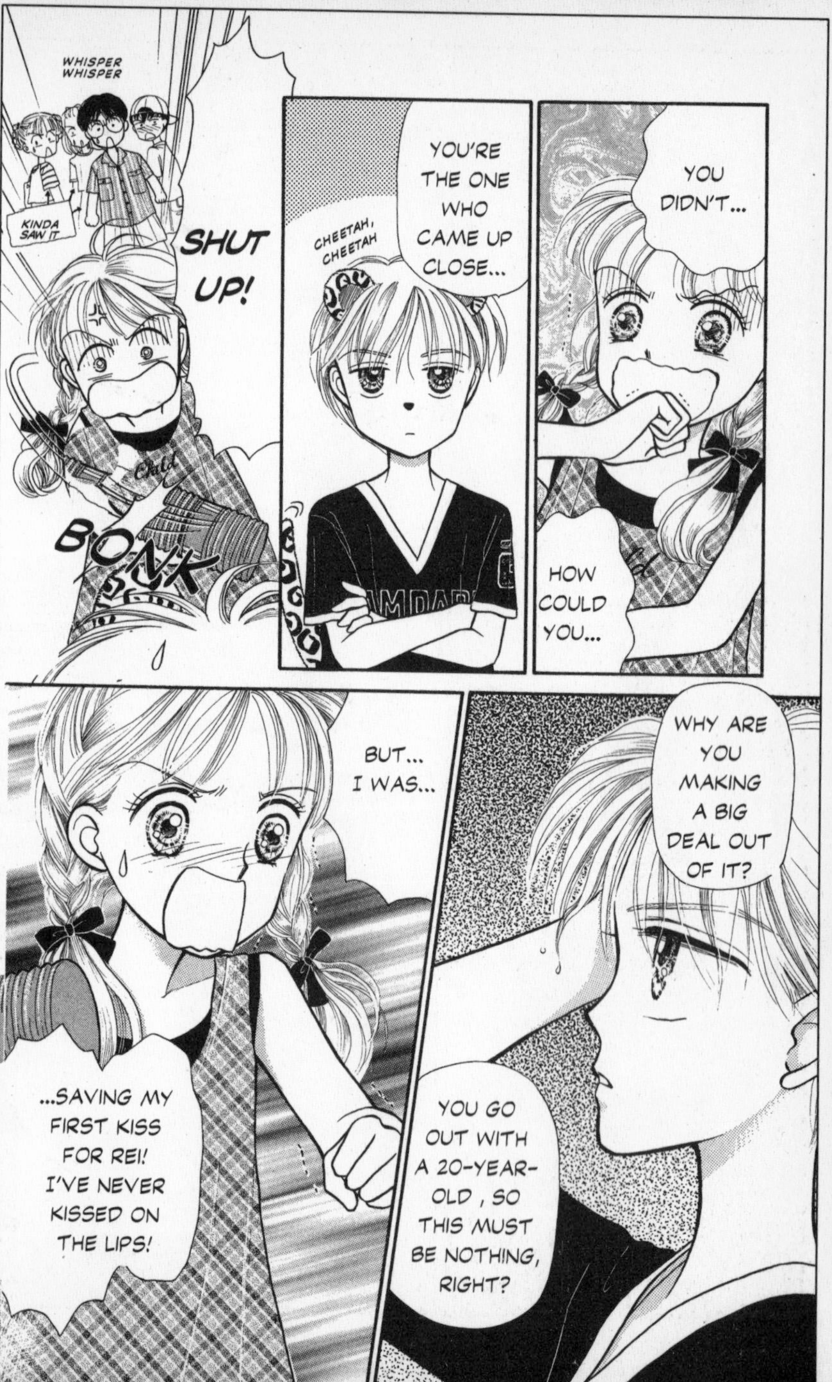
YOU DIDN'T...
HOW COULD YOU...
YOU'RE THE ONE WHO CAME UP CLOSE...
CHEETAH, CHEETAH
WHISPER WHISPER
KINDA SAW IT
SHUT UP!
BONK
WHY ARE YOU MAKING A BIG DEAL OUT OF IT?
YOU GO OUT WITH A 20-YEAR-OLD , SO THIS MUST BE NOTHING, RIGHT?
BUT... I WAS...
...SAVING MY FIRST KISS FOR REI! I'VE NEVER KISSED ON THE LIPS!

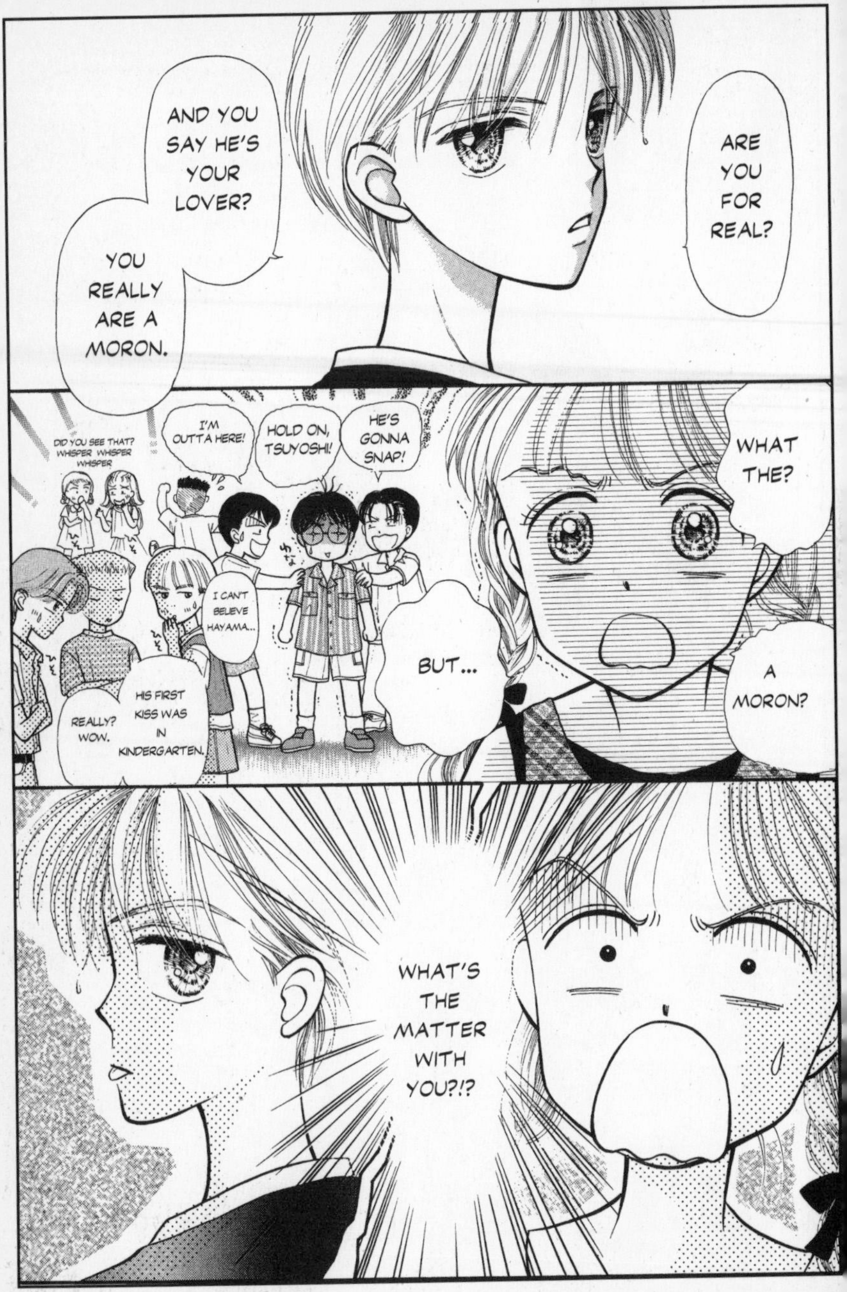
ARE YOU FOR REAL?
AND YOU SAY HE'S YOUR LOVER?
YOU REALLY ARE A MORON.
WHAT THE?
A MORON?
BUT...
HE'S GONNA SNAP!
HOLD ON, TSUYOSHI!
I'M OUTTA HERE!
I CAN'T BELIEVE HAYAMA...
HIS FIRST KISS WAS IN KINDERGARTEN.
REALLY? WOW.
DID YOU SEE THAT? WHISPER WHISPER WHISPER
WHAT'S THE MATTER WITH YOU?!?

CHILD'S TOY EXTRA:

CHILD'S TOY WEATHER REPORT

Tsuyoshi's version

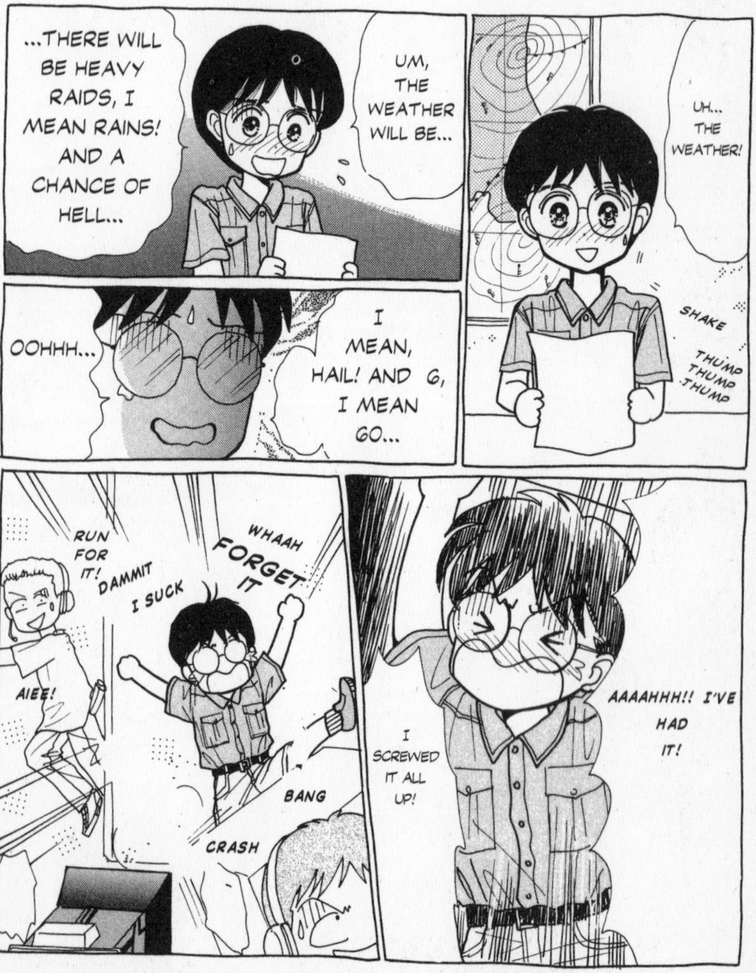
UH... THE WEATHER!
SHAKE
THUMP THUMP THUMP
UM, THE WEATHER WILL BE...
...THERE WILL BE HEAVY RAIDS, I MEAN RAINS! AND A CHANCE OF HELL...
I MEAN, HAIL! AND G, I MEAN GO...
OOHHH...
AAAAHHH!! I'VE HAD IT!
I SCREWED IT ALL UP!
WHAAH
FORGET IT
I SUCK
DAMMIT
RUN FOR IT!
AIEE!
BANG
CRASH

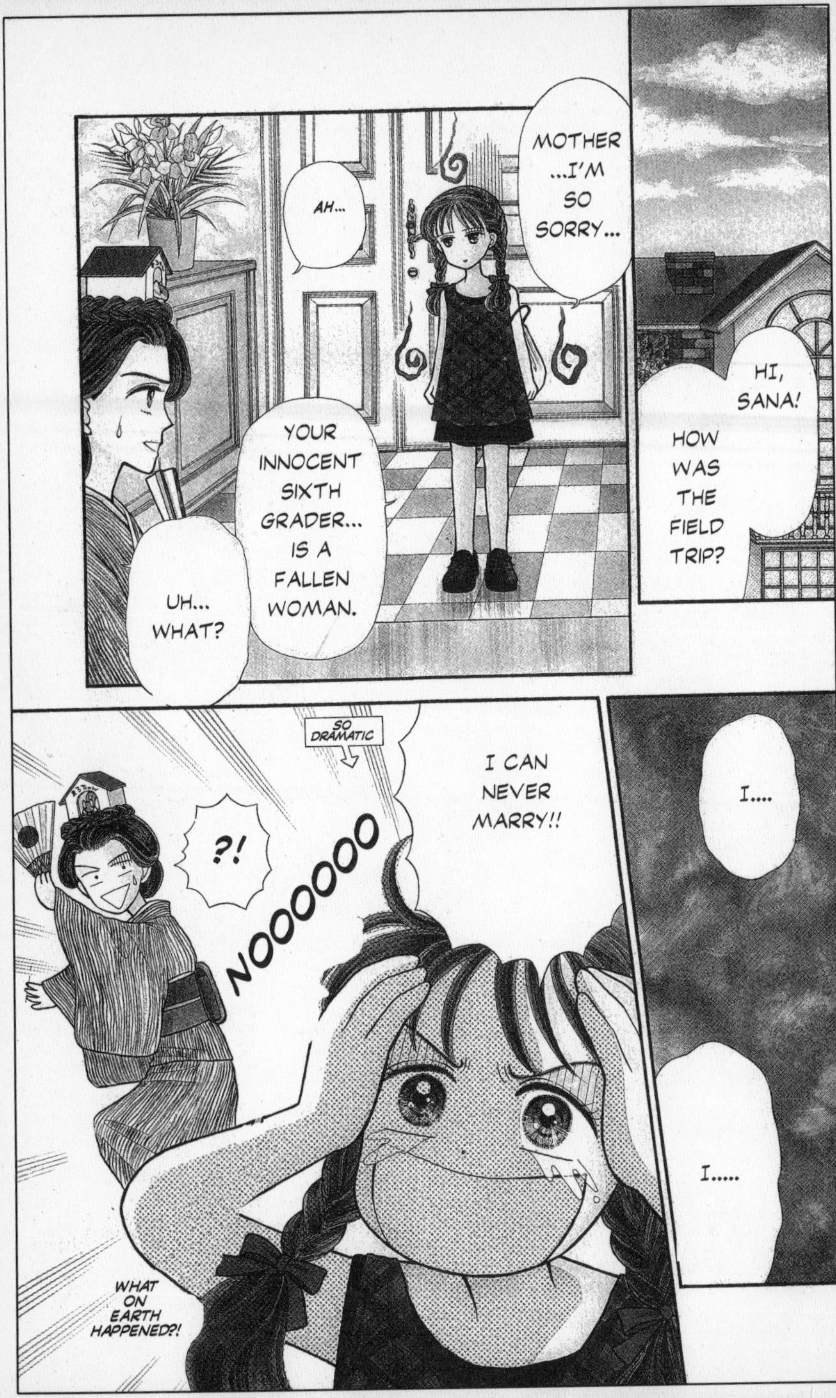
HI, SANA!
HOW WAS THE FIELD TRIP?
MOTHER ...I'M SO SORRY...
AH...
YOUR INNOCENT SIXTH GRADER... IS A FALLEN WOMAN.
UH... WHAT?
I....
I.....
I CAN NEVER MARRY!!
SO DRAMATIC
NOOOOOO
?!
WHAT ON EARTH HAPPENED?!

CHILD'S TOY EXTRA:

CHILD'S TOY WEATHER REPORT

Mariko's version

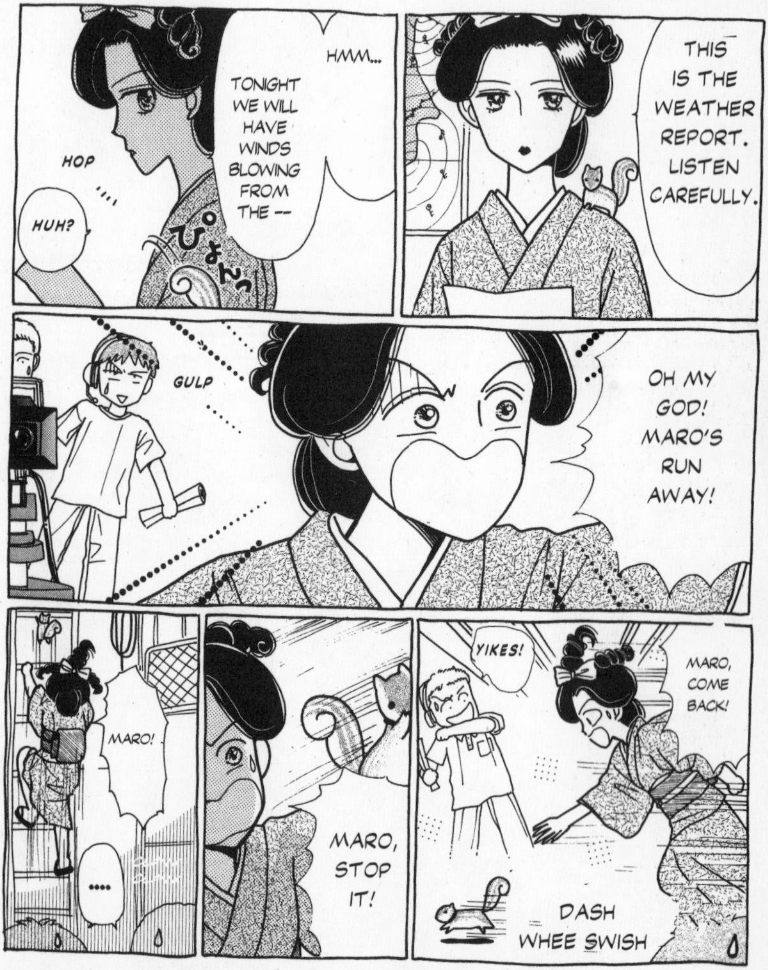
THIS IS THE WEATHER REPORT. LISTEN CAREFULLY.
HMM...
TONIGHT WE WILL HAVE WINDS BLOWING FROM THE --
HOP
....
HUH?
OH MY GOD! MARO'S RUN AWAY!
GULP
.....
YIKES!
MARO, COME BACK!
DASH
WHEE SWISH
MARO, STOP IT!
MARO!
....

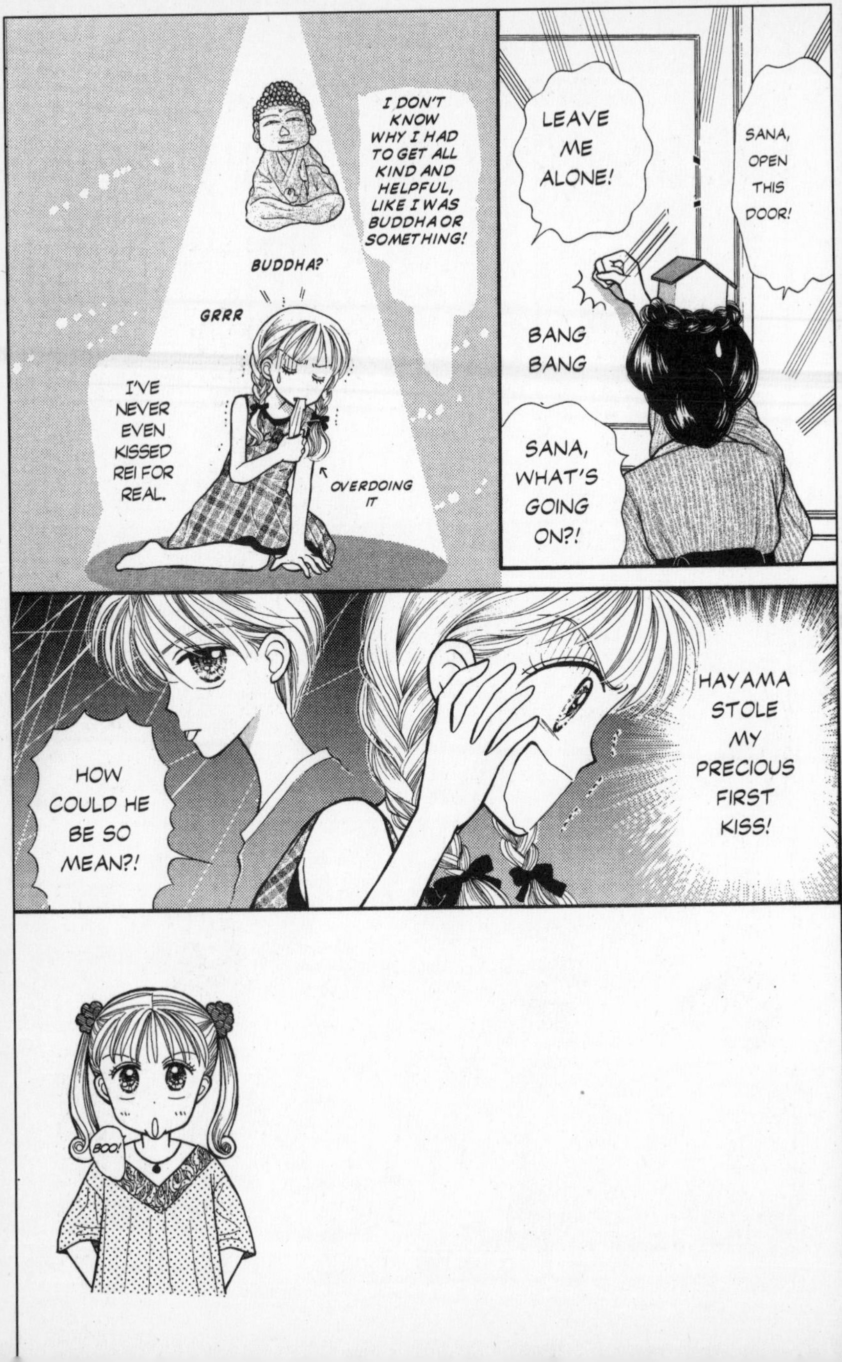
SANA, OPEN THIS DOOR!
LEAVE ME ALONE!
BANG BANG
SANA, WHAT'S GOING ON?!
I DON'T KNOW WHY I HAD TO GET ALL KIND AND HELPFUL, LIKE I WAS BUDDHA OR SOMETHING!
BUDDHA?
GRRR
I'VE NEVER EVEN KISSED REI FOR REAL.
OVERDOING IT
HAYAMA STOLE MY PRECIOUS FIRST KISS!
HOW COULD HE BE SO MEAN?!
BOO!

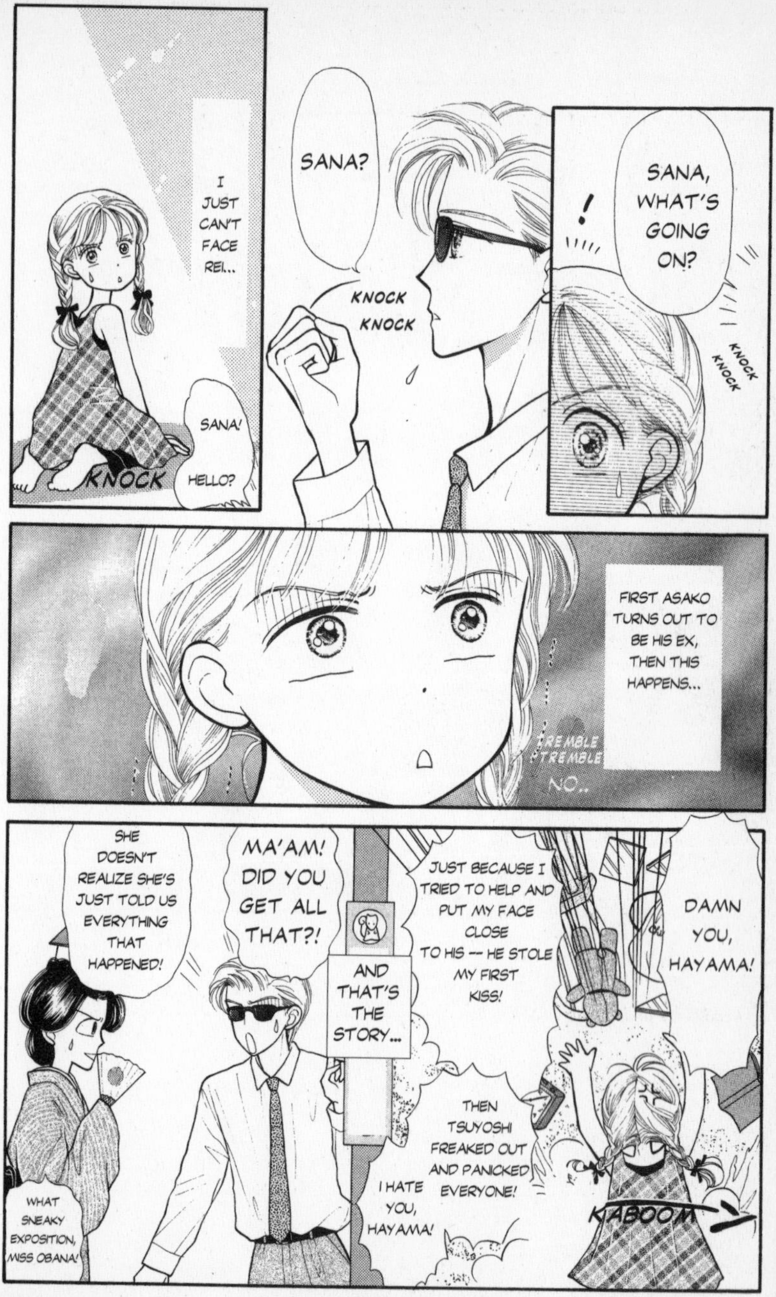
!
SANA, WHAT'S GOING ON?
KNOCK KNOCK
SANA?
KNOCK KNOCK
I JUST CAN'T FACE REI...
SANA!
HELLO?
KNOCK
FIRST ASAKO TURNS OUT TO BE HIS EX, THEN THIS HAPPENS...
TREMBLE TREMBLE
NO..
DAMN YOU, HAYAMA!
JUST BECAUSE I TRIED TO HELP AND PUT MY FACE CLOSE TO HIS -- HE STOLE MY FIRST KISS!
KABOOM
THEN TSUYOSHI FREAKED OUT AND PANICKED EVERYONE!
I HATE YOU, HAYAMA!
AND THAT'S THE STORY...
MA'AM! DID YOU GET ALL THAT?!
SHE DOESN'T REALIZE SHE'S JUST TOLD US EVERYTHING THAT HAPPENED!
WHAT SNEAKY EXPOSITION, MISS OBANA!

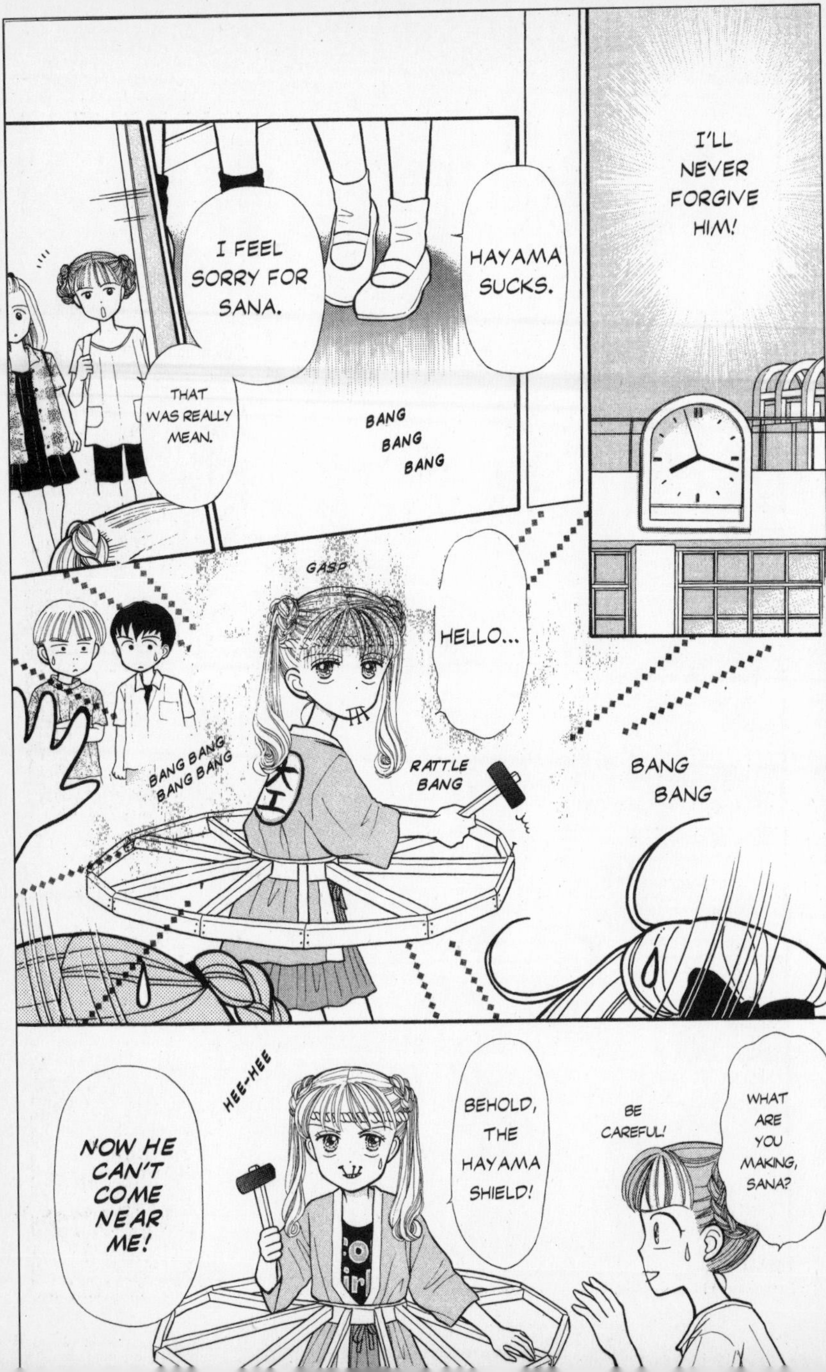
I'LL NEVER FORGIVE HIM!
HAYAMA SUCKS.
I FEEL SORRY FOR SANA.
THAT WAS REALLY MEAN.
BANG BANG BANG
HELLO...
GASP
BANG BANG
RATTLE BANG
BANG BANG BANG BANG
WHAT ARE YOU MAKING, SANA?
BE CAREFUL!
BEHOLD, THE HAYAMA SHIELD!
HEE-HEE
NOW HE CAN'T COME NEAR ME!

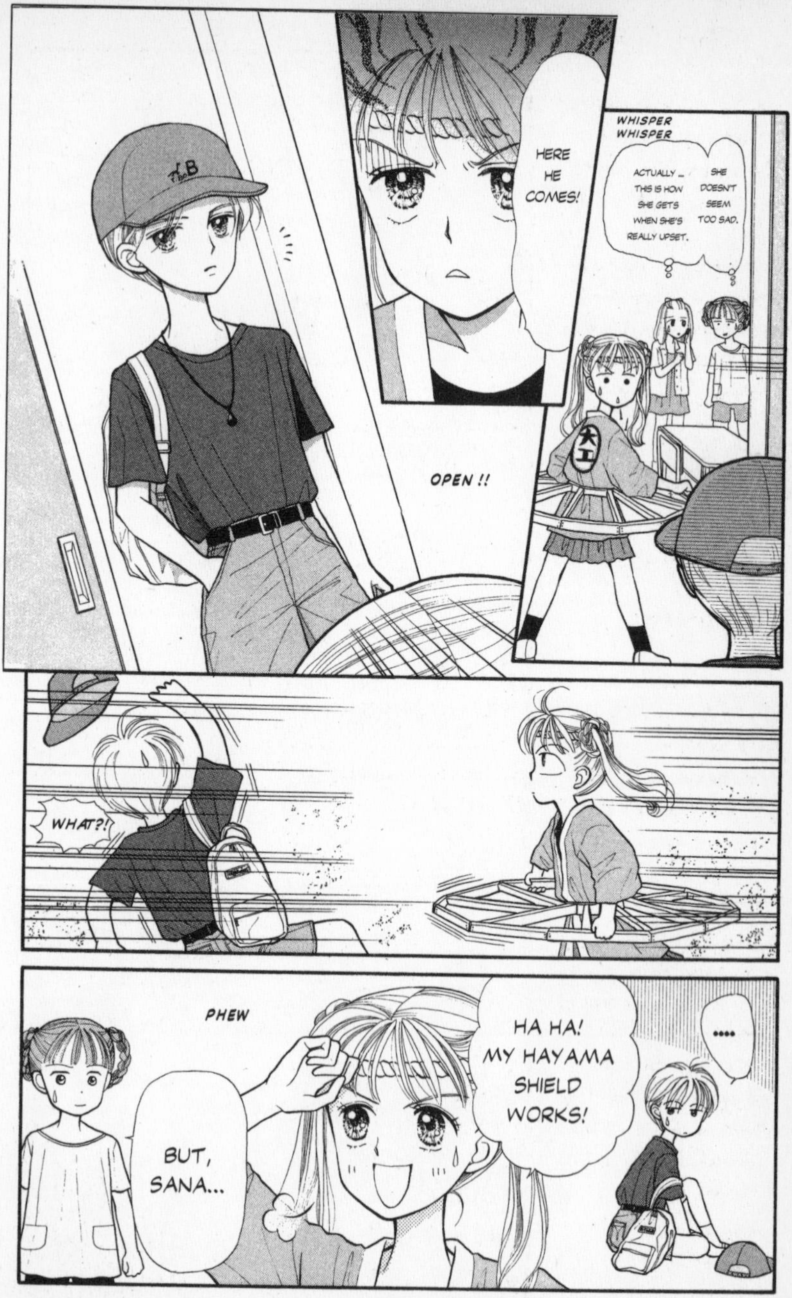
HERE HE COMES!
WHISPER WHISPER
SHE DOESN'T SEEM TOO SAD.
ACTUALLY ... THIS IS HOW SHE GETS WHEN SHE'S REALLY UPSET.
OPEN !!
WHAT?!
....
HA HA! MY HAYAMA SHIELD WORKS!
PHEW
BUT, SANA...

Part Two

Back then, anyone who tried out got into the Theater, so they said I was accepted. But then they told us how much it cost to join — $2000! My mom's face totally froze. So, I didn't get to join them after all. During my audition,

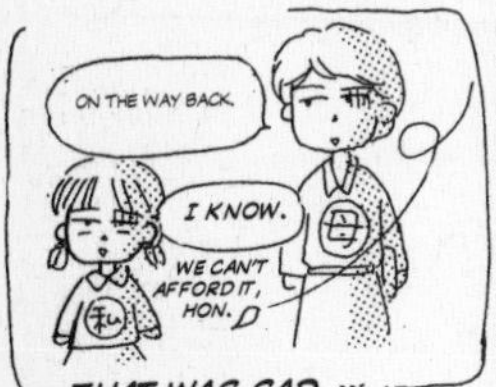
ON THE WAY BACK.
I KNOW.
WE CAN'T AFFORD IT, HON.
THAT WAS SAD. ···

the interviewer asked me what I was really good at. I told him, "drawing". He asked me to draw something, so I drew Benio-san (from the then-famous series Haikara-san Ga Tooru). When I look back on it, I realize that if I thought I was best at drawing all the way back then, I should've focused on becoming a comic book artist in the first place! But that's easy to say now. Hee-hee.

(To be continued...)

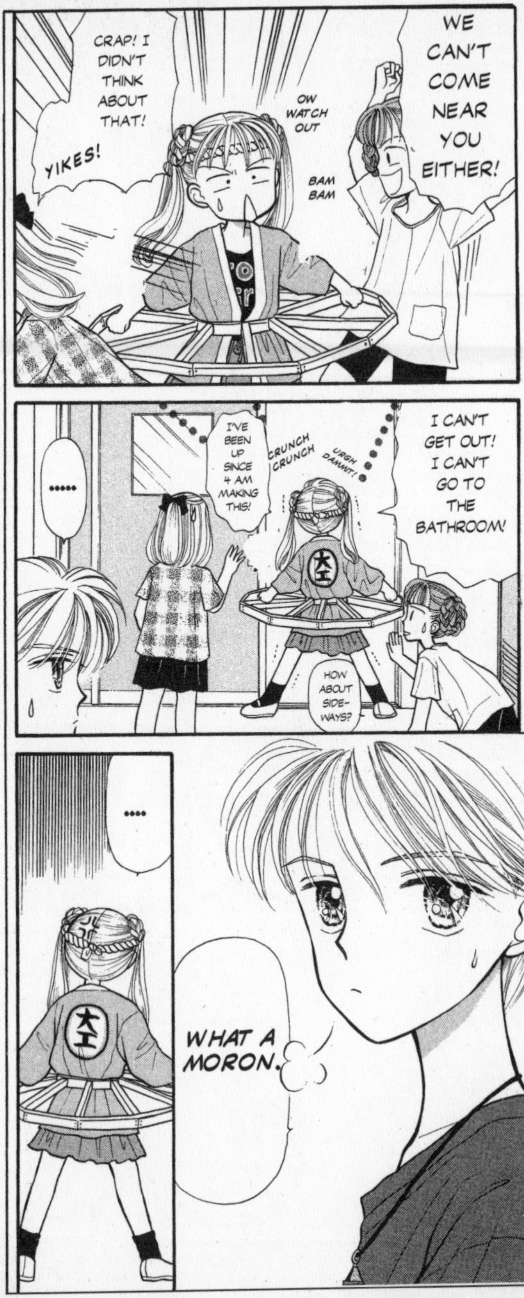
WE CAN'T COME NEAR YOU EITHER!
OW WATCH OUT
BAM BAM
CRAP! I DIDN'T THINK ABOUT THAT!
YIKES!
I CAN'T GET OUT! I CAN'T GO TO THE BATHROOM!
URGH DAMMIT!
CRUNCH CRUNCH
I'VE BEEN UP SINCE 4 AM MAKING THIS!
HOW ABOUT SIDEWAYS?
·····
WHAT A MORON.
····

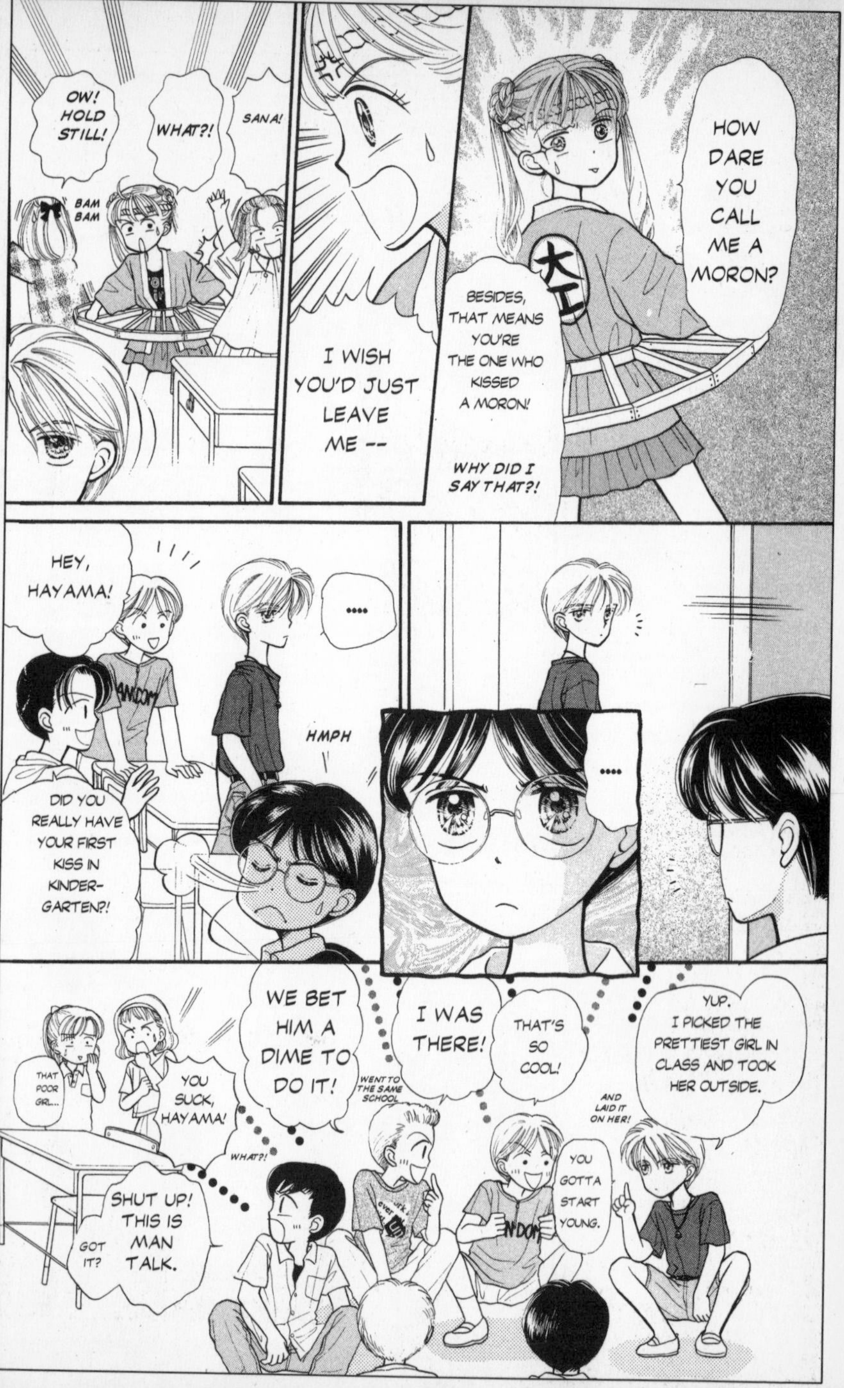
HOW DARE YOU CALL ME A MORON?
BESIDES, THAT MEANS YOU'RE THE ONE WHO KISSED A MORON!
WHY DID I SAY THAT?!
I WISH YOU'D JUST LEAVE ME --
SANA!
WHAT?!
OW! HOLD STILL!
BAM BAM
....
HEY, HAYAMA!
....
DID YOU REALLY HAVE YOUR FIRST KISS IN KINDER-GARTEN?!
HMPH
YUP. I PICKED THE PRETTIEST GIRL IN CLASS AND TOOK HER OUTSIDE.
AND LAID IT ON HER!
YOU GOTTA START YOUNG.
THAT'S SO COOL!
I WAS THERE!
WENT TO THE SAME SCHOOL
WE BET HIM A DIME TO DO IT!
WHAT?!
YOU SUCK, HAYAMA!
THAT POOR GIRL...
SHUT UP! THIS IS MAN TALK.
GOT IT?

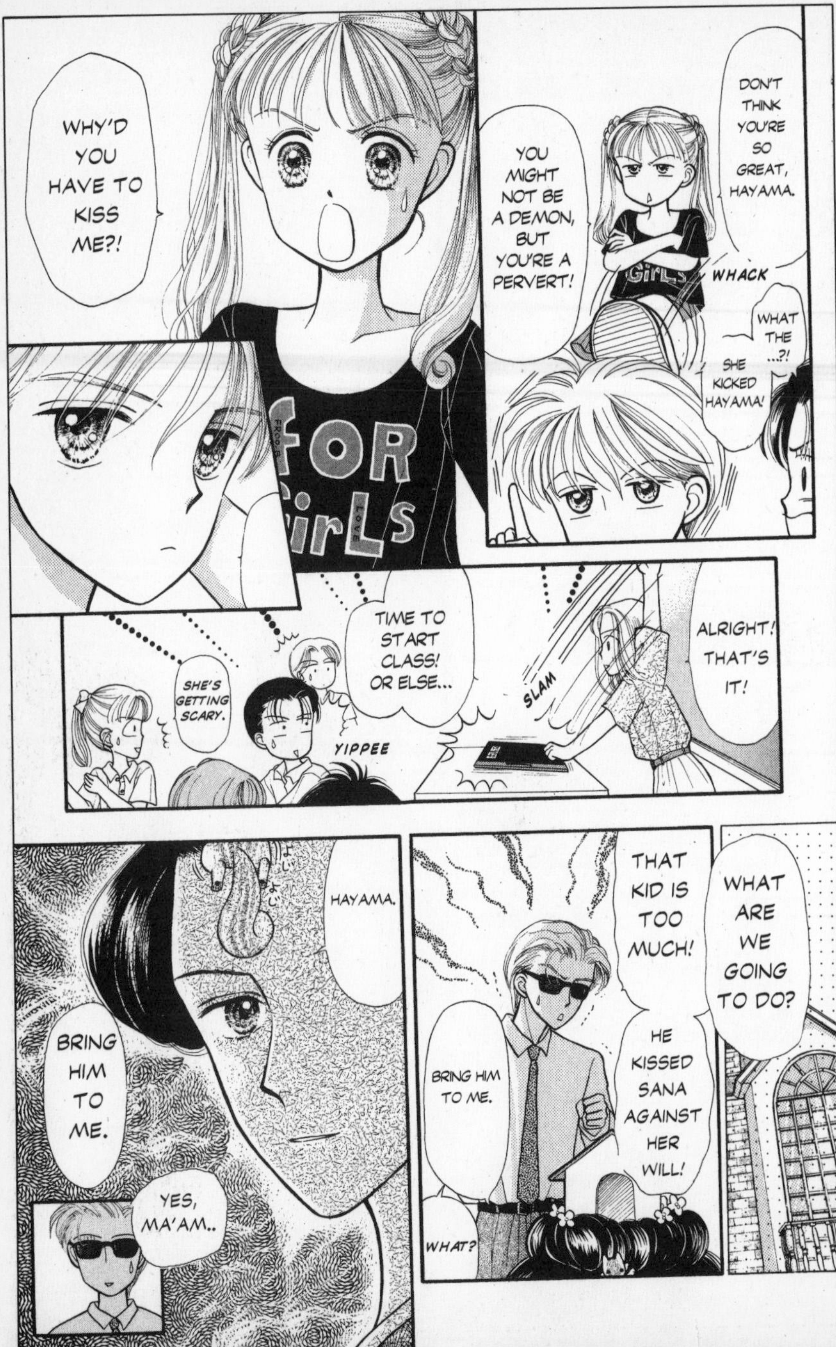
DON'T THINK YOU'RE SO GREAT, HAYAMA.
YOU MIGHT NOT BE A DEMON, BUT YOU'RE A PERVERT!
WHACK
WHAT THE ...?!
SHE KICKED HAYAMA!
WHY'D YOU HAVE TO KISS ME?!
ALRIGHT! THAT'S IT!
SLAM
TIME TO START CLASS! OR ELSE...
YIPPEE
SHE'S GETTING SCARY.
WHAT ARE WE GOING TO DO?
THAT KID IS TOO MUCH!
HE KISSED SANA AGAINST HER WILL!
BRING HIM TO ME.
WHAT?
HAYAMA.
よし よし
BRING HIM TO ME.
YES, MA'AM..

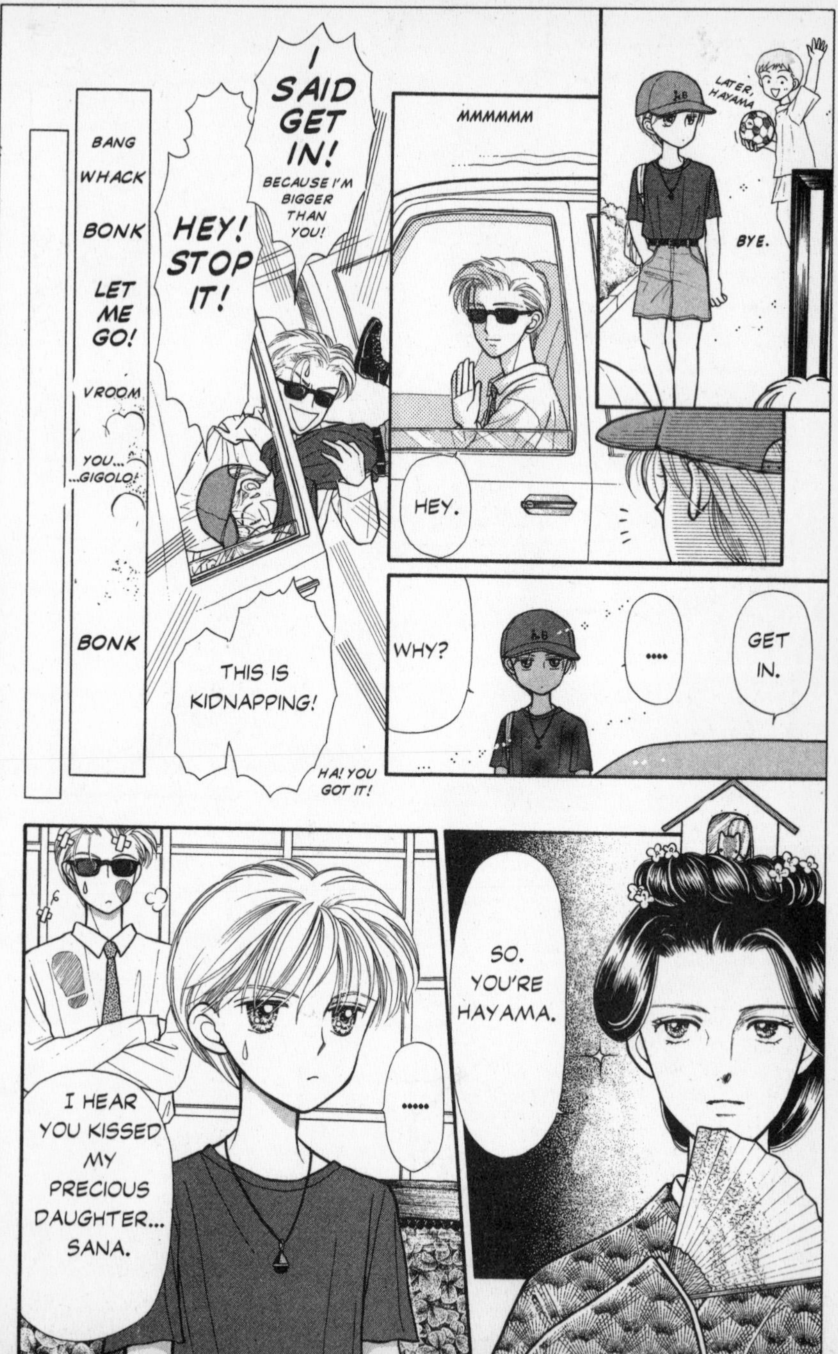
LATER, HAYAMA
BYE.
MMMMMM
HEY.
GET IN.
....
WHY?
I SAID GET IN!
BECAUSE I'M BIGGER THAN YOU!
HEY! STOP IT!
BANG
WHACK
BONK
LET ME GO!
VROOM
YOU... ...GIGOLO!
BONK
THIS IS KIDNAPPING!
HA! YOU GOT IT!
SO. YOU'RE HAYAMA.
.....
I HEAR YOU KISSED MY PRECIOUS DAUGHTER... SANA.

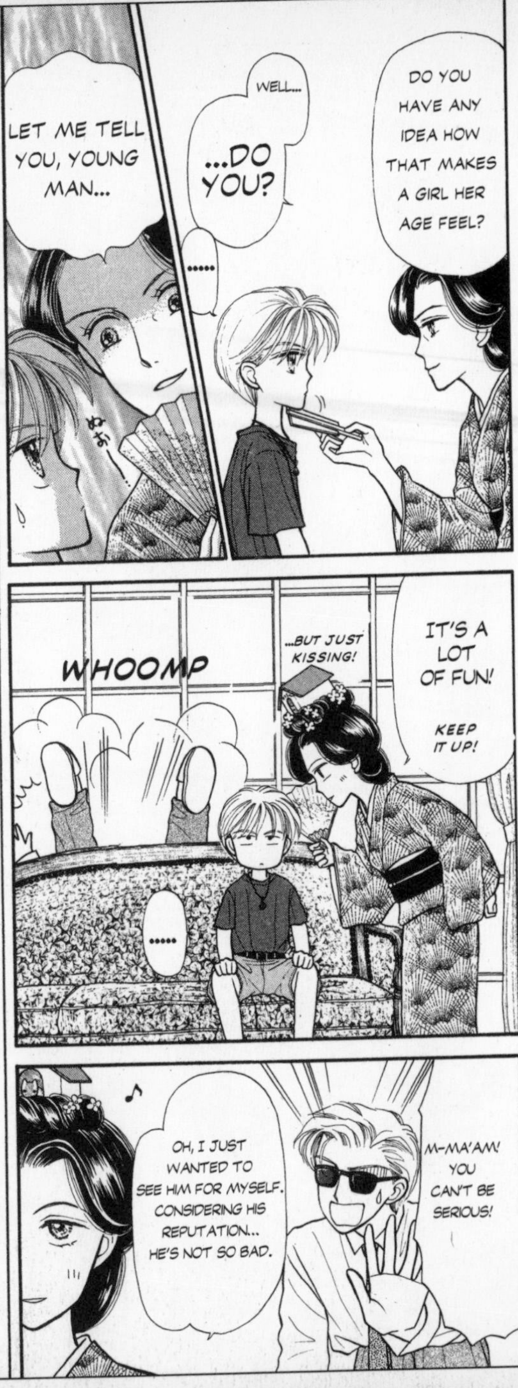
DO YOU HAVE ANY IDEA HOW THAT MAKES A GIRL HER AGE FEEL?
WELL...
...DO YOU?
......
LET ME TELL YOU, YOUNG MAN...
IT'S A LOT OF FUN!
KEEP IT UP!
...BUT JUST KISSING!
WHOOMP
......
M-MA'AM! YOU CAN'T BE SERIOUS!
OH, I JUST WANTED TO SEE HIM FOR MYSELF. CONSIDERING HIS REPUTATION... HE'S NOT SO BAD.

Part Three

When I auditioned for the Himawari Theater, they would tell me to "be angry" or "be happy"...to test my acting skills, I think. I was supposed to just do exactly what they told me to, but I improvised and added lines. I think they liked it. Looking back on it, the whole experience was kinda embarrassing.

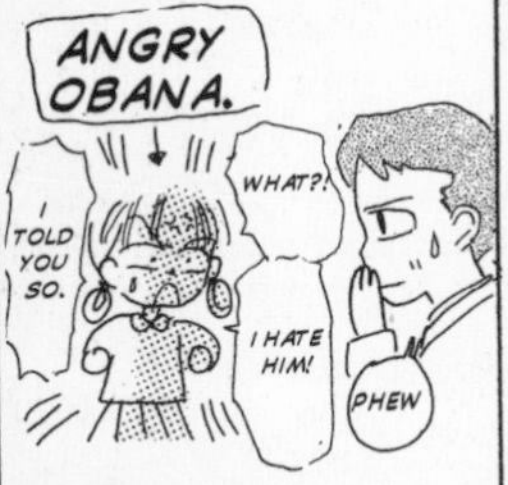
ANGRY OBANA.
I TOLD YOU SO.
WHAT?!
I HATE HIM!
PHEW

Also, they had me read various things out loud for voice training. As I was reading, I kept thinking about how stupid this stuff was.

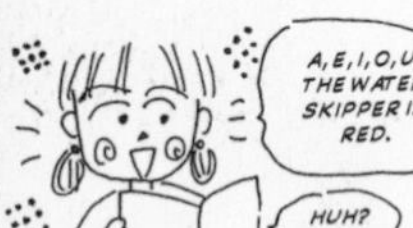
A, E, I, O, U. THE WATER SKIPPER IS RED.
HUH?

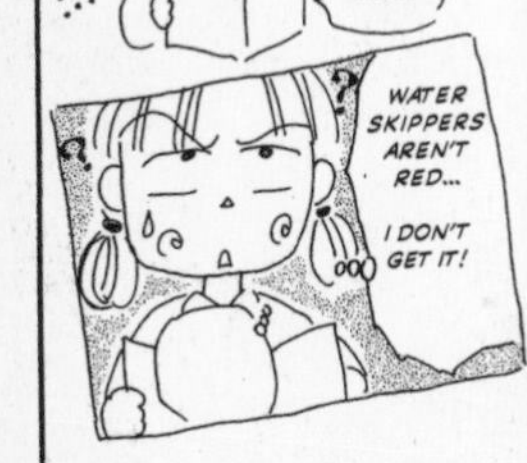
WATER SKIPPERS AREN'T RED...
I DON'T GET IT!

(To be continued.)

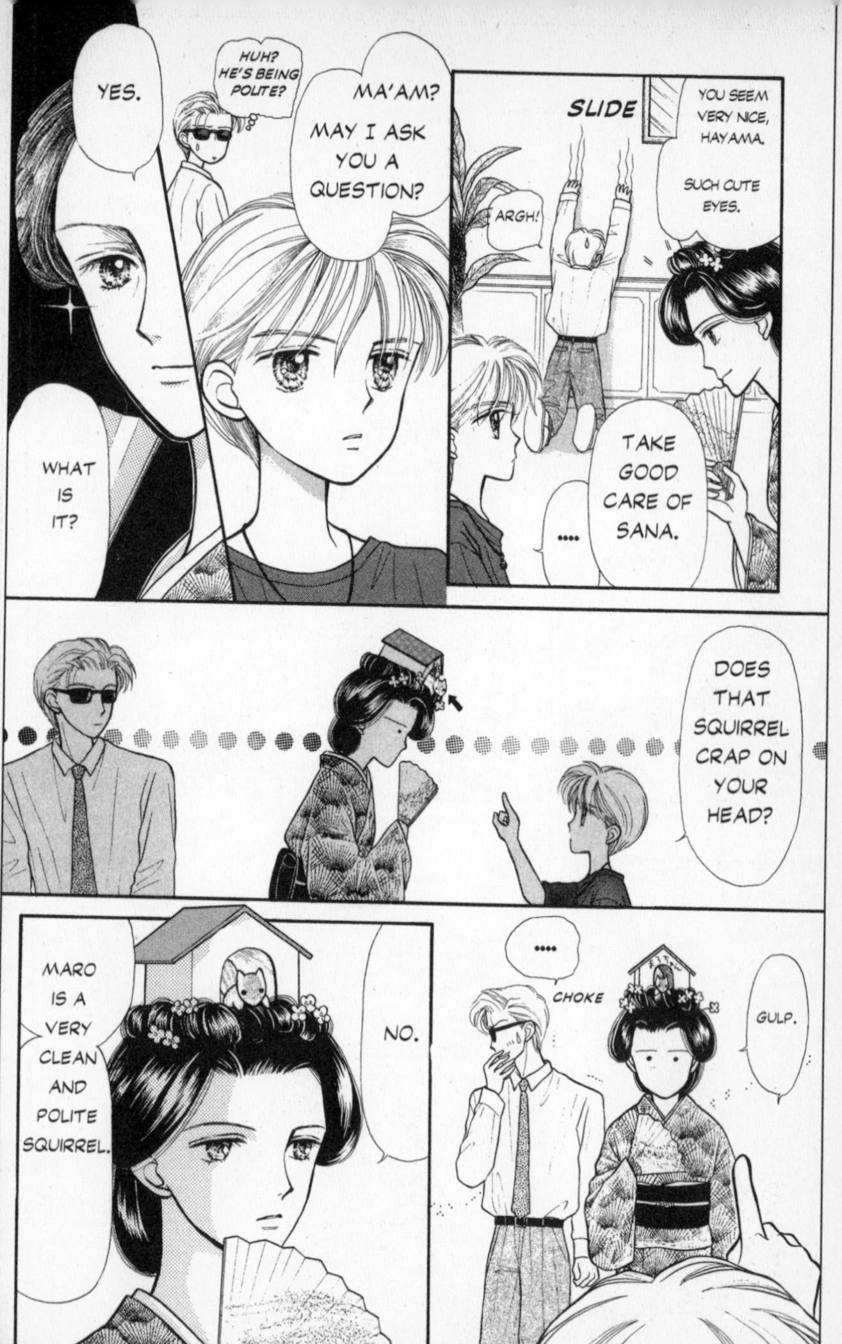
YOU SEEM VERY NICE, HAYAMA.
SUCH CUTE EYES.
SLIDE
ARGH!
TAKE GOOD CARE OF SANA.
....
MA'AM?
MAY I ASK YOU A QUESTION?
HUH? HE'S BEING POLITE?
YES.
WHAT IS IT?
DOES THAT SQUIRREL CRAP ON YOUR HEAD?
GULP.
....
CHOKE
NO.
MARO IS A VERY CLEAN AND POLITE SQUIRREL.

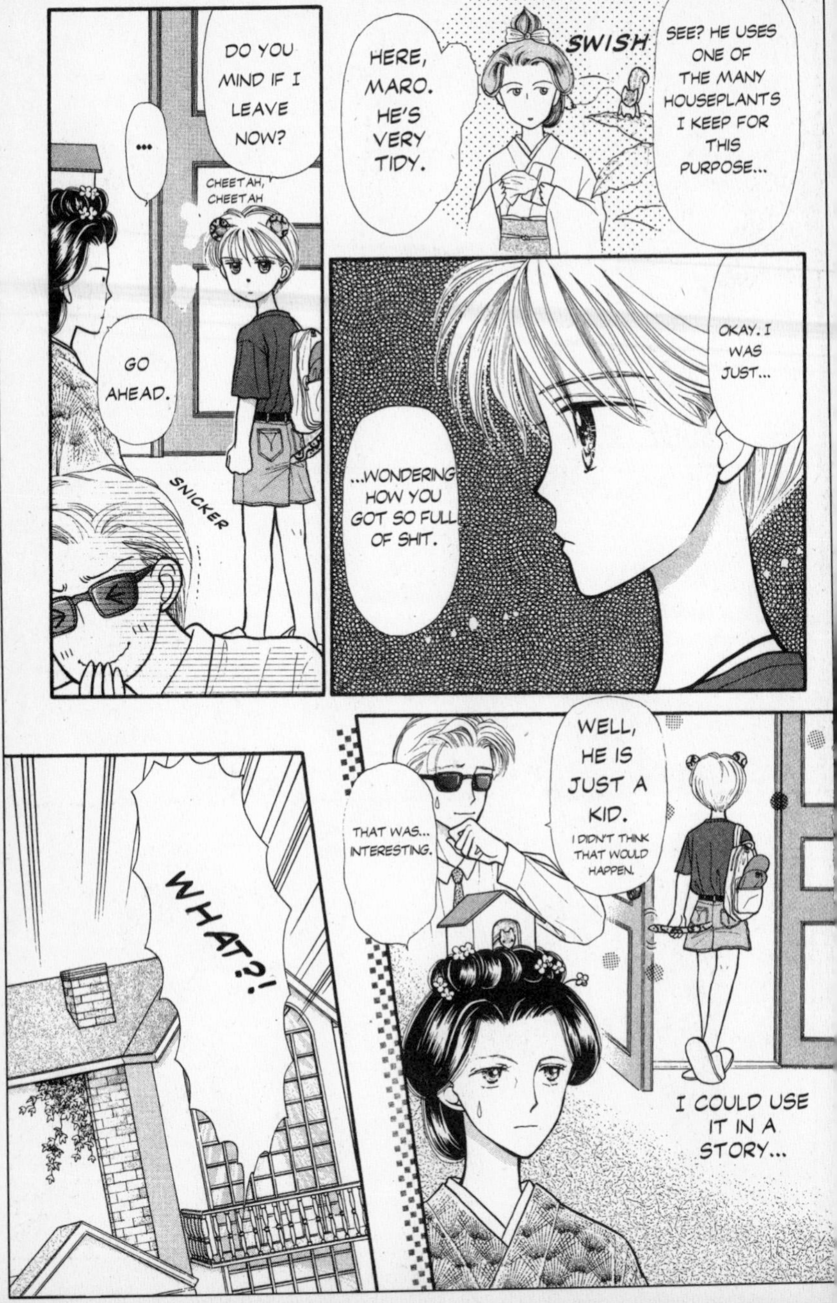
SEE? HE USES ONE OF THE MANY HOUSEPLANTS I KEEP FOR THIS PURPOSE...
SWISH
HERE, MARO. HE'S VERY TIDY.
OKAY. I WAS JUST...
...WONDERING HOW YOU GOT SO FULL OF SHIT.
DO YOU MIND IF I LEAVE NOW?
...
CHEETAH, CHEETAH
GO AHEAD.
SNICKER
WELL, HE IS JUST A KID.
I DIDN'T THINK THAT WOULD HAPPEN.
THAT WAS... INTERESTING.
I COULD USE IT IN A STORY...
WHAT?!

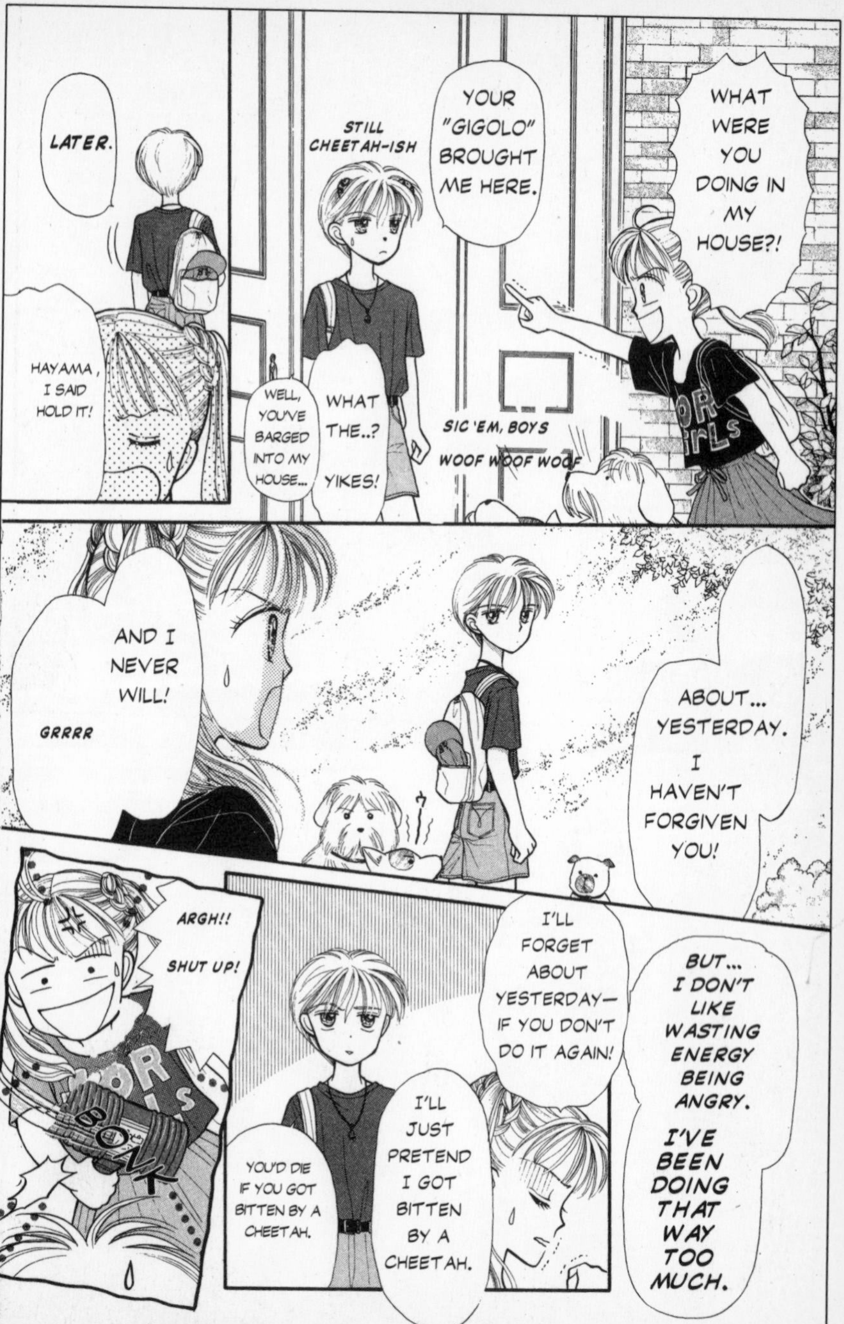
WHAT WERE YOU DOING IN MY HOUSE?!
YOUR "GIGOLO" BROUGHT ME HERE.
STILL CHEETAH-ISH
SIC 'EM, BOYS
WOOF WOOF WOOF
WHAT THE..? YIKES!
WELL, YOU'VE BARGED INTO MY HOUSE...
LATER.
HAYAMA, I SAID HOLD IT!
ABOUT... YESTERDAY. I HAVEN'T FORGIVEN YOU!
AND I NEVER WILL!
GRRRR
BUT... I DON'T LIKE WASTING ENERGY BEING ANGRY.
I'VE BEEN DOING THAT WAY TOO MUCH.
I'LL FORGET ABOUT YESTERDAY— IF YOU DON'T DO IT AGAIN!
I'LL JUST PRETEND I GOT BITTEN BY A CHEETAH.
YOU'D DIE IF YOU GOT BITTEN BY A CHEETAH.
ARGH!!
SHUT UP!
BONK

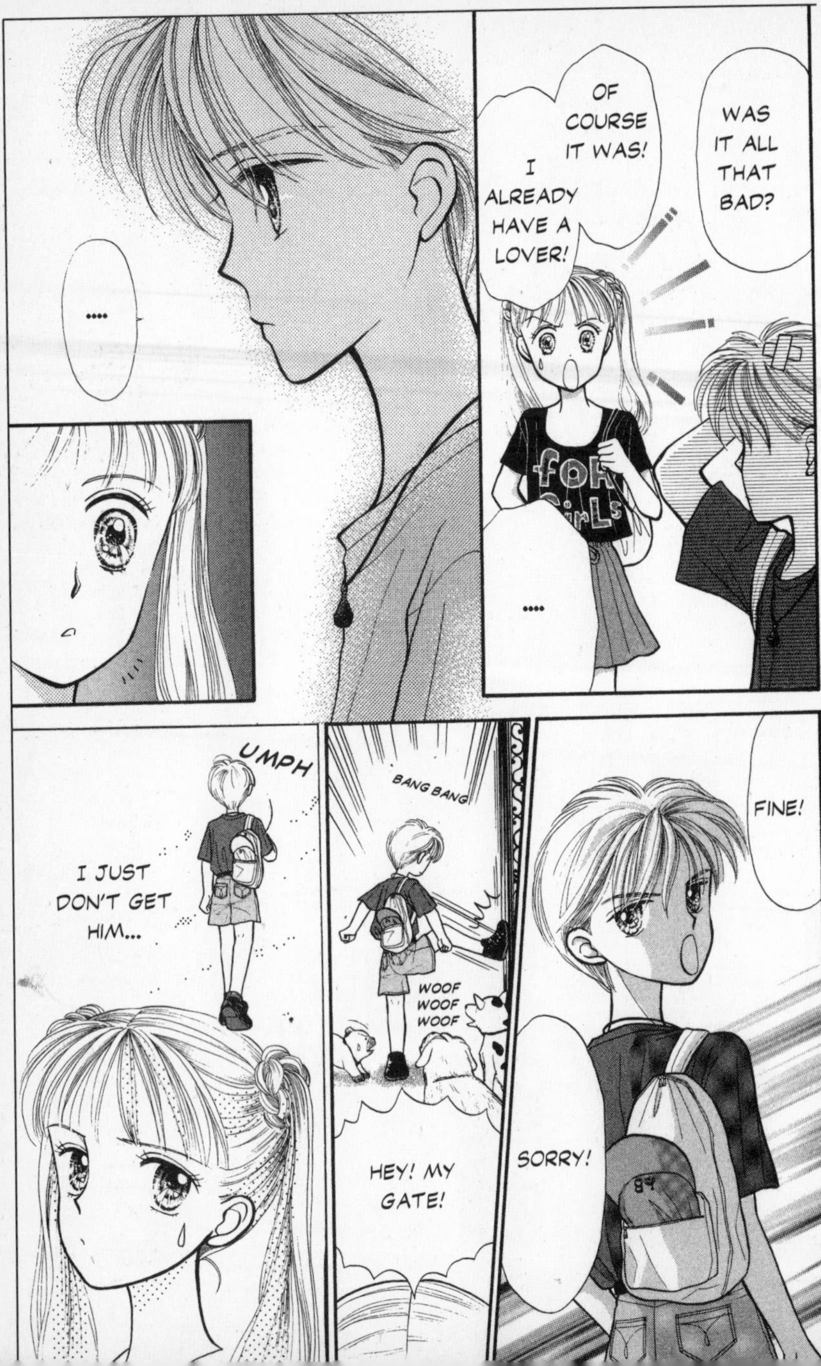
WAS IT ALL THAT BAD?
OF COURSE IT WAS!
I ALREADY HAVE A LOVER!
....
....
FINE!
SORRY!
BANG BANG
WOOF WOOF WOOF
HEY! MY GATE!
UMPH
I JUST DON'T GET HIM...

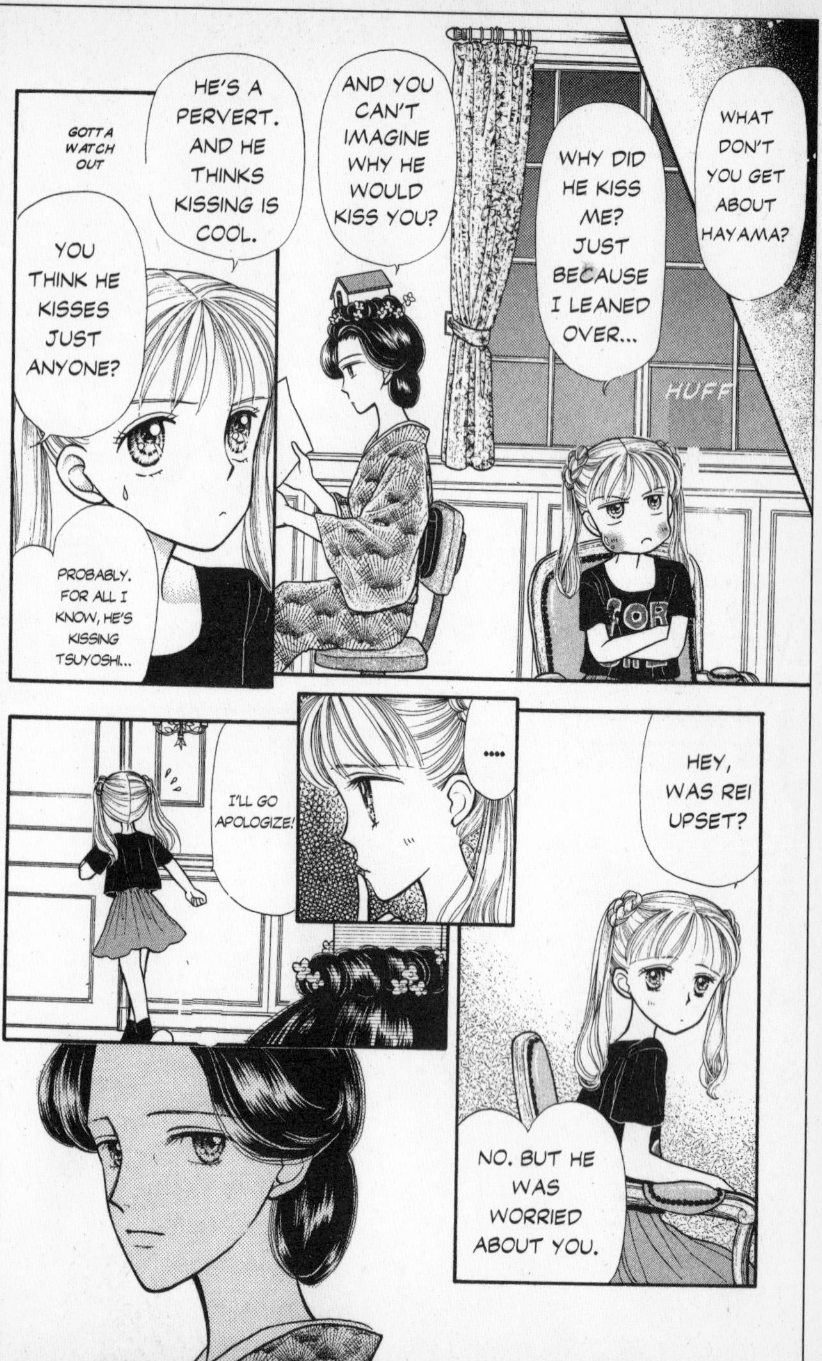
WHAT DON'T YOU GET ABOUT HAYAMA?
WHY DID HE KISS ME? JUST BECAUSE I LEANED OVER...
HUFF
AND YOU CAN'T IMAGINE WHY HE WOULD KISS YOU?
HE'S A PERVERT. AND HE THINKS KISSING IS COOL.
GOTTA WATCH OUT
YOU THINK HE KISSES JUST ANYONE?
PROBABLY. FOR ALL I KNOW, HE'S KISSING TSUYOSHI...
HEY, WAS REI UPSET?
NO. BUT HE WAS WORRIED ABOUT YOU.
....
I'LL GO APOLOGIZE!

Part Four

So, I didn't get to join Himawari Theater — but I was happy to just get a peek inside their world. It was a good experience. (Hee-hee.) And I'm certainly making good use of it now! Many of you write and say you want to be actresses like Sana. (Although some of you want to be comic book artists like me!) I totally understand. It's a dream a lot of young girls have. If you seriously want to be on TV, I hear that these days, it's better to join a talent agency or work as a model. Theater groups teach you to do many things (like dancing, acting, and singing) but don't necessarily get you work. I only put Sana in a theater group because of my past. By the way, remember my friend "S" that I told you about? She didn't try out for Himawari. She was discovered and asked to join. What a difference that made. Oh, well!

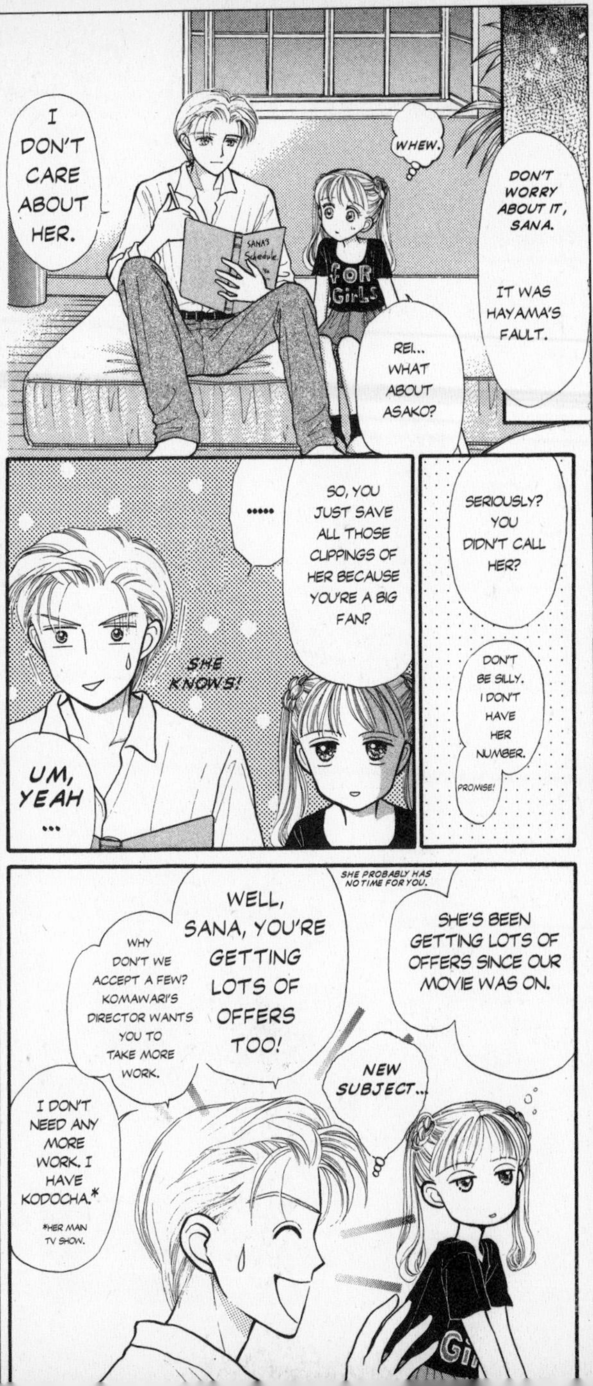
DON'T WORRY ABOUT IT, SANA.
IT WAS HAYAMA'S FAULT.
WHEW.
SANA'S Schedule
REI... WHAT ABOUT ASAKO?
I DON'T CARE ABOUT HER.
SERIOUSLY? YOU DIDN'T CALL HER?
DON'T BE SILLY. I DON'T HAVE HER NUMBER.
PROMISE!
SO, YOU JUST SAVE ALL THOSE CLIPPINGS OF HER BECAUSE YOU'RE A BIG FAN?
.....
SHE KNOWS!
UM, YEAH ...
SHE'S BEEN GETTING LOTS OF OFFERS SINCE OUR MOVIE WAS ON.
SHE PROBABLY HAS NO TIME FOR YOU.
WELL, SANA, YOU'RE GETTING LOTS OF OFFERS TOO!
WHY DON'T WE ACCEPT A FEW? KOMAWARI'S DIRECTOR WANTS YOU TO TAKE MORE WORK.
NEW SUBJECT...
I DON'T NEED ANY MORE WORK. I HAVE KODOCHA.*
*HER MAIN TV SHOW.

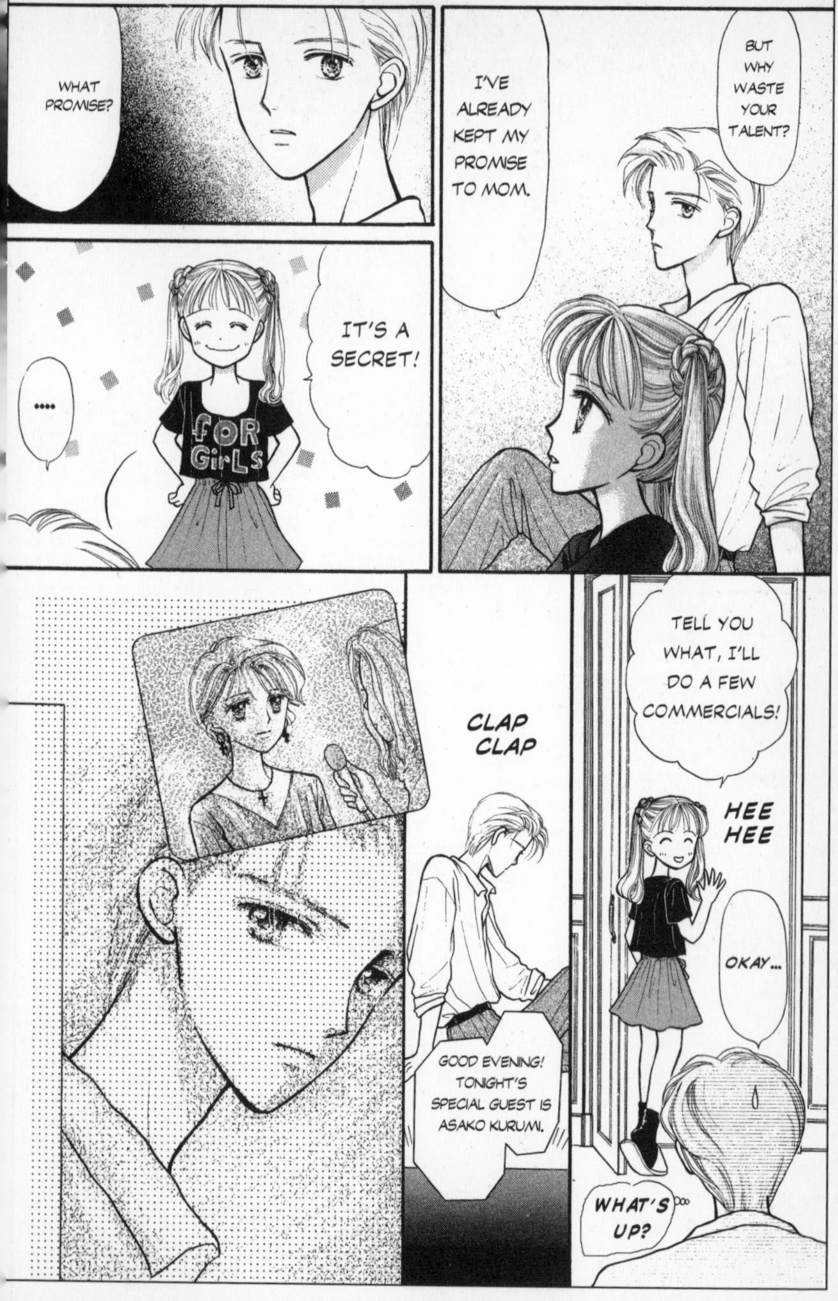
BUT WHY WASTE YOUR TALENT?
I'VE ALREADY KEPT MY PROMISE TO MOM.
WHAT PROMISE?
IT'S A SECRET!
....
TELL YOU WHAT, I'LL DO A FEW COMMERCIALS!
HEE HEE
OKAY...
WHAT'S UP?
CLAP CLAP
GOOD EVENING! TONIGHT'S SPECIAL GUEST IS ASAKO KURUMI.

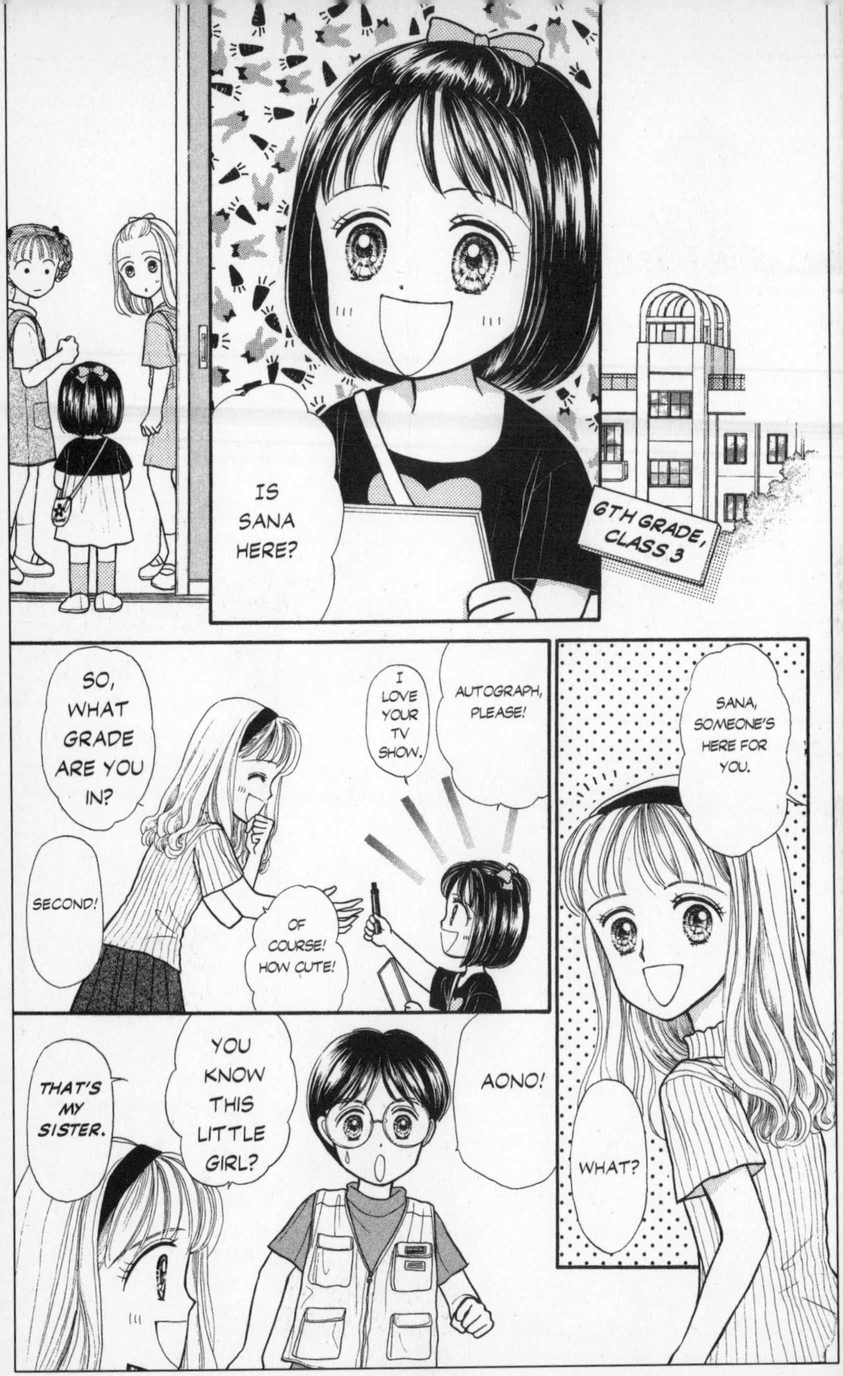
6TH GRADE, CLASS 3
IS SANA HERE?
SANA, SOMEONE'S HERE FOR YOU.
WHAT?
AUTOGRAPH, PLEASE!
I LOVE YOUR TV SHOW.
OF COURSE! HOW CUTE!
SO, WHAT GRADE ARE YOU IN?
SECOND!
AONO!
YOU KNOW THIS LITTLE GIRL?
THAT'S MY SISTER.

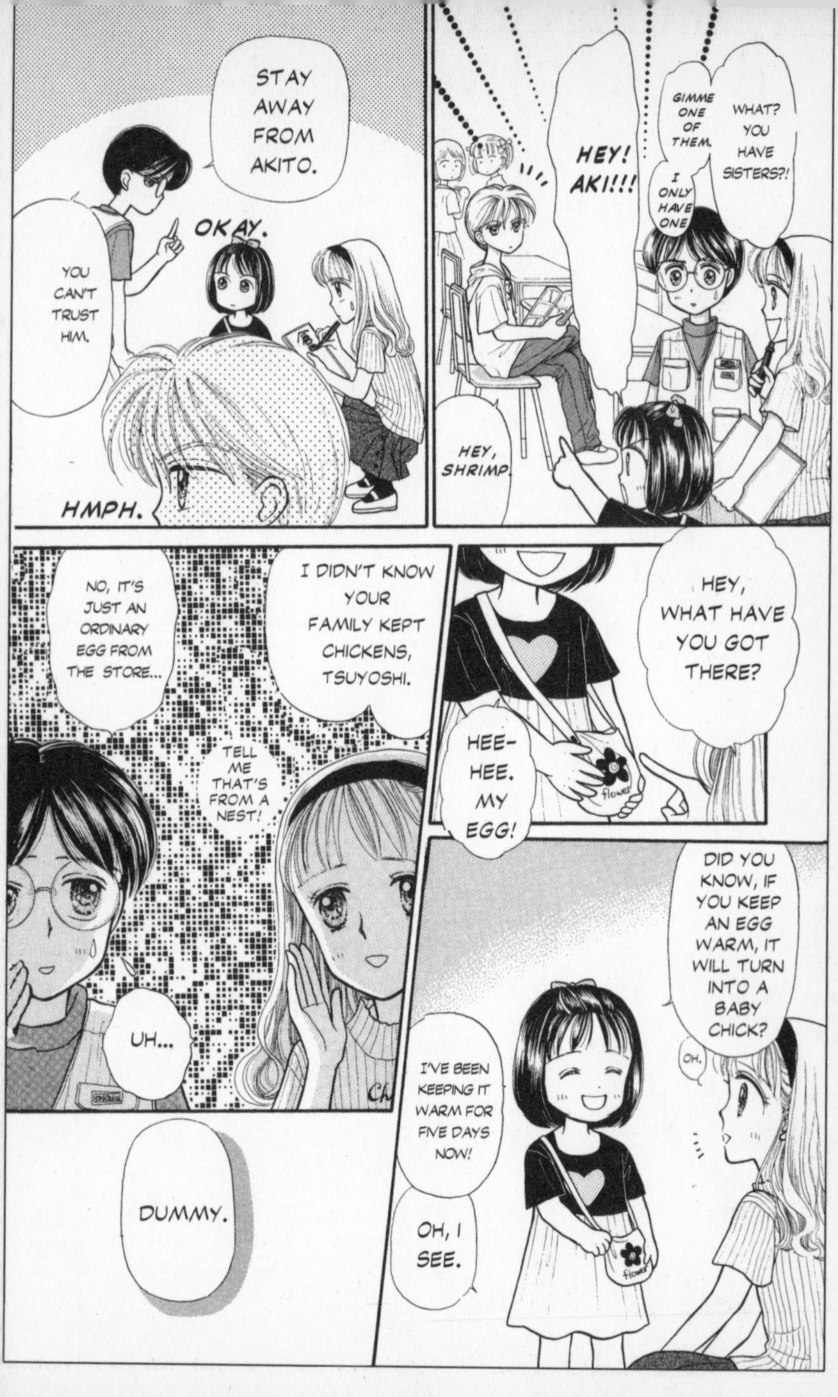
WHAT? YOU HAVE SISTERS?!
GIMME ONE OF THEM.
I ONLY HAVE ONE
HEY! AKI!!!
HEY, SHRIMP.
STAY AWAY FROM AKITO.
OKAY.
YOU CAN'T TRUST HIM.
HMPH.
HEY, WHAT HAVE YOU GOT THERE?
HEE-HEE. MY EGG!
DID YOU KNOW, IF YOU KEEP AN EGG WARM, IT WILL TURN INTO A BABY CHICK?
OH.
I'VE BEEN KEEPING IT WARM FOR FIVE DAYS NOW!
OH, I SEE.
I DIDN'T KNOW YOUR FAMILY KEPT CHICKENS, TSUYOSHI.
NO, IT'S JUST AN ORDINARY EGG FROM THE STORE...
TELL ME THAT'S FROM A NEST!
UH...
DUMMY.

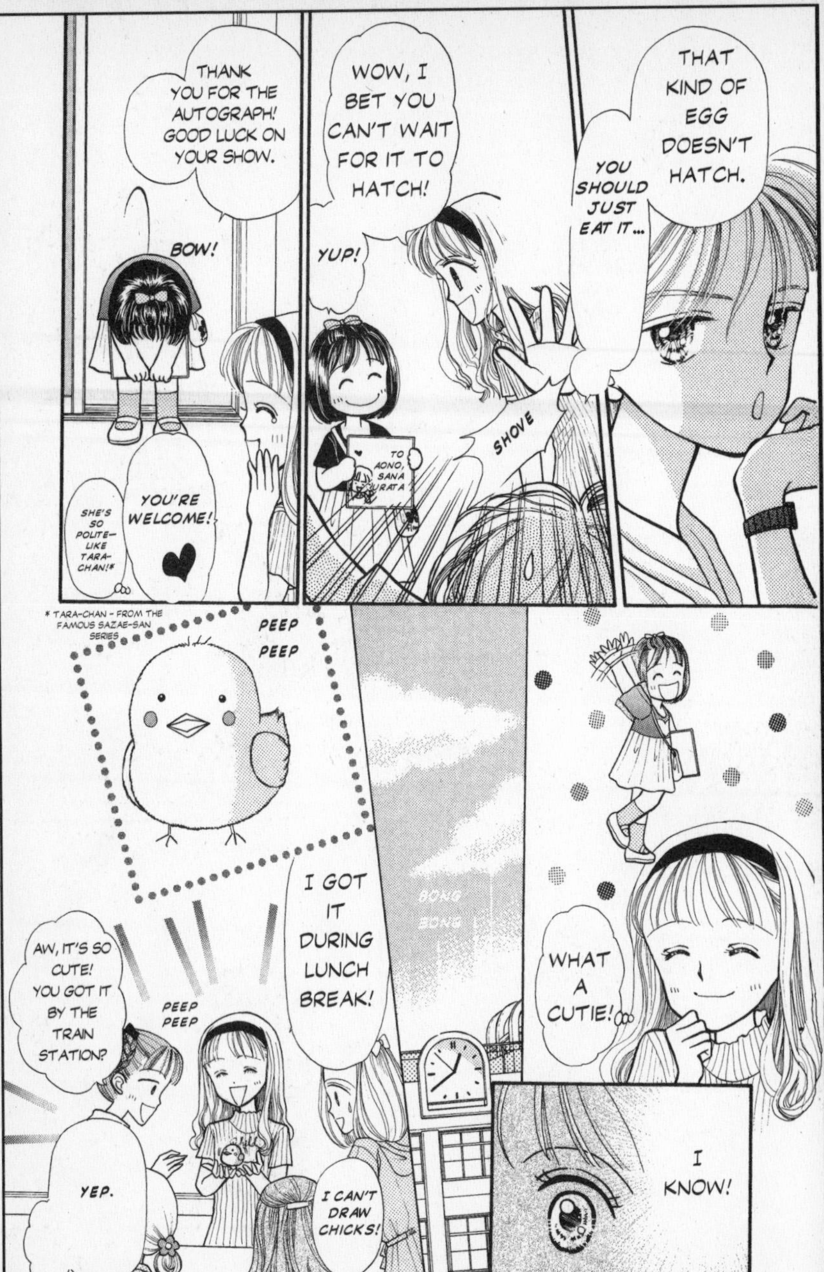
THANK YOU FOR THE AUTOGRAPH! GOOD LUCK ON YOUR SHOW.
BOW!
YOU'RE WELCOME!
SHE'S SO POLITE—LIKE TARA-CHAN!*
WOW, I BET YOU CAN'T WAIT FOR IT TO HATCH!
YUP!
TO AONO, SANA KURATA
SHOVE
THAT KIND OF EGG DOESN'T HATCH.
YOU SHOULD JUST EAT IT...
* TARA-CHAN - FROM THE FAMOUS SAZAE-SAN SERIES
PEEP PEEP
AW, IT'S SO CUTE! YOU GOT IT BY THE TRAIN STATION?
PEEP PEEP
YEP.
I GOT IT DURING LUNCH BREAK!
I CAN'T DRAW CHICKS!
BONG BONG
WHAT A CUTIE!
I KNOW!

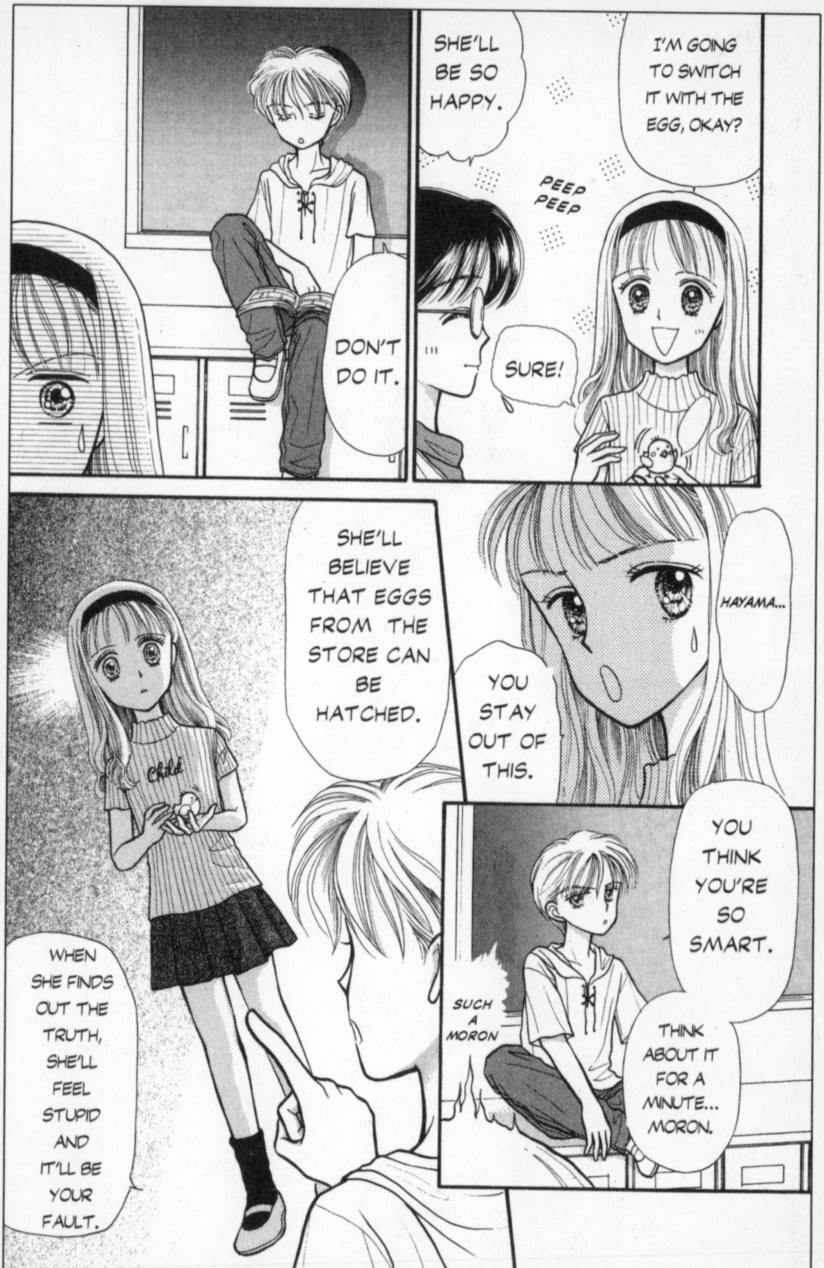
I'M GOING TO SWITCH IT WITH THE EGG, OKAY?
SHE'LL BE SO HAPPY.
PEEP PEEP
SURE!
DON'T DO IT.
HAYAMA...
YOU STAY OUT OF THIS.
YOU THINK YOU'RE SO SMART.
SUCH A MORON
THINK ABOUT IT FOR A MINUTE... MORON.
SHE'LL BELIEVE THAT EGGS FROM THE STORE CAN BE HATCHED.
WHEN SHE FINDS OUT THE TRUTH, SHE'LL FEEL STUPID AND IT'LL BE YOUR FAULT.

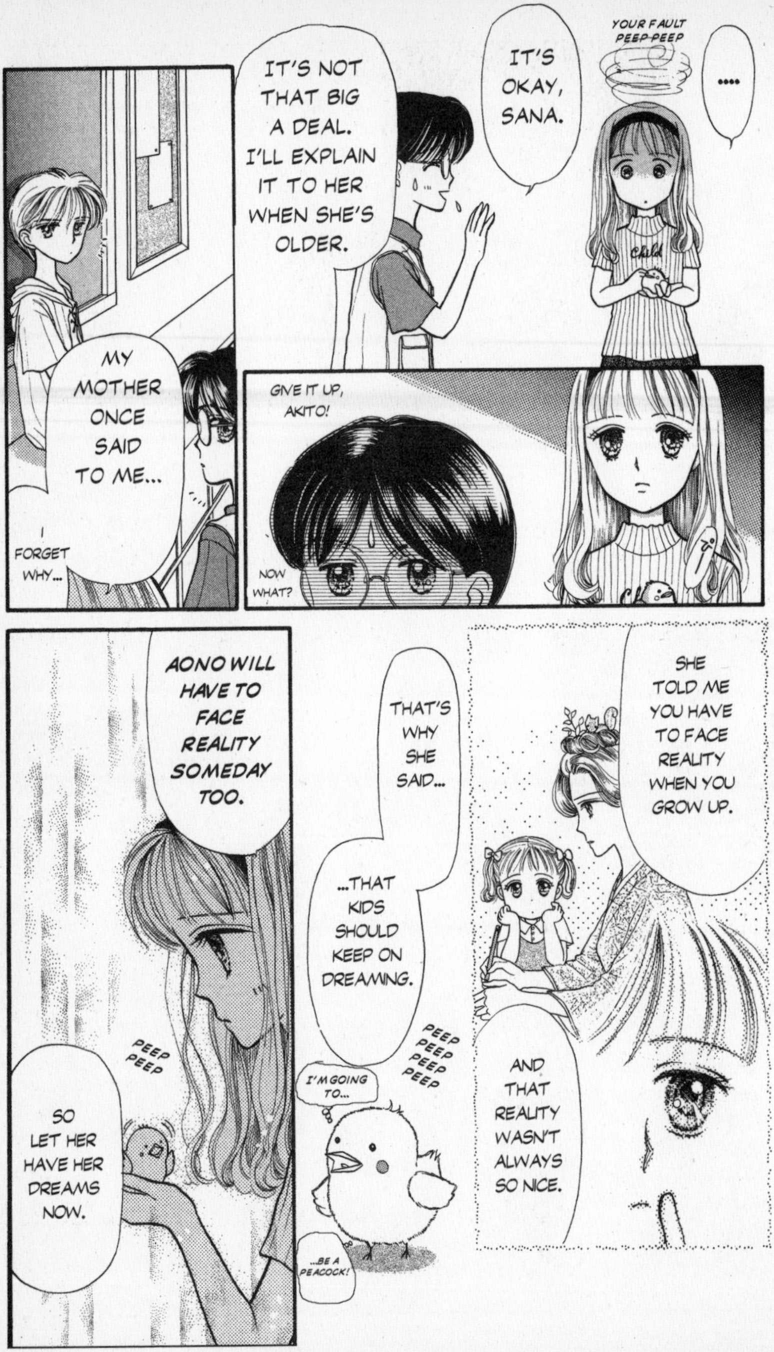
YOUR FAULT PEEP PEEP
....
IT'S OKAY, SANA.
IT'S NOT THAT BIG A DEAL. I'LL EXPLAIN IT TO HER WHEN SHE'S OLDER.
GIVE IT UP, AKITO!
NOW WHAT?
MY MOTHER ONCE SAID TO ME...
I FORGET WHY...
SHE TOLD ME YOU HAVE TO FACE REALITY WHEN YOU GROW UP.
AND THAT REALITY WASN'T ALWAYS SO NICE.
THAT'S WHY SHE SAID...
...THAT KIDS SHOULD KEEP ON DREAMING.
PEEP PEEP PEEP PEEP
I'M GOING TO...
...BE A PEACOCK!
AONO WILL HAVE TO FACE REALITY SOMEDAY TOO.
PEEP PEEP
SO LET HER HAVE HER DREAMS NOW.

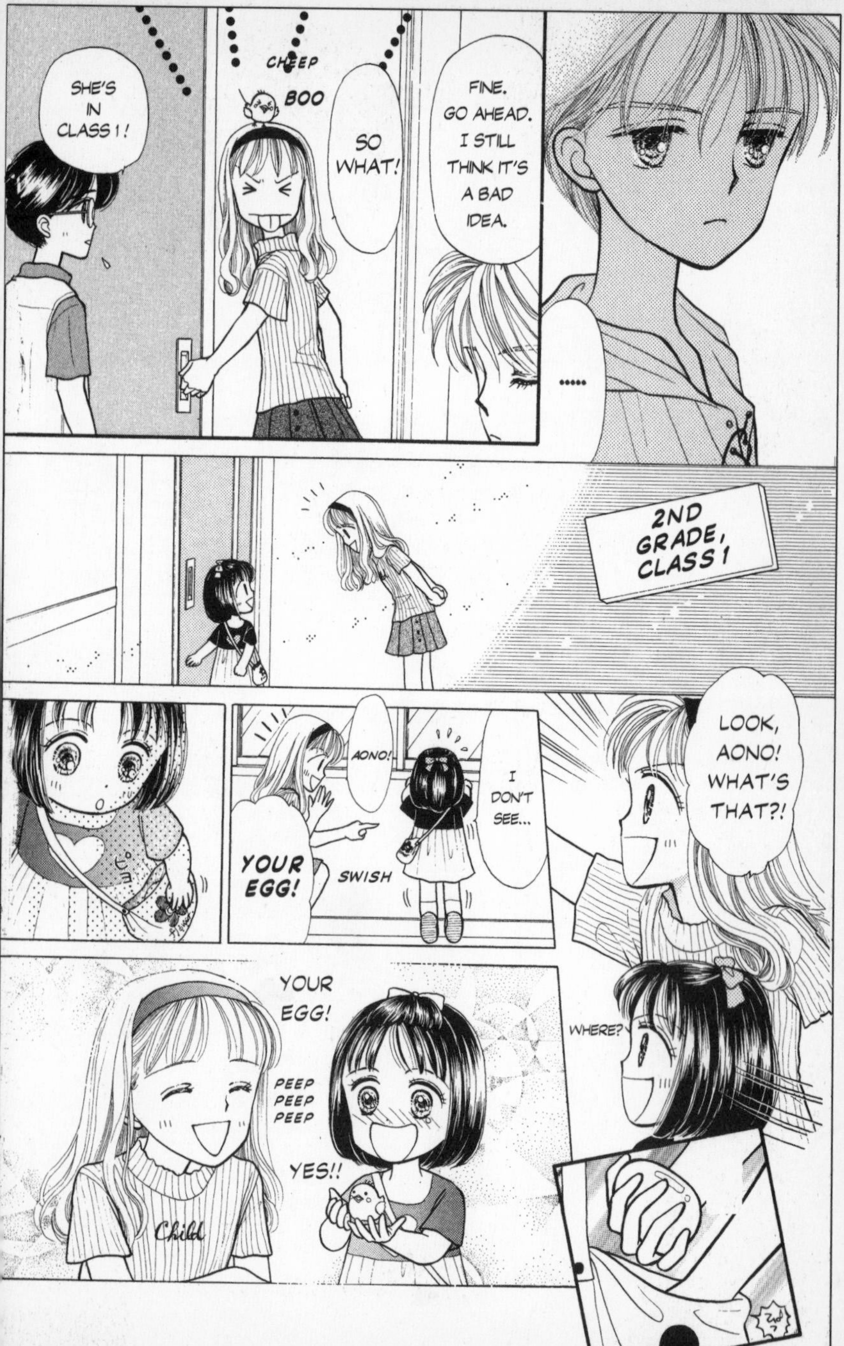

.....
FINE. GO AHEAD. I STILL THINK IT'S A BAD IDEA.
SO WHAT!
BOO
CHEEP
SHE'S IN CLASS 1!
2ND GRADE, CLASS 1
LOOK, AONO! WHAT'S THAT?!
I DON'T SEE...
AONO!
SWISH
YOUR EGG!
WHERE?
YOUR EGG!
PEEP PEEP PEEP
YES!!
Child

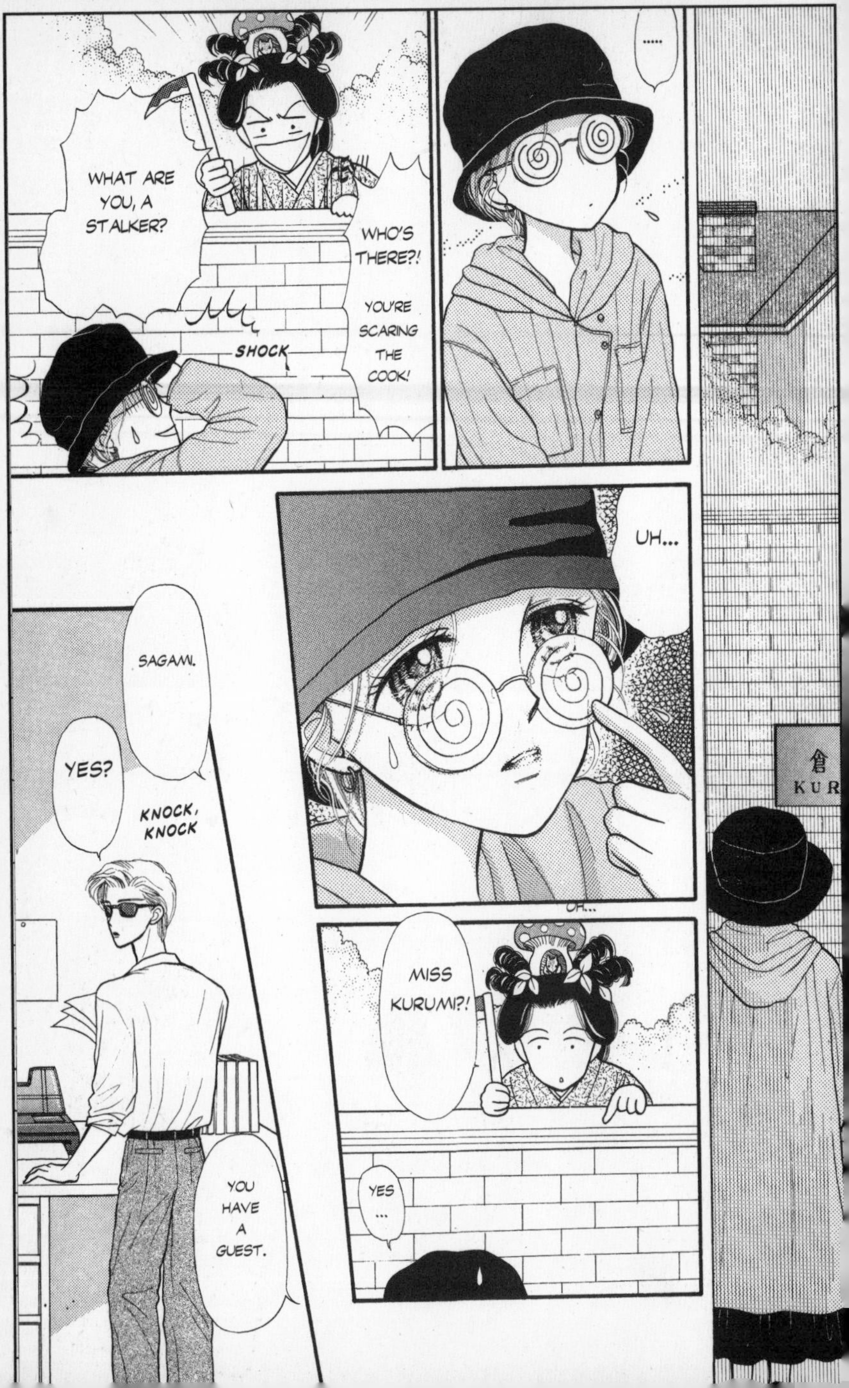

倉
KUR
.....
WHO'S THERE?!
YOU'RE SCARING THE COOK!
WHAT ARE YOU, A STALKER?
SHOCK
UH...
UH...
MISS KURUMI?!
YES ...
SAGAMI.
YES?
KNOCK, KNOCK
YOU HAVE A GUEST.

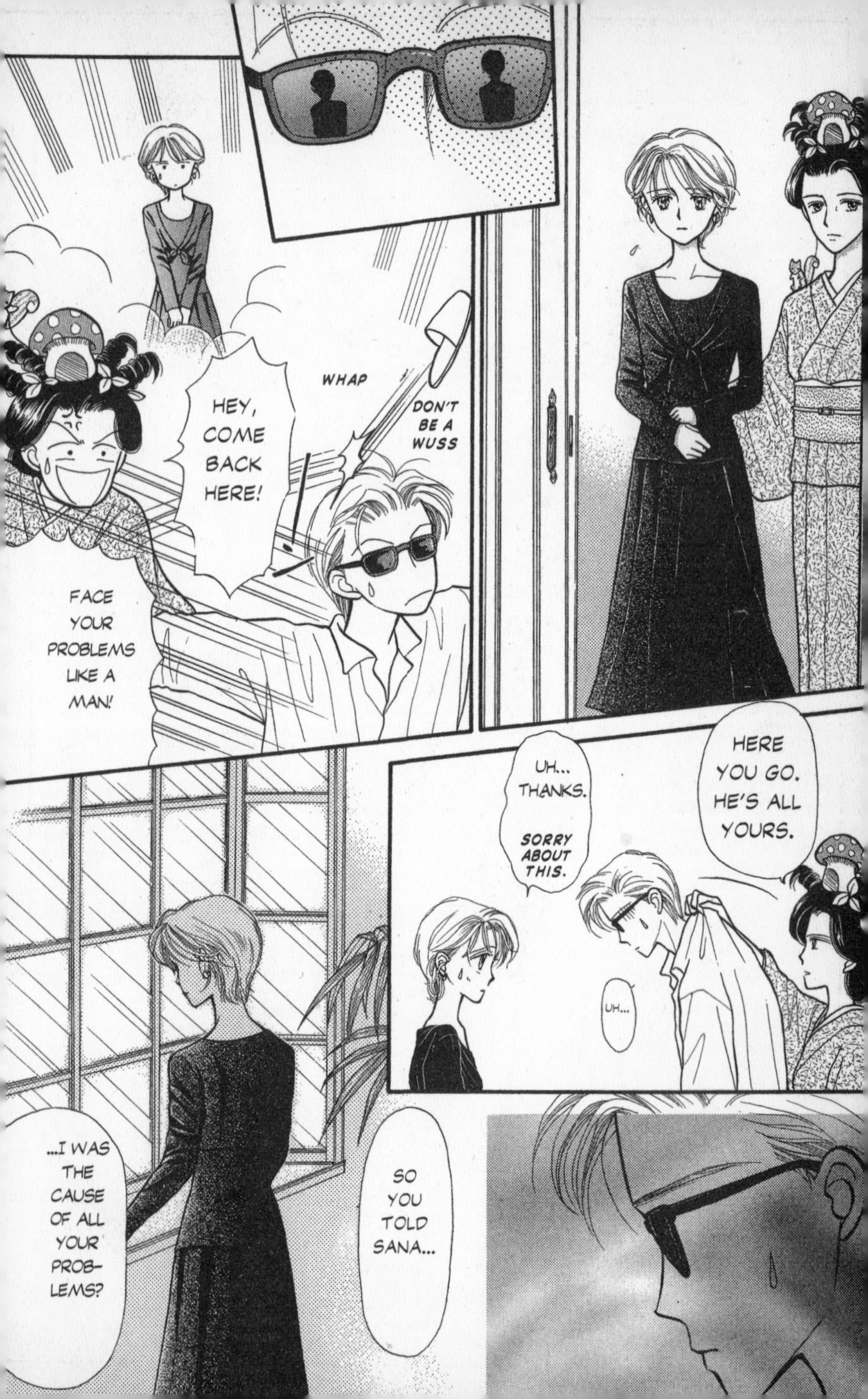
HEY, COME BACK HERE!
WHAP
DON'T BE A WUSS
FACE YOUR PROBLEMS LIKE A MAN!
HERE YOU GO. HE'S ALL YOURS.
UH... THANKS.
SORRY ABOUT THIS.
UH...
SO YOU TOLD SANA...
...I WAS THE CAUSE OF ALL YOUR PROB-LEMS?

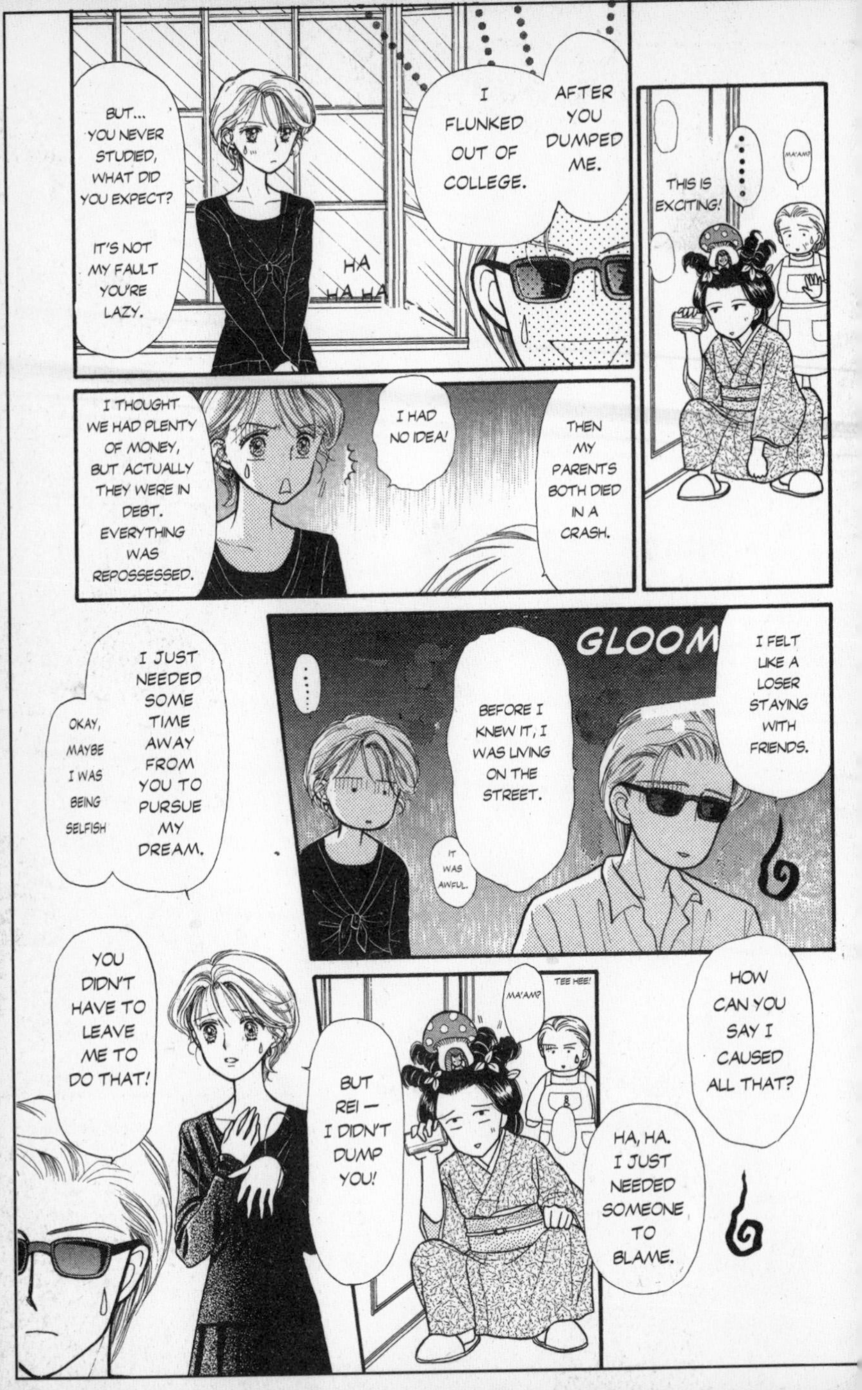
......
MA'AM?
THIS IS EXCITING!
AFTER YOU DUMPED ME.
I FLUNKED OUT OF COLLEGE.
HA HA HA
BUT... YOU NEVER STUDIED, WHAT DID YOU EXPECT? IT'S NOT MY FAULT YOU'RE LAZY.
THEN MY PARENTS BOTH DIED IN A CRASH.
I HAD NO IDEA!
I THOUGHT WE HAD PLENTY OF MONEY, BUT ACTUALLY THEY WERE IN DEBT. EVERYTHING WAS REPOSSESSED.
I FELT LIKE A LOSER STAYING WITH FRIENDS.
GLOOM
BEFORE I KNEW IT, I WAS LIVING ON THE STREET.
IT WAS AWFUL.
......
I JUST NEEDED SOME TIME AWAY FROM YOU TO PURSUE MY DREAM.
OKAY, MAYBE I WAS BEING SELFISH
HOW CAN YOU SAY I CAUSED ALL THAT?
HA, HA. I JUST NEEDED SOMEONE TO BLAME.
TEE HEE!
MA'AM?
BUT REI— I DIDN'T DUMP YOU!
YOU DIDN'T HAVE TO LEAVE ME TO DO THAT!

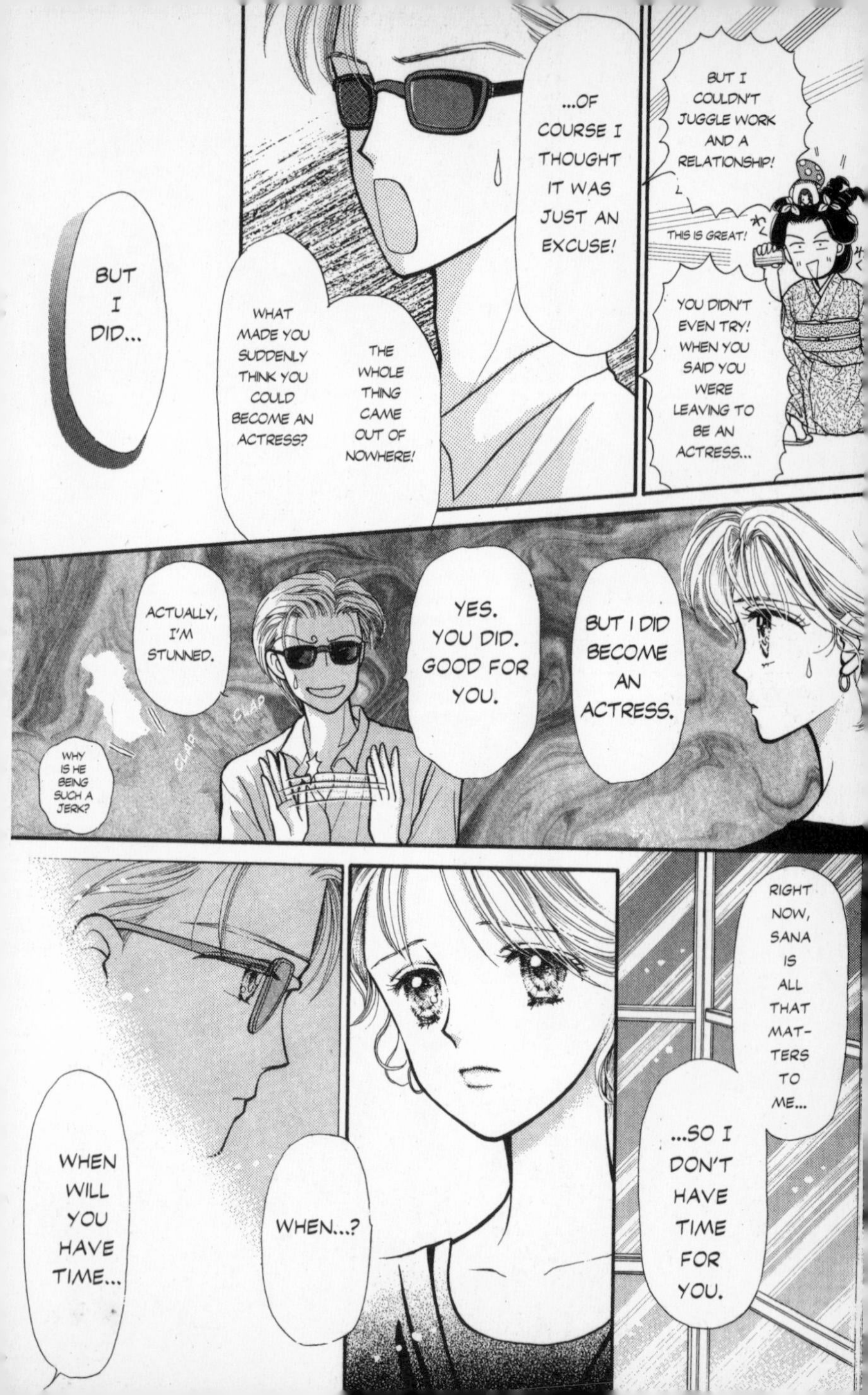
BUT I COULDN'T JUGGLE WORK AND A RELATIONSHIP!
THIS IS GREAT!
YOU DIDN'T EVEN TRY! WHEN YOU SAID YOU WERE LEAVING TO BE AN ACTRESS...
...OF COURSE I THOUGHT IT WAS JUST AN EXCUSE!
THE WHOLE THING CAME OUT OF NOWHERE!
WHAT MADE YOU SUDDENLY THINK YOU COULD BECOME AN ACTRESS?
BUT I DID...
BUT I DID BECOME AN ACTRESS.
YES. YOU DID. GOOD FOR YOU.
ACTUALLY, I'M STUNNED.
CLAP
CLAP
WHY IS HE BEING SUCH A JERK?
RIGHT NOW, SANA IS ALL THAT MATTERS TO ME...
...SO I DON'T HAVE TIME FOR YOU.
WHEN...?
WHEN WILL YOU HAVE TIME...

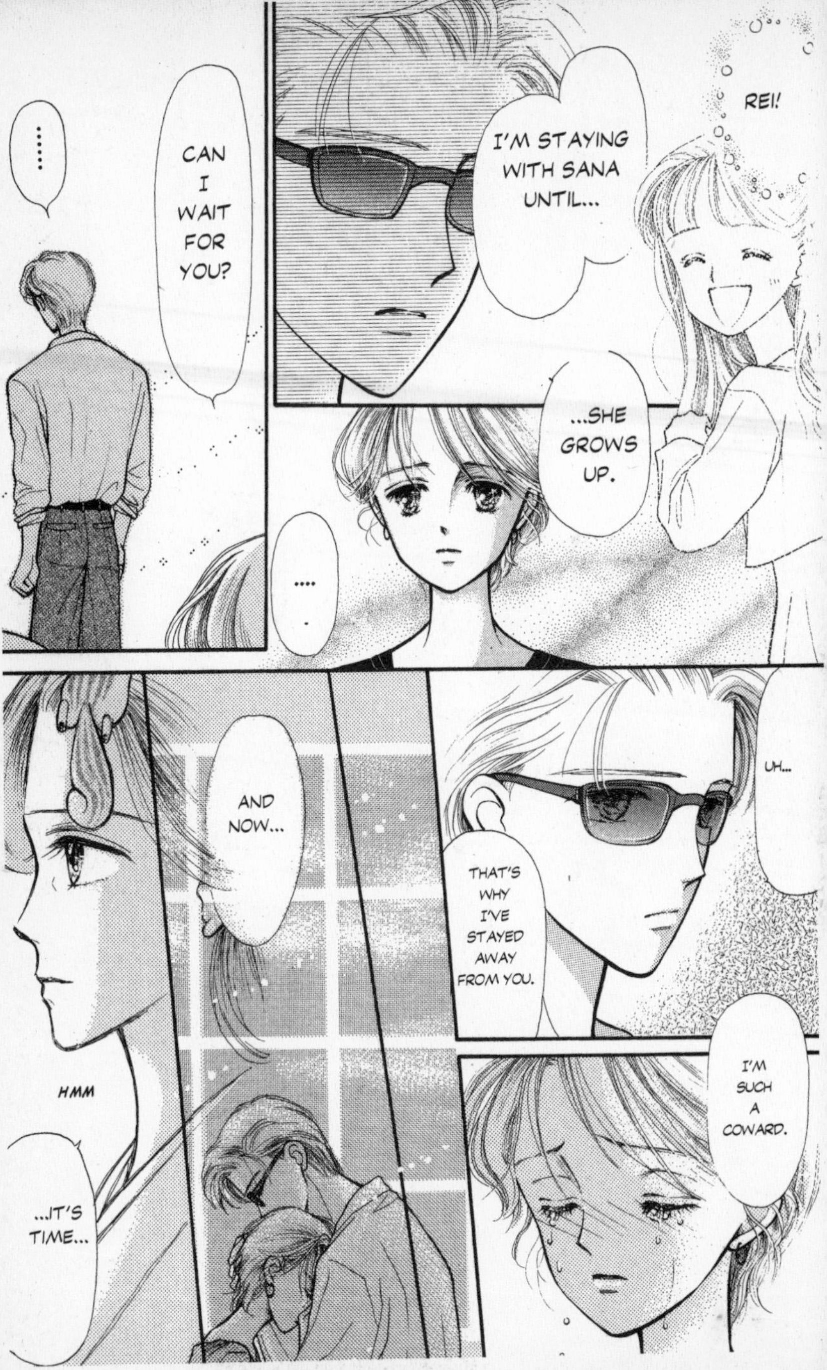
REI!
I'M STAYING WITH SANA UNTIL...
...SHE GROWS UP.
....
CAN I WAIT FOR YOU?
......
UH...
THAT'S WHY I'VE STAYED AWAY FROM YOU.
I'M SUCH A COWARD.
AND NOW...
HMM
...IT'S TIME...

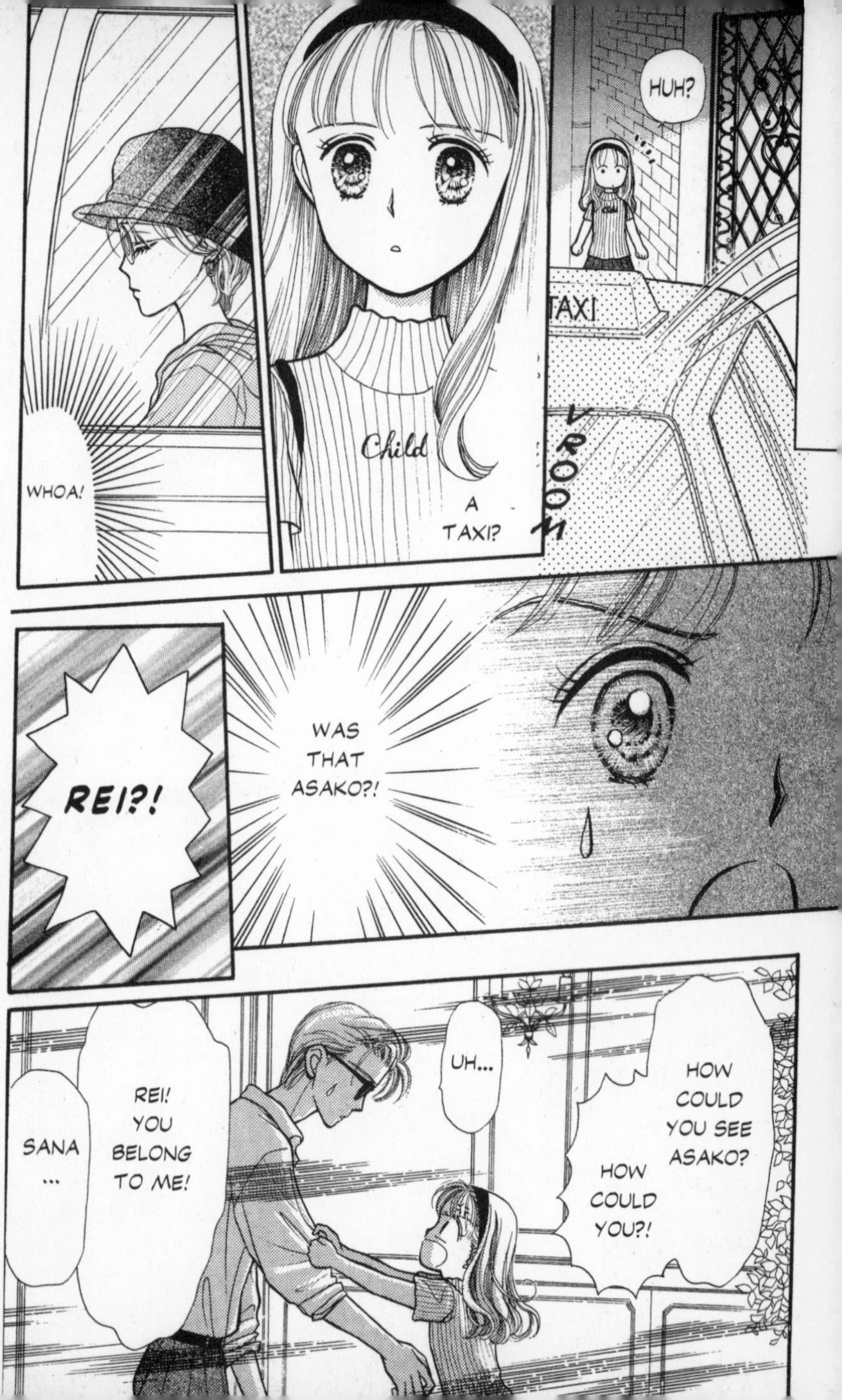
HUH?
TAXI
VROOM
A TAXI?
WHOA!
WAS THAT ASAKO?!
REI?!
HOW COULD YOU SEE ASAKO?
HOW COULD YOU?!
UH...
REI! YOU BELONG TO ME!
SANA ...

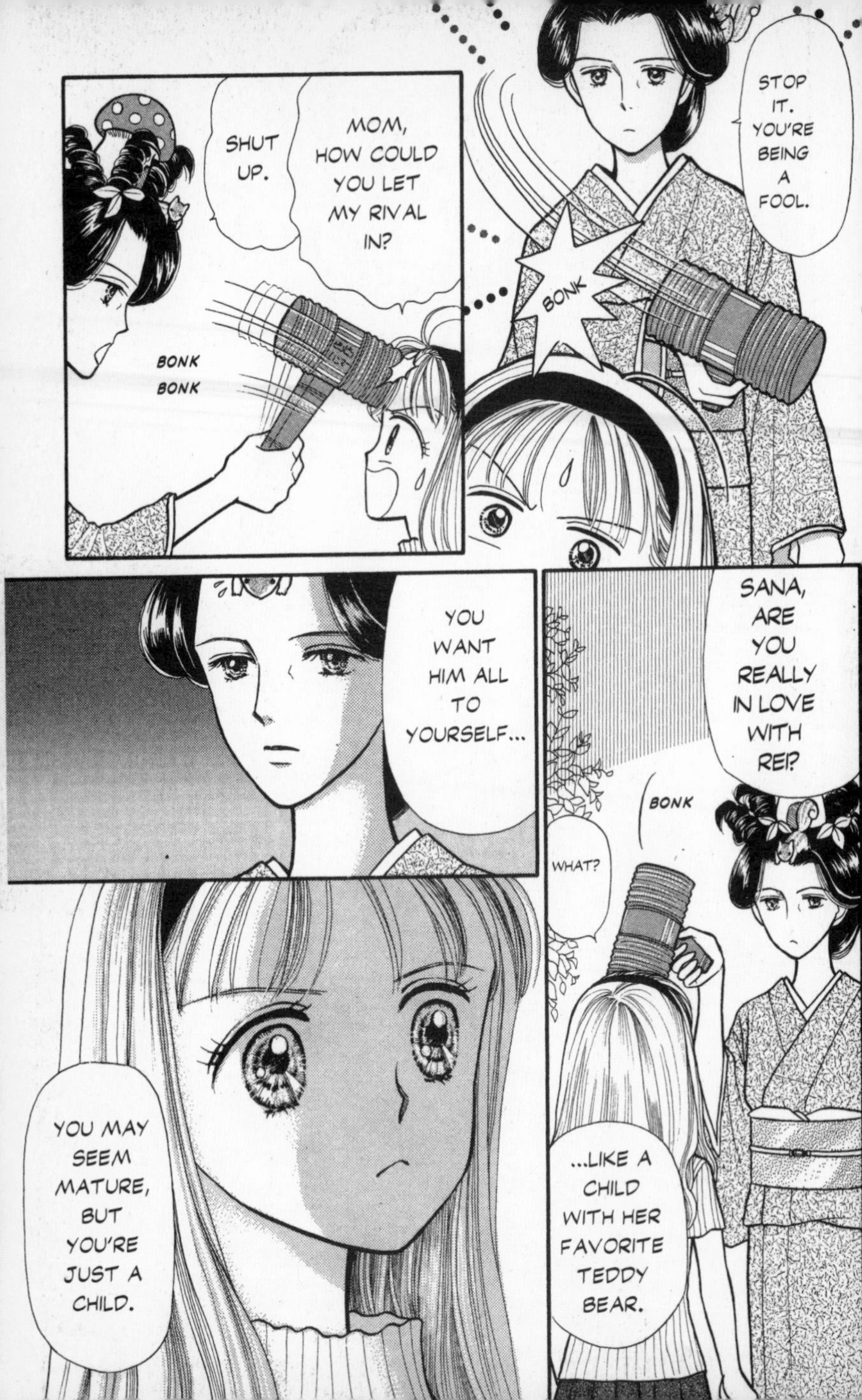
STOP IT. YOU'RE BEING A FOOL.
BONK
MOM, HOW COULD YOU LET MY RIVAL IN?
SHUT UP.
BONK BONK
SANA, ARE YOU REALLY IN LOVE WITH REI?
BONK
WHAT?
...LIKE A CHILD WITH HER FAVORITE TEDDY BEAR.
YOU WANT HIM ALL TO YOURSELF...
YOU MAY SEEM MATURE, BUT YOU'RE JUST A CHILD.

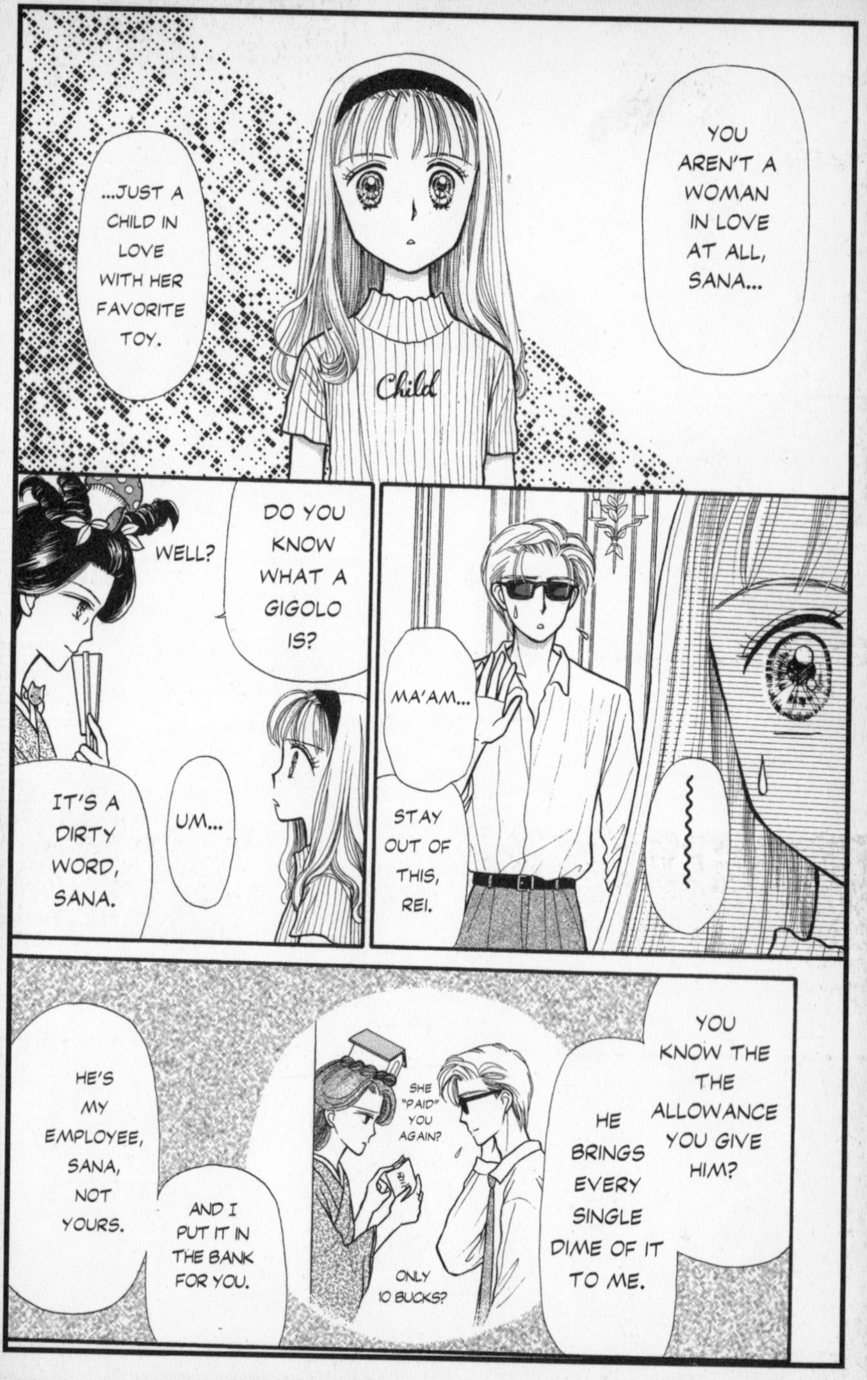
YOU AREN'T A WOMAN IN LOVE AT ALL, SANA...
...JUST A CHILD IN LOVE WITH HER FAVORITE TOY.
Child
MA'AM...
STAY OUT OF THIS, REI.
DO YOU KNOW WHAT A GIGOLO IS?
WELL?
UM...
IT'S A DIRTY WORD, SANA.
YOU KNOW THE THE ALLOWANCE YOU GIVE HIM?
HE BRINGS EVERY SINGLE DIME OF IT TO ME.
SHE "PAID" YOU AGAIN?
ONLY 10 BUCKS?
AND I PUT IT IN THE BANK FOR YOU.
HE'S MY EMPLOYEE, SANA, NOT YOURS.

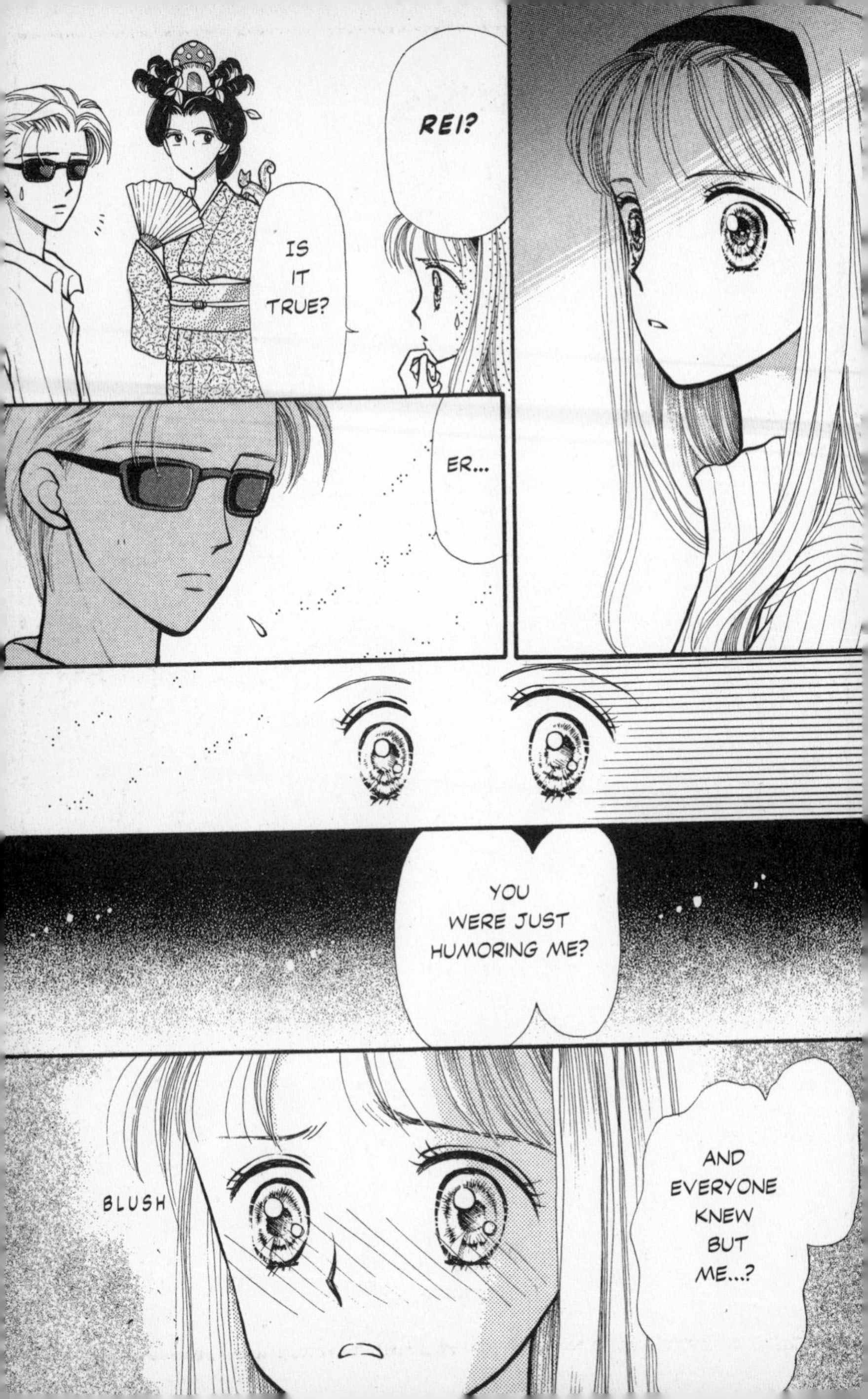
REI?
IS IT TRUE?
ER...
YOU WERE JUST HUMORING ME?
AND EVERYONE KNEW BUT ME...?
BLUSH

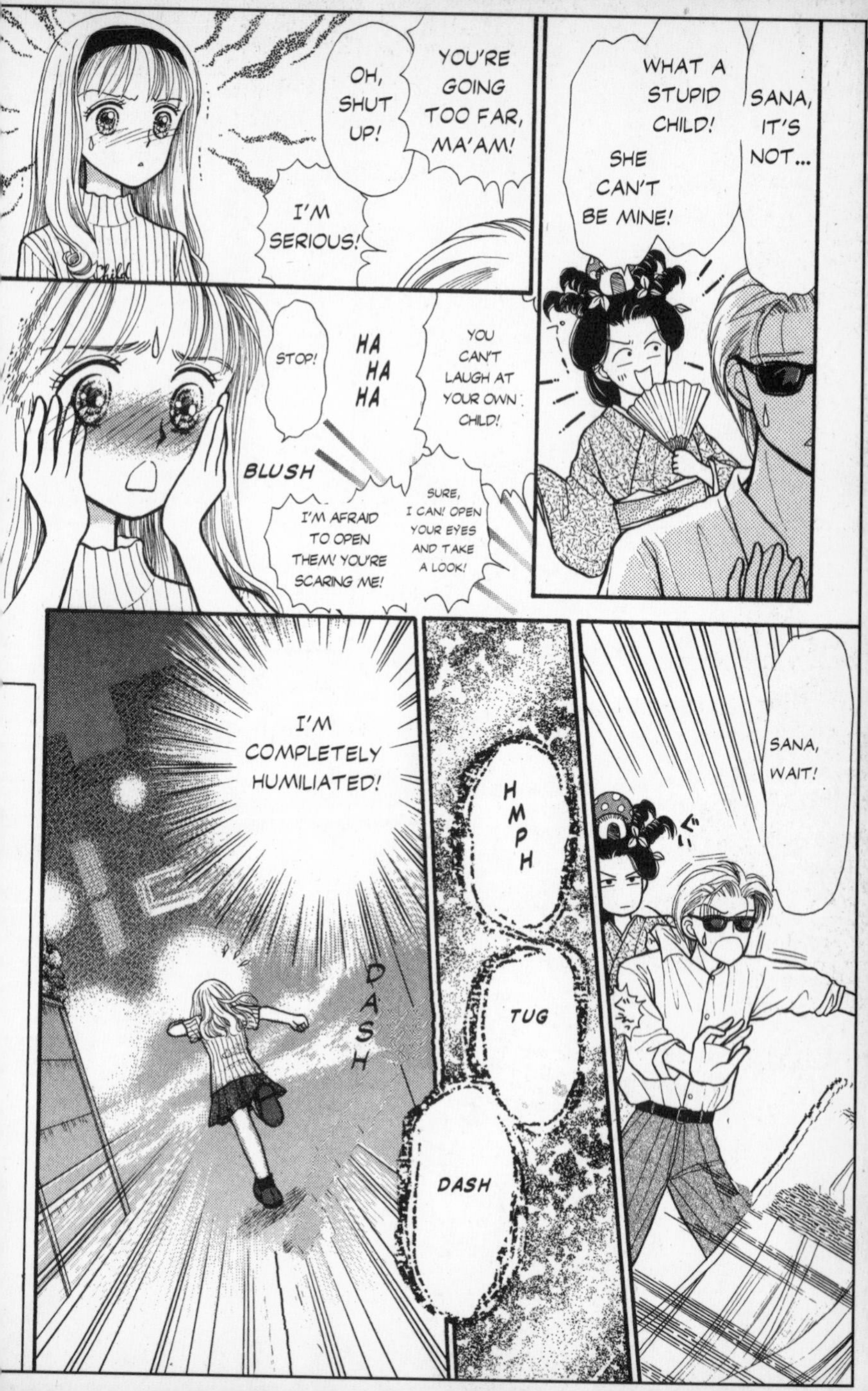
SANA, IT'S NOT...
WHAT A STUPID CHILD!
SHE CAN'T BE MINE!
YOU'RE GOING TOO FAR, MA'AM!
OH, SHUT UP!
I'M SERIOUS!
YOU CAN'T LAUGH AT YOUR OWN CHILD!
HA HA HA
STOP!
BLUSH
SURE, I CAN! OPEN YOUR EYES AND TAKE A LOOK!
I'M AFRAID TO OPEN THEM! YOU'RE SCARING ME!
SANA, WAIT!
HMPH
TUG
DASH
I'M COMPLETELY HUMILIATED!
DASH

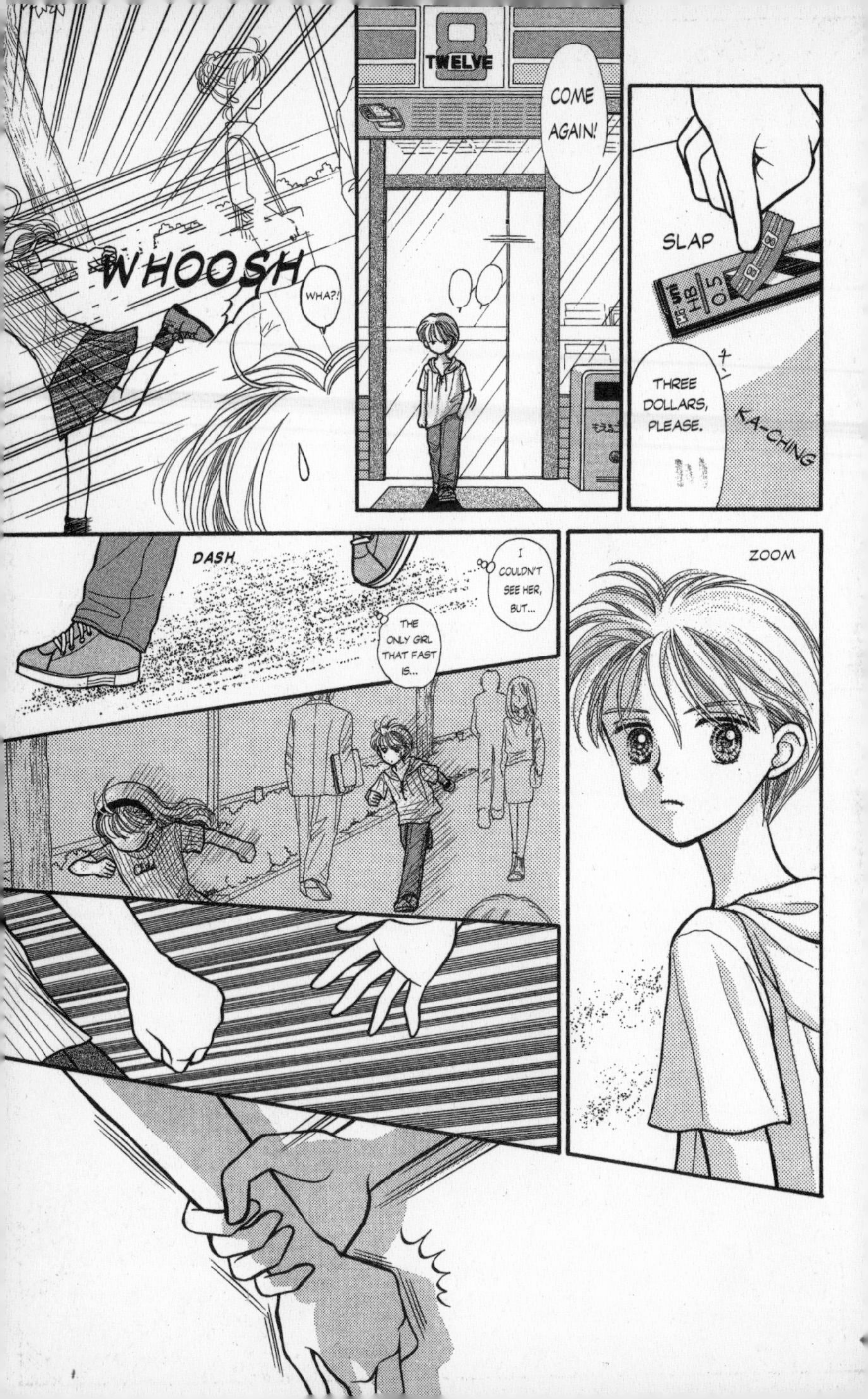
SLAP
THREE DOLLARS, PLEASE.
KA-CHING
COME AGAIN!
WHOOSH
WHA?!
ZOOM
DASH
I COULDN'T SEE HER, BUT...
THE ONLY GIRL THAT FAST IS...

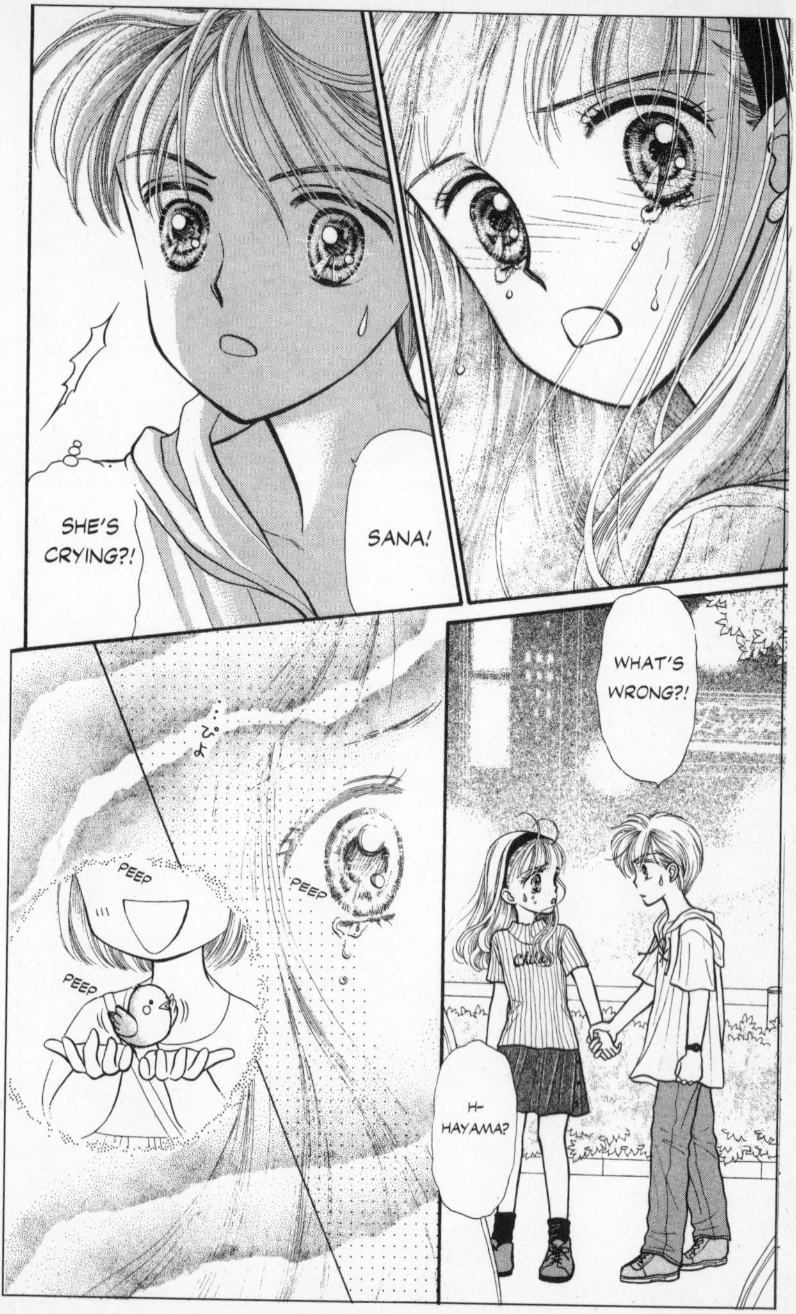
SANA!
SHE'S CRYING?!
WHAT'S WRONG?!
H- HAYAMA?
…ぴよ
PEEP
PEEP
PEEP

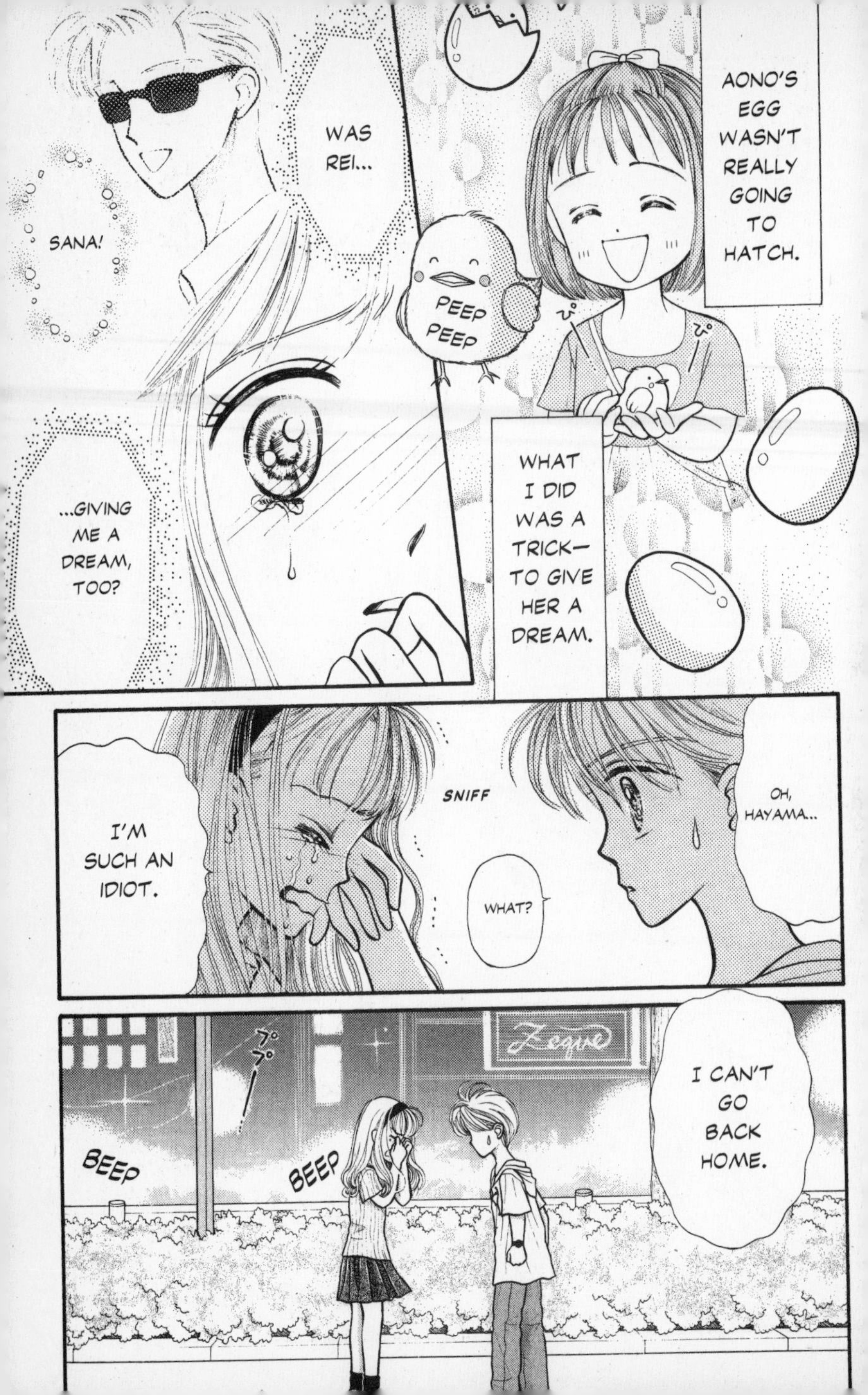
AONO'S EGG WASN'T REALLY GOING TO HATCH.
PEEP PEEP
WHAT I DID WAS A TRICK— TO GIVE HER A DREAM.
WAS REI...
SANA!
...GIVING ME A DREAM, TOO?
OH, HAYAMA...
WHAT?
SNIFF
I'M SUCH AN IDIOT.
I CAN'T GO BACK HOME.
BEEP
BEEP

CHILD'S TOY EXTRA:

CHILD'S TOY WEATHER REPORT

Rei's version

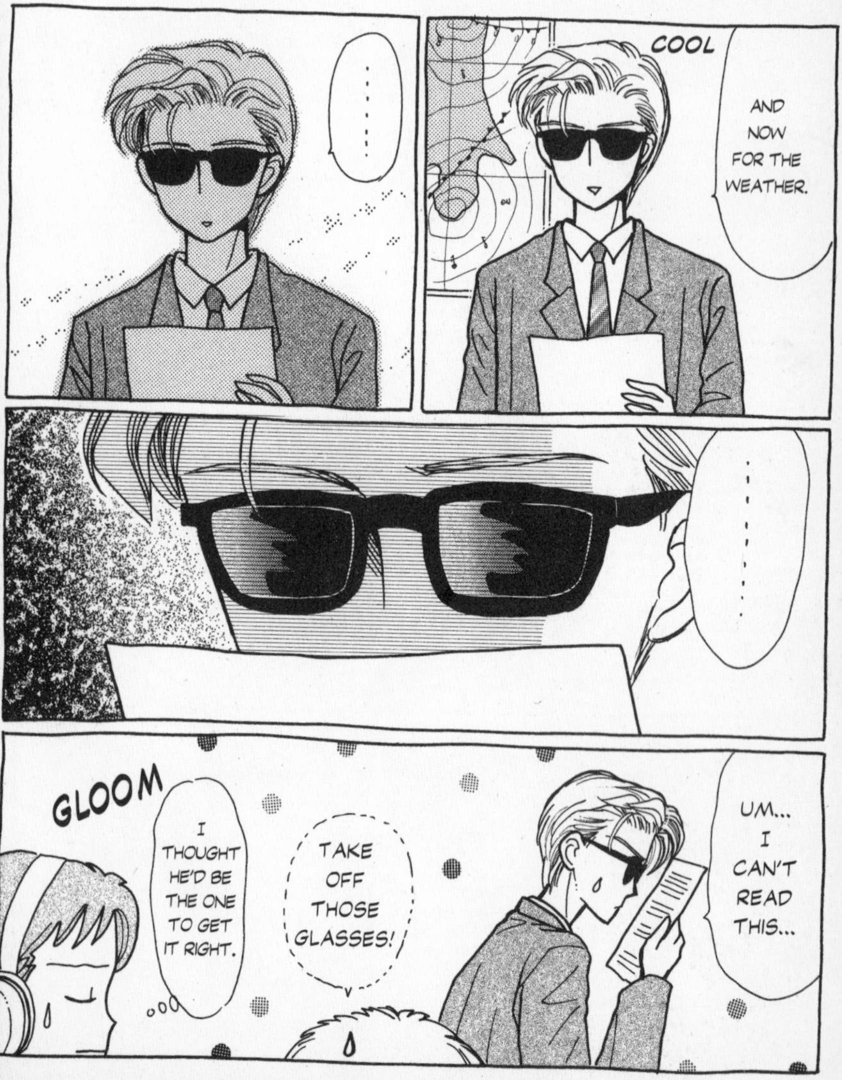
COOL
AND NOW FOR THE WEATHER.
......
......
UM... I CAN'T READ THIS...
TAKE OFF THOSE GLASSES!
I THOUGHT HE'D BE THE ONE TO GET IT RIGHT.
GLOOM

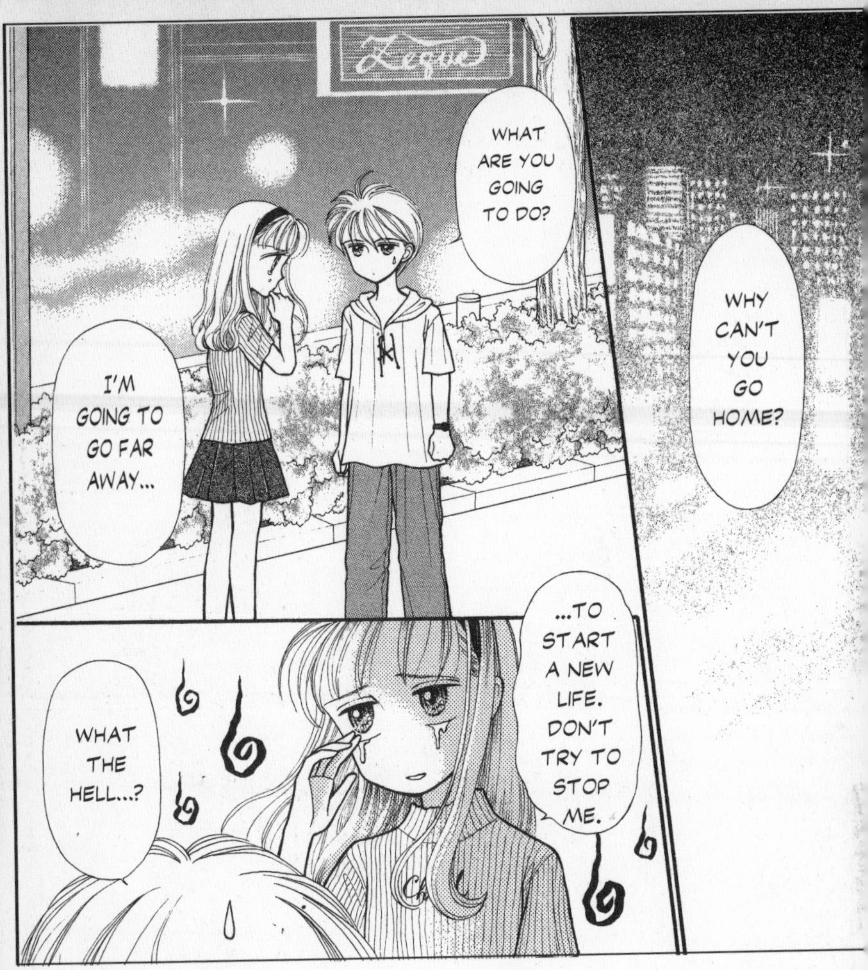
WHY CAN'T YOU GO HOME?
WHAT ARE YOU GOING TO DO?
I'M GOING TO GO FAR AWAY...
...TO START A NEW LIFE. DON'T TRY TO STOP ME.
WHAT THE HELL...?

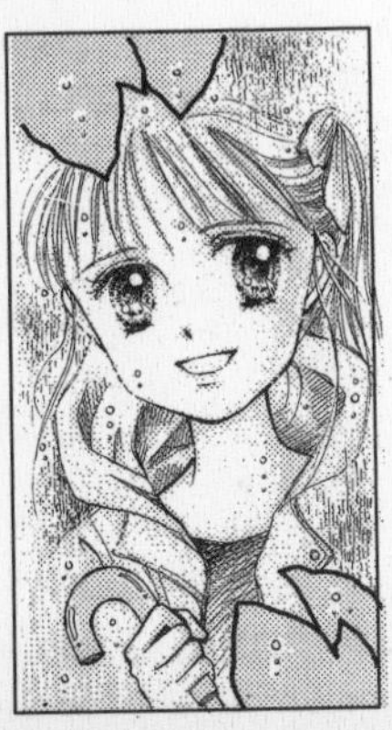

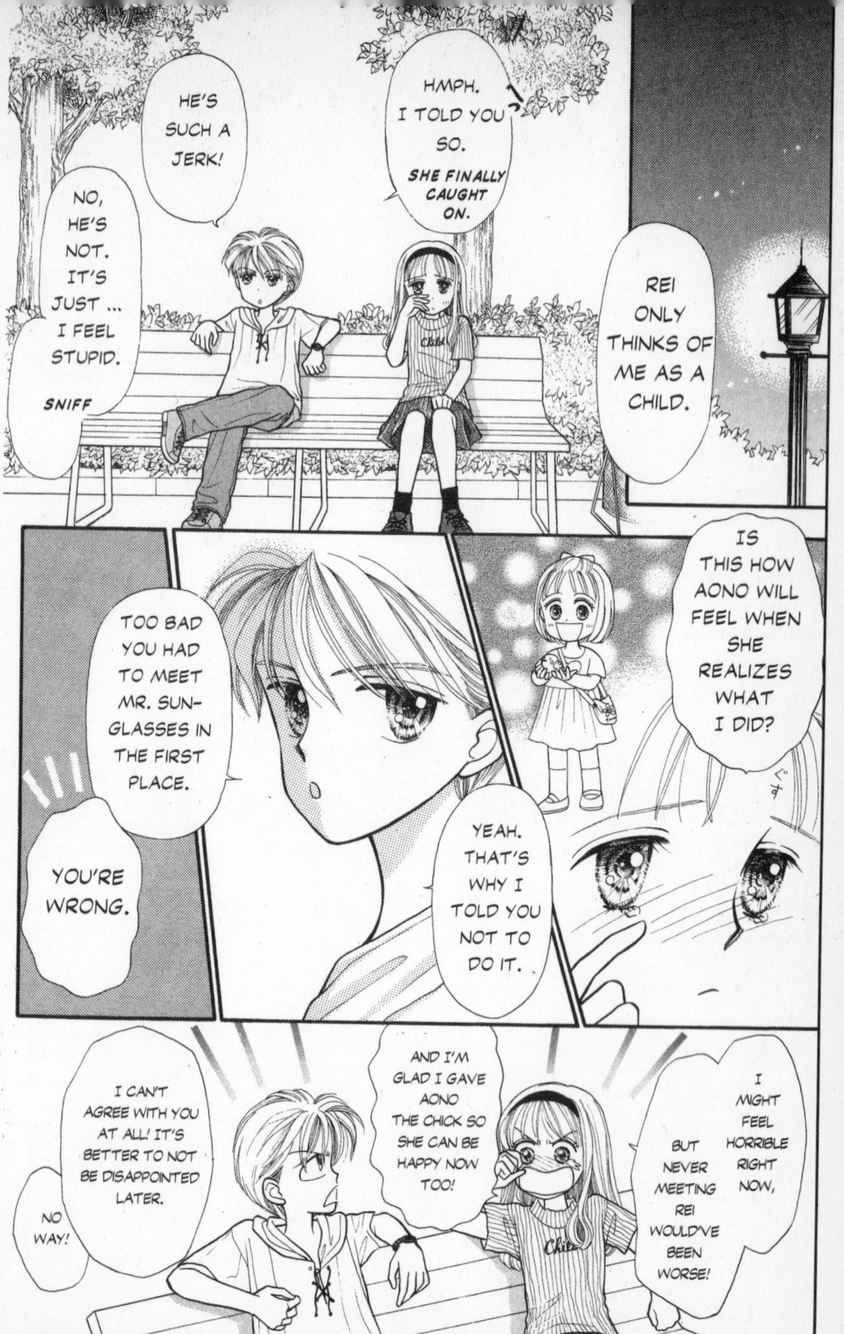
REI ONLY THINKS OF ME AS A CHILD.
HMPH. I TOLD YOU SO.
SHE FINALLY CAUGHT ON.
HE'S SUCH A JERK!
NO, HE'S NOT. IT'S JUST ... I FEEL STUPID.
SNIFF
IS THIS HOW AONO WILL FEEL WHEN SHE REALIZES WHAT I DID?
ぐす
YEAH. THAT'S WHY I TOLD YOU NOT TO DO IT.
TOO BAD YOU HAD TO MEET MR. SUN-GLASSES IN THE FIRST PLACE.
YOU'RE WRONG.
I MIGHT FEEL HORRIBLE RIGHT NOW,
BUT NEVER MEETING REI WOULD'VE BEEN WORSE!
AND I'M GLAD I GAVE AONO THE CHICK SO SHE CAN BE HAPPY NOW TOO!
I CAN'T AGREE WITH YOU AT ALL! IT'S BETTER TO NOT BE DISAPPOINTED LATER.
NO WAY!

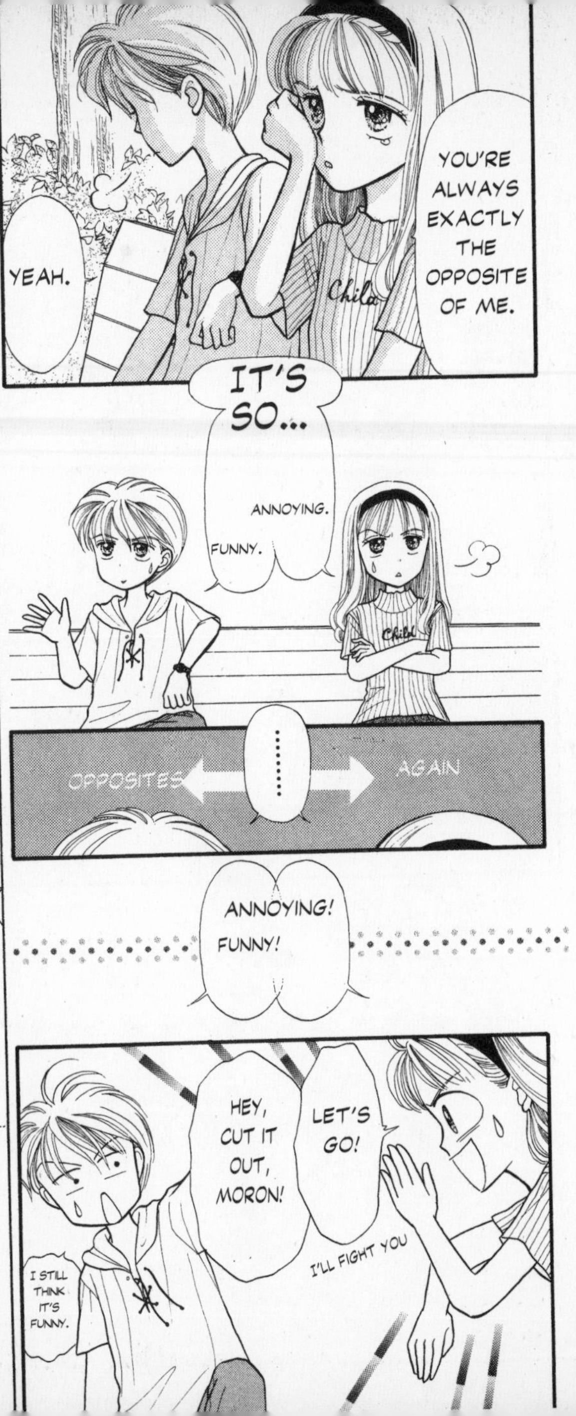
YOU'RE ALWAYS EXACTLY THE OPPOSITE OF ME.
YEAH.
IT'S SO...
ANNOYING.
FUNNY.
AGAIN
......
OPPOSITES
ANNOYING!
FUNNY!
LET'S GO!
HEY, CUT IT OUT, MORON!
I'LL FIGHT YOU
I STILL THINK IT'S FUNNY.

The Subject is Sushi

When it comes to food, I'm not a gourmet at all. Every time I eat in a really expensive restaurant, I get a horrible stomachache! (hee-hee) I'm the kind of woman who would rather have ramen noodles and play pool than enjoy a fancy meal. However, there's one food I'm really into—sushi. When I was little, I only ate cheap (and crappy) sushi, so I didn't like it very much. (how embarrassing to admit it) But when I got my first royalty check, I could finally afford Toku-jo* sushi and it was good!

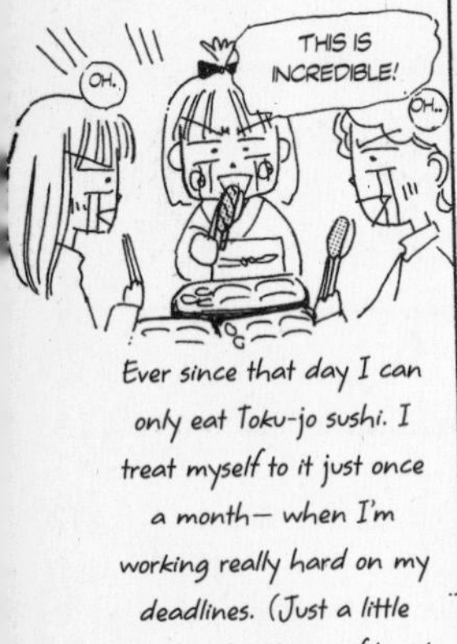
OH.
THIS IS INCREDIBLE!
OH..

Ever since that day I can only eat Toku-jo sushi. I treat myself to it just once a month— when I'm working really hard on my deadlines. (Just a little oasis in the desert of hard work, you know.) Thanks for making such great sushi, Dharma Sushi**!

*Toku-jo - really high grade sushi

**Dharma Sushi - a well-known sushi restaurant

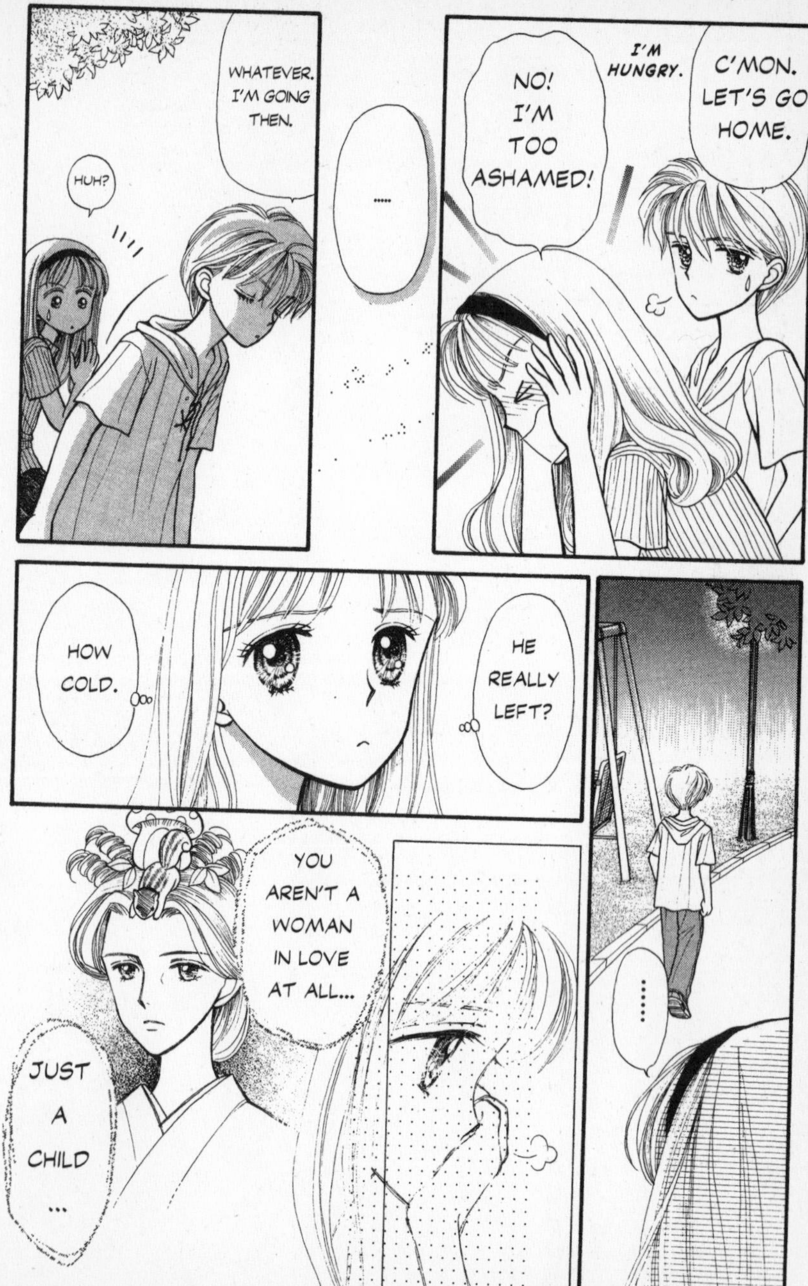
C'MON. LET'S GO HOME.
I'M HUNGRY.
NO! I'M TOO ASHAMED!
......
WHATEVER. I'M GOING THEN.
HUH?
......
HE REALLY LEFT?
HOW COLD.
YOU AREN'T A WOMAN IN LOVE AT ALL...
JUST A CHILD ...

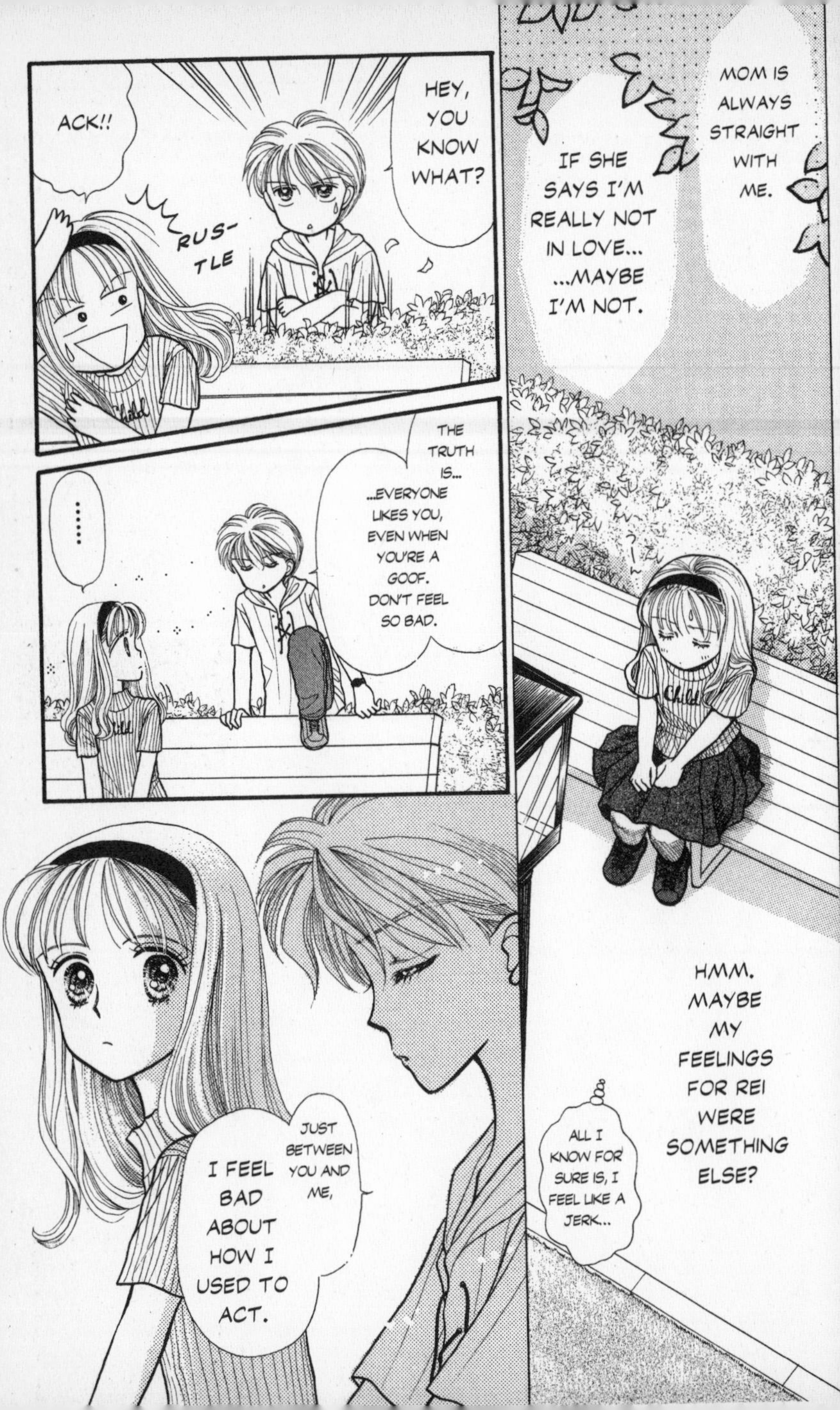
MOM IS ALWAYS STRAIGHT WITH ME.
IF SHE SAYS I'M REALLY NOT IN LOVE... ...MAYBE I'M NOT.
HMM. MAYBE MY FEELINGS FOR REI WERE SOMETHING ELSE?
ALL I KNOW FOR SURE IS, I FEEL LIKE A JERK...
HEY, YOU KNOW WHAT?
RUS-TLE
ACK!!
THE TRUTH IS...
...EVERYONE LIKES YOU, EVEN WHEN YOU'RE A GOOF. DON'T FEEL SO BAD.
......
JUST BETWEEN YOU AND ME,
I FEEL BAD ABOUT HOW I USED TO ACT.

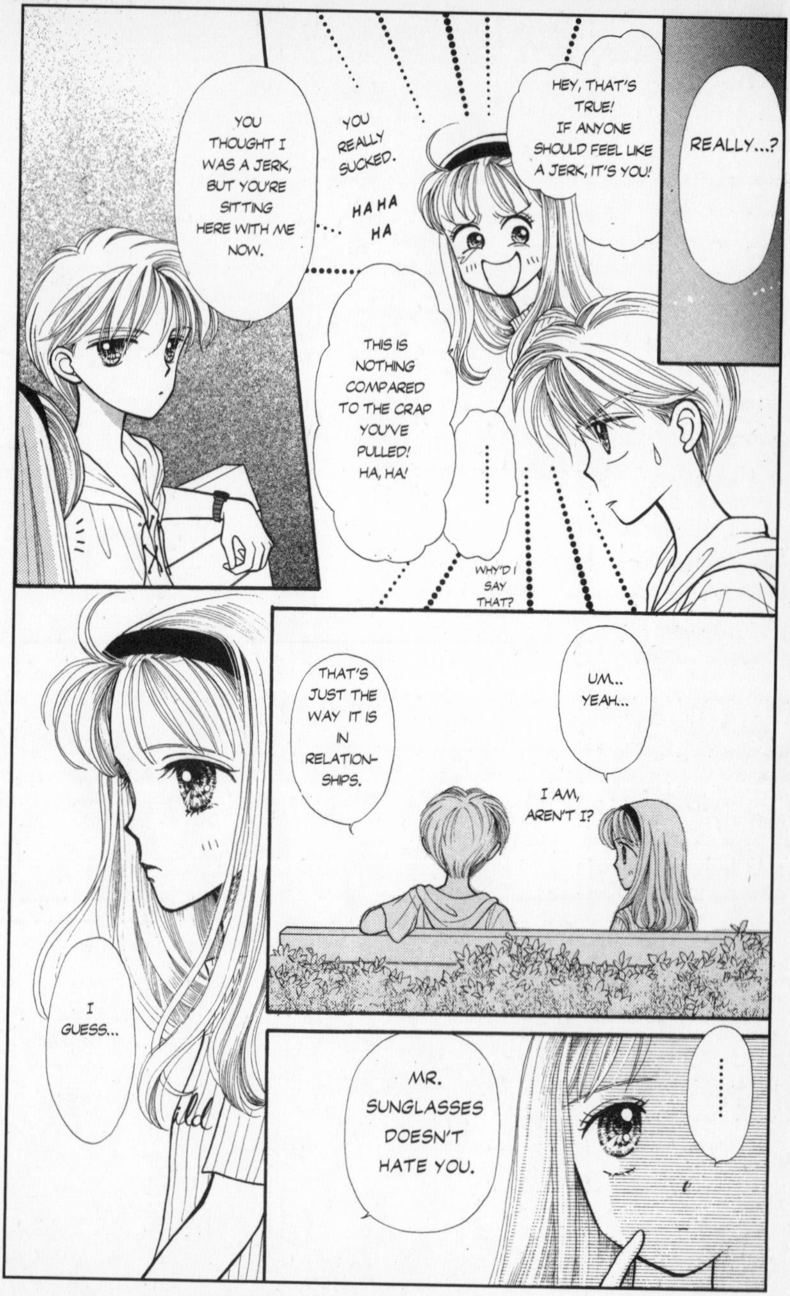
REALLY...?
HEY, THAT'S TRUE! IF ANYONE SHOULD FEEL LIKE A JERK, IT'S YOU!
YOU REALLY SUCKED.
HA HA HA
THIS IS NOTHING COMPARED TO THE CRAP YOU'VE PULLED! HA, HA!
......
WHY'D I SAY THAT?
YOU THOUGHT I WAS A JERK, BUT YOU'RE SITTING HERE WITH ME NOW.
UM... YEAH...
I AM, AREN'T I?
THAT'S JUST THE WAY IT IS IN RELATIONSHIPS.
......
MR. SUNGLASSES DOESN'T HATE YOU.
I GUESS...

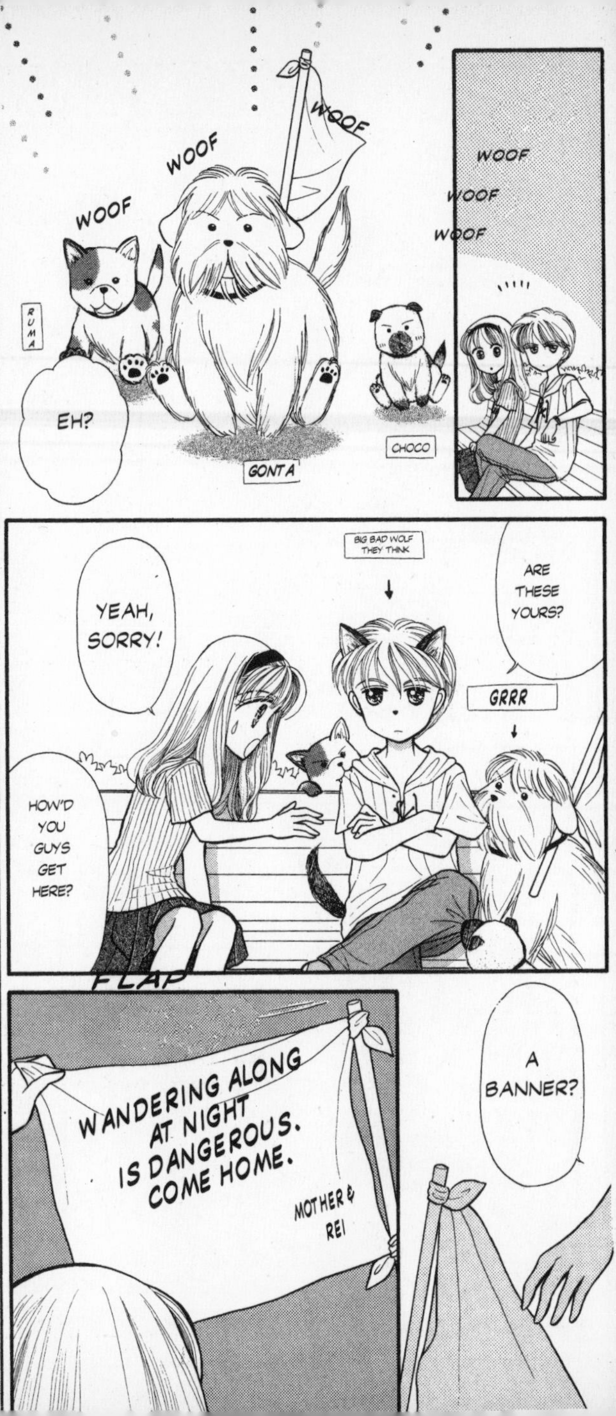
WOOF
WOOF
WOOF
!!!!
WOOF
WOOF
WOOF
RUMA
GONTA
CHOCO
EH?
ARE THESE YOURS?
BIG BAD WOLF THEY THINK
GRRR
YEAH, SORRY!
HOW'D YOU GUYS GET HERE?
A BANNER?
FLAP
WANDERING ALONG AT NIGHT IS DANGEROUS. COME HOME.
MOTHER & REI

My Alarming Clock

I can never get up in the morning. I always hit the snooze button and go back to sleep. When I was in high school, I was tardy more than anyone else in my class! I thought I'd better do something about it, so I bought an alarm clock that was like a mole hitter game. It worked! It was so hard to hit the moles, I got up on time for days. But after about a month, I got so good at hitting the moles when the alarm went off ...

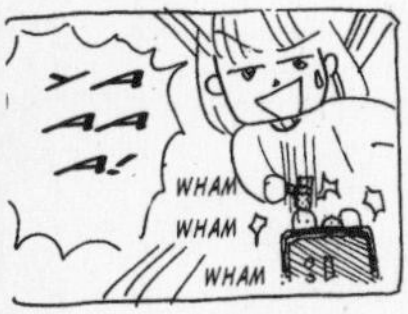
YAAAA!
WHAM
WHAM
WHAM

...I could hit them all real fast and...

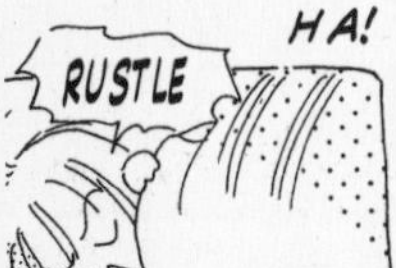
HA!
RUSTLE
ZZZZ.

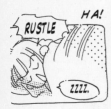

...go right back to sleep!

(To be continued.)

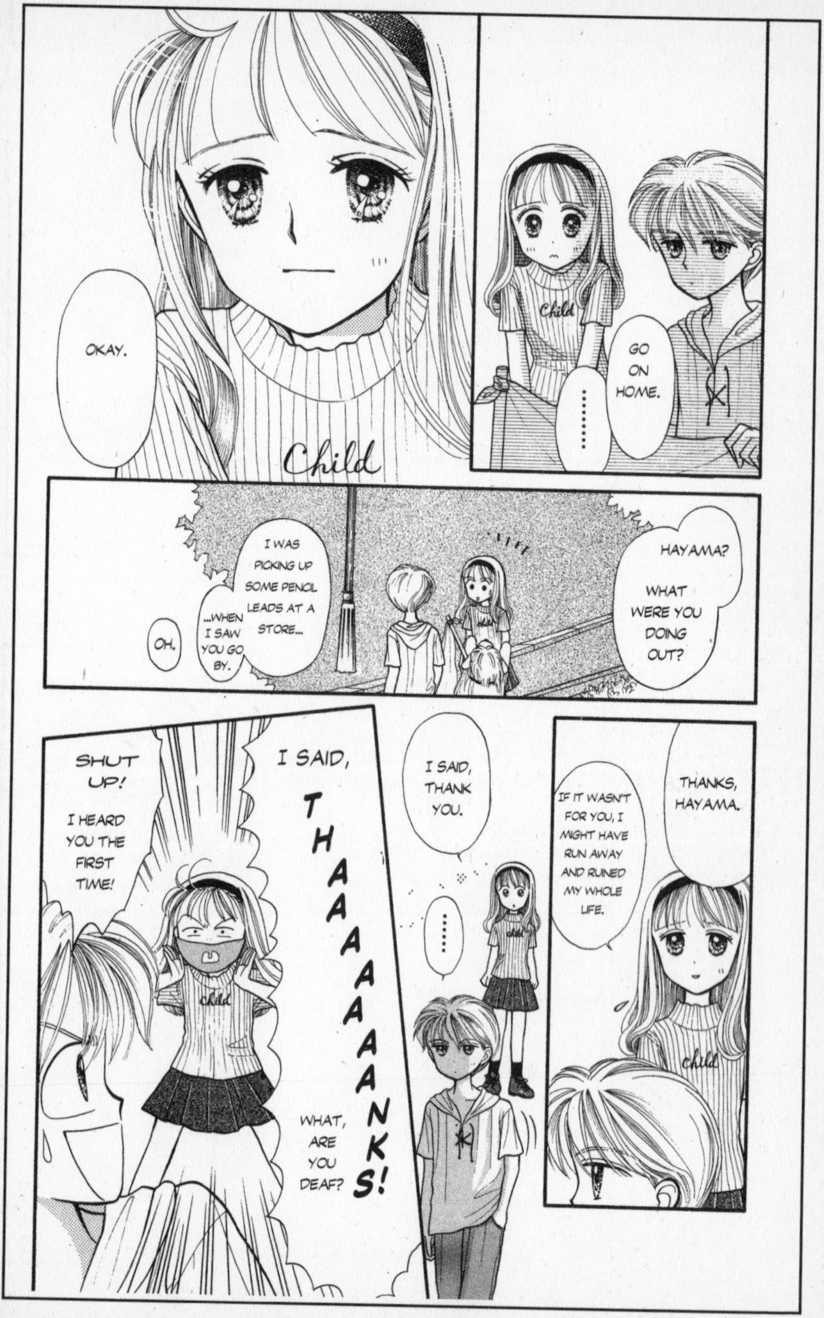
GO ON HOME.
......
OKAY.
HAYAMA? WHAT WERE YOU DOING OUT?
I WAS PICKING UP SOME PENCIL LEADS AT A STORE...
...WHEN I SAW YOU GO BY.
OH.
THANKS, HAYAMA.
IF IT WASN'T FOR YOU, I MIGHT HAVE RUN AWAY AND RUINED MY WHOLE LIFE.
I SAID, THANK YOU.
......
I SAID, THAAAAAAANKS!
WHAT, ARE YOU DEAF?
SHUT UP! I HEARD YOU THE FIRST TIME!
Child
Child
Child
Child
Child

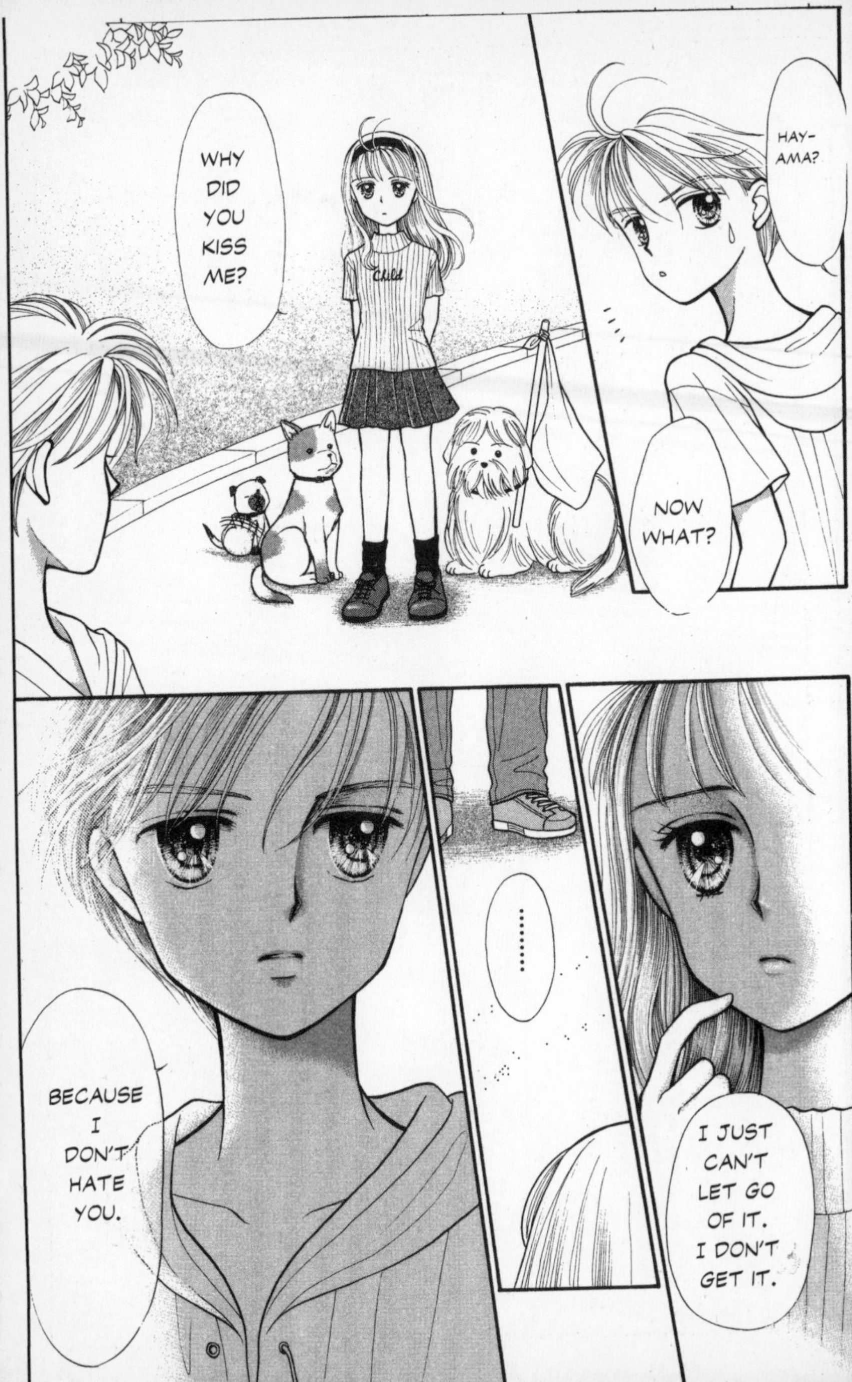
HAY-AMA?
NOW WHAT?
WHY DID YOU KISS ME?
Child
I JUST CAN'T LET GO OF IT. I DON'T GET IT.
......
BECAUSE I DON'T HATE YOU.

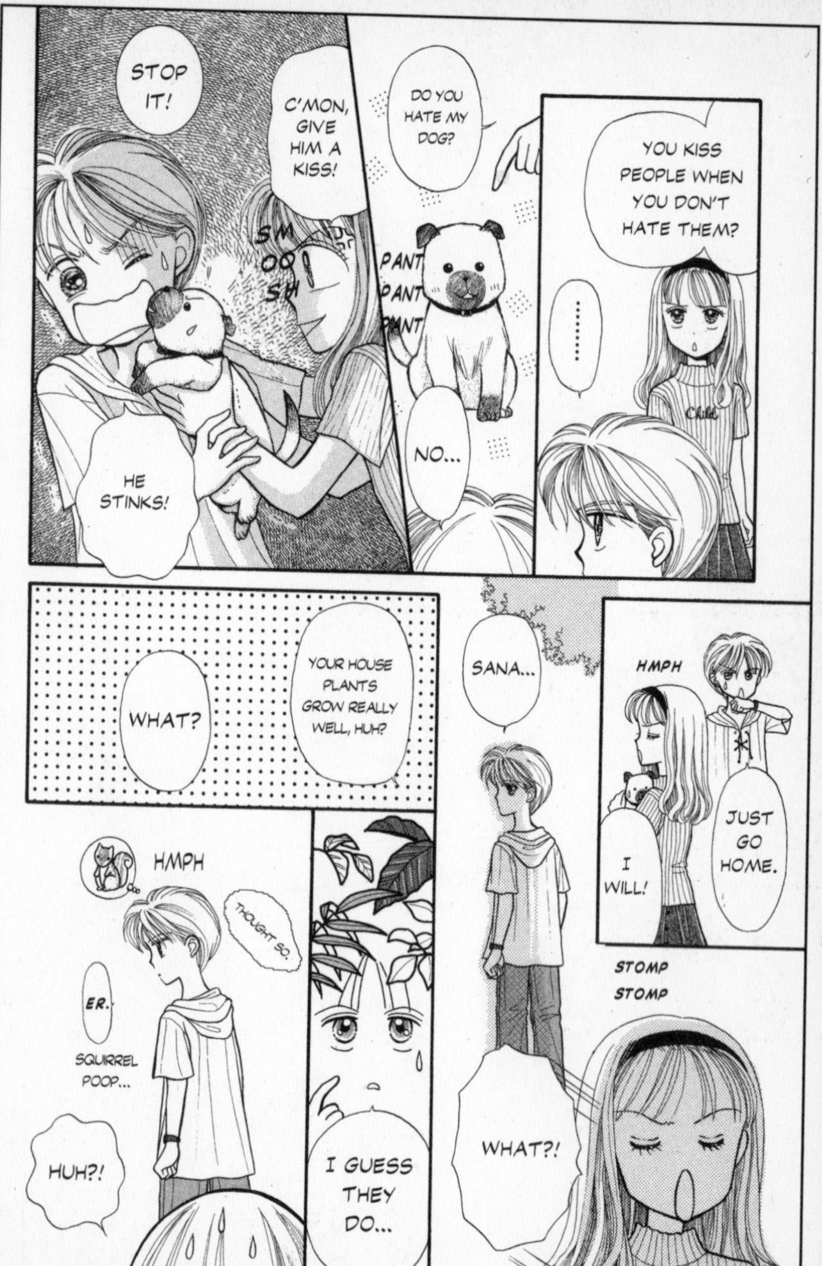
YOU KISS PEOPLE WHEN YOU DON'T HATE THEM?
......
DO YOU HATE MY DOG?
PANT PANT PANT
NO...
C'MON, GIVE HIM A KISS!
STOP IT!
SMOOSH
HE STINKS!
HMPH
JUST GO HOME.
I WILL!
STOMP STOMP
WHAT?!
SANA...
YOUR HOUSE PLANTS GROW REALLY WELL, HUH?
WHAT?
I GUESS THEY DO...
HMPH
THOUGHT SO.
ER.
SQUIRREL POOP...
HUH?!

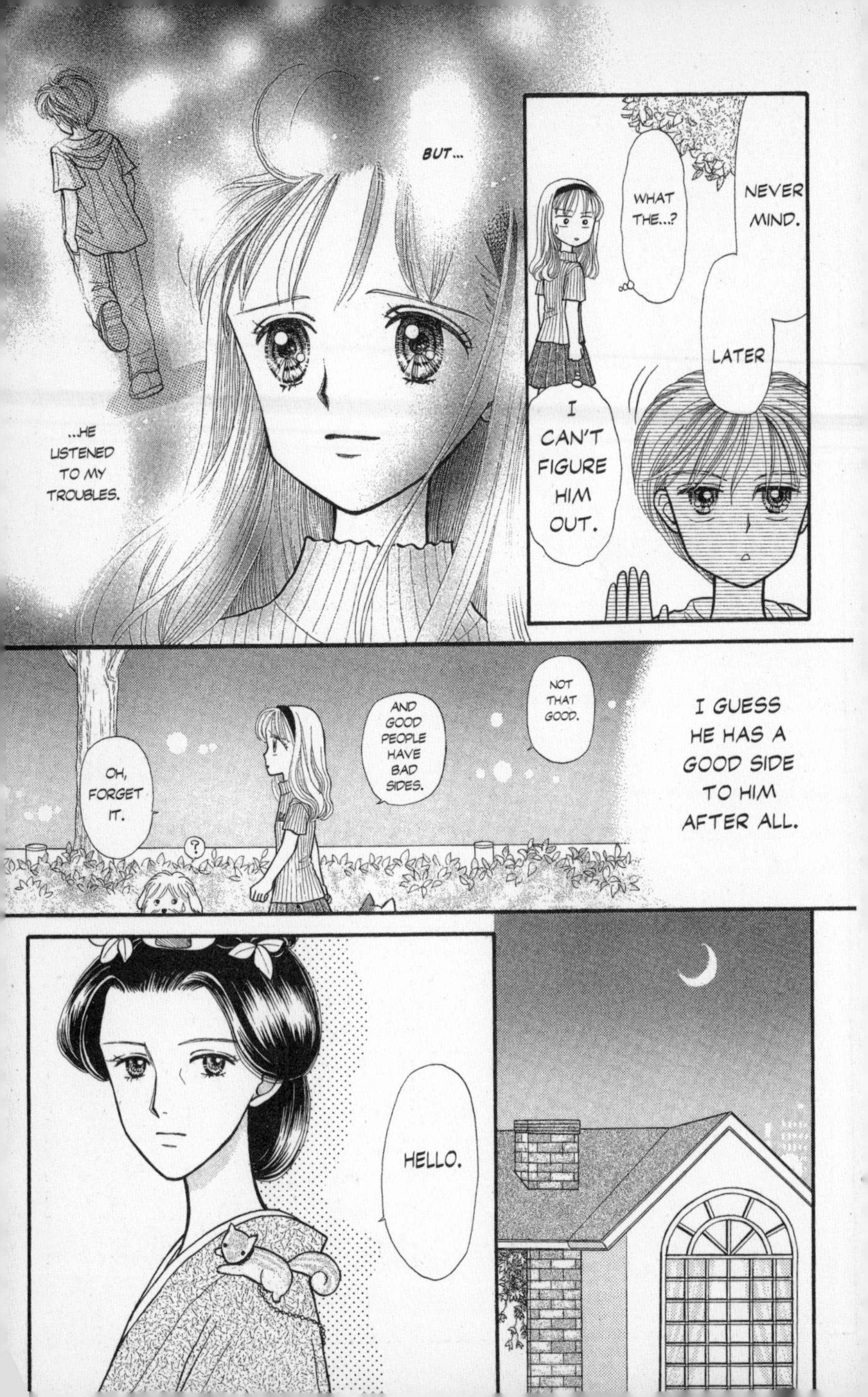
NEVER MIND.
LATER
WHAT THE...?
I CAN'T FIGURE HIM OUT.
BUT...
...HE LISTENED TO MY TROUBLES.
I GUESS HE HAS A GOOD SIDE TO HIM AFTER ALL.
NOT THAT GOOD.
AND GOOD PEOPLE HAVE BAD SIDES.
?
OH, FORGET IT.
HELLO.

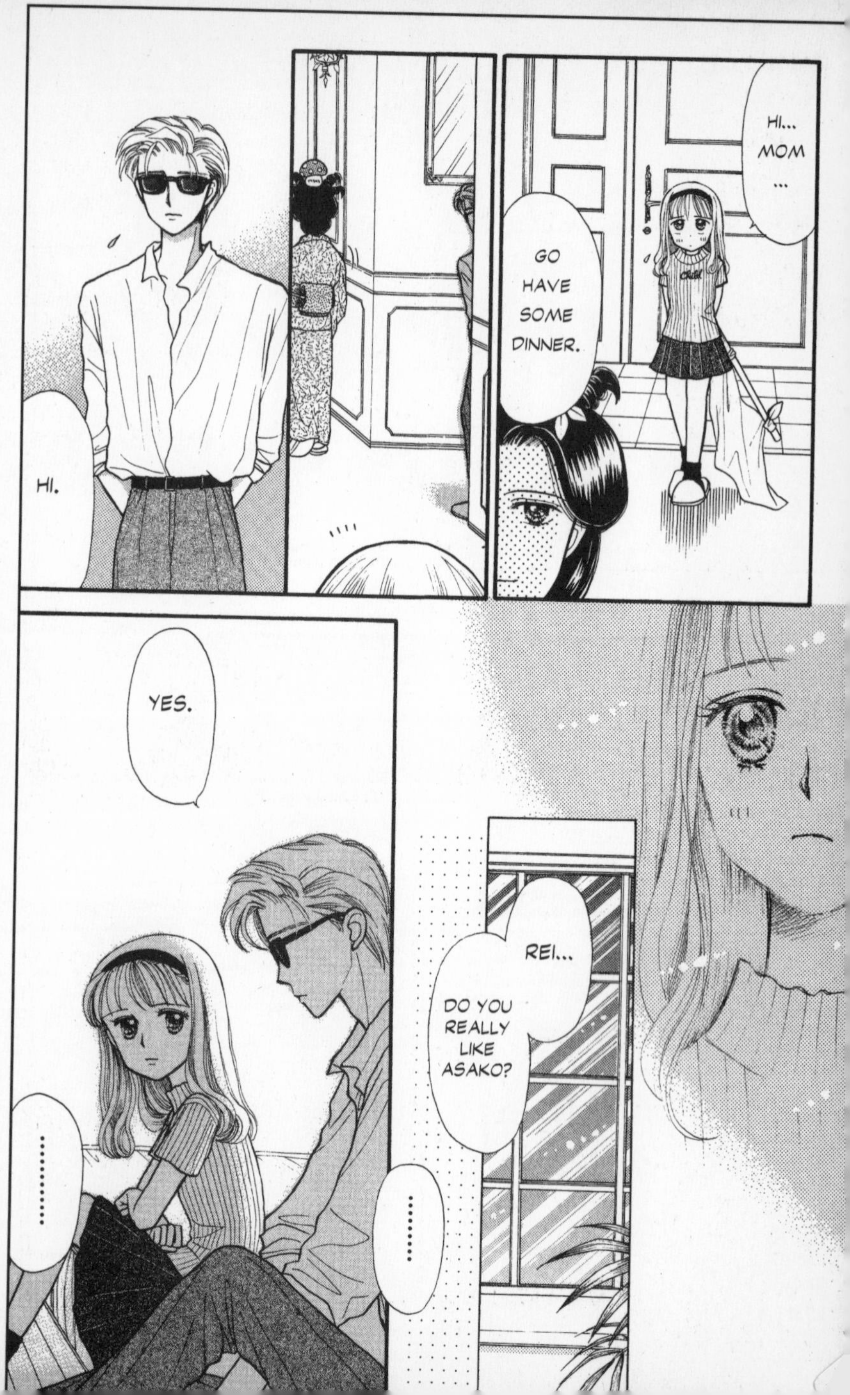
HI... MOM ...
GO HAVE SOME DINNER.
HI.
REI...
DO YOU REALLY LIKE ASAKO?
......
YES.
....

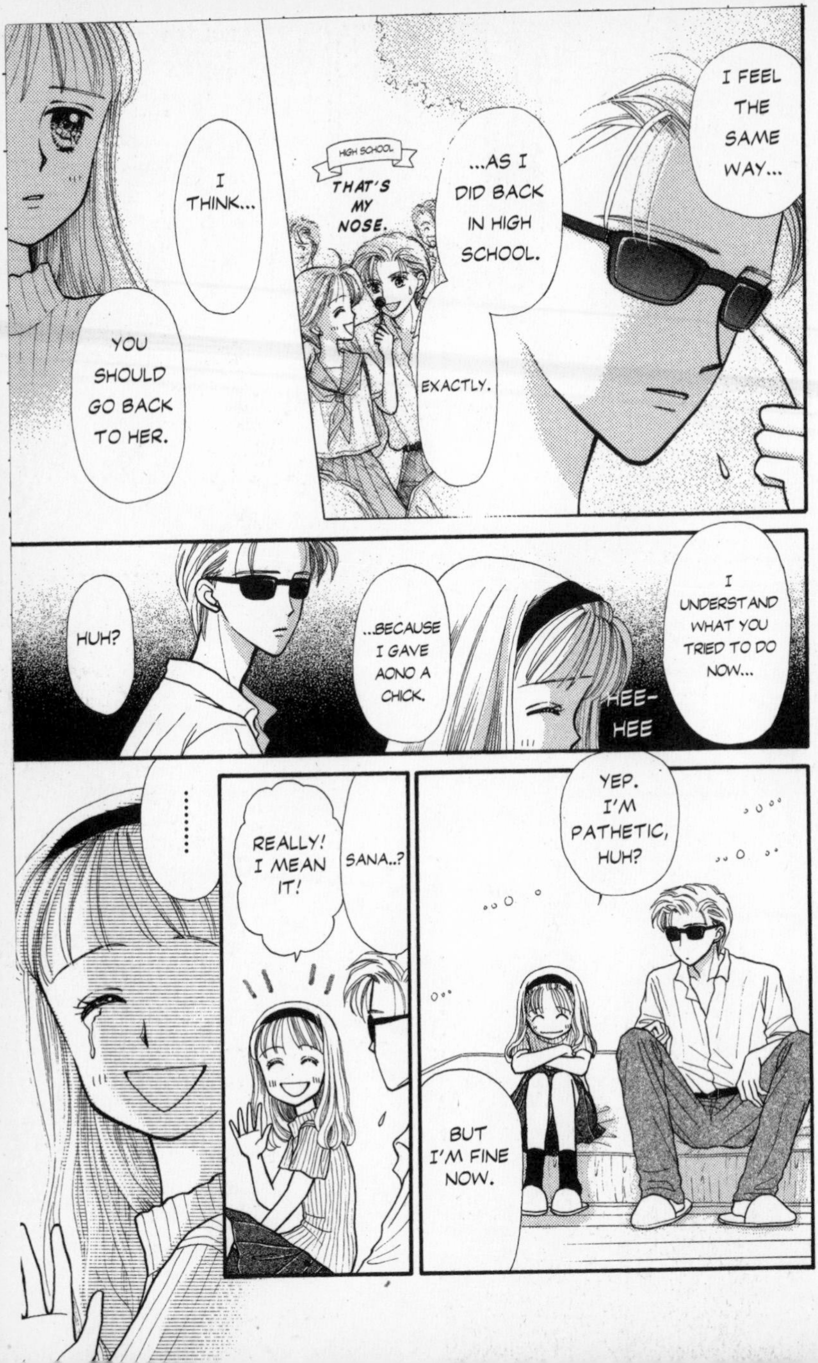
I FEEL THE SAME WAY...
...AS I DID BACK IN HIGH SCHOOL.
HIGH SCHOOL
THAT'S MY NOSE.
EXACTLY.
I THINK...
YOU SHOULD GO BACK TO HER.
I UNDERSTAND WHAT YOU TRIED TO DO NOW...
HEE-HEE
...BECAUSE I GAVE AONO A CHICK.
HUH?
YEP. I'M PATHETIC, HUH?
BUT I'M FINE NOW.
SANA..?
REALLY! I MEAN IT!
......

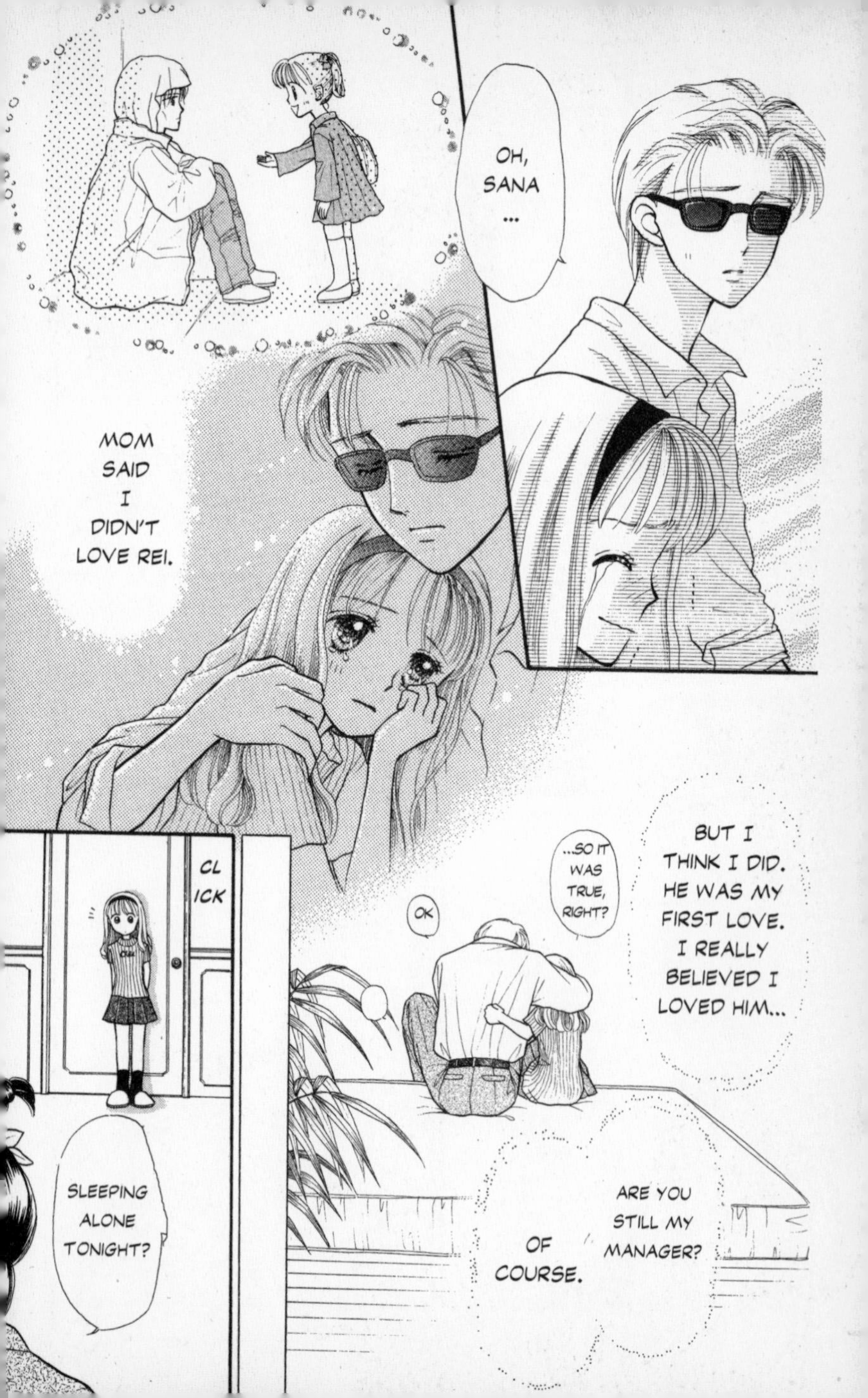
OH, SANA ...
MOM SAID I DIDN'T LOVE REI.
BUT I THINK I DID. HE WAS MY FIRST LOVE. I REALLY BELIEVED I LOVED HIM...
...SO IT WAS TRUE, RIGHT?
OK
ARE YOU STILL MY MANAGER?
OF COURSE.
CL ICK
SLEEPING ALONE TONIGHT?

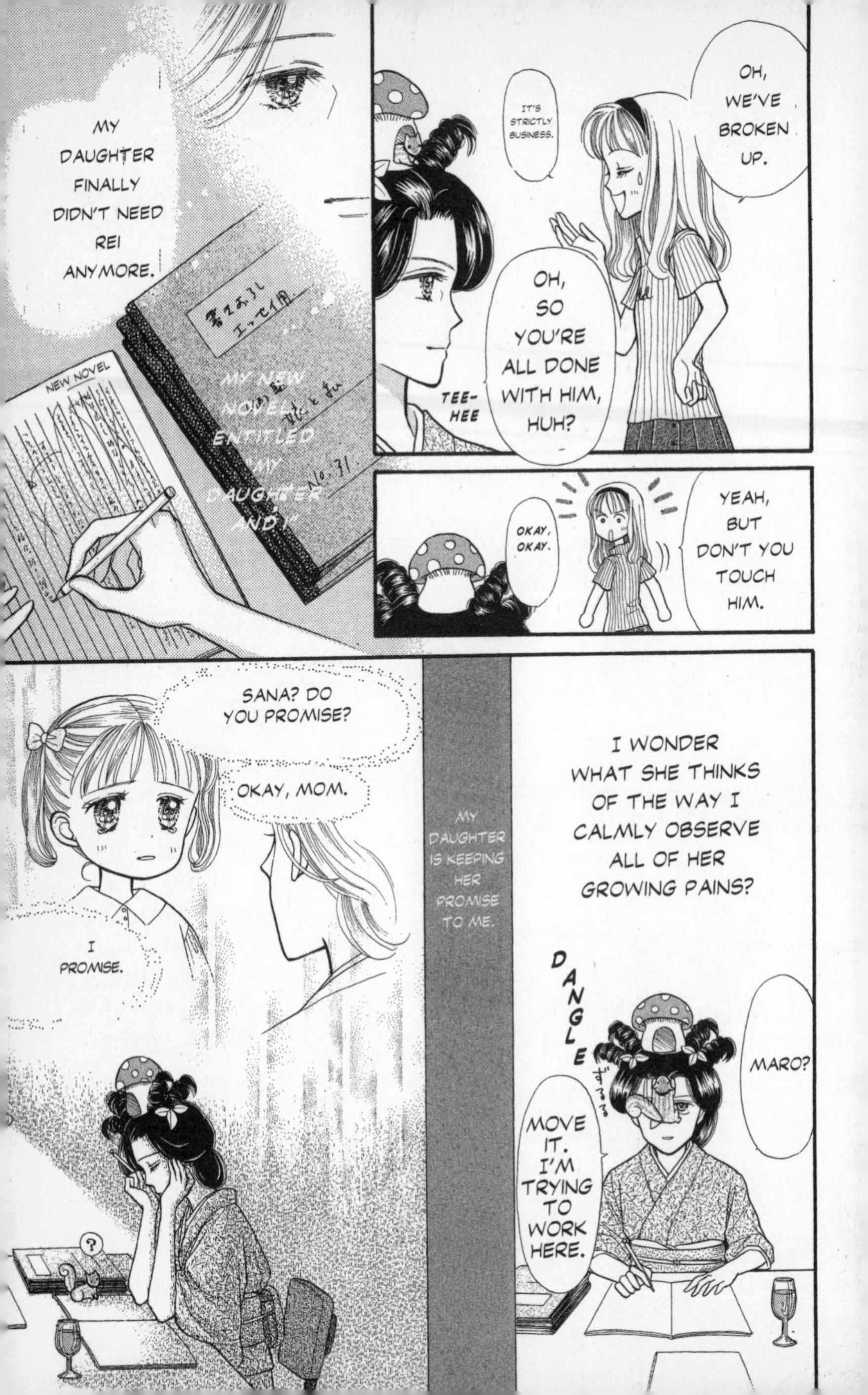
OH, WE'VE BROKEN UP.
IT'S STRICTLY BUSINESS.
OH, SO YOU'RE ALL DONE WITH HIM, HUH?
TEE-HEE
YEAH, BUT DON'T YOU TOUCH HIM.
OKAY, OKAY.
MY DAUGHTER FINALLY DIDN'T NEED REI ANYMORE.
NEW NOVEL
MY NEW NOVEL ENTITLED "MY DAUGHTER AND I"
No. 31
I WONDER WHAT SHE THINKS OF THE WAY I CALMLY OBSERVE ALL OF HER GROWING PAINS?
MARO?
DANGLE
MOVE IT. I'M TRYING TO WORK HERE.
MY DAUGHTER IS KEEPING HER PROMISE TO ME.
SANA? DO YOU PROMISE?
OKAY, MOM.
I PROMISE.

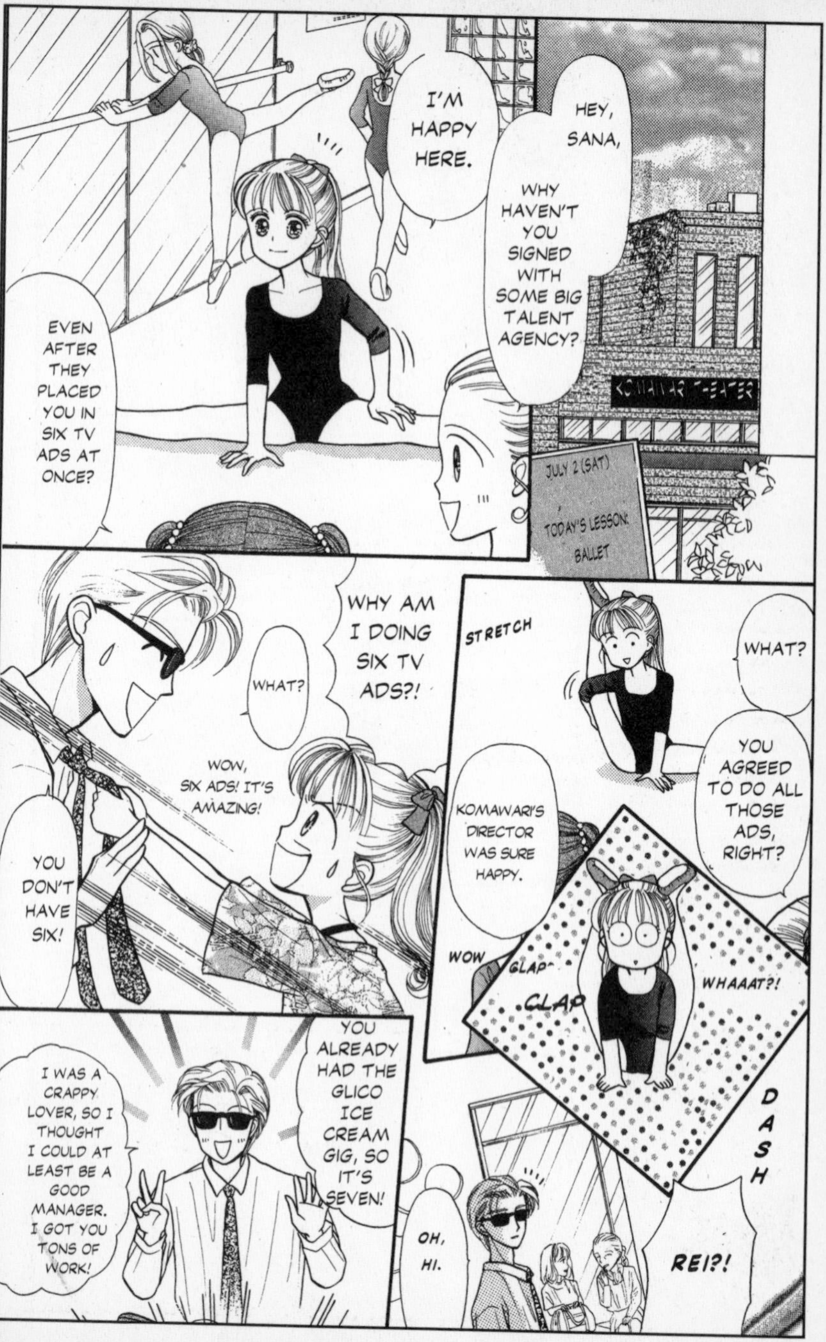
JULY 2 (SAT)
TODAY'S LESSON: BALLET
HEY, SANA, WHY HAVEN'T YOU SIGNED WITH SOME BIG TALENT AGENCY?
I'M HAPPY HERE.
EVEN AFTER THEY PLACED YOU IN SIX TV ADS AT ONCE?
STRETCH
WHAT?
YOU AGREED TO DO ALL THOSE ADS, RIGHT?
KOMAWARI'S DIRECTOR WAS SURE HAPPY.
WOW
CLAP
CLAP
WHAAAT?!
WHY AM I DOING SIX TV ADS?!
WHAT?
WOW, SIX ADS! IT'S AMAZING!
YOU DON'T HAVE SIX!
DASH
REI?!
OH, HI.
YOU ALREADY HAD THE GLICO ICE CREAM GIG, SO IT'S SEVEN!
I WAS A CRAPPY LOVER, SO I THOUGHT I COULD AT LEAST BE A GOOD MANAGER. I GOT YOU TONS OF WORK!

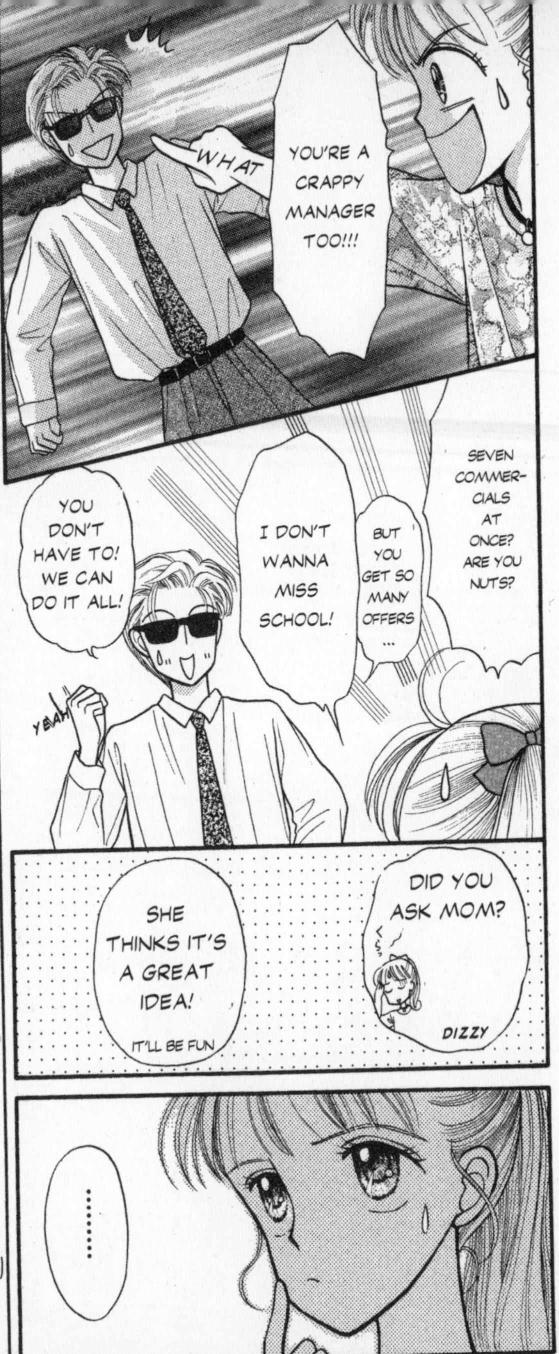
YOU'RE A CRAPPY MANAGER TOO!!!
WHAT
SEVEN COMMERCIALS AT ONCE? ARE YOU NUTS?
BUT YOU GET SO MANY OFFERS ...
I DON'T WANNA MISS SCHOOL!
YOU DON'T HAVE TO! WE CAN DO IT ALL!
YEAH
DID YOU ASK MOM?
DIZZY
SHE THINKS IT'S A GREAT IDEA!
IT'LL BE FUN
......

Part Two

So, I looked for a better alarm clock. In this one catalogue I found a pillow that vibrates your head to wake you up. I thought it sounded like it would work—but then I figured having my head shook around every morning would just make me more stupid, so I didn't get it. On Christmas, my sister gave me the "Little Bear's Music Group". It's a clock with five cute little toy bears who played music in the morning. This one worked pretty well—because the bears worked so hard to play their music, I felt sorry for them and woke up feeling refreshed. But, then I got used to that, too. (Now it sounds to me like a lullaby.) But finally, I found the ultimate alarm clock - it's my cat, Nao! Every day I have to get up to stop Nao from messing up my desk. Finally, I can wake up in the morning!

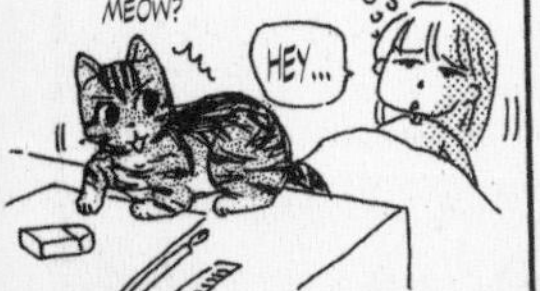
MEOW?
HEY...

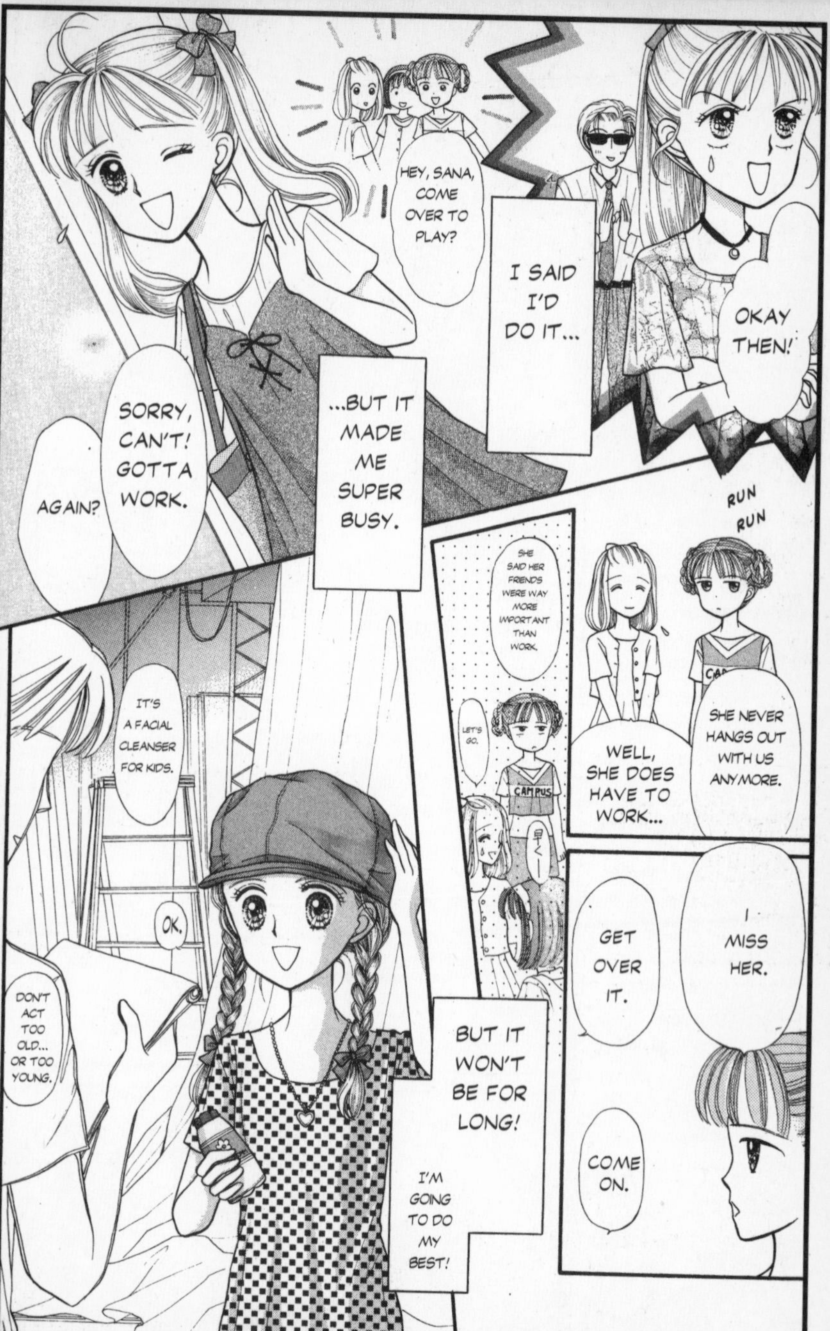
OKAY THEN!
I SAID I'D DO IT...
HEY, SANA, COME OVER TO PLAY?
SORRY, CAN'T! GOTTA WORK.
AGAIN?
...BUT IT MADE ME SUPER BUSY.
RUN RUN
SHE NEVER HANGS OUT WITH US ANYMORE.
WELL, SHE DOES HAVE TO WORK...
SHE SAID HER FRIENDS WERE WAY MORE IMPORTANT THAN WORK.
LET'S GO.
I MISS HER.
GET OVER IT.
COME ON.
IT'S A FACIAL CLEANSER FOR KIDS.
OK.
DON'T ACT TOO OLD... OR TOO YOUNG.
BUT IT WON'T BE FOR LONG!
I'M GOING TO DO MY BEST!

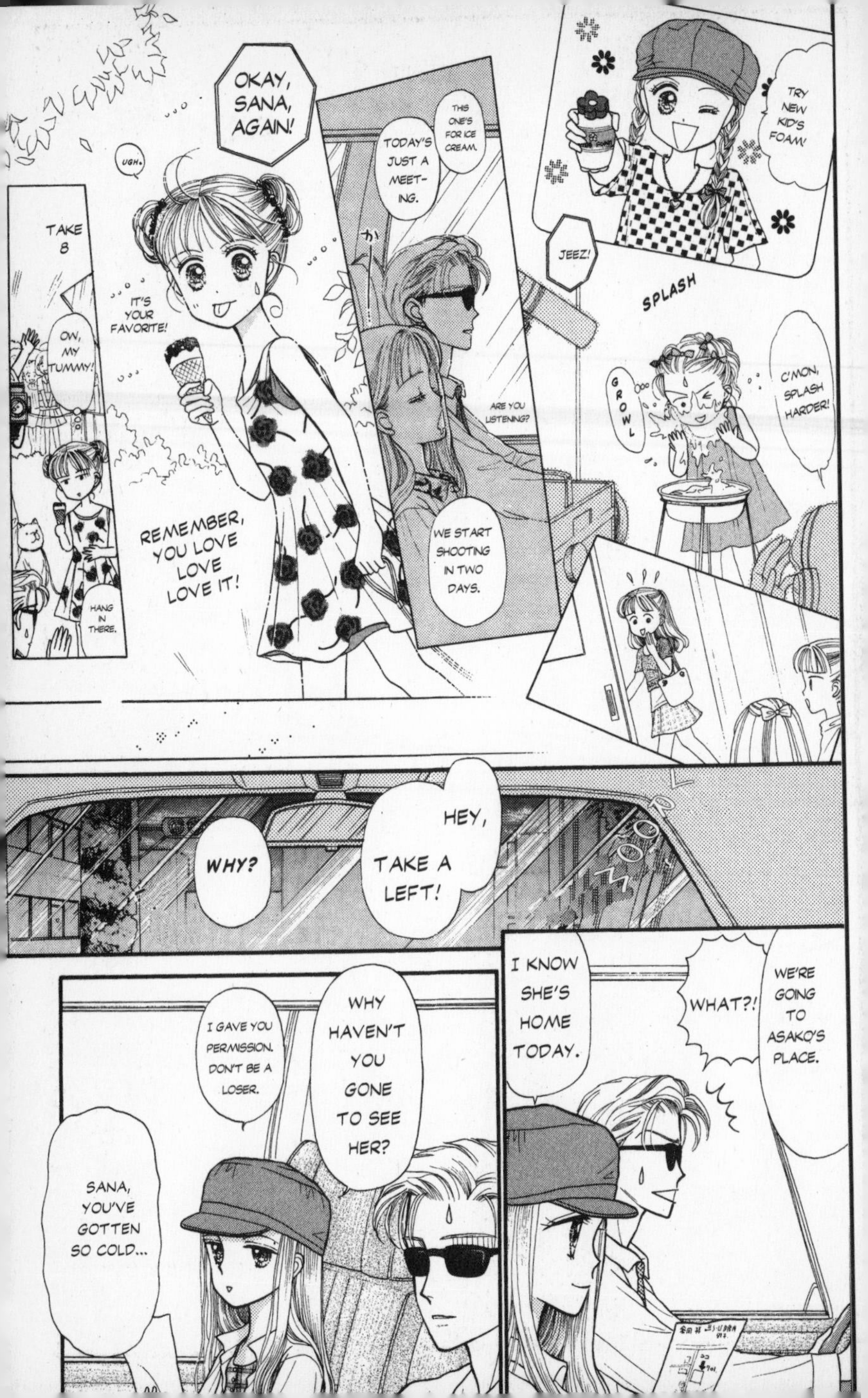
TRY NEW KID'S FOAM!
JEEZ!
SPLASH
C'MON, SPLASH HARDER!
GROWL
THIS ONE'S FOR ICE CREAM.
TODAY'S JUST A MEET-ING.
ARE YOU LISTENING?
WE START SHOOTING IN TWO DAYS.
OKAY, SANA, AGAIN!
UGH.
IT'S YOUR FAVORITE!
REMEMBER, YOU LOVE LOVE LOVE IT!
TAKE 8
OW, MY TUMMY!
HANG IN THERE.
HEY, TAKE A LEFT!
WHY?
WE'RE GOING TO ASAKO'S PLACE.
WHAT?!
I KNOW SHE'S HOME TODAY.
WHY HAVEN'T YOU GONE TO SEE HER?
I GAVE YOU PERMISSION. DON'T BE A LOSER.
SANA, YOU'VE GOTTEN SO COLD...

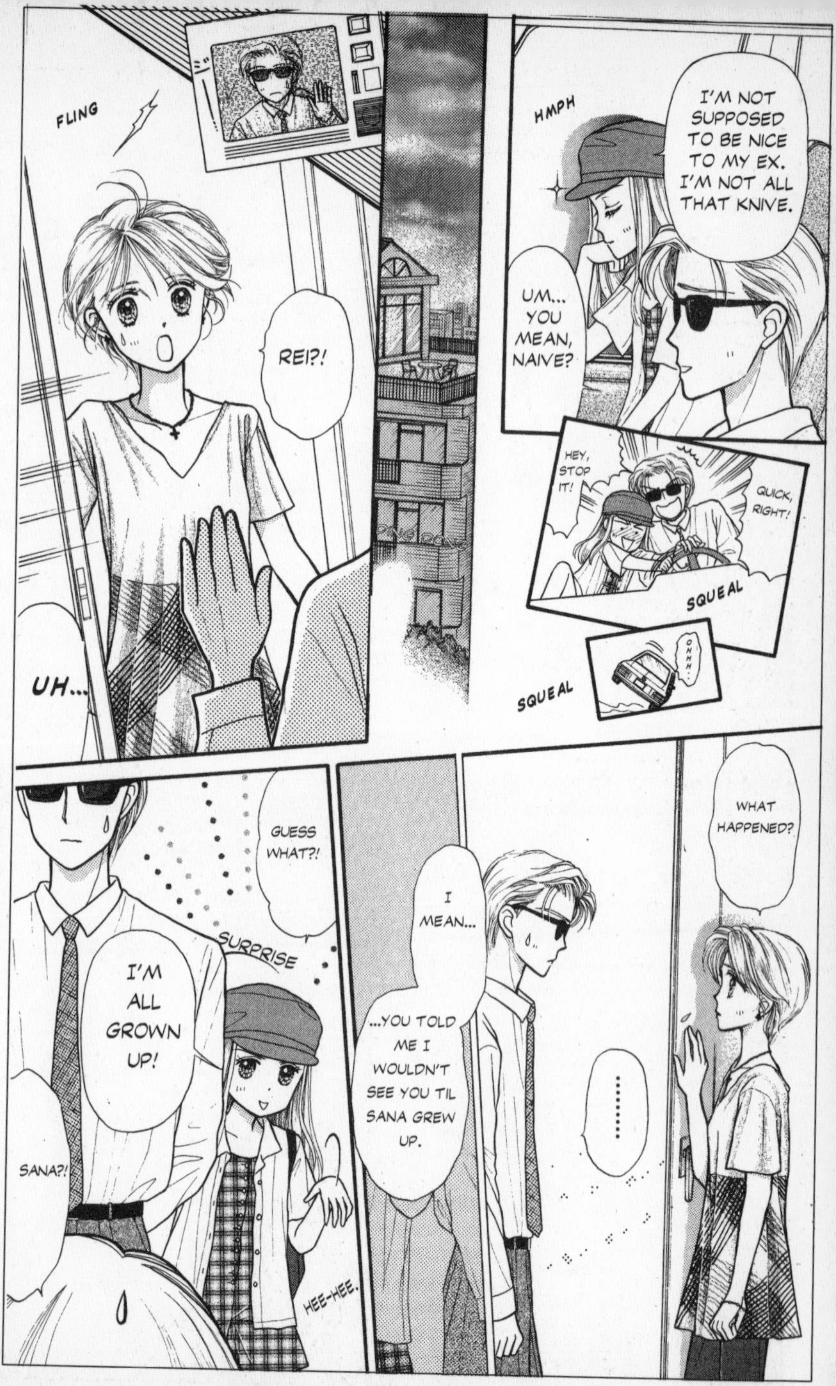
HMPH
I'M NOT SUPPOSED TO BE NICE TO MY EX. I'M NOT ALL THAT KNIVE.
UM... YOU MEAN, NAIVE?
HEY, STOP IT!
QUICK, RIGHT!
SQUEAL
OHHH..
SQUEAL
DING DONG
FLING
REI?!
UH...
WHAT HAPPENED?
......
I MEAN...
...YOU TOLD ME I WOULDN'T SEE YOU TIL SANA GREW UP.
GUESS WHAT?!
SURPRISE
I'M ALL GROWN UP!
SANA?!
HEE-HEE.

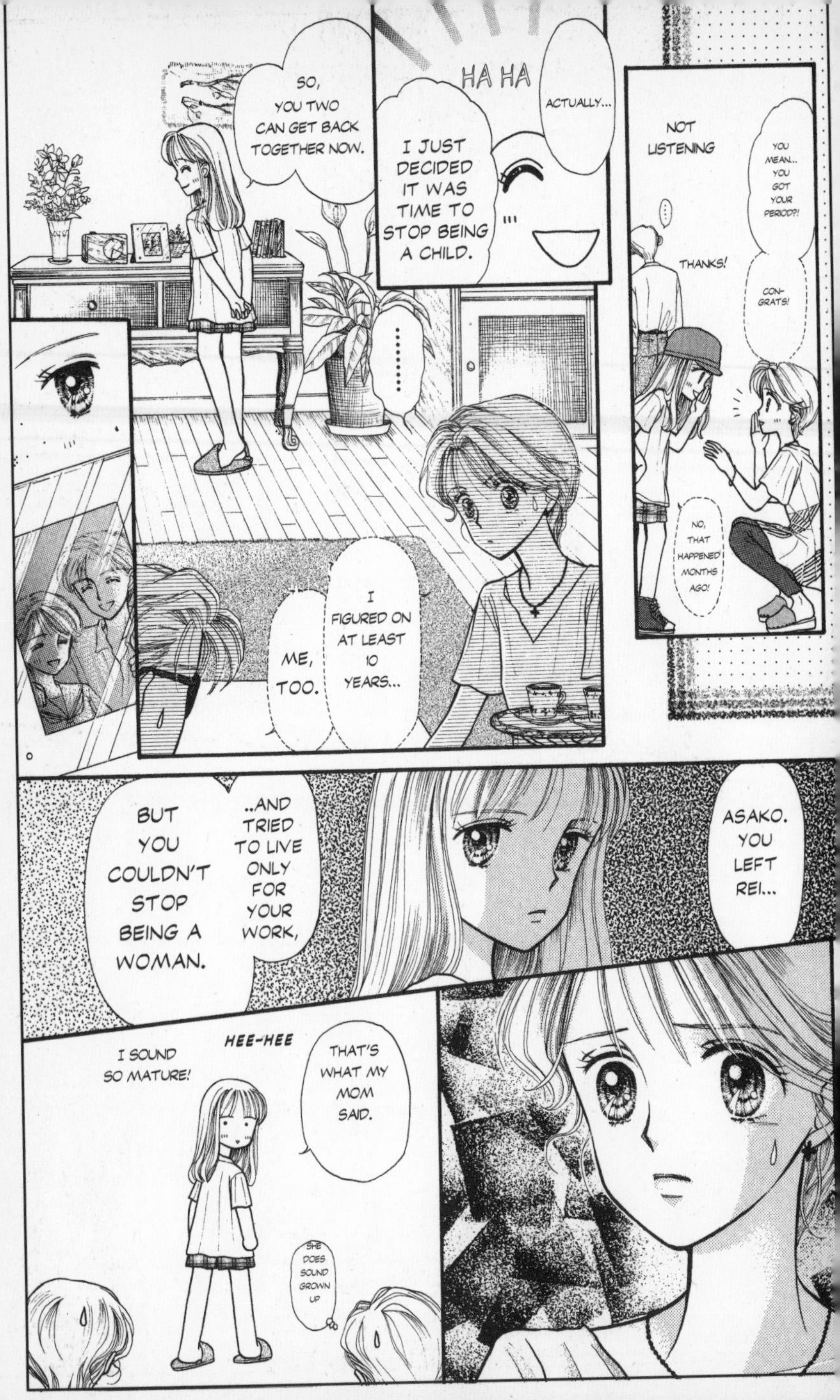
NOT LISTENING
YOU MEAN.. YOU GOT YOUR PERIOD?!
...
THANKS!
CON-GRATS!
NO, THAT HAPPENED MONTHS AGO!
HA HA
ACTUALLY...
I JUST DECIDED IT WAS TIME TO STOP BEING A CHILD.
SO, YOU TWO CAN GET BACK TOGETHER NOW.
......
I FIGURED ON AT LEAST 10 YEARS...
ME, TOO.
ASAKO. YOU LEFT REI...
..AND TRIED TO LIVE ONLY FOR YOUR WORK,
BUT YOU COULDN'T STOP BEING A WOMAN.
THAT'S WHAT MY MOM SAID.
HEE-HEE
I SOUND SO MATURE!
SHE DOES SOUND GROWN UP

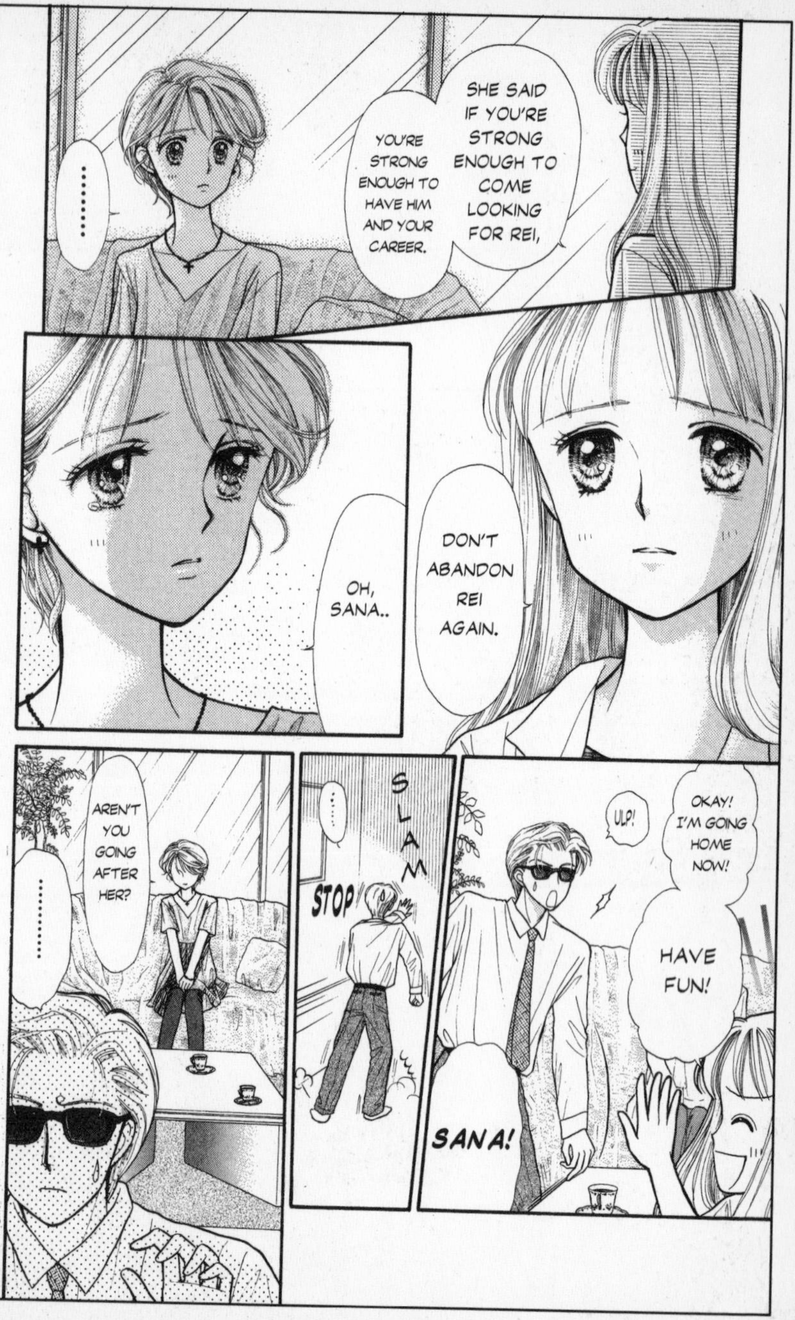
SHE SAID IF YOU'RE STRONG ENOUGH TO COME LOOKING FOR REI,
YOU'RE STRONG ENOUGH TO HAVE HIM AND YOUR CAREER.
......
DON'T ABANDON REI AGAIN.
OH, SANA..
OKAY! I'M GOING HOME NOW!
ULP!
HAVE FUN!
SANA!
SLAM
......
STOP
AREN'T YOU GOING AFTER HER?
......

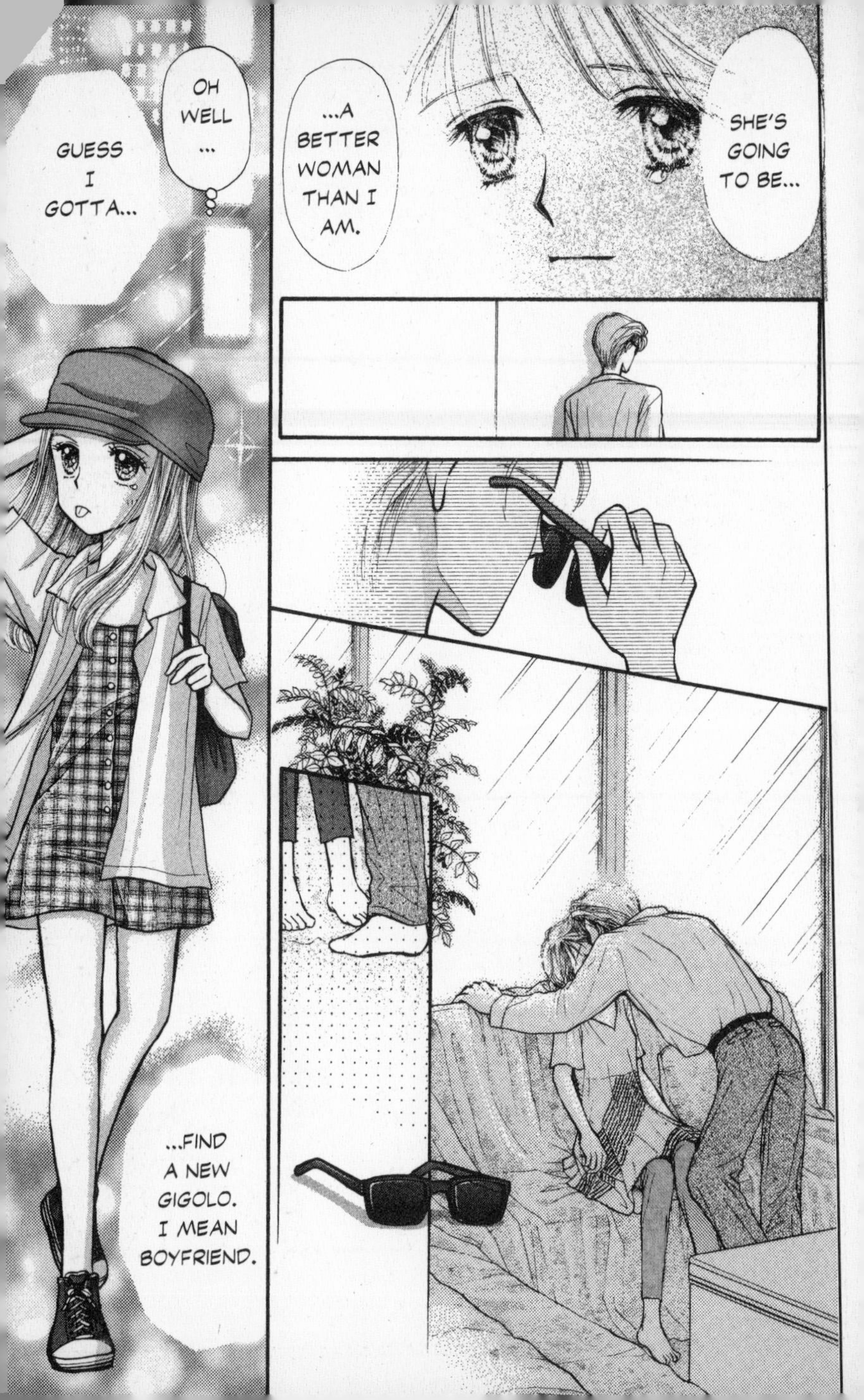
SHE'S GOING TO BE...
...A BETTER WOMAN THAN I AM.
OH WELL ...
GUESS I GOTTA...
...FIND A NEW GIGOLO. I MEAN BOYFRIEND.

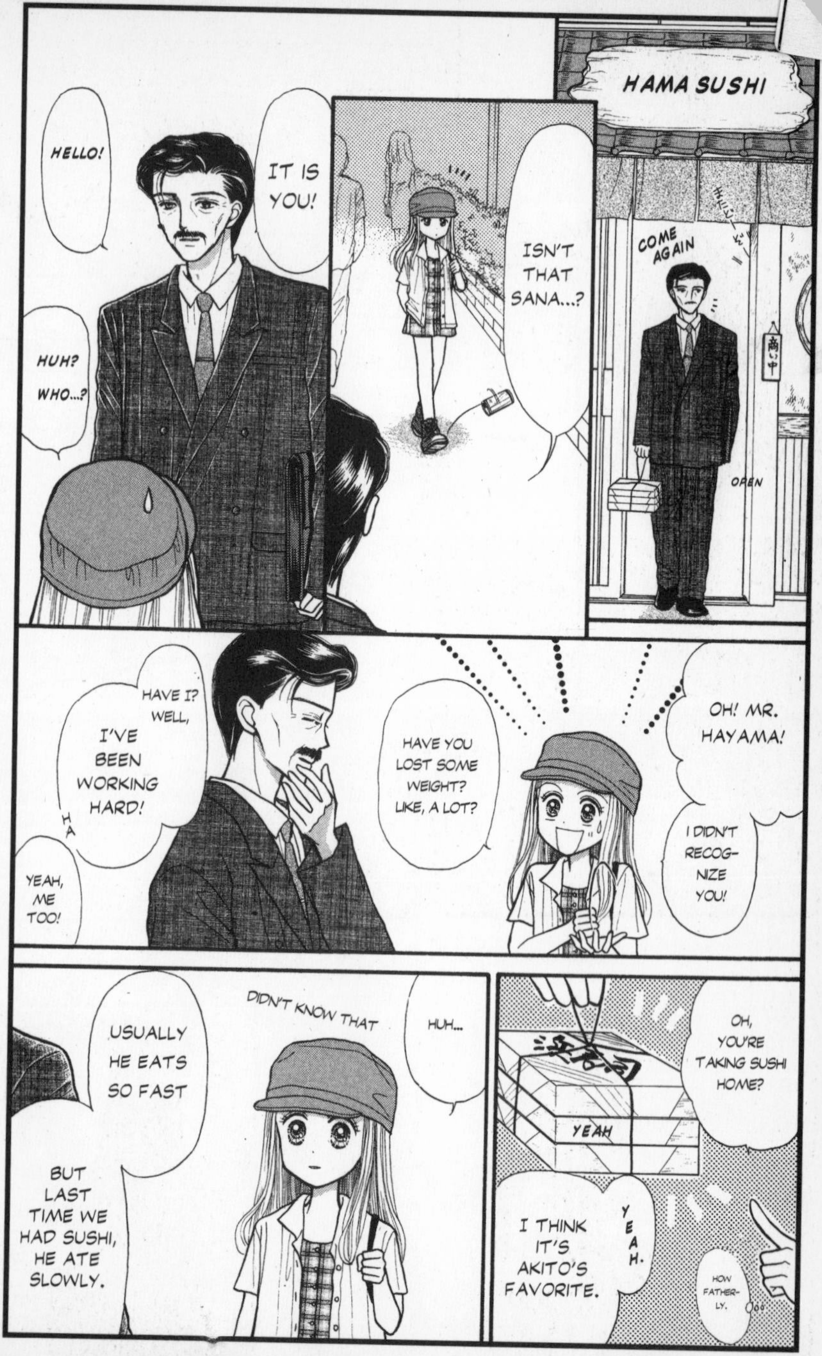
HAMA SUSHI
COME AGAIN
OPEN
ISN'T THAT SANA...?
IT IS YOU!
HELLO!
HUH? WHO...?
OH! MR. HAYAMA!
I DIDN'T RECOG-NIZE YOU!
HAVE YOU LOST SOME WEIGHT? LIKE, A LOT?
HAVE I? WELL, I'VE BEEN WORKING HARD!
HA
YEAH, ME TOO!
OH, YOU'RE TAKING SUSHI HOME?
YEAH
YEAH.
I THINK IT'S AKITO'S FAVORITE.
HOW FATHER-LY.
HUH...
DIDN'T KNOW THAT
USUALLY HE EATS SO FAST
BUT LAST TIME WE HAD SUSHI, HE ATE SLOWLY.

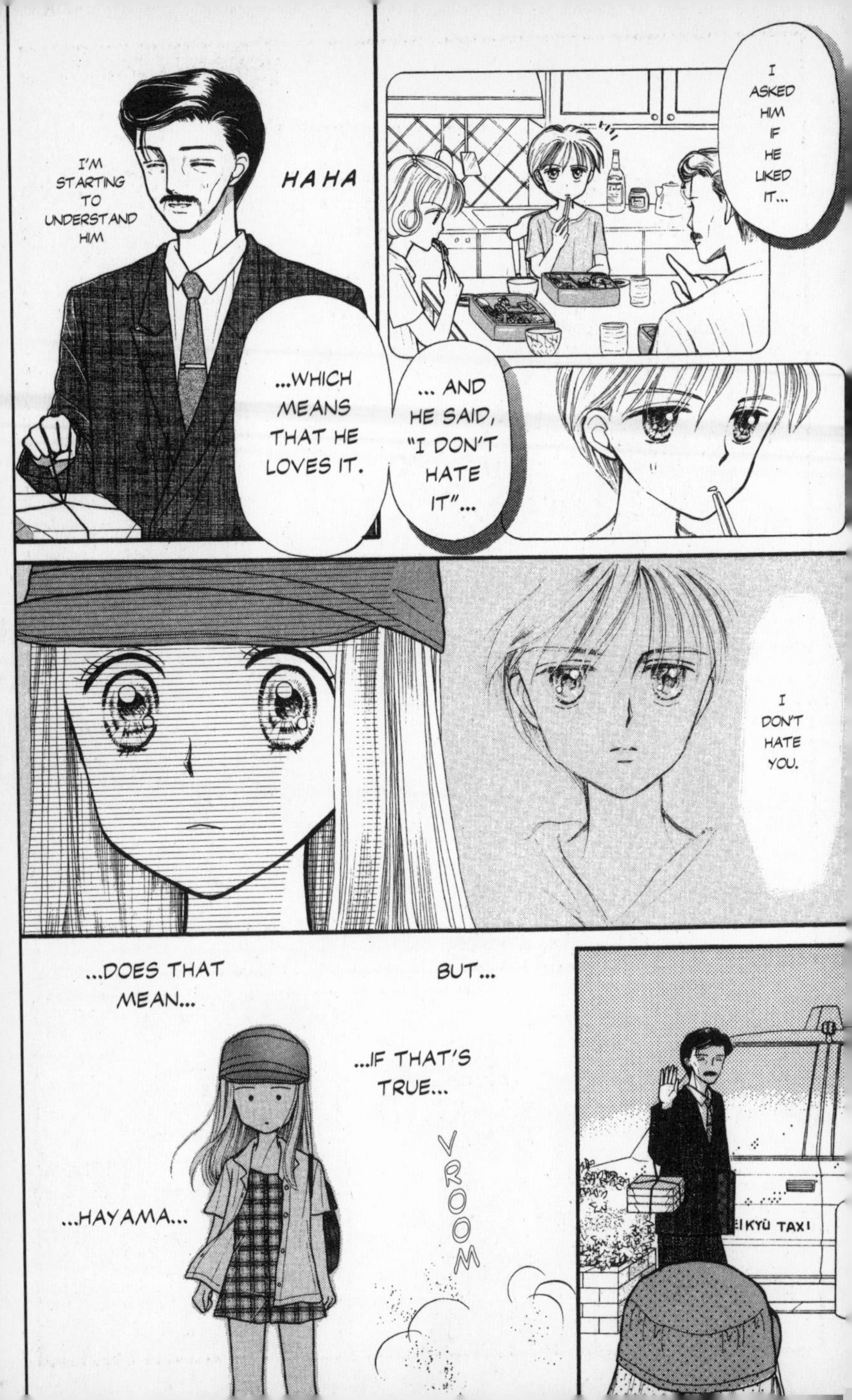
I ASKED HIM IF HE LIKED IT...
... AND HE SAID, "I DON'T HATE IT"...
...WHICH MEANS THAT HE LOVES IT.
HA HA
I'M STARTING TO UNDERSTAND HIM
I DON'T HATE YOU.
EIKYŪ TAXI
BUT...
...IF THAT'S TRUE...
...DOES THAT MEAN...
VROOM
...HAYAMA...

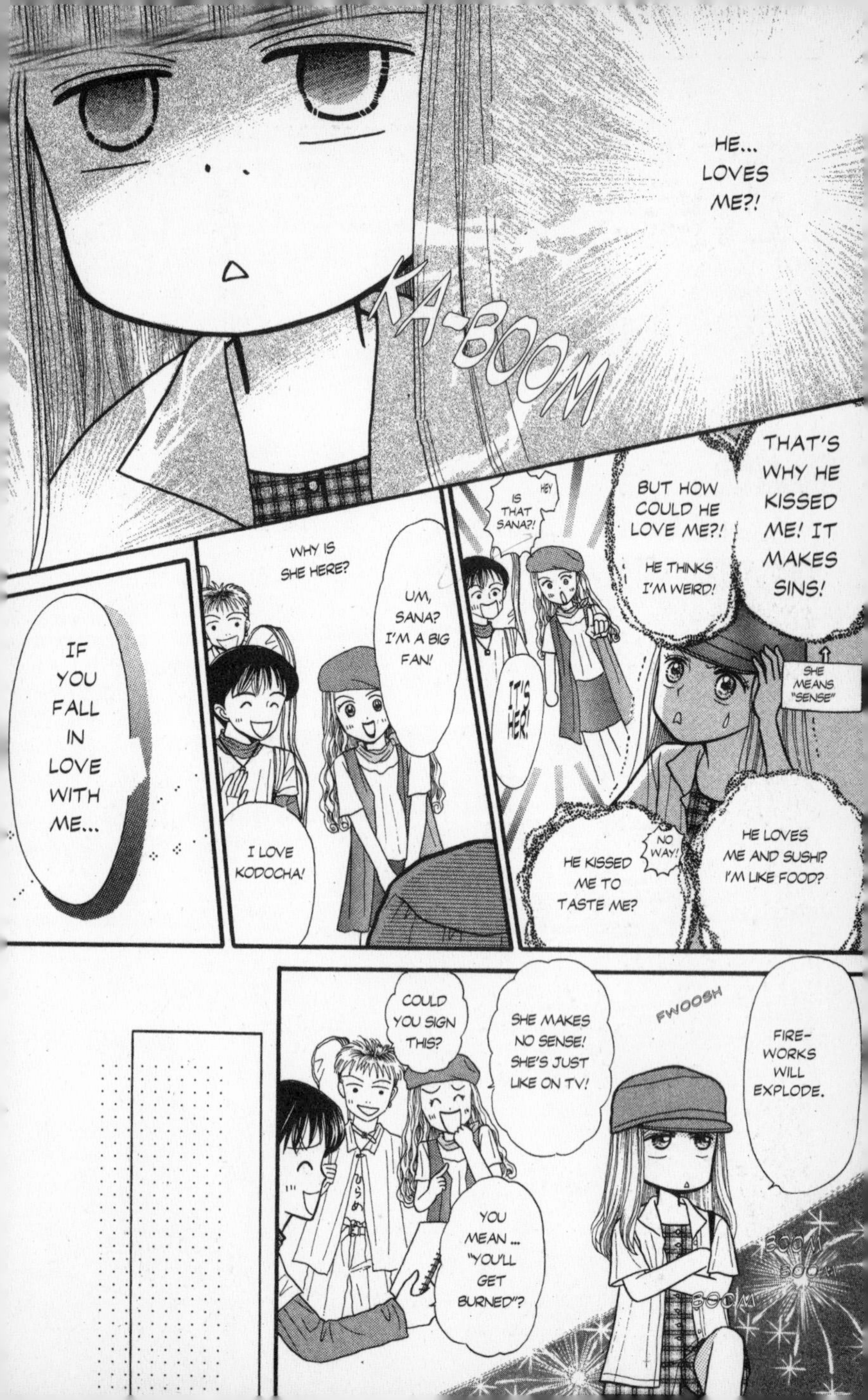
HE... LOVES ME?!
KA-BOOM
THAT'S WHY HE KISSED ME! IT MAKES SINS!
SHE MEANS "SENSE"
BUT HOW COULD HE LOVE ME?! HE THINKS I'M WEIRD!
HEY
IS THAT SANA?!
IT'S HER!
HE LOVES ME AND SUSHI? I'M LIKE FOOD?
NO WAY!
HE KISSED ME TO TASTE ME?
UM, SANA? I'M A BIG FAN!
WHY IS SHE HERE?
I LOVE KODOCHA!
IF YOU FALL IN LOVE WITH ME...
FIRE-WORKS WILL EXPLODE.
FWOOSH
SHE MAKES NO SENSE! SHE'S JUST LIKE ON TV!
COULD YOU SIGN THIS?
YOU MEAN ... "YOU'LL GET BURNED"?
BOOM
BOOM
BOOM

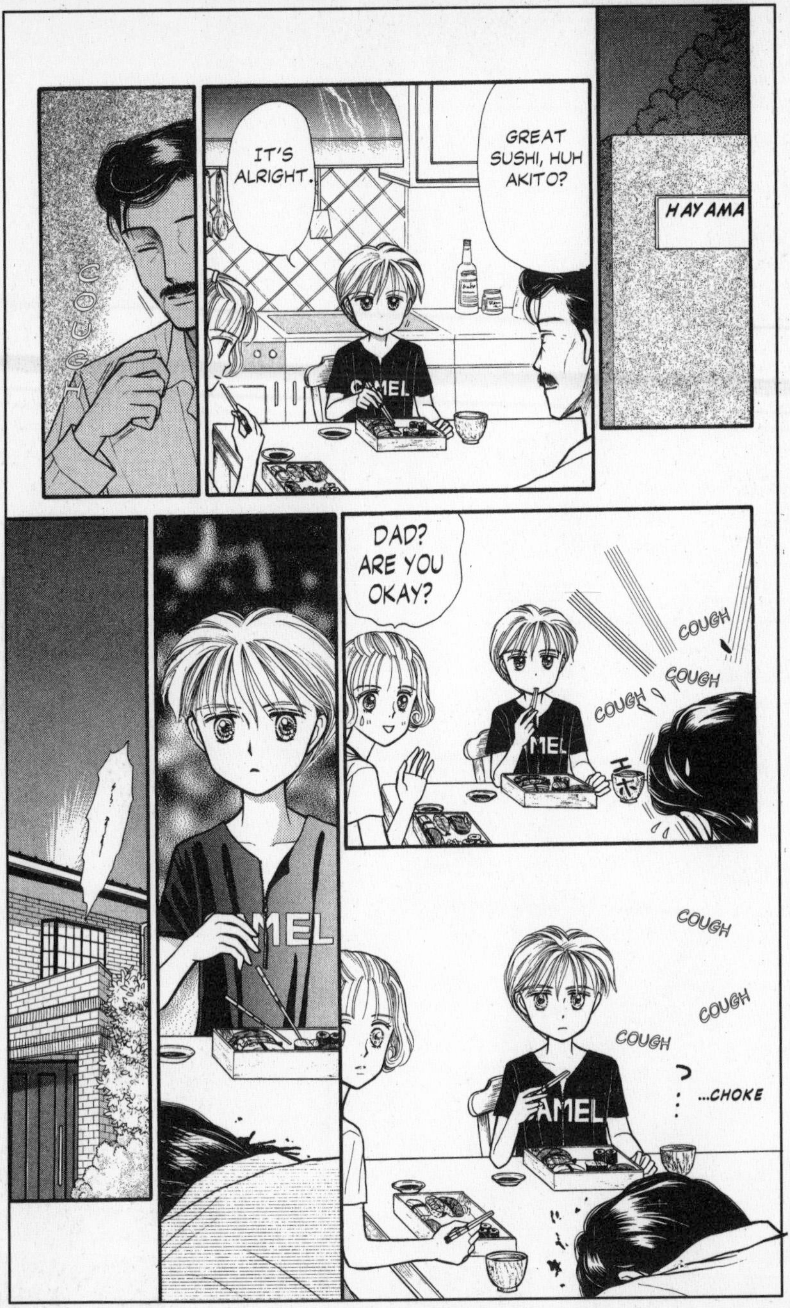

HAYAMA
GREAT SUSHI, HUH AKITO?
IT'S ALRIGHT.
COUGH
DAD? ARE YOU OKAY?
COUGH
COUGH
COUGH
COUGH
COUGH
COUGH
...CHOKE

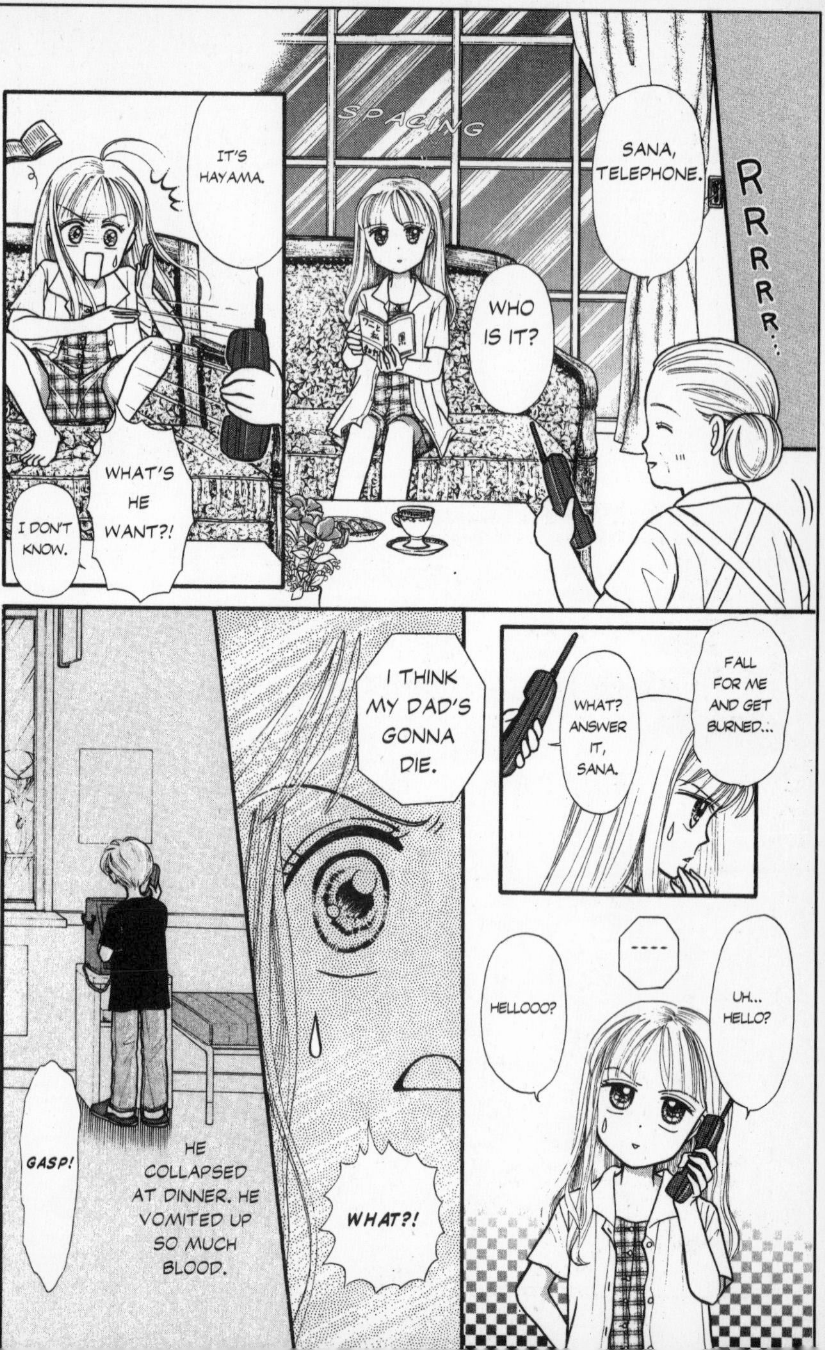
RRRRR...
SANA, TELEPHONE.
SPACING
WHO IS IT?
IT'S HAYAMA.
WHAT'S HE WANT?!
I DON'T KNOW.
FALL FOR ME AND GET BURNED...
WHAT? ANSWER IT, SANA.
UH... HELLO?

HELLOOO?
I THINK MY DAD'S GONNA DIE.
WHAT?!
HE COLLAPSED AT DINNER. HE VOMITED UP SO MUCH BLOOD.
GASP!

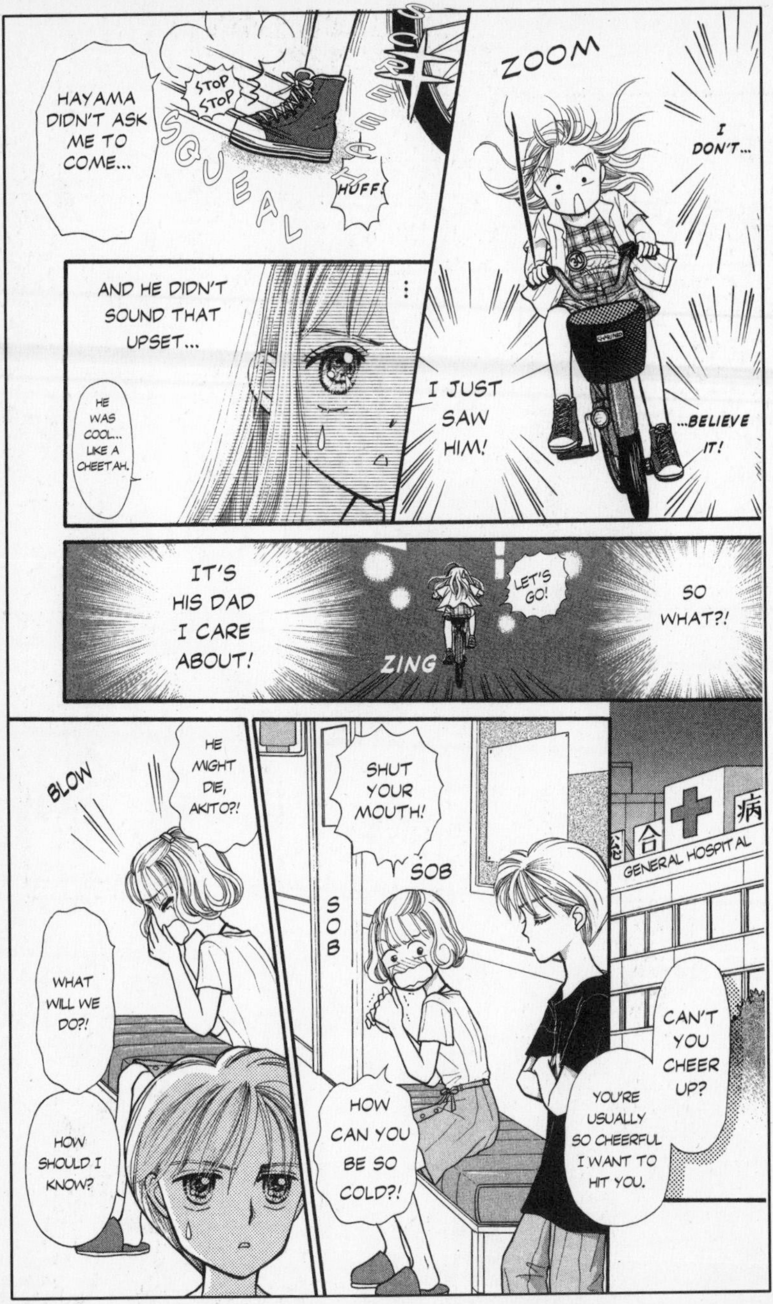
ZOOM
I DON'T...
...BELIEVE IT!
I JUST SAW HIM!
HAYAMA DIDN'T ASK ME TO COME...
STOP STOP
SCREECH
SQUEAL
HUFF!
AND HE DIDN'T SOUND THAT UPSET...
...
HE WAS COOL... LIKE A CHEETAH.
SO WHAT?!
LET'S GO!
IT'S HIS DAD I CARE ABOUT!
ZING
GENERAL HOSPITAL
CAN'T YOU CHEER UP?
YOU'RE USUALLY SO CHEERFUL I WANT TO HIT YOU.
SHUT YOUR MOUTH!
SOB
SOB
HOW CAN YOU BE SO COLD?!
HE MIGHT DIE, AKITO?!
BLOW
WHAT WILL WE DO?!
HOW SHOULD I KNOW?

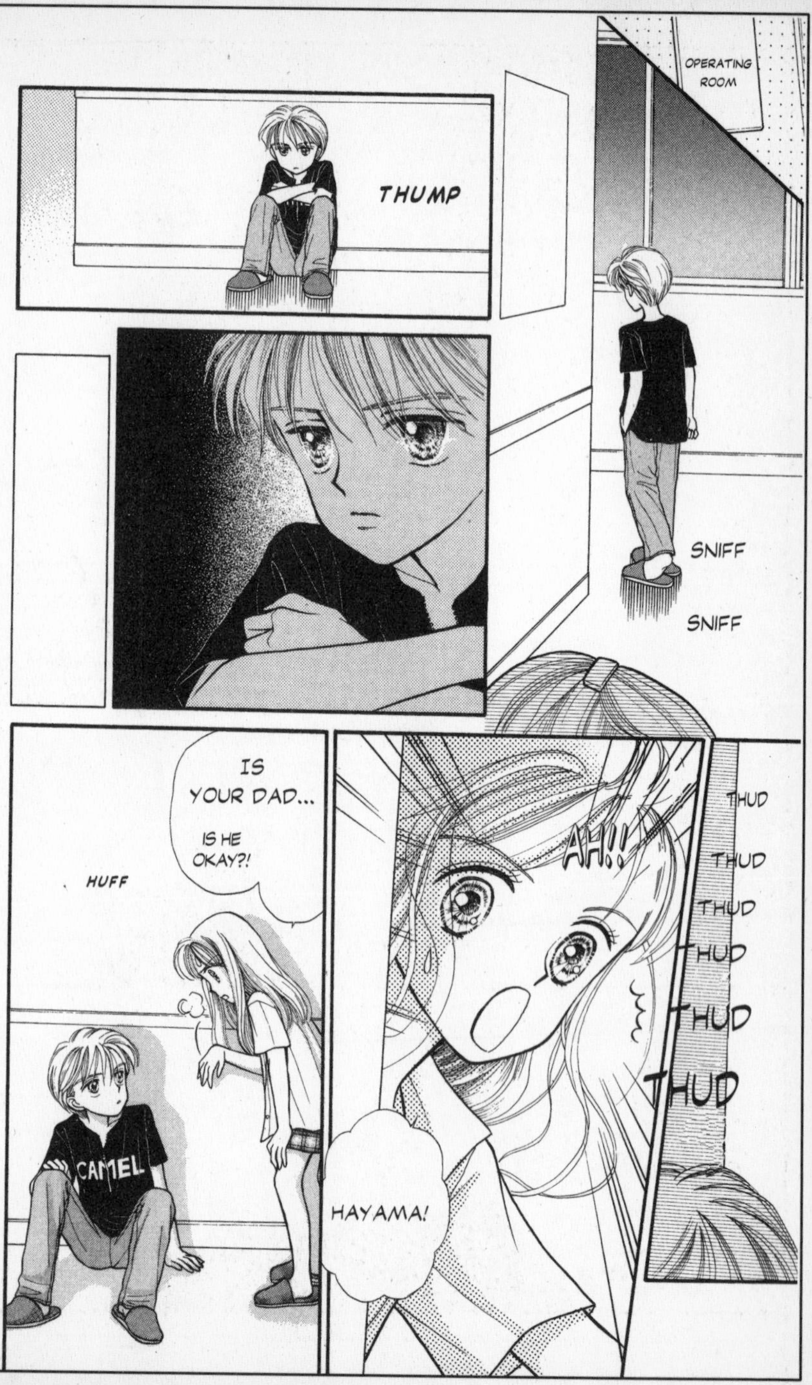
OPERATING ROOM
SNIFF
SNIFF
THUMP
THUD
THUD
THUD
THUD
THUD
THUD
AH!!
HAYAMA!
HUFF
IS YOUR DAD...
IS HE OKAY?!
CAMEL

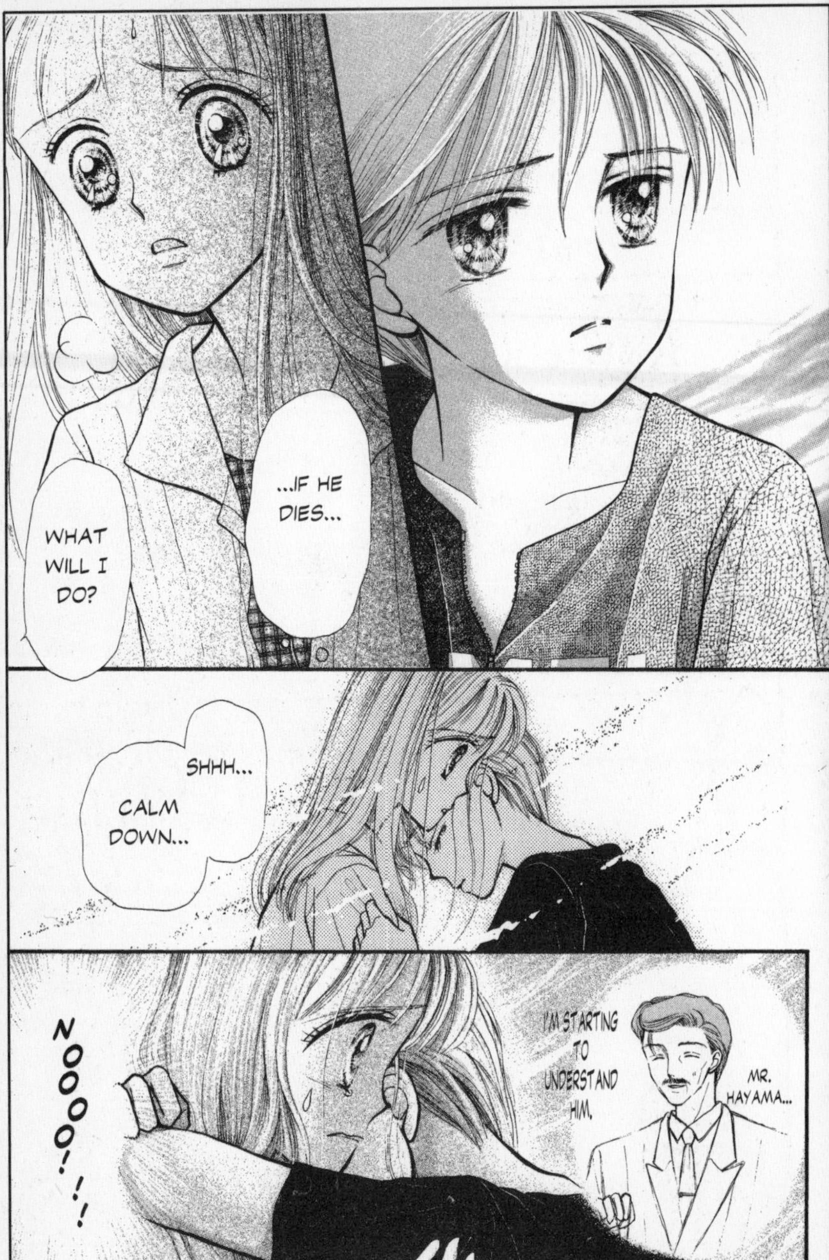
...IF HE DIES...
WHAT WILL I DO?
SHHH... CALM DOWN...
MR. HAYAMA...
I'M STARTING TO UNDERSTAND HIM.
NOOOOO!!!

CHILD'S TOY EXTRA:

CHILD'S TOY WEATHER REPORT

Ribon magazine's editor-in-chief Mr. Nah's version

TODAY'S WEATHER ...
......
IT RAINS WHEN IT RAINS.
IT'S SUNNY WHEN IT'S SUNNY.
THAT'S HOW LIFE IS.
......
RIBON
......

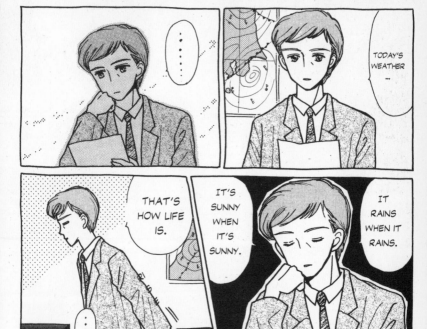

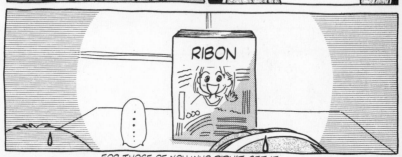

FOR THOSE OF YOU WHO DIDN'T GET IT...
MR. NAH IS THE VERY TOP BOSS OF
RIBON MAGAZINE (WHERE CHILD'S TOY WAS FIRST PUBLISHED).

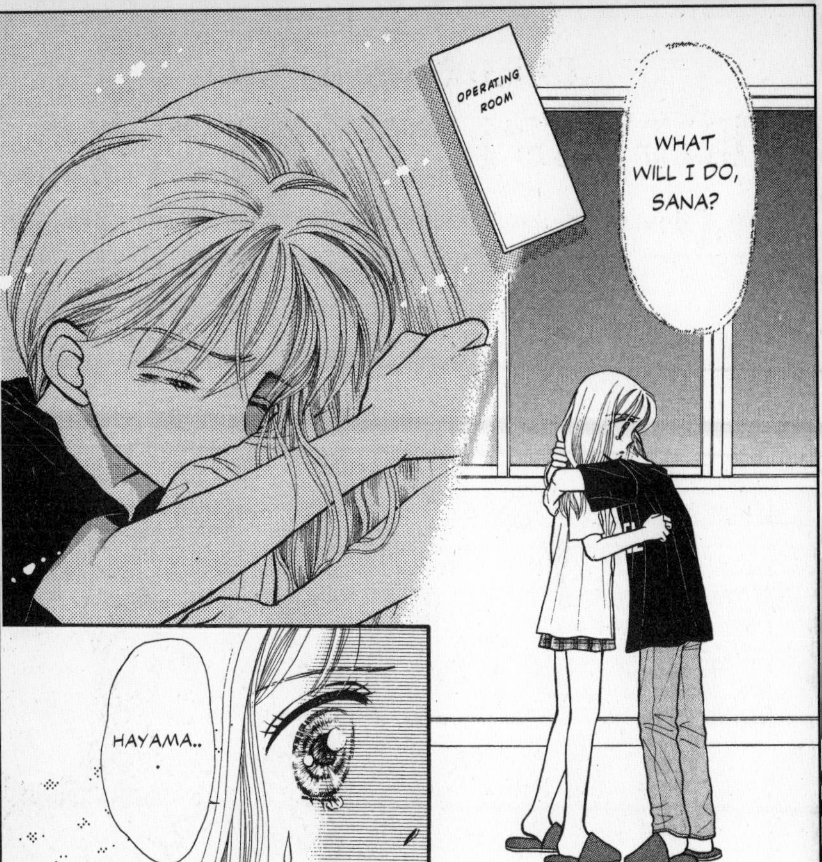
OPERATING ROOM
WHAT WILL I DO, SANA?
HAYAMA..

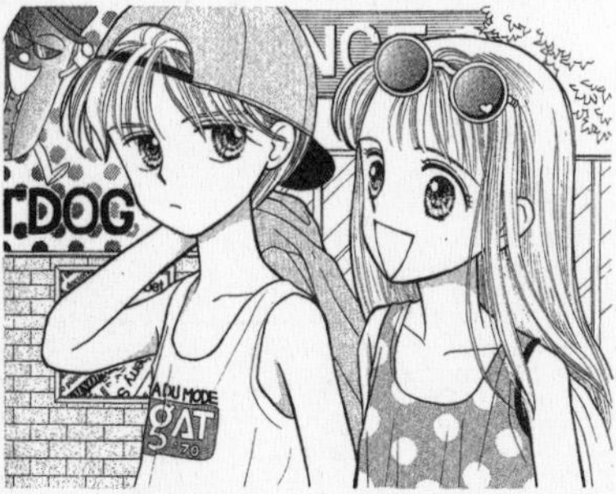

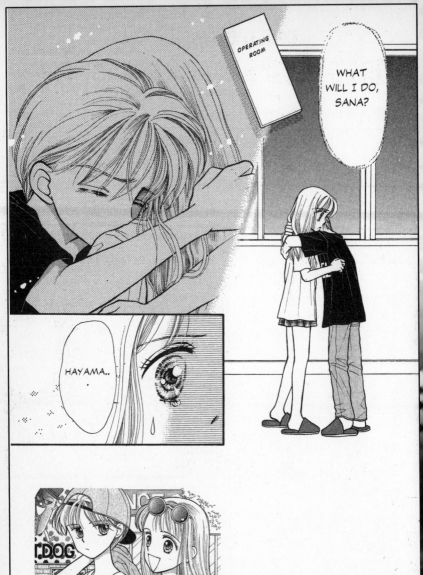

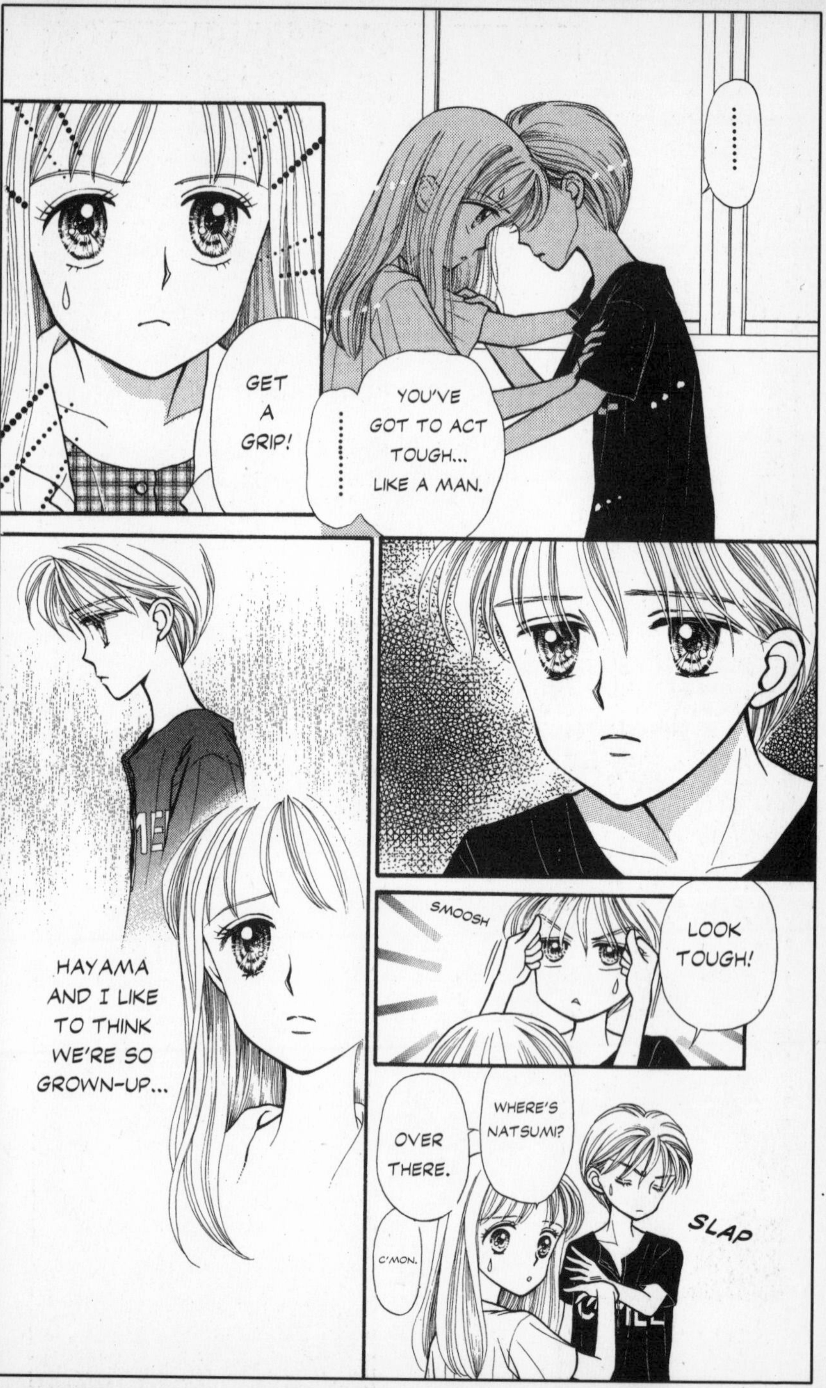
......
YOU'VE GOT TO ACT TOUGH... LIKE A MAN.
......
GET A GRIP!
SMOOSH
LOOK TOUGH!
WHERE'S NATSUMI?
OVER THERE.
SLAP
C'MON.
HAYAMA AND I LIKE TO THINK WE'RE SO GROWN-UP...

SOMETHING LIKE THIS...

...MAKES US REALIZE...

...WE'RE STILL JUST KIDS.

WITHOUT OUR PARENTS...

...WE'D HAVE NO IDEA WHAT TO DO.

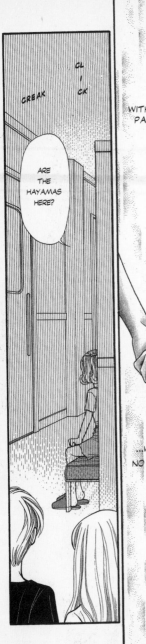

CL I CK

CREAK

ARE THE HAYAMAS HERE?

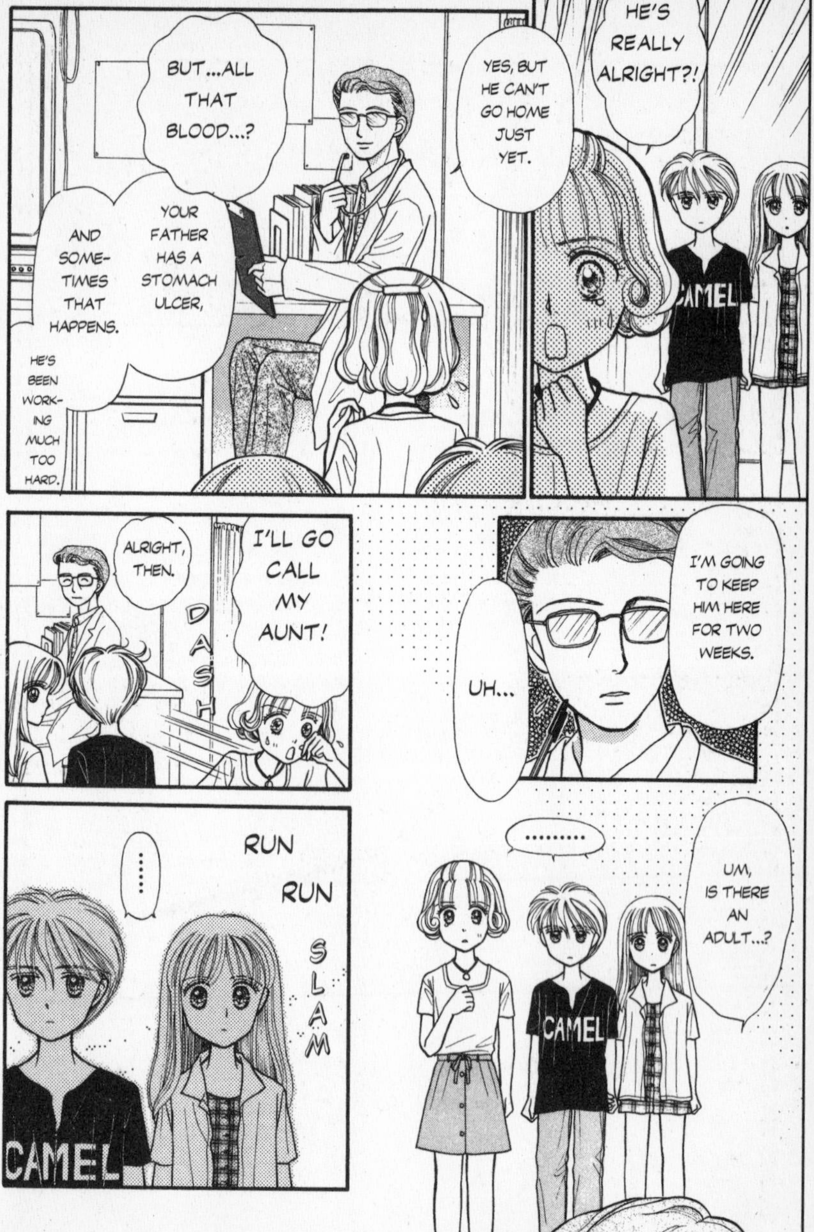
HE'S REALLY ALRIGHT?!
YES, BUT HE CAN'T GO HOME JUST YET.
BUT...ALL THAT BLOOD...?
YOUR FATHER HAS A STOMACH ULCER,
AND SOME-TIMES THAT HAPPENS.
HE'S BEEN WORK-ING MUCH TOO HARD.
I'M GOING TO KEEP HIM HERE FOR TWO WEEKS.
UH...
UM, IS THERE AN ADULT...?
....
ALRIGHT, THEN.
I'LL GO CALL MY AUNT!
DASH
.....
RUN
RUN
SLAM
CAMEL

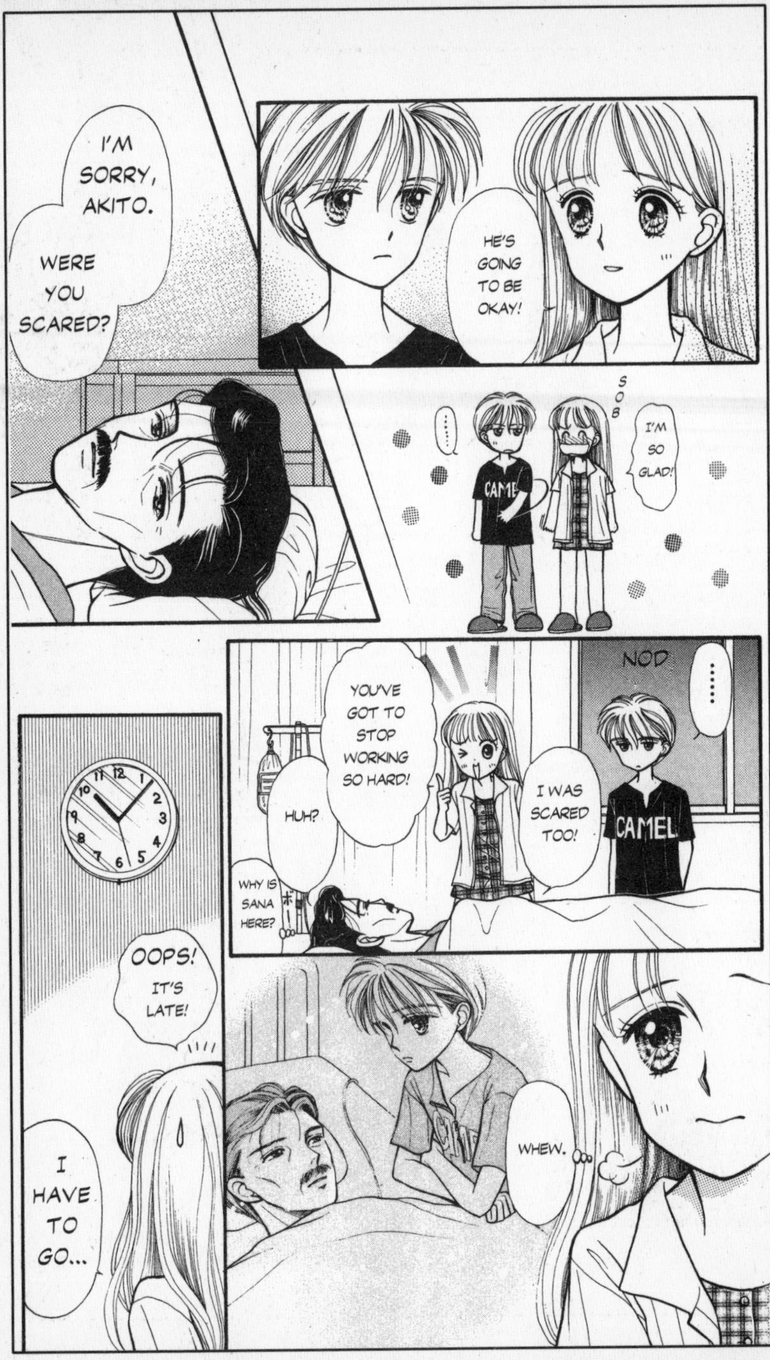
HE'S GOING TO BE OKAY!
SOB
I'M SO GLAD!
......
I'M SORRY, AKITO.
WERE YOU SCARED?
NOD
......
I WAS SCARED TOO!
YOU'VE GOT TO STOP WORKING SO HARD!
HUH?
WHY IS SANA HERE?
WHEW.
OOPS! IT'S LATE!
I HAVE TO GO...

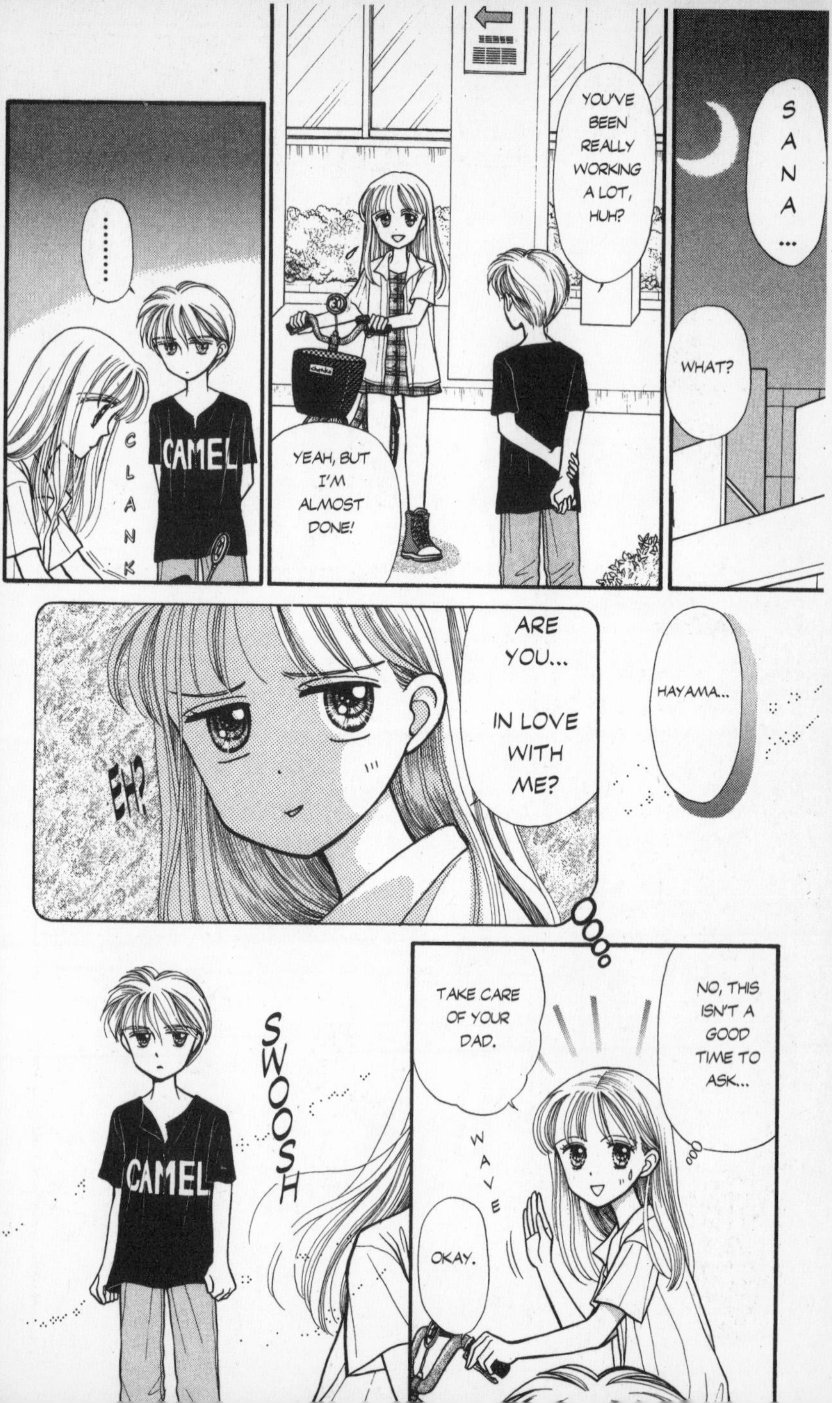
SANA...
WHAT?
YOU'VE BEEN REALLY WORKING A LOT, HUH?
YEAH, BUT I'M ALMOST DONE!
......
CLANK
CAMEL
HAYAMA...
ARE YOU... IN LOVE WITH ME?
EH?
NO, THIS ISN'T A GOOD TIME TO ASK...
TAKE CARE OF YOUR DAD.
WAVE
OKAY.
SWOOSH
CAMEL

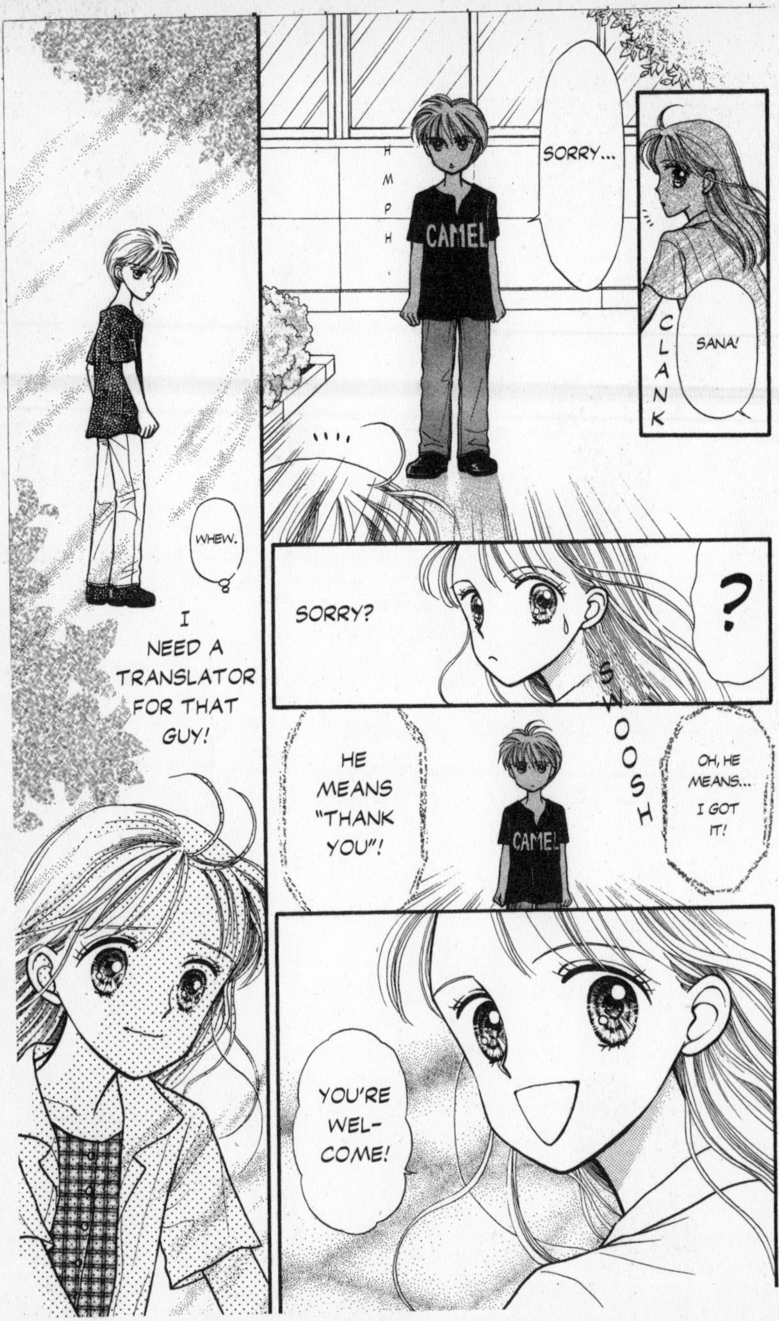

CLANK
SANA!
SORRY...
HMPH.
''''
?
SORRY?
SWOOSH
OH, HE MEANS... I GOT IT!
HE MEANS "THANK YOU"!
YOU'RE WEL-COME!
WHEW.
I NEED A TRANSLATOR FOR THAT GUY!

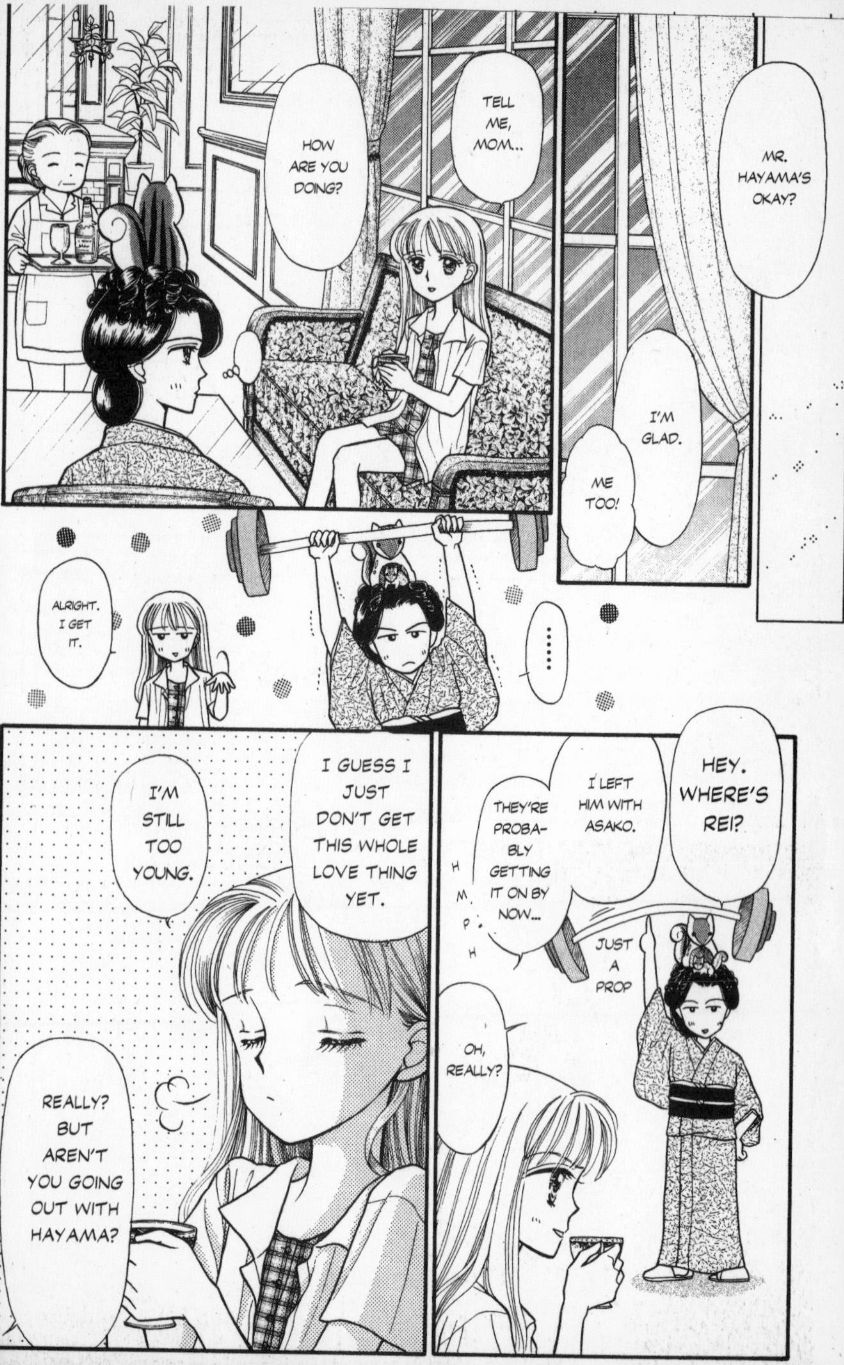
MR. HAYAMA'S OKAY?
I'M GLAD.
ME TOO!
TELL ME, MOM...
HOW ARE YOU DOING?
......
ALRIGHT. I GET IT.
HEY. WHERE'S REI?
I LEFT HIM WITH ASAKO.
THEY'RE PROBA-BLY GETTING IT ON BY NOW...
HMPH
JUST A PROP
OH, REALLY?
I GUESS I JUST DON'T GET THIS WHOLE LOVE THING YET.
I'M STILL TOO YOUNG.
REALLY? BUT AREN'T YOU GOING OUT WITH HAYAMA?

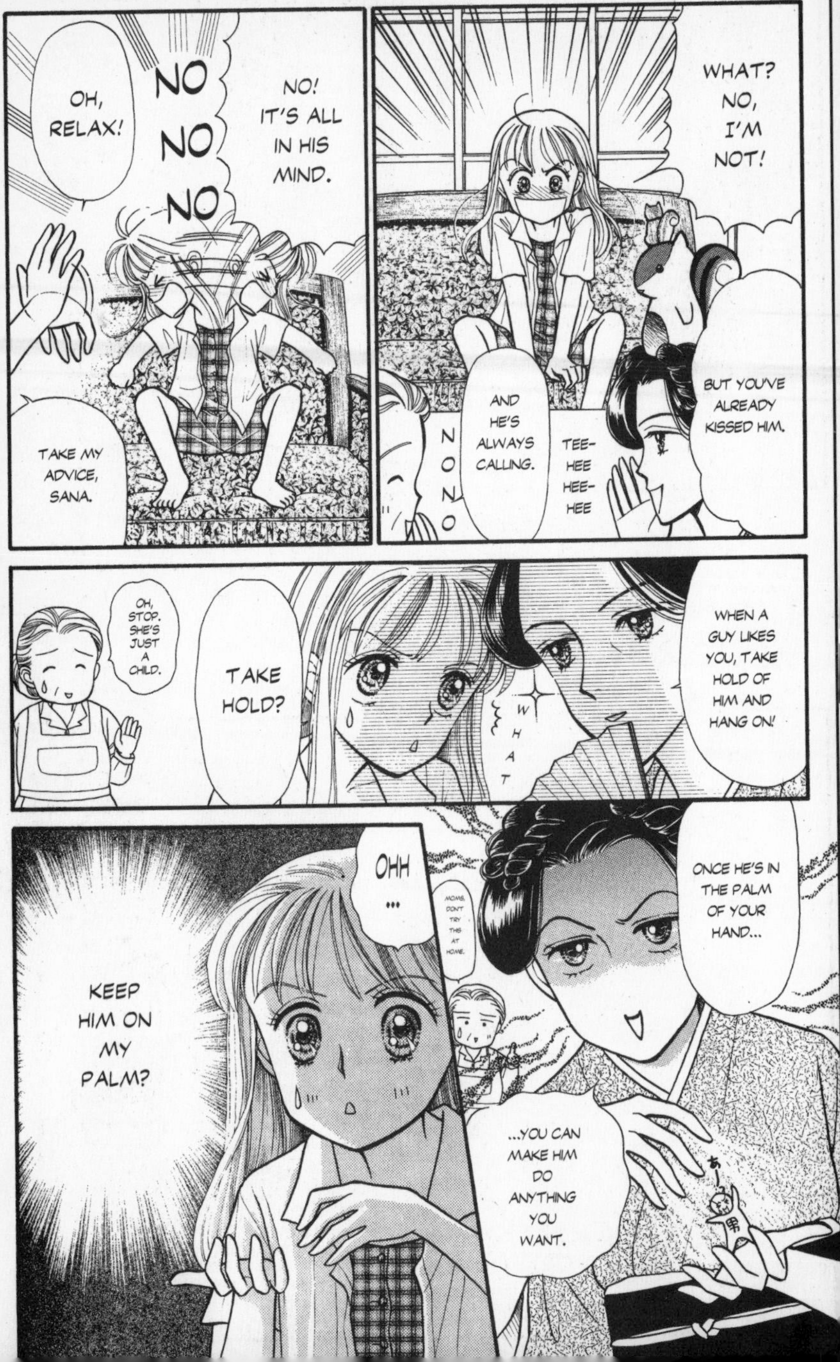
WHAT? NO, I'M NOT!
BUT YOU'VE ALREADY KISSED HIM.
TEE-HEE HEE-HEE
AND HE'S ALWAYS CALLING.
NO NO
NO! IT'S ALL IN HIS MIND.
NO NO NO
OH, RELAX!
TAKE MY ADVICE, SANA.
WHEN A GUY LIKES YOU, TAKE HOLD OF HIM AND HANG ON!
WHAT
TAKE HOLD?
OH, STOP. SHE'S JUST A CHILD.
ONCE HE'S IN THE PALM OF YOUR HAND...
OHH ...
MOMS, DON'T TRY THIS AT HOME.
...YOU CAN MAKE HIM DO ANYTHING YOU WANT.
男
KEEP HIM ON MY PALM?

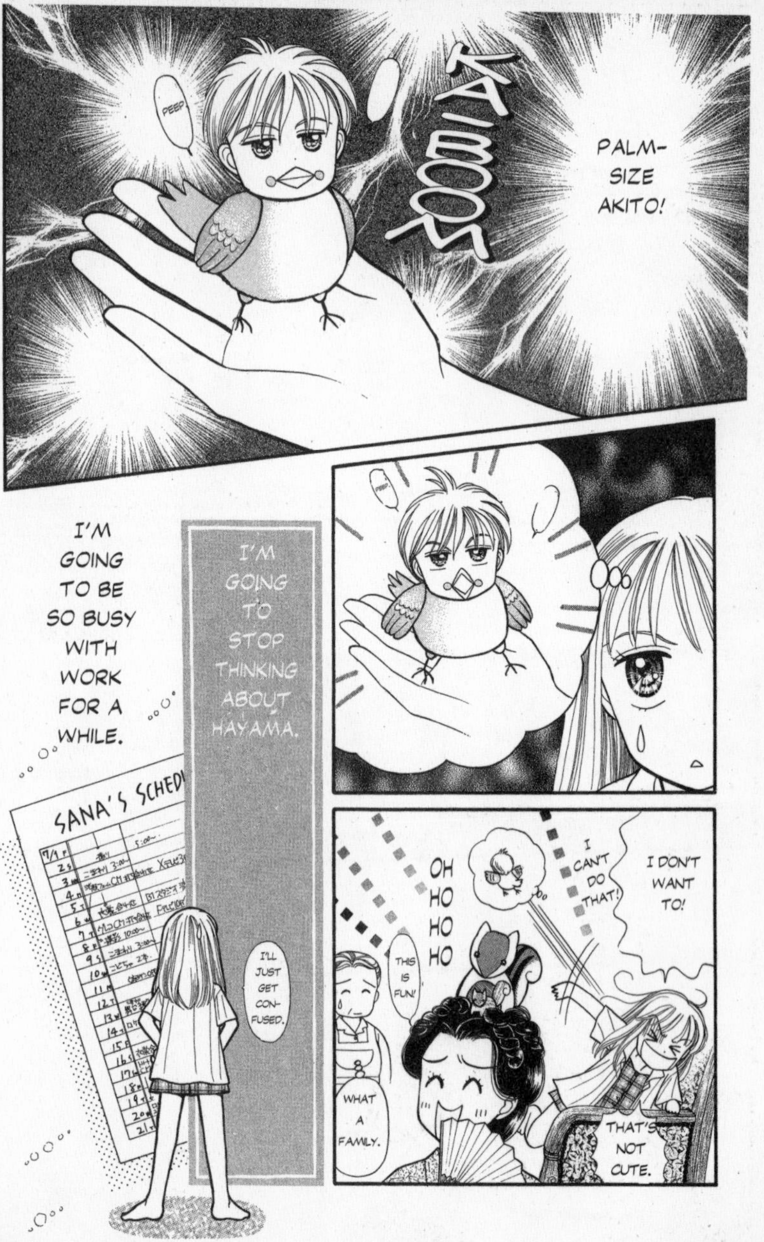
PALM-SIZE AKITO!
KA-BOOM
PEEP
PEEP
I DON'T WANT TO!
I CAN'T DO THAT!
OH HO HO HO
THIS IS FUN!
THAT'S NOT CUTE.
WHAT A FAMILY.
I'M GOING TO STOP THINKING ABOUT HAYAMA.
I'M GOING TO BE SO BUSY WITH WORK FOR A WHILE.
I'LL JUST GET CON-FUSED.
SANA'S SCHED

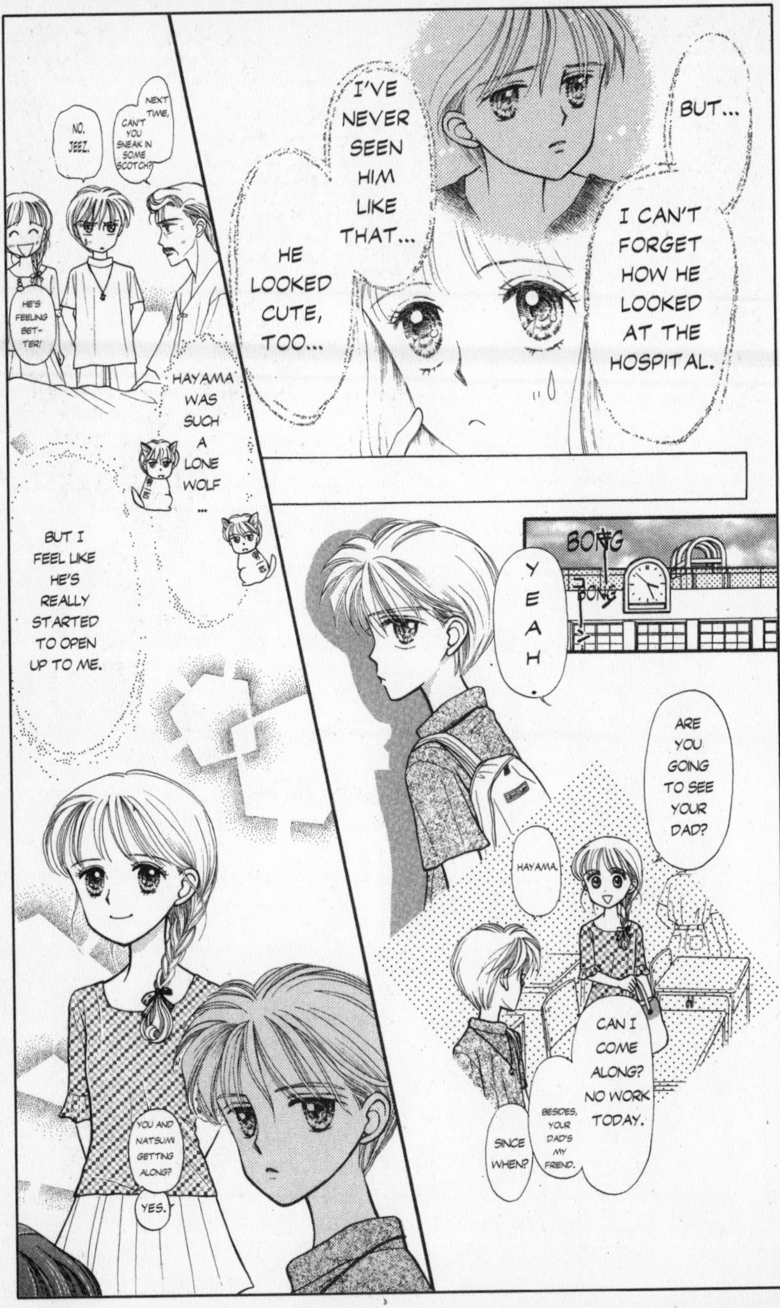
I'VE NEVER SEEN HIM LIKE THAT...
BUT...
I CAN'T FORGET HOW HE LOOKED AT THE HOSPITAL.
HE LOOKED CUTE, TOO...
BONG
BONG
HAYAMA.
ARE YOU GOING TO SEE YOUR DAD?
YEAH.
CAN I COME ALONG? NO WORK TODAY.
BESIDES, YOUR DAD'S MY FRIEND.
SINCE WHEN?
NEXT TIME, CAN'T YOU SNEAK IN SOME SCOTCH?
NO. JEEZ.
HE'S FEELING BETTER!
HAYAMA WAS SUCH A LONE WOLF...
BUT I FEEL LIKE HE'S REALLY STARTED TO OPEN UP TO ME.
YOU AND NATSUMI GETTING ALONG?
YES.

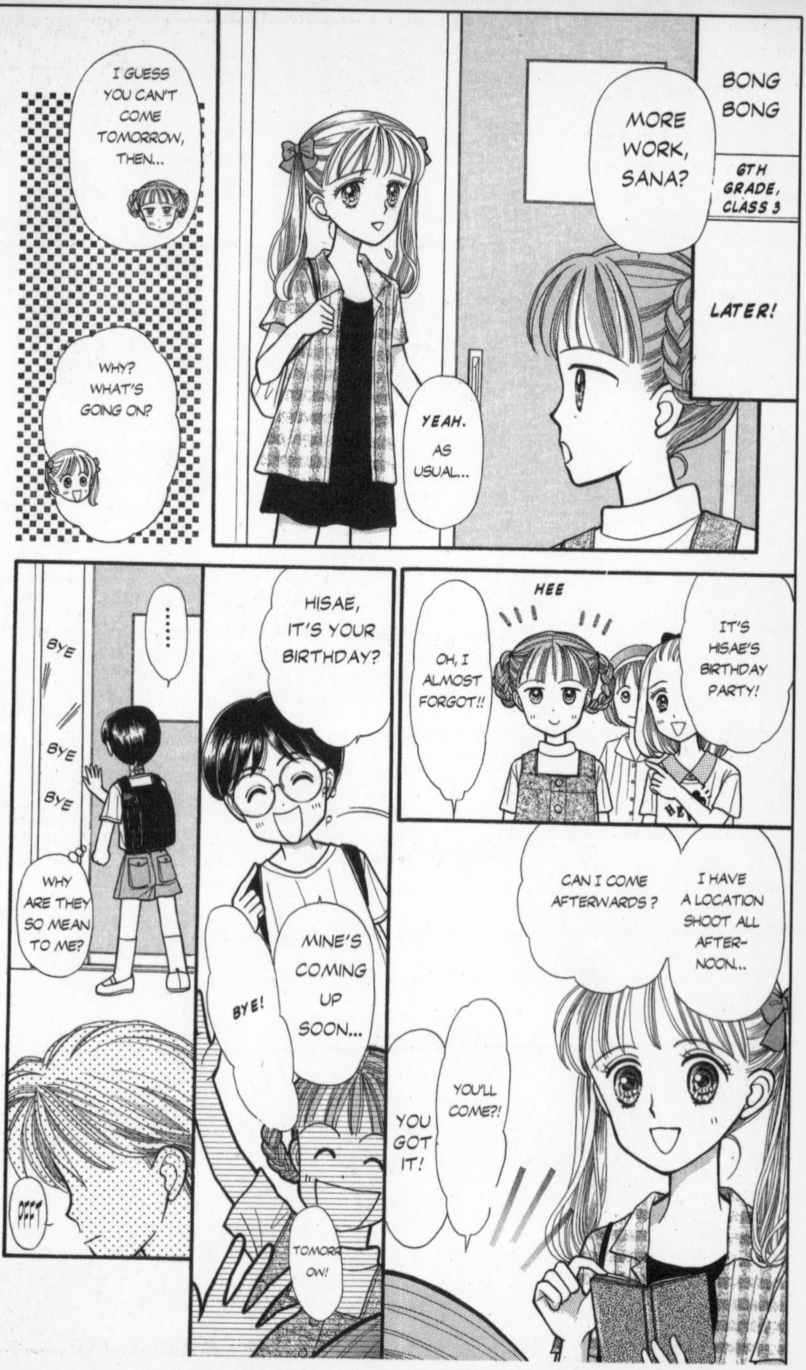
BONG BONG
6TH GRADE, CLASS 3
LATER!
MORE WORK, SANA?
YEAH. AS USUAL...
I GUESS YOU CAN'T COME TOMORROW, THEN...
WHY? WHAT'S GOING ON?
IT'S HISAE'S BIRTHDAY PARTY!
HEE
OH, I ALMOST FORGOT!!
I HAVE A LOCATION SHOOT ALL AFTER-NOON...
CAN I COME AFTERWARDS?
YOU'LL COME?!
YOU GOT IT!
HISAE, IT'S YOUR BIRTHDAY?
MINE'S COMING UP SOON...
BYE!
TOMORR OW!
......
BYE
BYE
BYE
WHY ARE THEY SO MEAN TO ME?
PFFT

All About Dodge Ball

Writing so much about elementary school makes me think a lot about my elementary school days. Did you have to play dodge ball in elementary school? We did, and I hated it. I was totally scared of the ball and trying to hit people with it made me really nervous. But even though I was freaking out I somehow always managed to stay on the court until the very end. When the game was finally over I felt like the whole world had come to a stop. When I got a little older, I learned about cutting class, so after that I always avoided dodge ball. I don't know what it was. I liked other ball games and I was even on a basketball team! I just didn't like dodge ball!

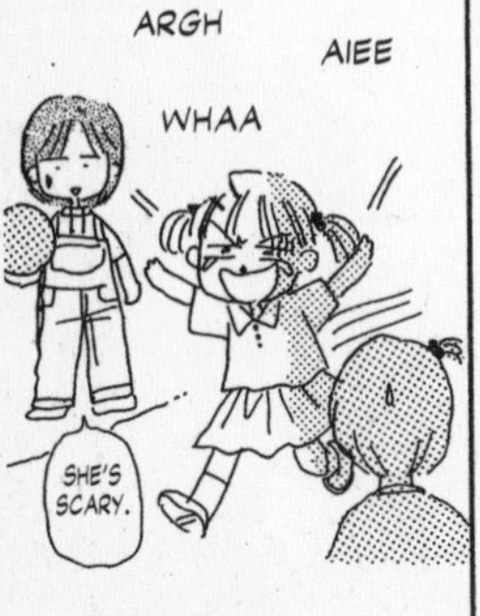
AIEE
ARGH
WHAA
SHE'S SCARY.

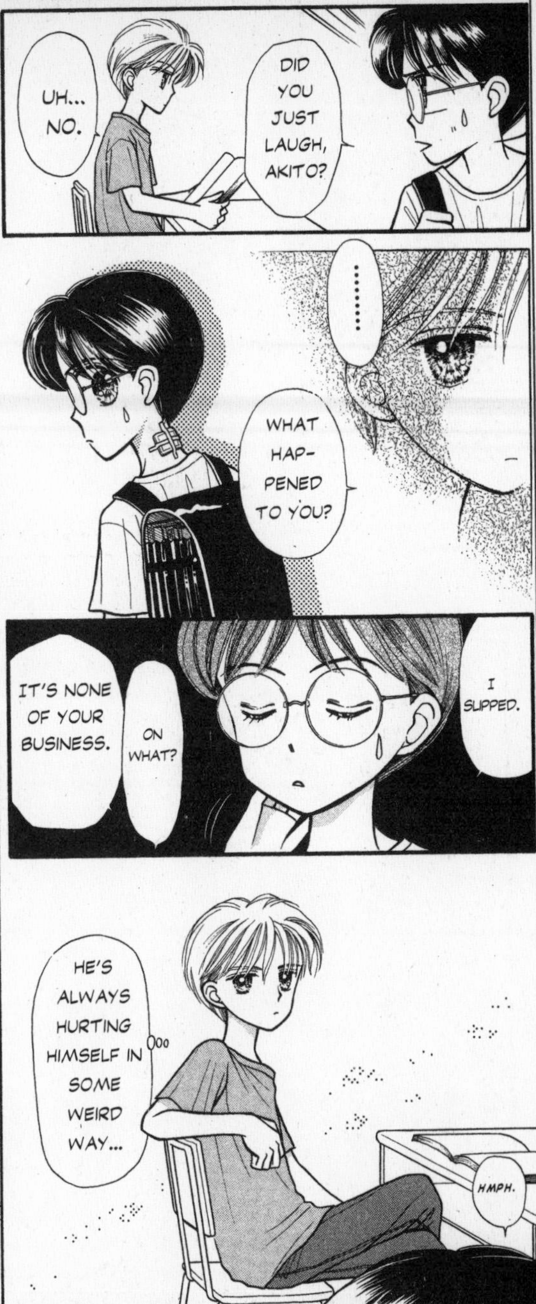
DID YOU JUST LAUGH, AKITO?
UH... NO.
......
WHAT HAP-PENED TO YOU?
I SLIPPED.
ON WHAT?
IT'S NONE OF YOUR BUSINESS.
HMPH.
HE'S ALWAYS HURTING HIMSELF IN SOME WEIRD WAY...

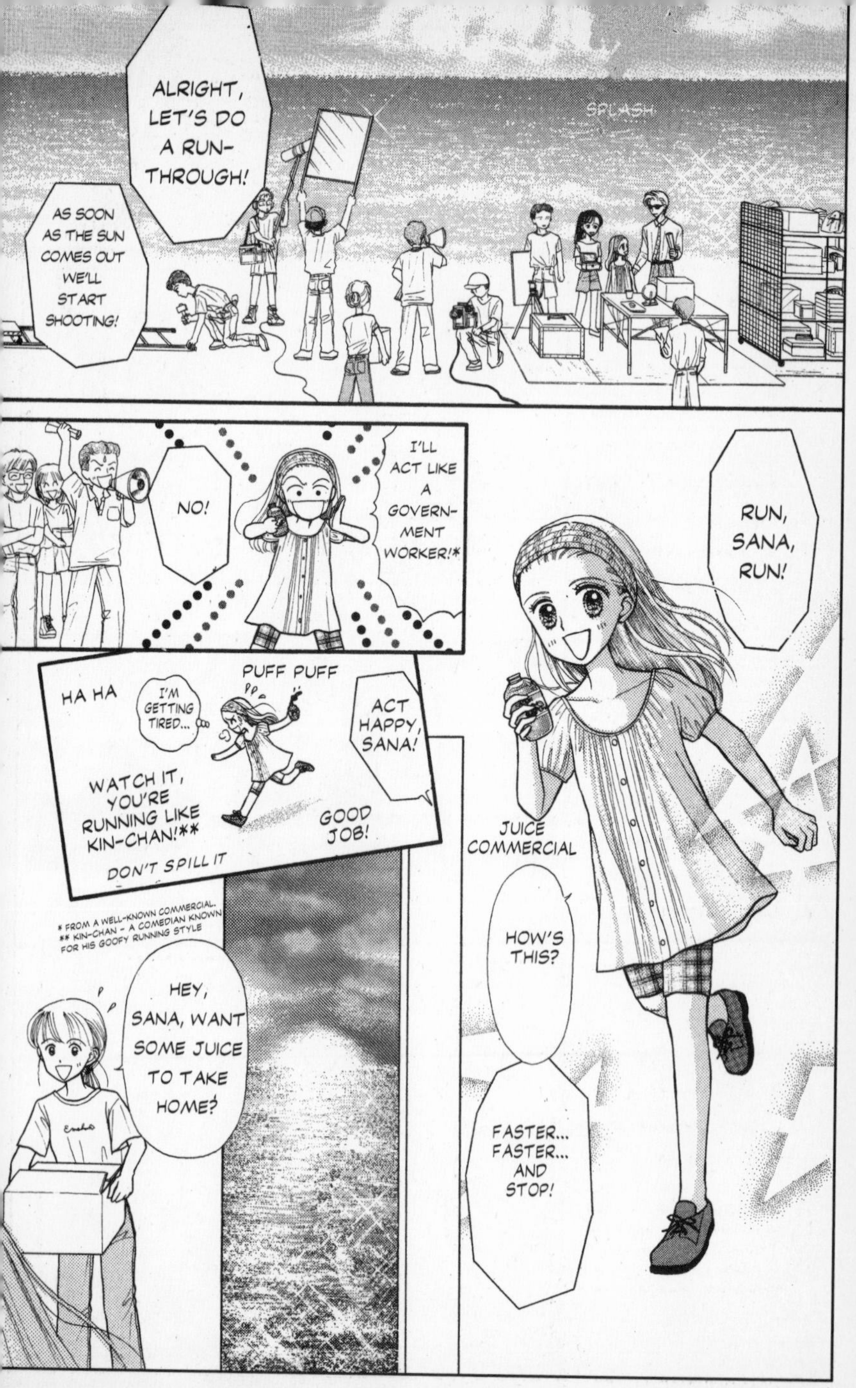
SPLASH
ALRIGHT, LET'S DO A RUN-THROUGH!
AS SOON AS THE SUN COMES OUT WE'LL START SHOOTING!
RUN, SANA, RUN!
JUICE COMMERCIAL
HOW'S THIS?
FASTER... FASTER... AND STOP!
I'LL ACT LIKE A GOVERNMENT WORKER!*
NO!
ACT HAPPY, SANA!
PUFF PUFF
I'M GETTING TIRED...
HA HA
GOOD JOB!
WATCH IT, YOU'RE RUNNING LIKE KIN-CHAN!**
DON'T SPILL IT
HEY, SANA, WANT SOME JUICE TO TAKE HOME?

* FROM A WELL-KNOWN COMMERCIAL.
** KIN-CHAN - A COMEDIAN KNOWN FOR HIS GOOFY RUNNING STYLE

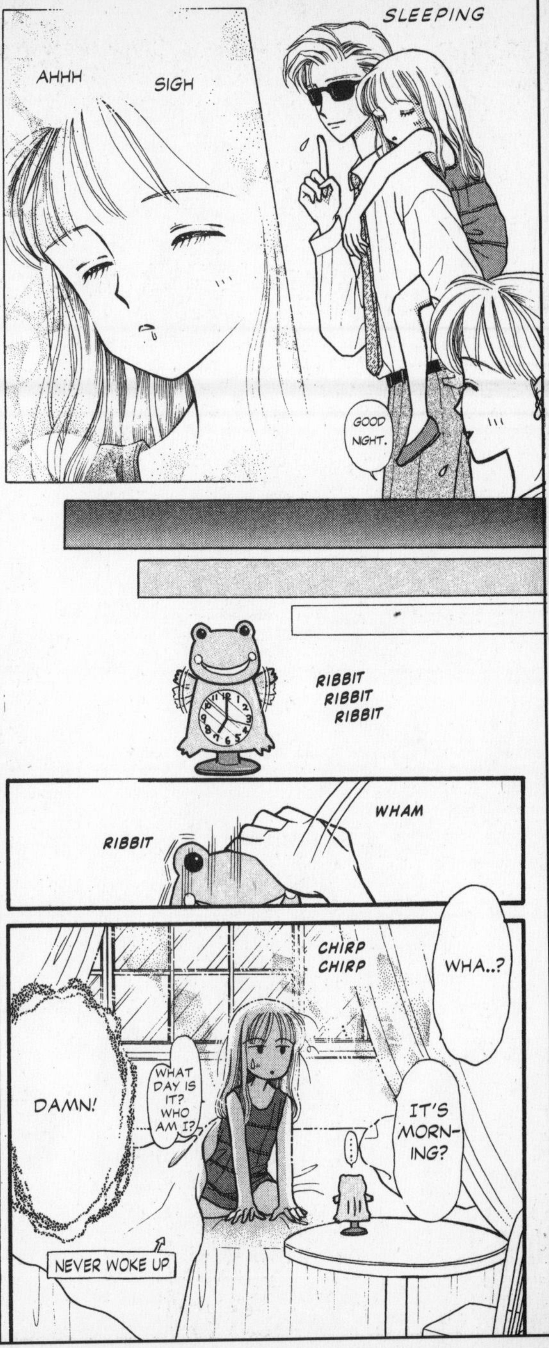
SLEEPING
GOOD NIGHT.
SIGH
AHHH
RIBBIT RIBBIT RIBBIT
WHAM
RIBBIT
WHA..?
IT'S MORN-ING?
CHIRP CHIRP
WHAT DAY IS IT? WHO AM I?
DAMN!
NEVER WOKE UP

Extra Work

I'm doing a lot of work making drawings for Kodocha inserts* for Ribon Magazine and others. I knew it was going to be a lot of work, but didn't realize how hard it was actually going to be until I started doing it. Now that I'm doing all this extra work, I only have one day to work on the color piece for each story - when I'd rather have five! I'm not real happy about it, but my fans seem to really like the extras — so I'm gonna hang in there!

I was really happy to find out Kie-chan from Appare TV show** uses the "World Note" (one of the inserts I did). I'd love to see you guys using them too! If you get hold of any, please let me know what you think!

*Lots of Japanese magazines have inserts like she's talking about all kinds of stuff like postcards, stickers and notepads, featuring popular characters.

**a child actress that partly inspired Sana.

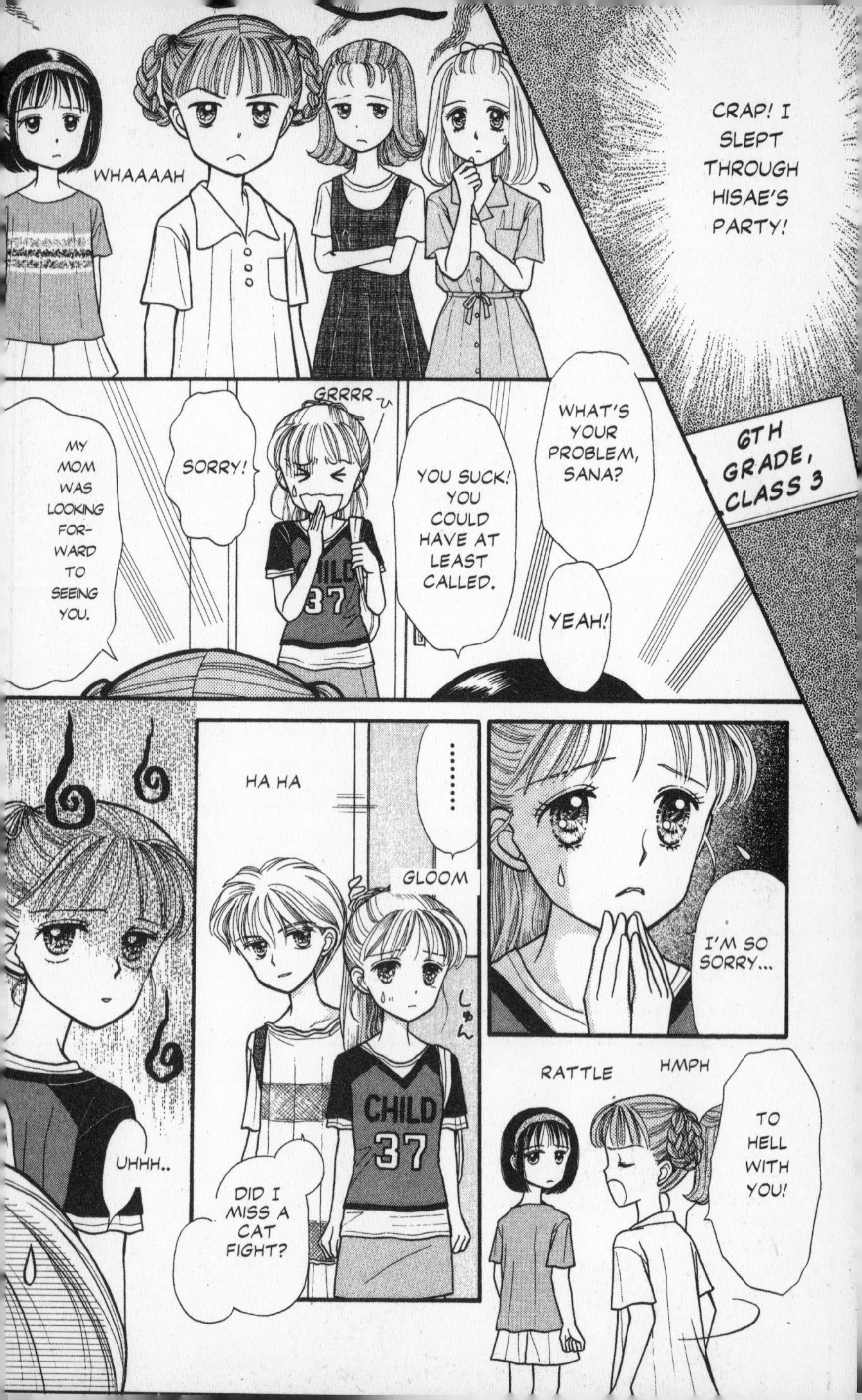
CRAP! I SLEPT THROUGH HISAE'S PARTY!
6TH GRADE, CLASS 3
WHAAAAH
WHAT'S YOUR PROBLEM, SANA?
YEAH!
YOU SUCK! YOU COULD HAVE AT LEAST CALLED.
GRRRR
SORRY!
MY MOM WAS LOOKING FOR-WARD TO SEEING YOU.
I'M SO SORRY...
HMPH
TO HELL WITH YOU!
RATTLE
......
HA HA
GLOOM
しゅん
DID I MISS A CAT FIGHT?
UHHH..

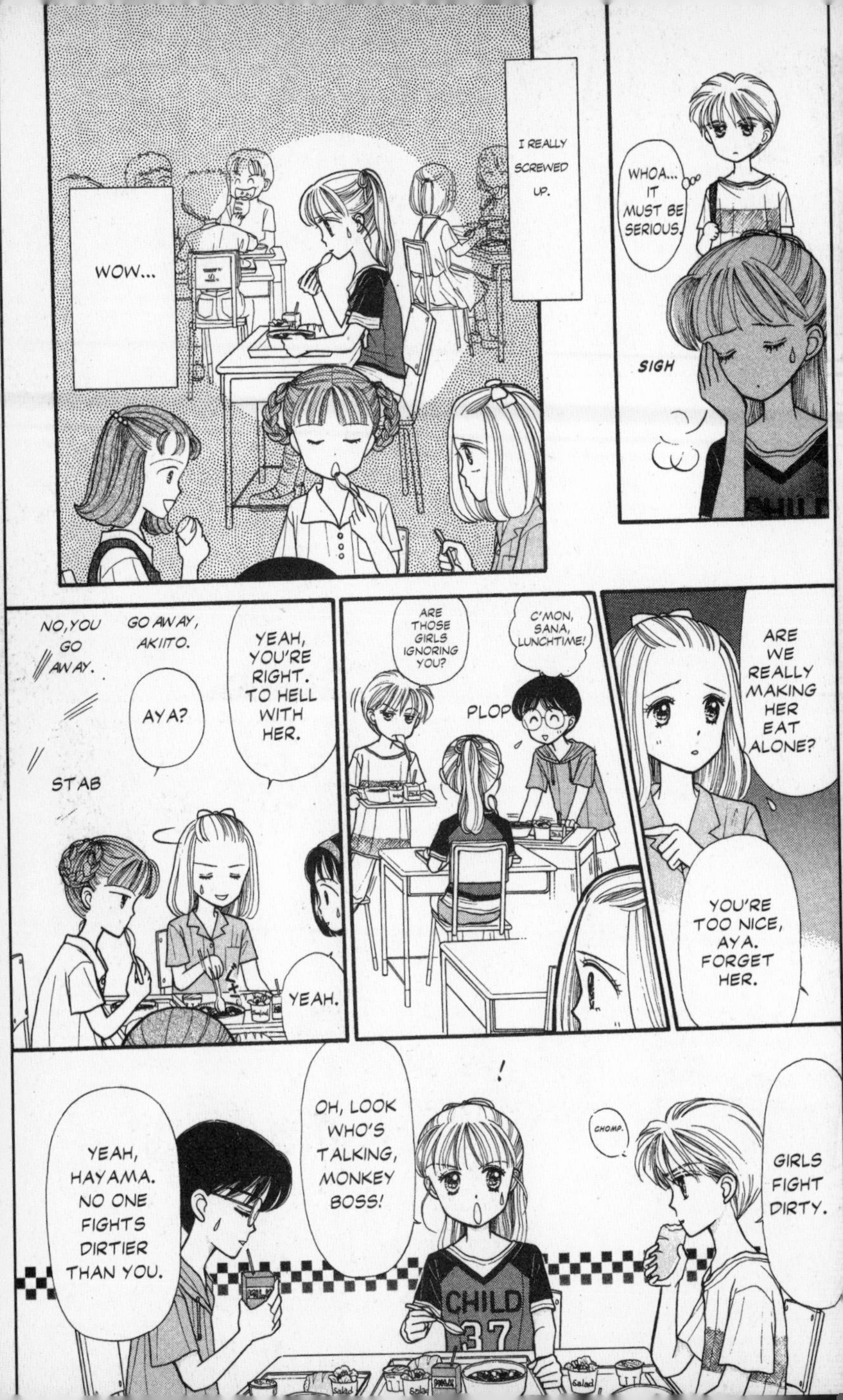

WHOA... IT MUST BE SERIOUS.
SIGH
I REALLY SCREWED UP.
WOW...
ARE WE REALLY MAKING HER EAT ALONE?
YOU'RE TOO NICE, AYA. FORGET HER.
C'MON, SANA, LUNCHTIME!
ARE THOSE GIRLS IGNORING YOU?
PLOP
YEAH, YOU'RE RIGHT. TO HELL WITH HER.
GO AWAY, AKIITO.
NO, YOU GO AWAY.
AYA?
STAB
YEAH.
GIRLS FIGHT DIRTY.
CHOMP.
!
OH, LOOK WHO'S TALKING, MONKEY BOSS!
YEAH, HAYAMA. NO ONE FIGHTS DIRTIER THAN YOU.

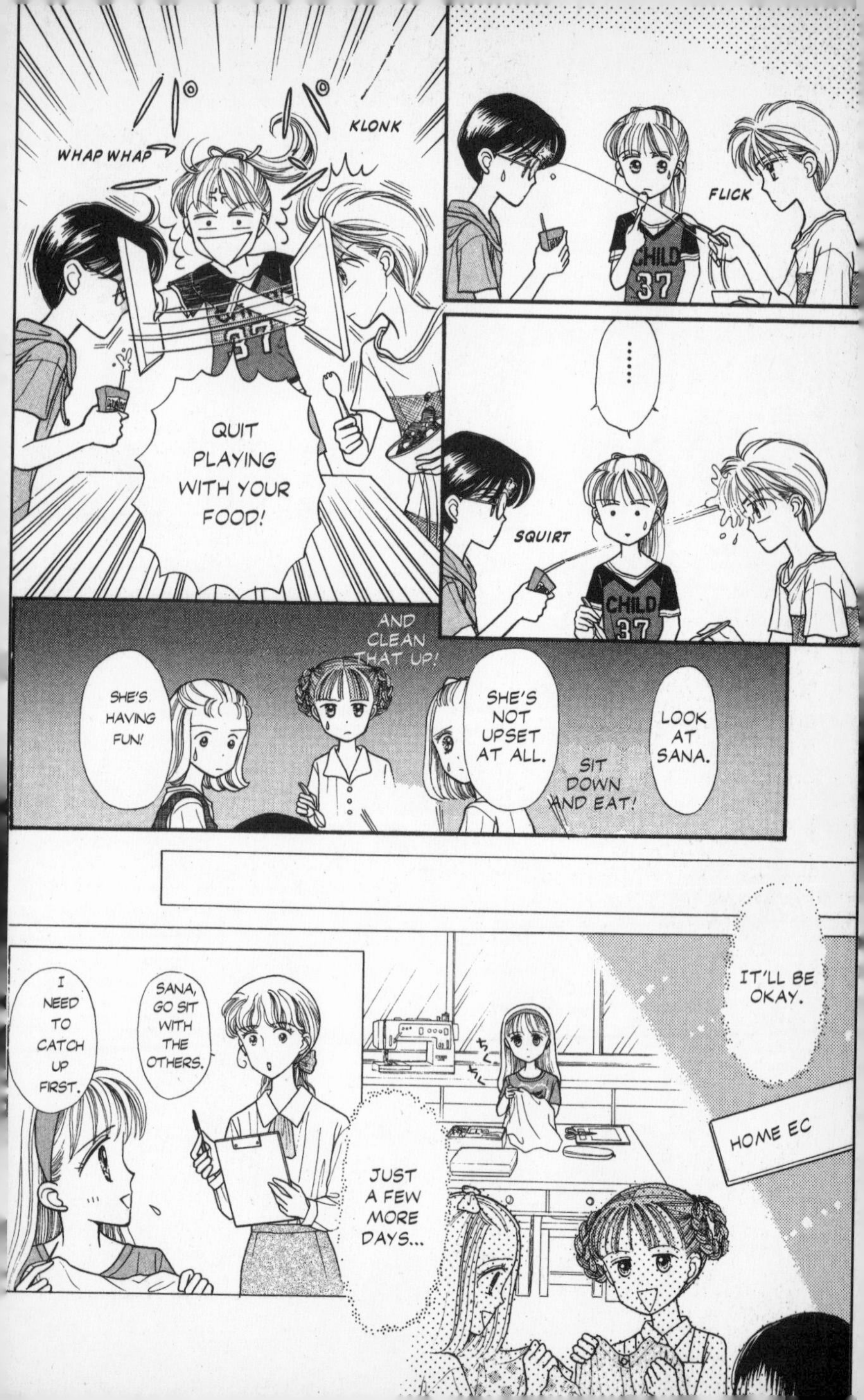
FLICK
......
SQUIRT
KLONK
WHAP WHAP
QUIT PLAYING WITH YOUR FOOD!
LOOK AT SANA.
SHE'S NOT UPSET AT ALL.
SIT DOWN AND EAT!
AND CLEAN THAT UP!
SHE'S HAVING FUN!
HOME EC
IT'LL BE OKAY.
JUST A FEW MORE DAYS...
SANA, GO SIT WITH THE OTHERS.
I NEED TO CATCH UP FIRST.

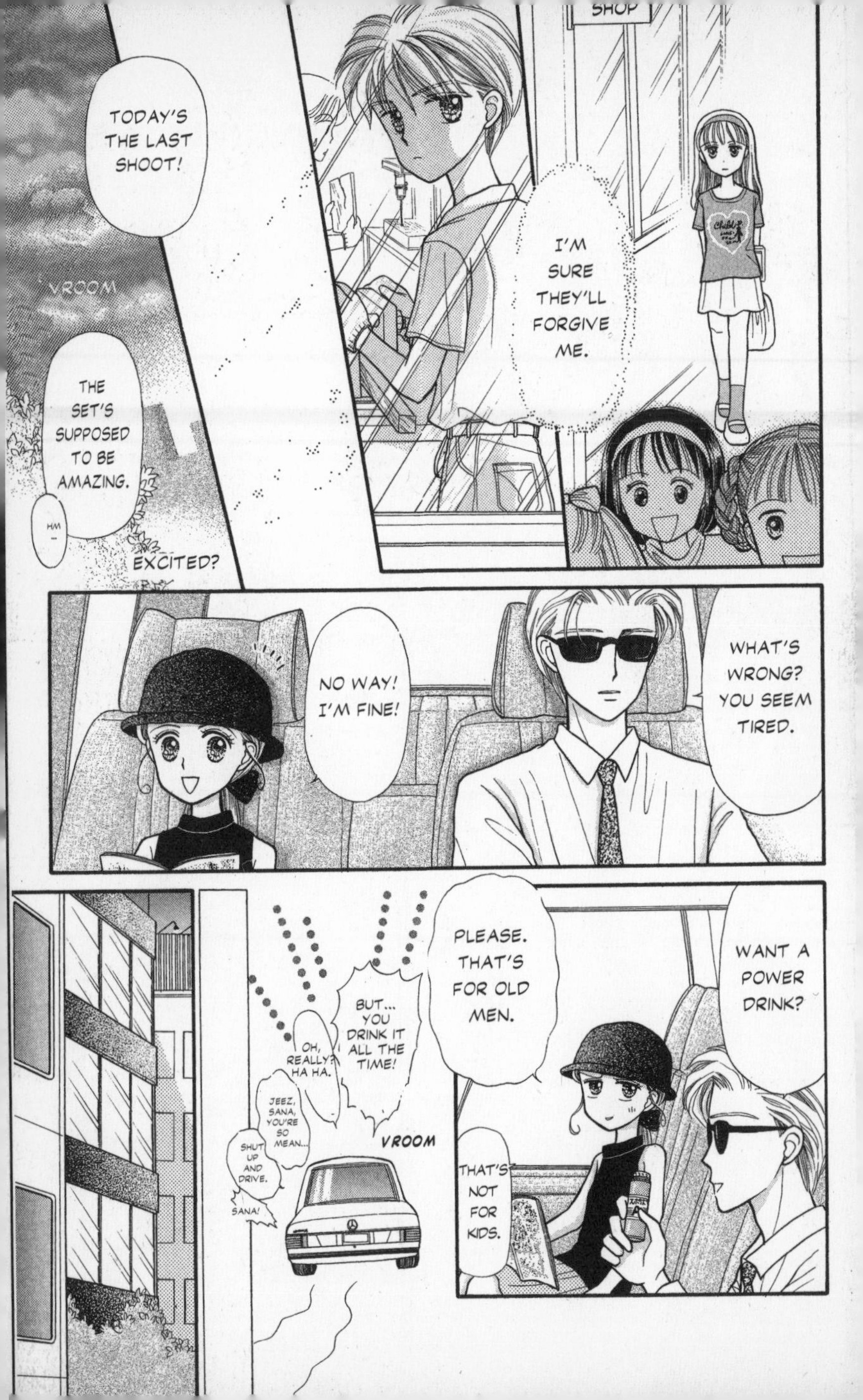
SHOP
I'M SURE THEY'LL FORGIVE ME.
TODAY'S THE LAST SHOOT!
VROOM
THE SET'S SUPPOSED TO BE AMAZING.
EXCITED?
HM ...
WHAT'S WRONG? YOU SEEM TIRED.
NO WAY! I'M FINE!
WANT A POWER DRINK?
PLEASE. THAT'S FOR OLD MEN.
THAT'S NOT FOR KIDS.
BUT... YOU DRINK IT ALL THE TIME!
OH, REALLY? HA HA.
JEEZ, SANA, YOU'RE SO MEAN...
SHUT UP AND DRIVE.
SANA!
VROOM

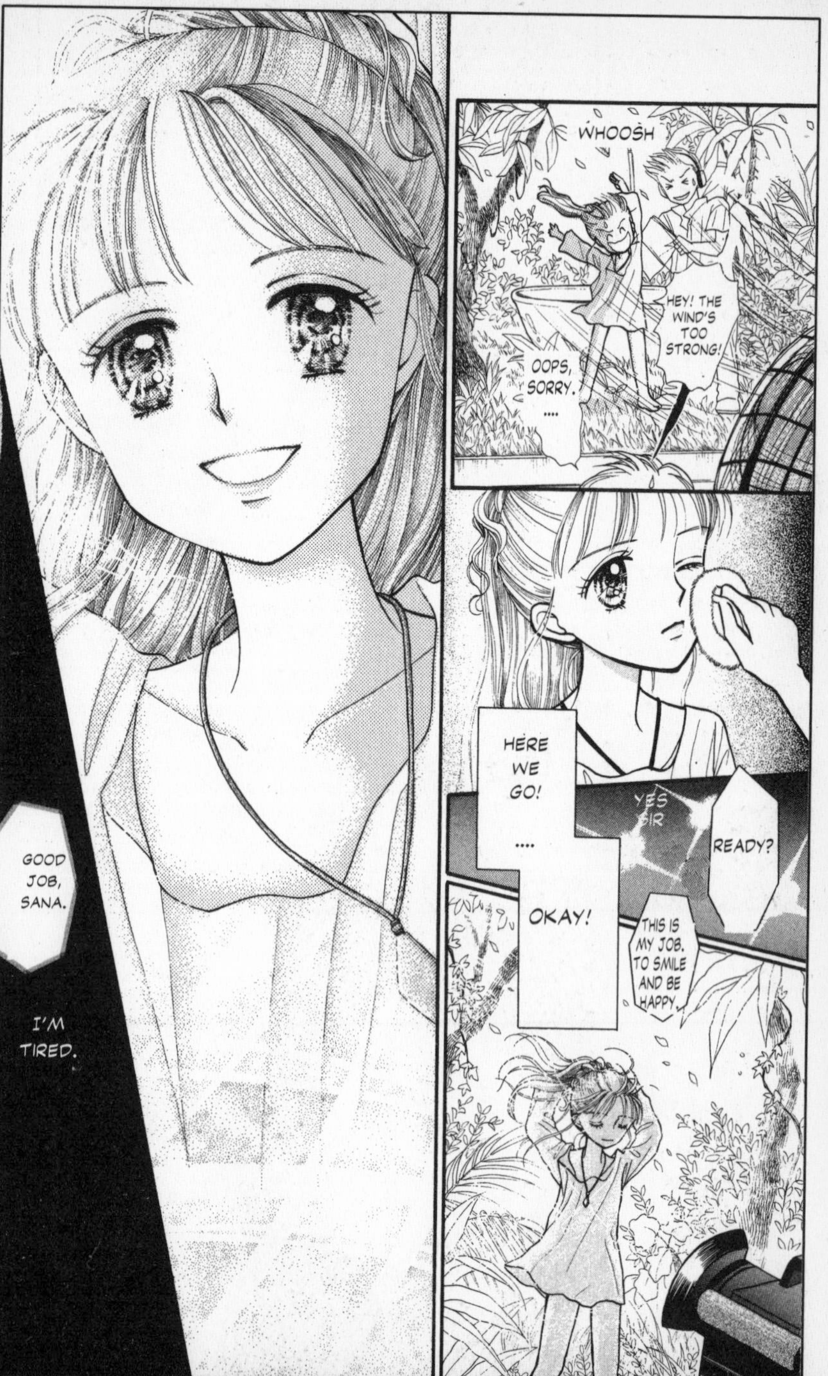
WHOOSH
HEY! THE WIND'S TOO STRONG!
OOPS, SORRY.
....
READY?
YES SIR
HERE WE GO!
....
OKAY!
THIS IS MY JOB. TO SMILE AND BE HAPPY.
GOOD JOB, SANA.
I'M TIRED.

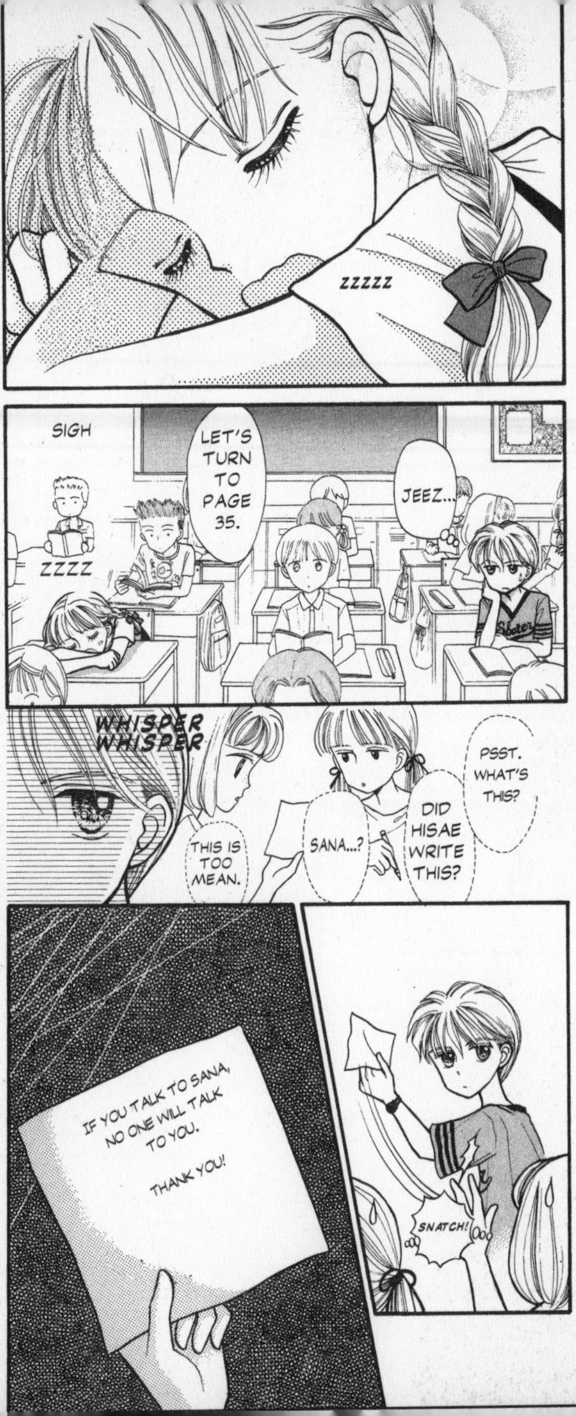
ZZZZZ
JEEZ...
LET'S TURN TO PAGE 35.
SIGH
ZZZZ
PSST. WHAT'S THIS?
WHISPER WHISPER
DID HISAE WRITE THIS?
SANA...?
THIS IS TOO MEAN.
SNATCH!
IF YOU TALK TO SANA, NO ONE WILL TALK TO YOU.
THANK YOU!

The Last Word

Well, it looks like I'm getting close to the end!* Thank you for reading this far. In book 1, I told you I was going to try and make this four volumes...but now I'm not sure if I'm going to make it. (Editor's note: Actually, Miss Obana ended up writing ten whole books! Yay!) I am sort of extending the story (for a good reason — what is it?). That's why the plot has been developing so slowly. Hee-hee. But fans seem to be enjoying the extra sub-plots I've been throwing in, so I'm getting to have fun and I'm happy about it. You'll see two new characters later: They'll be interacting with Akito & Sana. I'll make this a really exciting drama, so please keep reading!

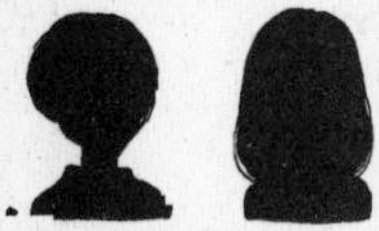

(Here they are, identities disguised!)
They're in the dark...
This one's already appeared in Ribon magazine!

See you in book 3!

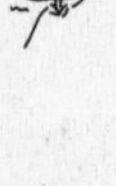

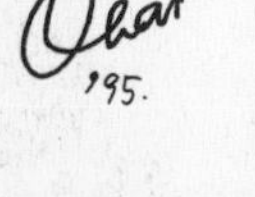
Miho Obana
'95.

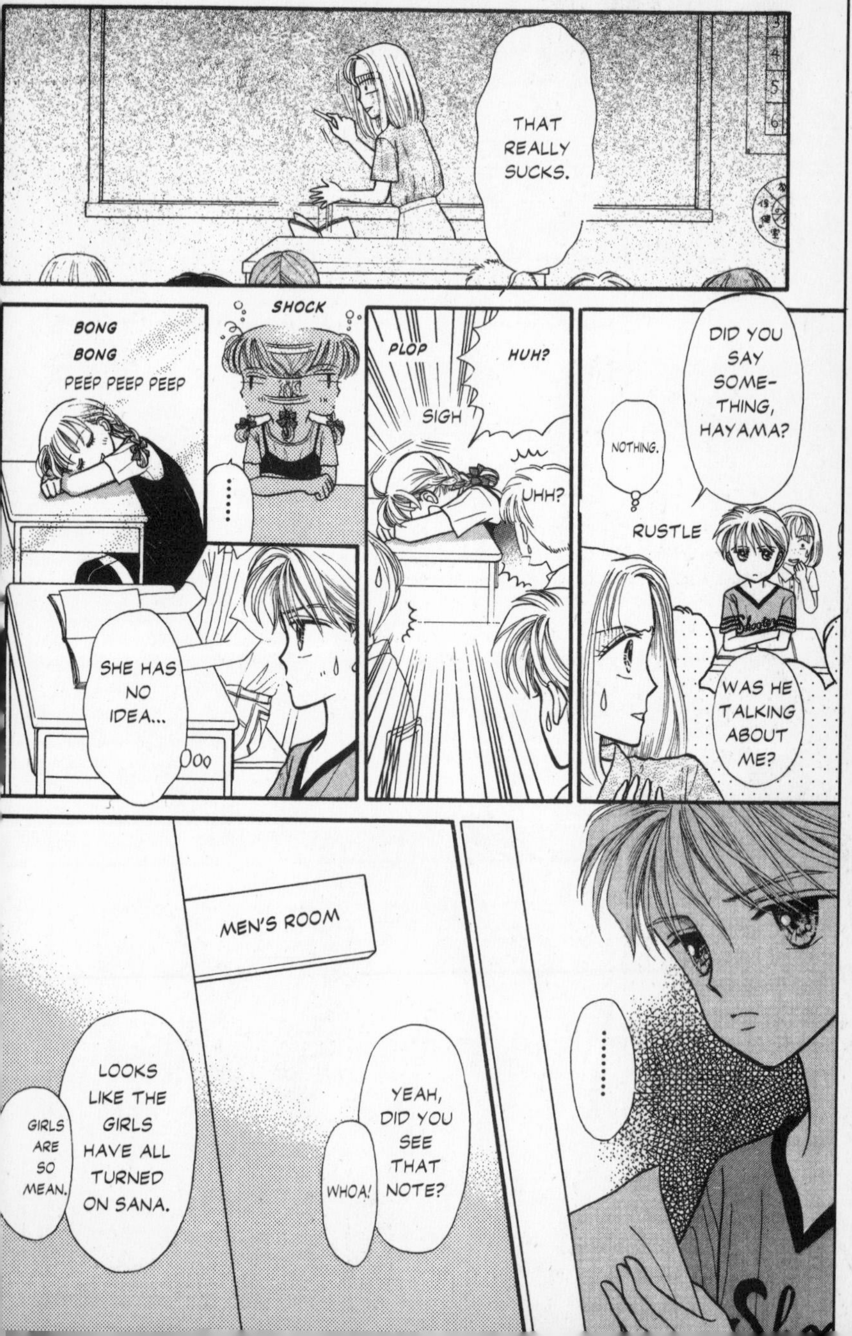
THAT REALLY SUCKS.
DID YOU SAY SOME-THING, HAYAMA?
NOTHING.
RUSTLE
WAS HE TALKING ABOUT ME?
HUH?
PLOP
SIGH
UHH?
SHOCK
BONG BONG
PEEP PEEP PEEP
......
SHE HAS NO IDEA...
......
MEN'S ROOM
YEAH, DID YOU SEE THAT NOTE?
WHOA!
LOOKS LIKE THE GIRLS HAVE ALL TURNED ON SANA.
GIRLS ARE SO MEAN.

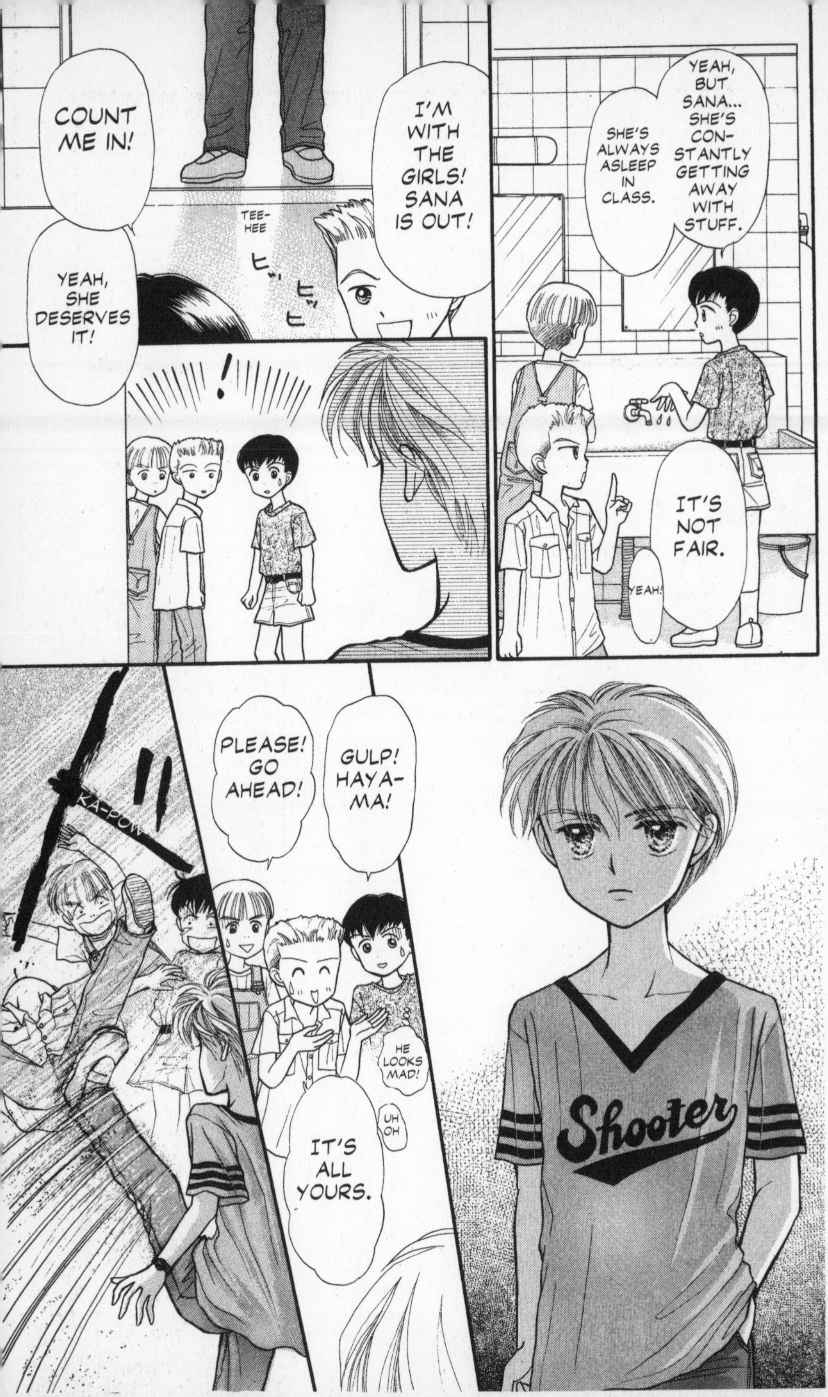
YEAH, BUT SANA... SHE'S CON-STANTLY GETTING AWAY WITH STUFF.
SHE'S ALWAYS ASLEEP IN CLASS.
IT'S NOT FAIR.
YEAH!
I'M WITH THE GIRLS! SANA IS OUT!
TEE-HEE
COUNT ME IN!
YEAH, SHE DESERVES IT!
!
GULP! HAYA-MA!
PLEASE! GO AHEAD!
HE LOOKS MAD!
UH OH
IT'S ALL YOURS.
KA-PON

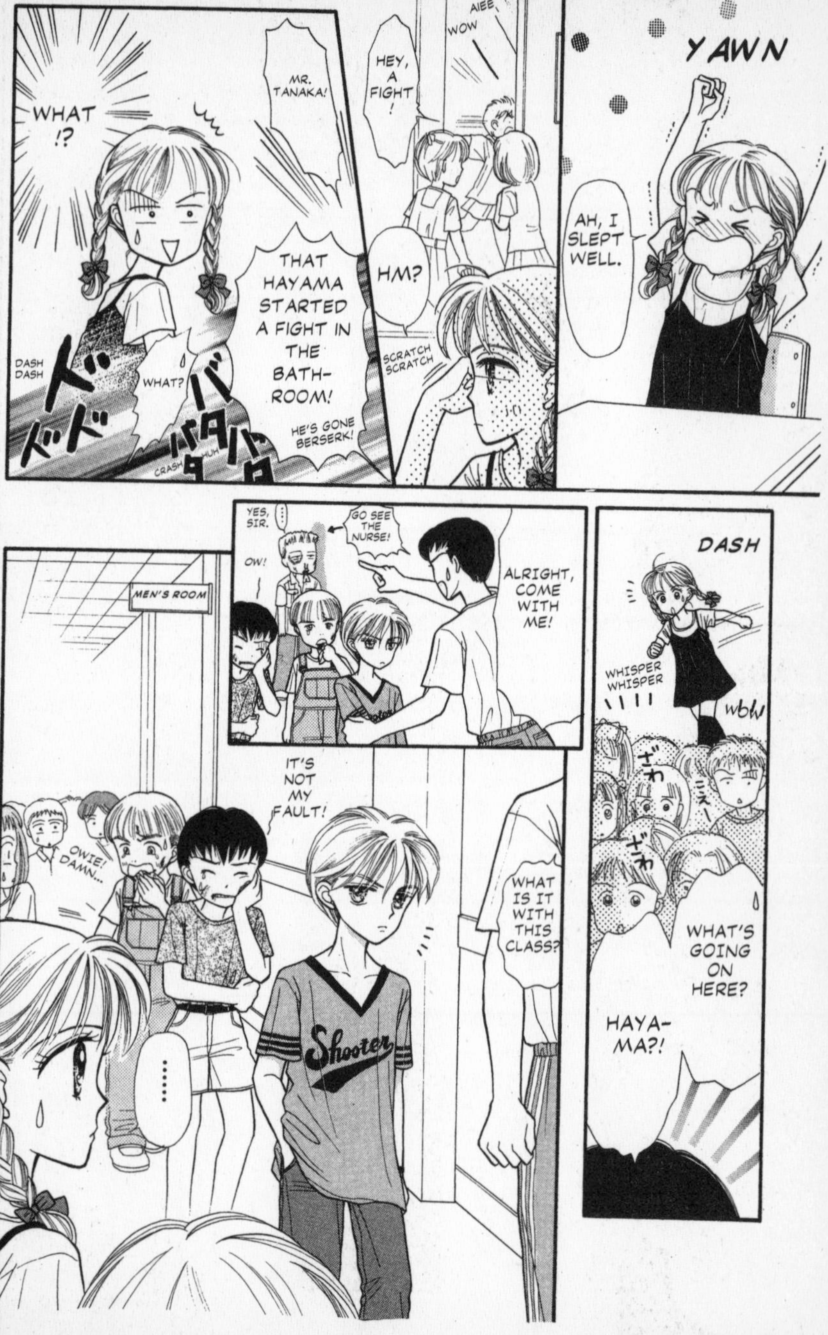
YAWN
AH, I SLEPT WELL.
AIEE
WOW
HEY, A FIGHT!
HM?
SCRATCH SCRATCH
MR. TANAKA!
WHAT!?
THAT HAYAMA STARTED A FIGHT IN THE BATHROOM!
HE'S GONE BERSERK!
DASH DASH
WHAT?
CRASH
HUH
DASH
WHISPER WHISPER
WHAT'S GOING ON HERE?
HAYAMA?!
ALRIGHT, COME WITH ME!
GO SEE THE NURSE!
YES, SIR.
OW!
MEN'S ROOM
IT'S NOT MY FAULT!
WHAT IS IT WITH THIS CLASS?
OWIE! DAMN...
......

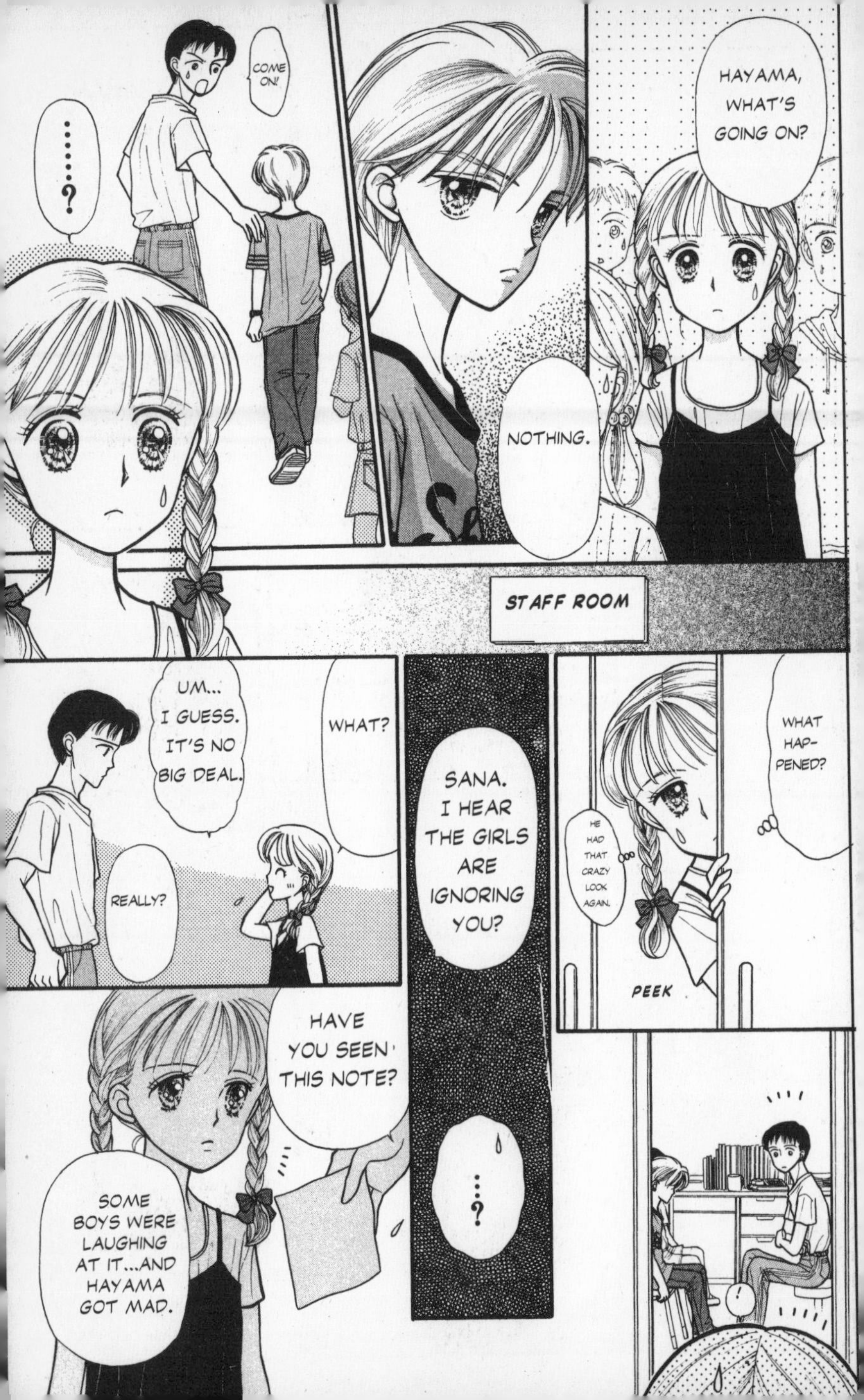
HAYAMA, WHAT'S GOING ON?
NOTHING.
COME ON!
......?
STAFF ROOM
WHAT HAP-PENED?
HE HAD THAT CRAZY LOOK AGAIN.
PEEK
SANA. I HEAR THE GIRLS ARE IGNORING YOU?
...?
WHAT?
UM... I GUESS. IT'S NO BIG DEAL.
REALLY?
HAVE YOU SEEN THIS NOTE?
SOME BOYS WERE LAUGHING AT IT...AND HAYAMA GOT MAD.

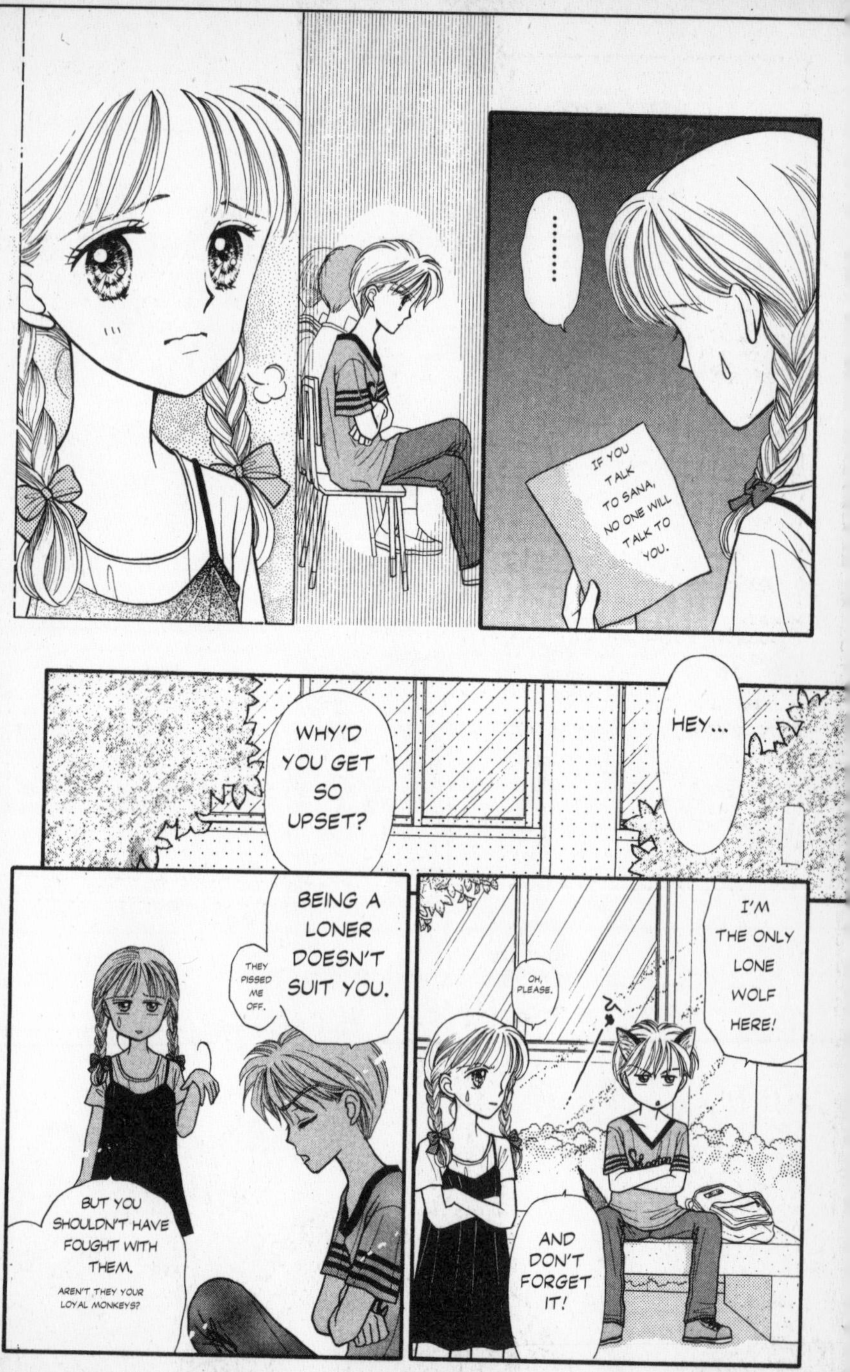
......
IF YOU TALK TO SANA, NO ONE WILL TALK TO YOU.
HEY...
WHY'D YOU GET SO UPSET?
I'M THE ONLY LONE WOLF HERE!
OH, PLEASE.
AND DON'T FORGET IT!
BEING A LONER DOESN'T SUIT YOU.
THEY PISSED ME OFF.
BUT YOU SHOULDN'T HAVE FOUGHT WITH THEM.
AREN'T THEY YOUR LOYAL MONKEYS?

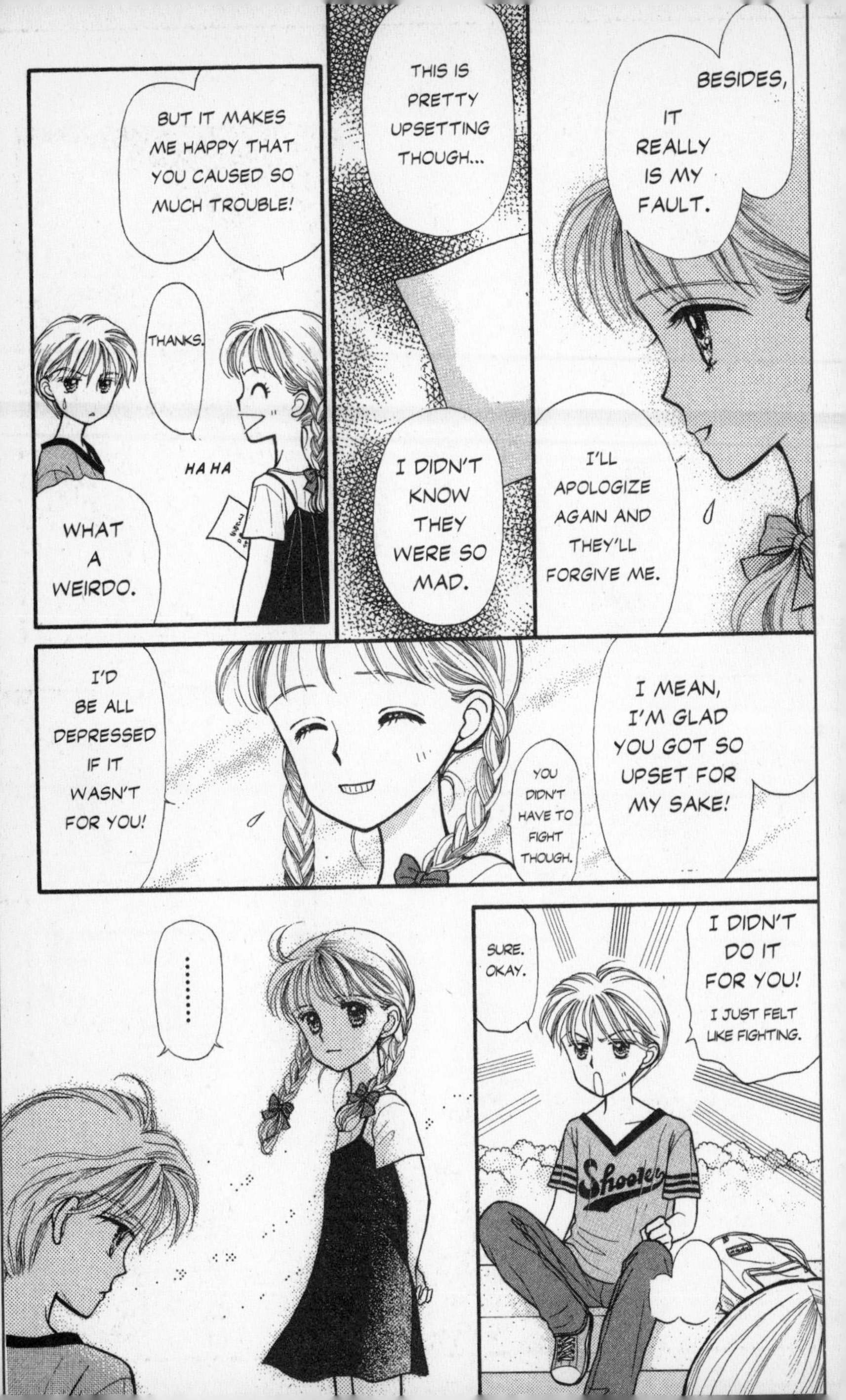
BESIDES, IT REALLY IS MY FAULT.
I'LL APOLOGIZE AGAIN AND THEY'LL FORGIVE ME.
THIS IS PRETTY UPSETTING THOUGH...
I DIDN'T KNOW THEY WERE SO MAD.
BUT IT MAKES ME HAPPY THAT YOU CAUSED SO MUCH TROUBLE!
THANKS.
HA HA
WHAT A WEIRDO.
I MEAN, I'M GLAD YOU GOT SO UPSET FOR MY SAKE!
YOU DIDN'T HAVE TO FIGHT THOUGH.
I'D BE ALL DEPRESSED IF IT WASN'T FOR YOU!
I DIDN'T DO IT FOR YOU!
I JUST FELT LIKE FIGHTING.
SURE. OKAY.
......
Shooter

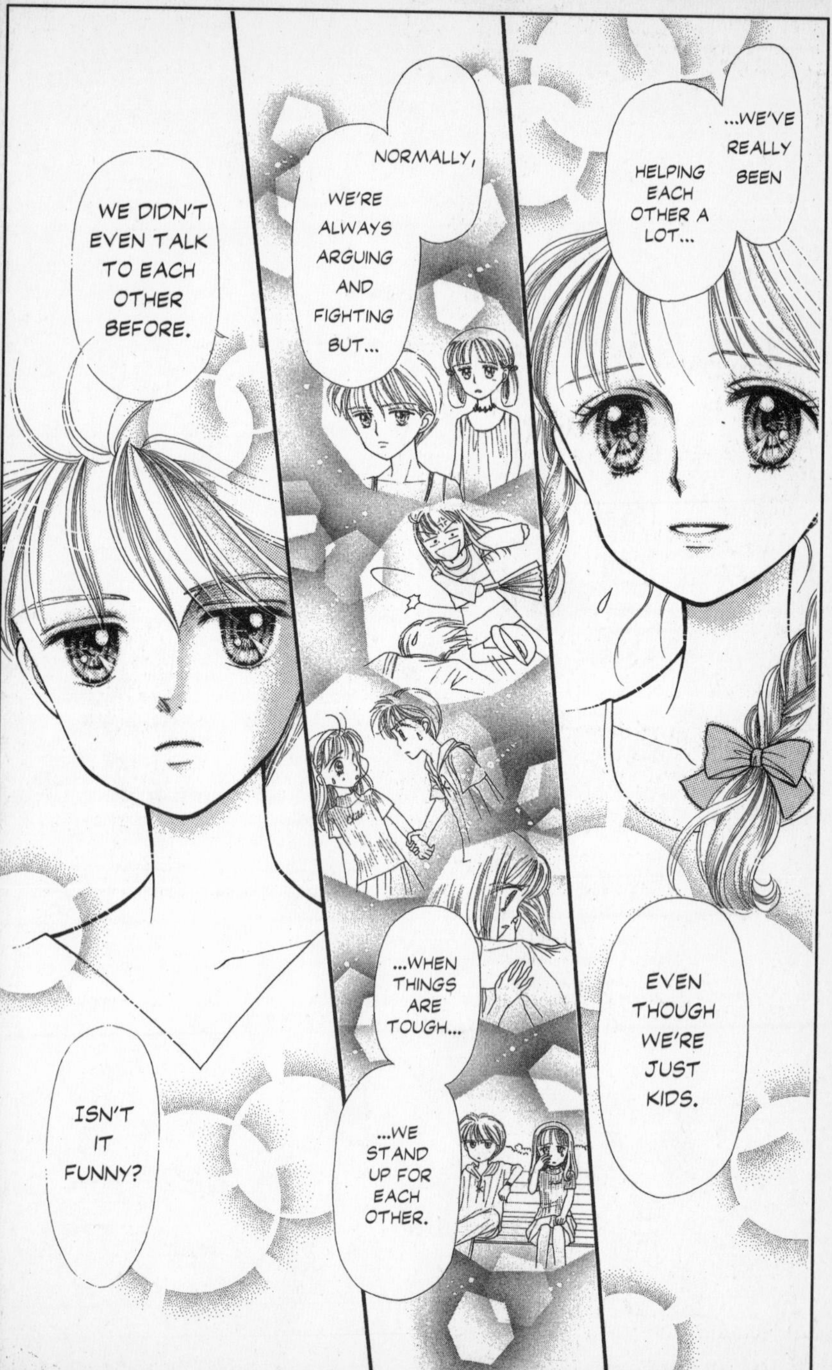
...WE'VE REALLY BEEN HELPING EACH OTHER A LOT...
EVEN THOUGH WE'RE JUST KIDS.
NORMALLY, WE'RE ALWAYS ARGUING AND FIGHTING BUT...
...WHEN THINGS ARE TOUGH...
...WE STAND UP FOR EACH OTHER.
WE DIDN'T EVEN TALK TO EACH OTHER BEFORE.
ISN'T IT FUNNY?

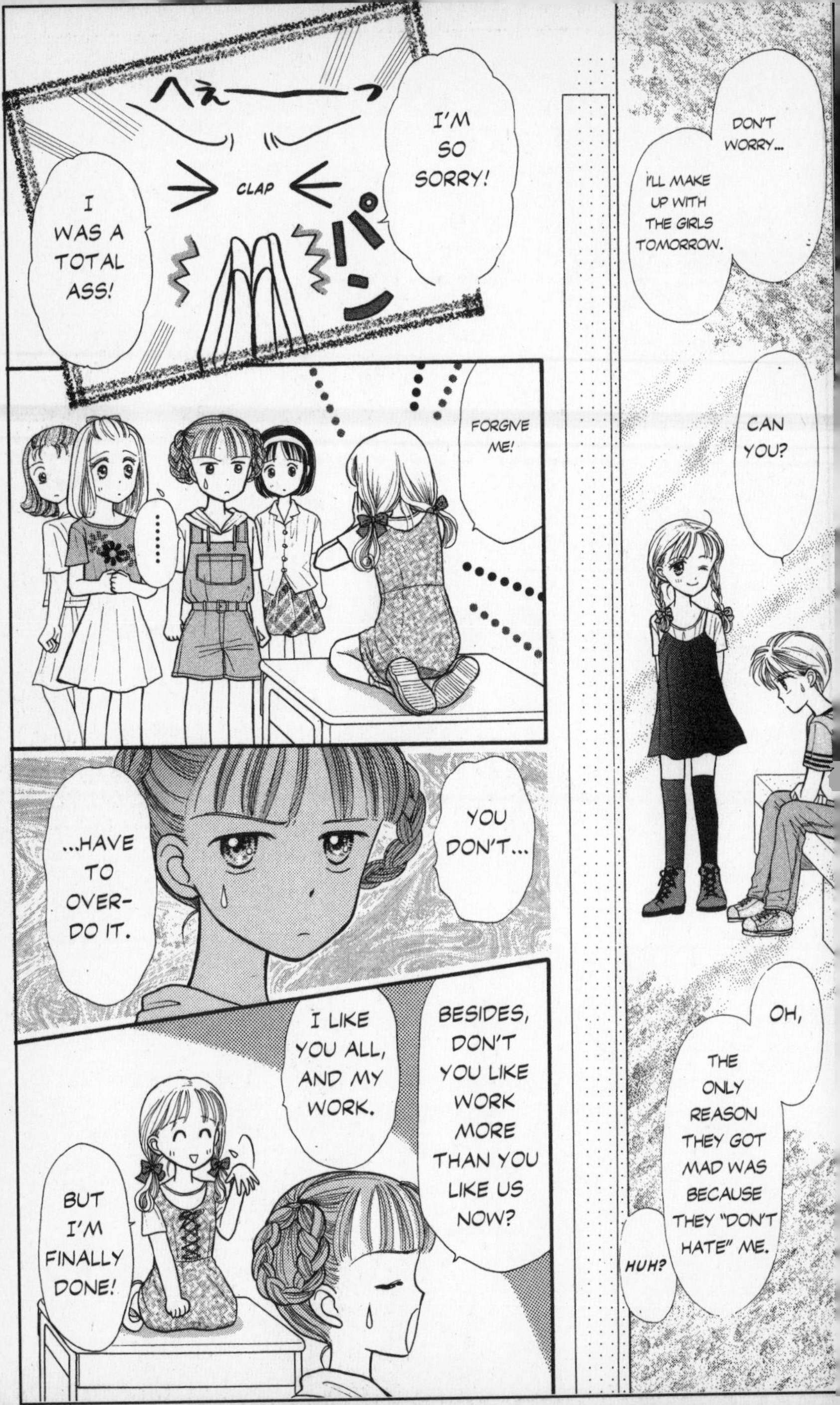
DON'T WORRY...
I'LL MAKE UP WITH THE GIRLS TOMORROW.
CAN YOU?
OH, THE ONLY REASON THEY GOT MAD WAS BECAUSE THEY "DON'T HATE" ME.
HUH?
I'M SO SORRY!
へえーーっ
パン
CLAP
I WAS A TOTAL ASS!
FORGIVE ME!
......
YOU DON'T...
...HAVE TO OVER-DO IT.
BESIDES, DON'T YOU LIKE WORK MORE THAN YOU LIKE US NOW?
I LIKE YOU ALL, AND MY WORK.
BUT I'M FINALLY DONE!

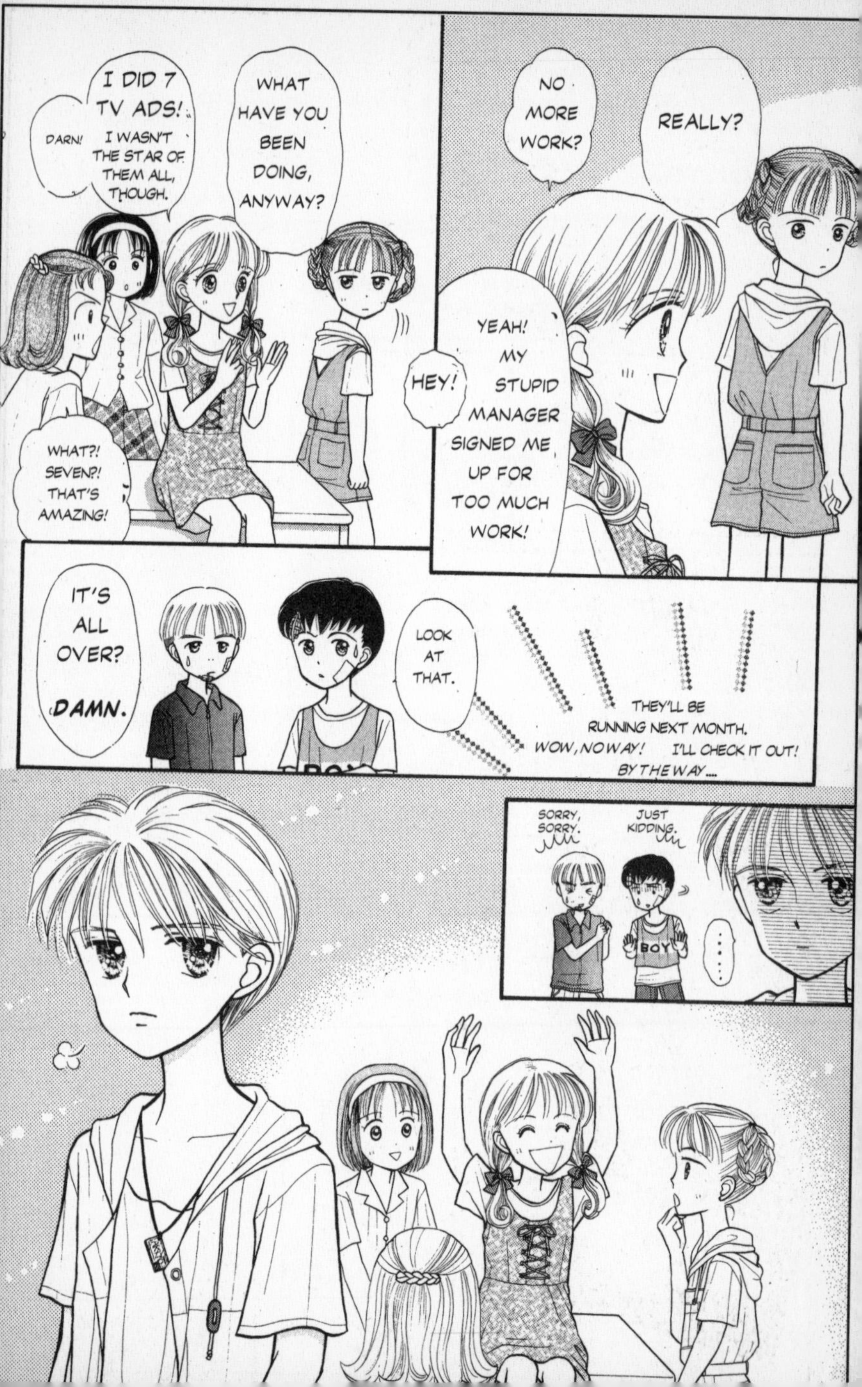
REALLY?
NO MORE WORK?
YEAH! MY STUPID MANAGER SIGNED ME UP FOR TOO MUCH WORK!
HEY!
WHAT HAVE YOU BEEN DOING, ANYWAY?
I DID 7 TV ADS! I WASN'T THE STAR OF THEM ALL, THOUGH.
DARN!
WHAT?! SEVEN?! THAT'S AMAZING!
THEY'LL BE RUNNING NEXT MONTH.
I'LL CHECK IT OUT!
WOW, NO WAY!
BY THE WAY....
LOOK AT THAT.
IT'S ALL OVER?
DAMN.
JUST KIDDING.
SORRY, SORRY.
......

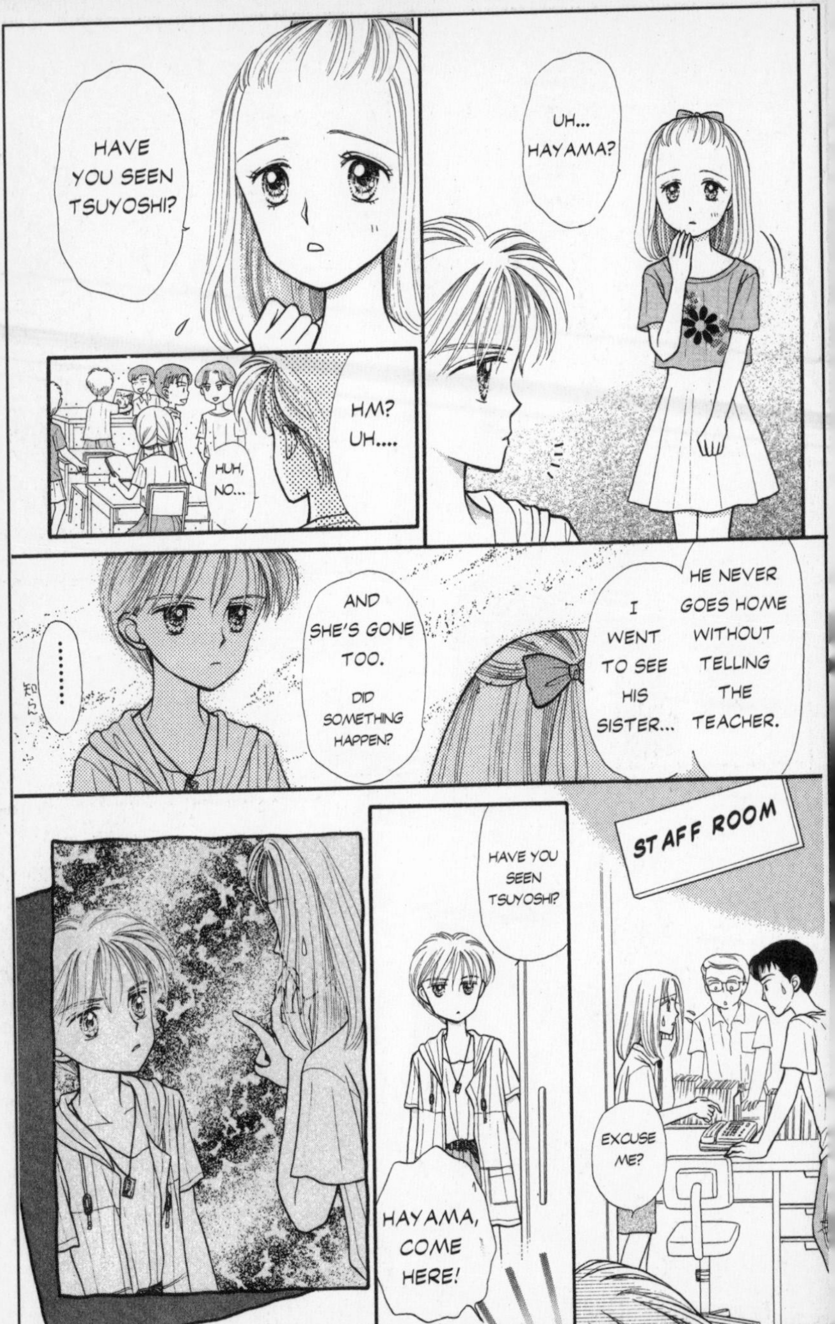
UH... HAYAMA?
HAVE YOU SEEN TSUYOSHI?
HM? UH....
HUH, NO...
HE NEVER GOES HOME WITHOUT TELLING THE TEACHER.
I WENT TO SEE HIS SISTER...
AND SHE'S GONE TOO.
DID SOMETHING HAPPEN?
....
STAFF ROOM
EXCUSE ME?
HAVE YOU SEEN TSUYOSHI?
HAYAMA, COME HERE!

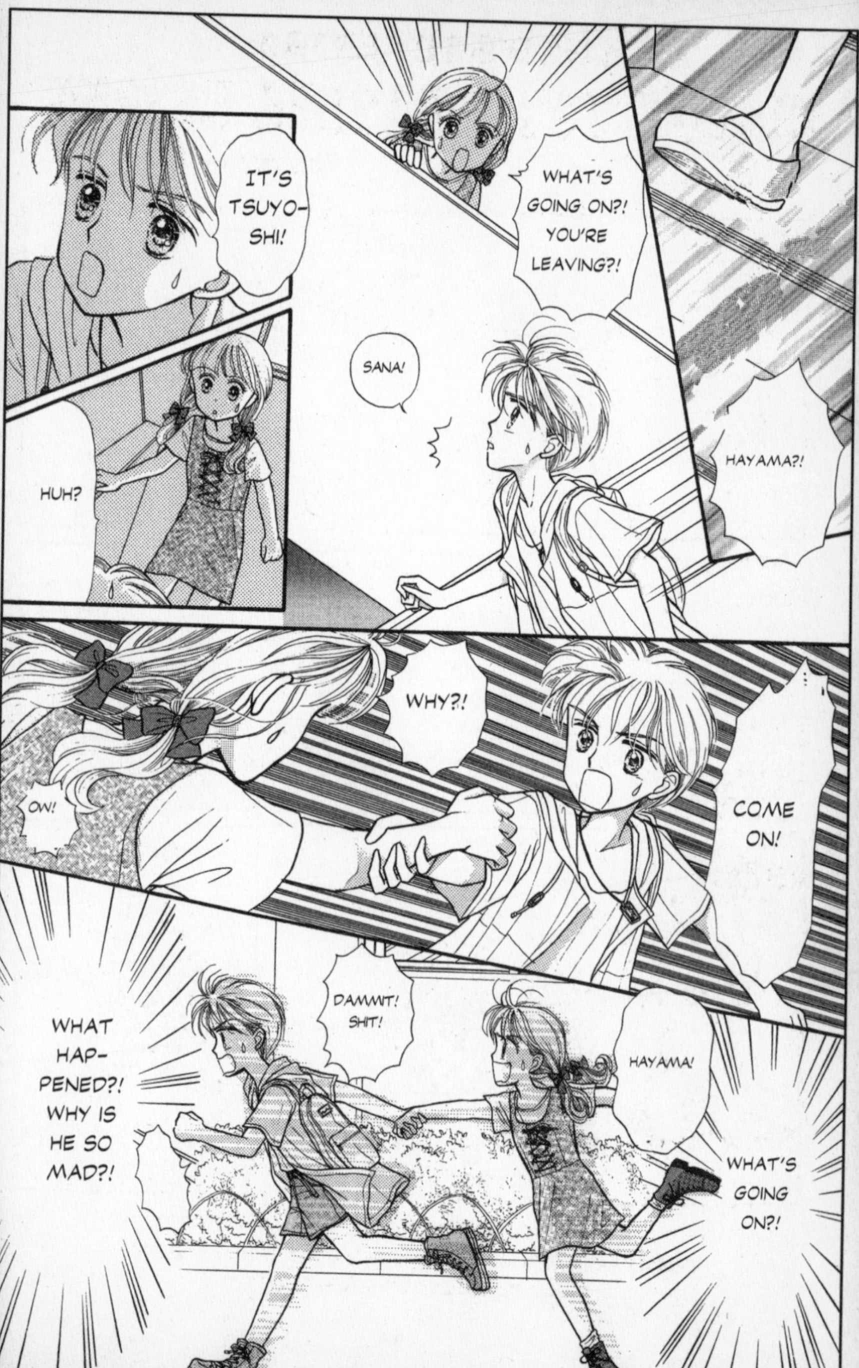
HAYAMA?!
WHAT'S GOING ON?! YOU'RE LEAVING?!
SANA!
IT'S TSUYO-SHI!
HUH?
COME ON!
WHY?!
OW!
WHAT'S GOING ON?!
HAYAMA!
DAMMIT! SHIT!
WHAT HAP-PENED?! WHY IS HE SO MAD?!

CHILD'S TOY EXTRA:
CHILD'S TOY WEATHER REPORT
Tommy's version

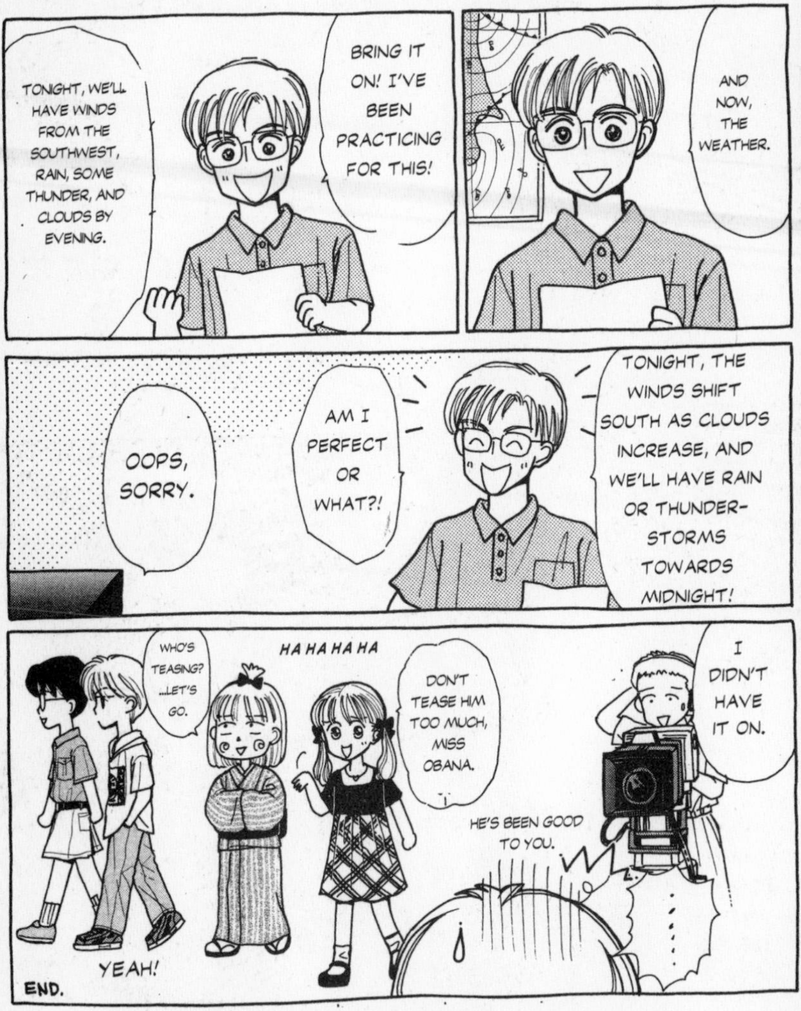
AND NOW, THE WEATHER.
BRING IT ON! I'VE BEEN PRACTICING FOR THIS!
TONIGHT, WE'LL HAVE WINDS FROM THE SOUTHWEST, RAIN, SOME THUNDER, AND CLOUDS BY EVENING.
TONIGHT, THE WINDS SHIFT SOUTH AS CLOUDS INCREASE, AND WE'LL HAVE RAIN OR THUNDER-STORMS TOWARDS MIDNIGHT!
AM I PERFECT OR WHAT?!
OOPS, SORRY.
I DIDN'T HAVE IT ON.
HE'S BEEN GOOD TO YOU.
DON'T TEASE HIM TOO MUCH, MISS OBANA.
HA HA HA HA HA
WHO'S TEASING? ...LET'S GO.
YEAH!
END.

FOR THOSE OF YOU WHO DON'T GET IT...TOMMY TELLS COMIC ARTISTS HOW MANY PAGES TO DO AND HELPS THEM WORK OUT THEIR STORIES.

Coming Next!

What is Kodocha? It's the smash-hit comedy series from Japan about what happens when child star Sana Kurata tries to "fix" the problems of everyone around her. And there are a LOT of problems to solve. Her mom just announced that she's going to publish a new book sharing all of Sana's family secrets with the world. Even though Sana initially gives her blessing, she soon begins to doubt herself—and her mom's devotion. When her main man, Hayama, offers his unexpected support, she feels loads better...until a hottie named Naozumi enters the picture and threatens to bust their bond. There are going to be a few brawls in the halls when this controversial page-turner hits the streets!

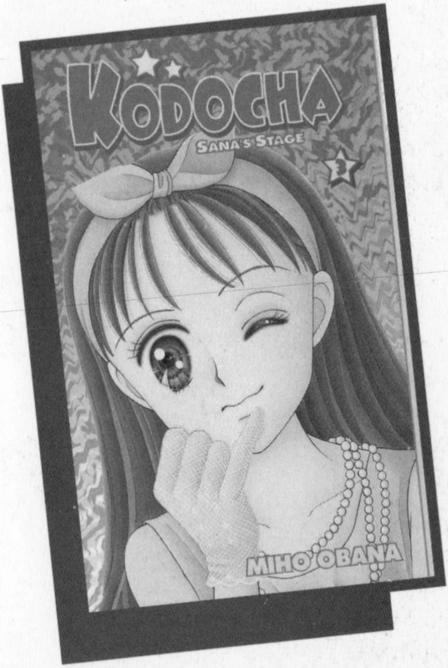
KODOCHA
SANA'S STAGE
3
MIHO OBANA

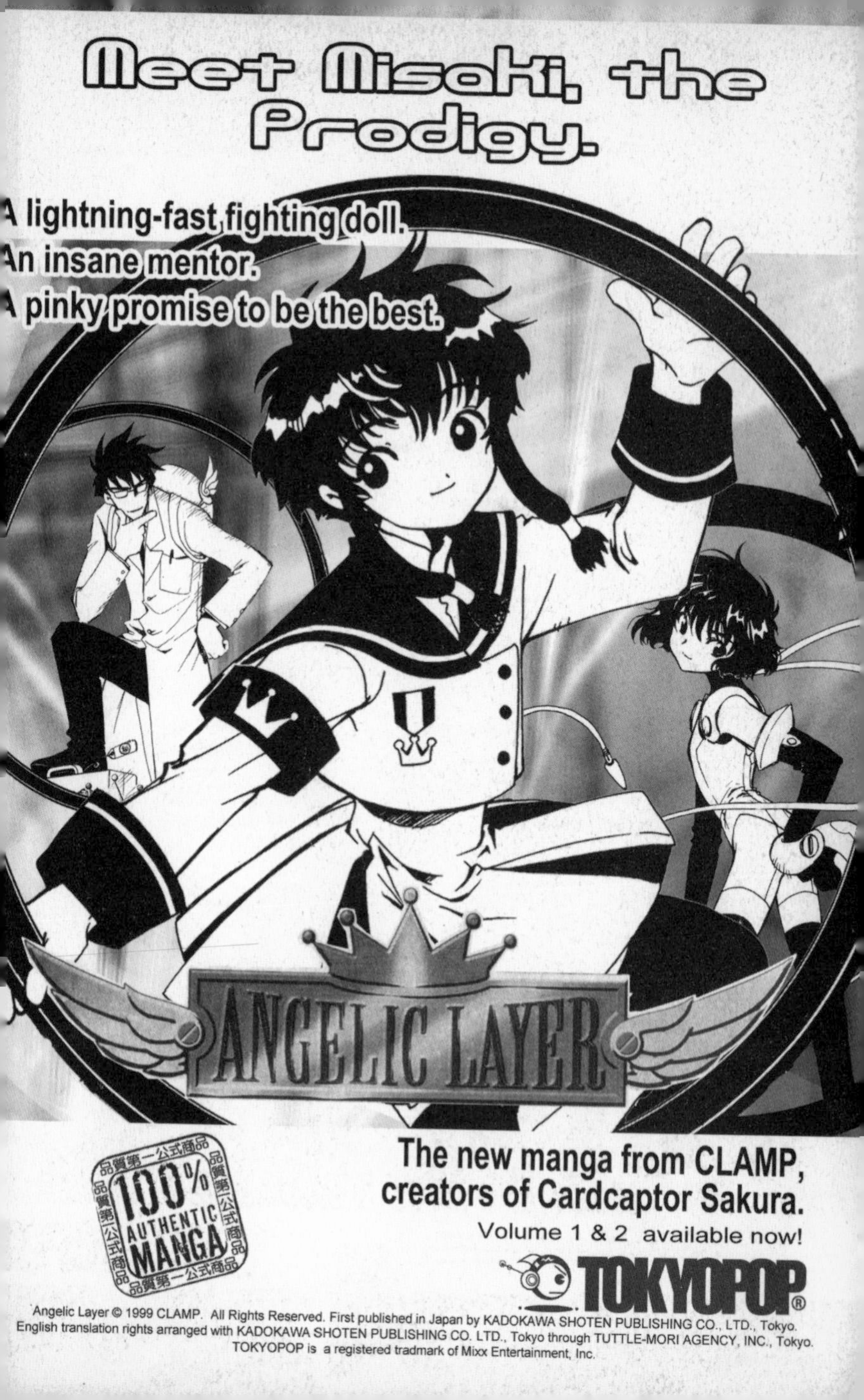
Meet Misaki, the Prodigy.
A lightning-fast fighting doll.
An insane mentor.
A pinky promise to be the best.
ANGELIC LAYER
品質第一公式商品
100% AUTHENTIC MANGA
The new manga from CLAMP, creators of Cardcaptor Sakura.
Volume 1 & 2 available now!
TOKYOPOP®
Angelic Layer © 1999 CLAMP. All Rights Reserved. First published in Japan by KADOKAWA SHOTEN PUBLISHING CO., LTD., Tokyo. English translation rights arranged with KADOKAWA SHOTEN PUBLISHING CO. LTD., Tokyo through TUTTLE-MORI AGENCY, INC., Tokyo. TOKYOPOP is a registered trademark of Mixx Entertainment, Inc.

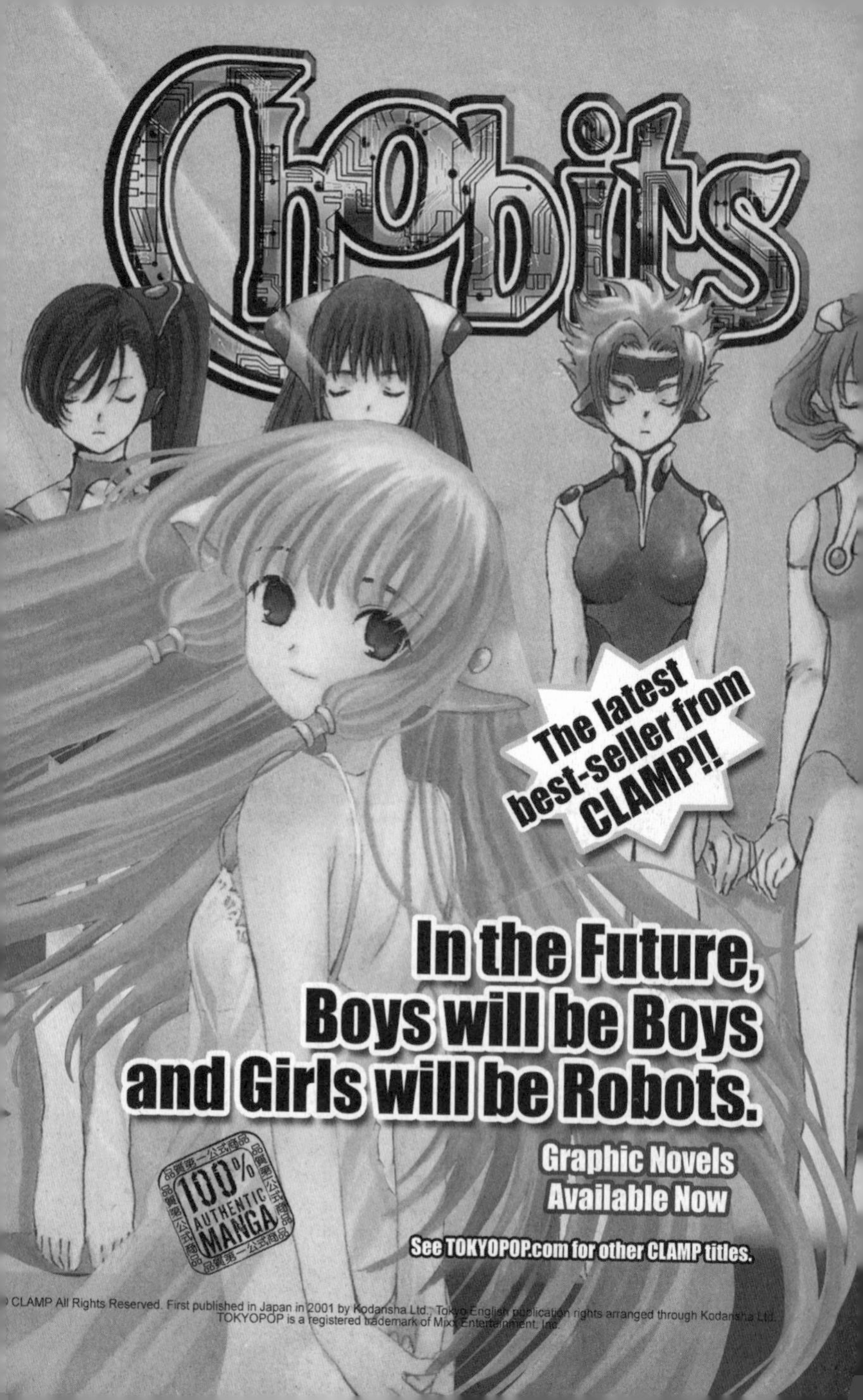

Chobits
The latest best-seller from CLAMP!!
In the Future, Boys will be Boys and Girls will be Robots.
Graphic Novels Available Now
100% AUTHENTIC MANGA
See TOKYOPOP.com for other CLAMP titles.
CLAMP All Rights Reserved. First published in Japan in 2001 by Kodansha Ltd., Tokyo English publication rights arranged through Kodansha Ltd.
TOKYOPOP is a registered trademark of Mixx Entertainment, Inc.

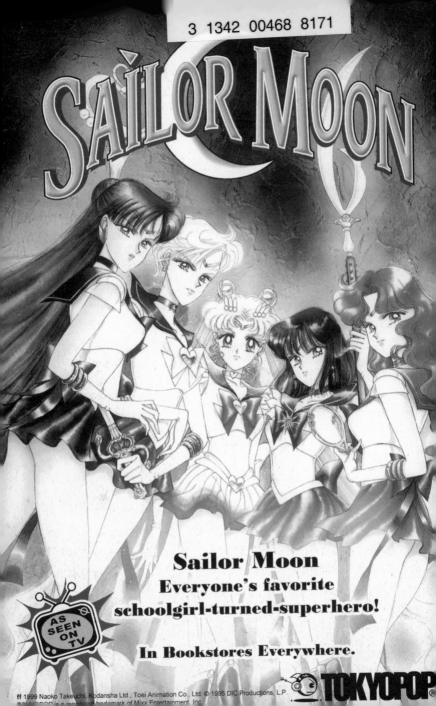

5-08

STOP!

This is the back of the book.

You wouldn't want to spoil a great ending!

This book is printed "manga-style," in the authentic Japanese right-to-left format. Since none of the artwork has been flipped or altered, readers get to experience the story just as the creator intended. You've been asking for it, so TOKYOPOP® delivered: authentic, hot-off-the-press, and far more fun!

1
I GOT THE STUFF, MOM.
WHAT'S THAT?
NOTHING
I STOPPED IN TO VISIT AKITO'S DAD.
THAT'S FINE.
2
HOW'S
A LITTLE MORE TO THE LEFT...
TSUYOSHI, WHERE'S DADDY?
WELL... HE'S...
3
TELL YOU WHAT, AONO, I'LL BE DAD FROM NOW ON.
SILLY, YOU CAN'T BE A DAD. YOU HAVE HAIR!
4
NOT ALL DADS ARE BALD, SHRIMP.
SHAKE
5
MOM, THE PHONE WON'T REACH THE OUTLET FROM HERE.
REALLY?

DIRECTIONS:

If this is your first time reading manga-style, here's a quick guide to help you understand how it works.

It's easy...just start in the top right panel and follow the numbers. Have fun, and look for more 100% authentic manga from TOKYOPOP®!